Dissolving Illusions

Disease, Vaccines, and the Forgotten History

Suzanne Humphries, MD

and

Roman Bystrianyk

Rally of the Anti-Vaccination League of Canada, Old City Hall
November 13, 1919
Photographer: William James
Thanks to the City of Toronto Archives

ISBN: 1480216895
ISBN-13: 978-1480216891

Those who have had to take detailed notice of the immunisation accidents of the past few years know that to get the truth of what really went wrong generally calls for the resources of something like the secret service.

– Charles Cyril Okell, MC, MA, ScD, FRCP, 1938

Often have I wished that this work, for its own sake and the great issues involved, had been in more competent and less occupied hands, but the results of any investigations as to the effects of vaccination are given with the fervent hope that at least, they may promote inquiry, induce impartial consideration, and elucidate the truth on so important a question affecting the public health.

– J. T. Biggs, Member of the Leicester Town Council and its Sanitary Committee for more than 22 years. 1912

The fatal tendency of mankind to leave off thinking about a thing when it is no longer doubtful, is the cause of half their errors.

– John Stuart Mill (1806–1873)

Authors' Notes

The format of this book is somewhat unconventional, as it is filled with many direct quotes from a wide variety of historical and medical sources. We decided on this format to give you unfiltered information that will help you gain better insight into the true history of disease and vaccination. Oftentimes each quote tells a unique, self-contained story that can draw the reality of the past into view much better than a distilled summary would.

The book contains more than 50 graphs that are based on meticulously researched data. Each graph lists the references upon which the data is based. The graphs provide—in most cases—a never-before-seen view of the history of disease from the 1800s into the 1900s. They provide foundational evidence for the points presented in the text.

The book also includes many photographs extracted from numerous historic sources. Most of the photographs are presented with the exact captions that appeared in the original work.

Throughout the book, **bold text** indicates something that we think warrants special attention.

For more information related to the book, please visit *www.dissolvingillusions.com*. There you can see photos, full-color graphs, and other information that appears in this book.

Dedications

To Bryan, Kyle, and Dylan, whose entry into this world inspired this investigation, and to Meryl, whose steadfast support, help, and love kept this project moving forward.

– Roman Bystrianyk

To all who continue to move forward with the Truth, despite tyranny nipping at their heels.

– Suzanne Humphries, MD

Acknowledgments

Foreword: Dr. Jayne L. M. Donegan

Editor: Jennifer Hutchinson

Cover Design: Valerie Lovelace, Thunderbunny Designs,
www.thunderbunnydesigns.com

Cover Photo: Arthur Smith, Jr. August 1915
(approximately 1 year after vaccination)

Special Thanks

Our thanks go to a great many people, including the following:

The staff of the New York Academy of Medicine Rare Book and History of Medicine Collections for providing some extremely valuable documents.

The Harvey Cushing/John Hay Whitney Medical Library at Yale for its outstanding historical books and wealth of statistical information.

Gary Null, who inspired Roman to think independently and to "pursue the truth no matter where it may take you."

Clifford G. Miller, who supplied some excellent historical documents.

John Scudamore for providing some of the original raw mortality data for England and Wales.

Heather H. Georghiou, a local history librarian, and others at the Newburgh Free Library, who helped acquire some historical information.

Joseph Lieby for his meticulous research on Arthur Smith Jr.

To our many friends who helped make this book into what it is, including Sandy Lefebvre; Alisa Hunt, PhD; Marshall P. Johnson; and Robert Mariano.

Cindy M. Nicholas, RN, for her outstanding vetting of information and her words of wisdom and support.

Suzanne's dear friends Serena and Petros for their wisdom and guidance.

Dr. Jennifer Craig and Dr. J. F. for all their invaluable help.

J. T. Biggs, whose dedication to public health and dogged pursuit of the truth culminated in his 784-page book written in 1912 on the question of vaccination and sanitation.

The scientists and researchers who, throughout the years, have done a great deal of important work that we were able to reference.

The few scientists in academia today who take the risks involved in reporting the truth about vaccines and vaccine components.

The countless souls who acquired, compiled, and maintained an enormous amount of statistical information.

Roman's parents, who were always there when he needed them.

Meryl Barr's seemingly infinite inspiration and support.

All parents who dedicate long hours of self-education in order to care for the precious lives that have been bestowed upon them.

Contents

Foreword by Dr. Jayne L. M. Donegan

Vaccination is regarded as the most important health advance in the 20th century by most health professionals and laypeople. Although the dramatic decreases in morbidity and mortality from diseases that occurred in the course of the 20th century have been credited to the introduction of specific vaccines, scant acknowledgment has been given to improving social conditions.

Despite questioning the safety and efficacy of vaccination by reputable medical men since its introduction, debate has been, and is, increasingly discouraged.

Information published in scientific journals is used to support this position, other views being regarded as "unscientific."

It was a received "article of faith" for me and my contemporaries, that vaccination was **the** single most useful health intervention that had ever been introduced. Along with all my medical and nursing colleagues, I was taught that vaccines were the reason children and adults stopped dying from diseases for which there are vaccines.

We were told that other diseases, such as scarlet fever, rheumatic fever, typhus, typhoid, cholera, and so on, for which there are no vaccines at the time, diminished both in incidence and mortality (ability to kill) due to better social conditions.

You would think—as medical students who are supposed to be moderately intelligent—that some of us would have asked, "But if deaths from these diseases decreased due to improved social conditions, mightn't the ones for which there are vaccines also have decreased at the same time, for the same reason?" But we didn't.

The medical curriculum is so overloaded with information that you just have to learn what you hear, as you hear it: nonvaccinatable diseases into the social conditions box and vaccinatable diseases into the vaccines box and then on to the next subject.

Everything I was taught and read in textbooks, both before I qualified as a doctor and through all my post-graduate training, reinforced this view.

Along with most doctors, I regarded parents who would not vaccinate their children as ignorant or, if not ignorant, sociopathic, for withholding what I believed was a lifesaving intervention and putting everybody else at risk by reducing herd immunity.

Indeed, at special clinics in the 1980s, I used to counsel parents who wouldn't vaccinate their children against whooping cough—which was regarded as the problematic vaccine in those days. I acknowledged that there were dangers associated with the vaccine. I was a truthful doctor, but I told them the official line: that the disease was 10 times more likely to cause death or disability than the vaccine, so **any sane person** would choose to vaccinate.

What changed?

In 1994 there was a massive measles/rubella vaccination campaign in the UK. Seven million schoolchildren were vaccinated against measles and rubella to protect them from an epidemic of measles, which was said to be imminent.

In those days, there was only one measles shot in the schedule—it is a live viral vaccine and was supposed to be like the wild measles virus. We were told, "One dose and you are immune for life." I did realize that one shot, however, might not protect every child—no vaccine is one hundred percent effective—but the chief medical officer said that even *two* shots of this "one-shot vaccine" would not necessarily protect children when the epidemic came and that they would need a *third.* He also said that the best way to vaccinate children was *en masse* to "break the chain of transmission."

This left me in a quandary. Obviously, the risk-to-benefit ratio of the vaccine was in favor of the vaccine if it was safer than the disease and if it stopped your child from getting the disease. This is what most parents expect to happen and certainly what they are encouraged to believe.

But if children can have the one-shot vaccine twice and still get the disease so they need to have a *third* shot, this means they can be exposed to all the risks of the vaccine two or three times . . . *and* at the same time, all the risks of the disease as well. Did I need to reevaluate what I had been saying to parents?

Also, if the **best way** of "breaking the **chain of transmission**" of an **infectious disease** was to vaccinate *en masse,* why did we vaccinate babies with all those different vaccines at two, three, and four months of age (UK schedule)? Why didn't we just wait for two or three years and then vaccinate all those who had been born in the interim en masse to break the chain of transmission?

This was the start of my long, slow journey researching vaccination and disease ecology and learning about other models and philosophies of health and natural hygiene such as those used by the great pioneers who cleaned up our cities and built clean water supplies and sewage systems.

I spent hours in libraries looking at archived journals and textbooks and the Office for National Statistics (ONS) getting out dusty volumes from the middle of the 19th century to make graphs of death rates from diseases for which we have vaccines but which, for some reason, have not been drawn—or made available to doctors or parents by the ONS or the Department of Health.

I read what prominent men of science, medical officers for health, and doctors wrote about vaccination and its sequelae that never made it into today's textbooks, and found out what anyone with even a passing acquaintance with disease figures of the 19th and 20th century knew. For example, by the 1950s when the whooping cough vaccine was introduced, data showed that whooping cough was killing only 1 percent of the numbers of people who used to die in England and Wales 50 years before.

Official data showed that the same happened with measles. Indeed, when the measles vaccine was introduced to the UK in 1968, the death rate continued to drop steadily, even though the initial uptake of the vaccine was only 30 percent and didn't get above 50 percent until the 1980s.

Even the much-heralded success story of smallpox vaccination was not what it seemed. The enforcement of the compulsory smallpox vaccination law in 1867, when the death rate was already falling, was accompanied by an increase in the deaths from 100 to 400 deaths per million.

After overcoming an awful lot of fear, I came to the gradual realization that it was true what people on the outside had been telling me, that "health is the only immunity." We don't need protecting *from out there.*

We get infectious diseases when our bodies need to have a periodic cleanout. Children, especially, benefit from childhood spotty rashes, or "exanthems" as they are called, at appropriate times in order to make developmental leaps, so long as they are treated appropriately. In my experience, the worst complications of childhood infections are caused by standard medical treatment, which involves suppression of all the symptoms.

Has this knowledge helped my career? It has certainly enabled me to give better advice to parents about treating childhood illness and to be able to provide parents with enough information to give truly informed consent for medical interventions such as vaccination.

My research also led me to being asked, in 2002, to act as an expert witness for the mothers of two unvaccinated children whose absent fathers were applying to the court for a vaccination enforcement order. I wrote a report based on my research, fully referenced, carefully using the methods and results of the studies I quoted to give my opinion, rather than the conclusions of the authors, which are often not supported by their results.

The experts for the fathers and the children were members of the Joint Committee on Vaccination and Immunisation (JCVI). They recommended vaccination for both children. If they had advised that vaccination was not necessary for these individual children, they would have been seen to be contradicting government health policy based on JCVI recommendations, which is a conflict of interest that was not explored in the case.

The judge decided that my opinion was less valid than theirs, and the mothers lost their case. When it went to appeal, one of the appeal judges called my evidence "junk science," and on this basis I was charged with Serious Professional Misconduct by the General Medical Council (GMC) of the UK, which could have resulted in being struck off the Medical Register, banned from practicing as a doctor, and losing my livelihood.

In 2007, after a long, drawn-out case lasting three and a half years, the GMC panel completely exonerated me. They did not merely acquit me, but said they were "sure that in the reports you provided you did not fail to be objective, independent and unbiased."

The successful outcome notwithstanding, the case took an inevitable and heavy toll on my children, our family, and my professional life.

In their meticulously researched book, Dr. Suzanne Humphries and Mr. Roman Bystrianyk take you right back to the roots of disease and the connection between living conditions, nutrition, and health.

They systematically piece together the information you need to pierce the myth that vaccination is what saved us from the infective scourges of the past. More worryingly, they also show how vaccines may be instrumental in creating a many-headed *hydra* of overt and covert disease, which is hardly recognised, barely understood, and may well be of immense consequence to our children and future generations.

With all this information there, waiting to be found, why don't more doctors go and look for it?

Why do doctors not even entertain the possibility that the Universal Childhood Vaccination Program may not be the unmitigated success that it is portrayed to be?

Why do doctors not even consider that there may be other ways of achieving health that are better and longer lasting?

In my opinion, the biggest obstacle to independent research and thinking is the professional consequence of stepping out of line and being seen to be different—as I know to my cost. As George Bernard Shaw says in his preface to "The Doctor's Dilemma" 1906:

> *Doctors are just like other Englishmen: most of them have no honour and no conscience: what they commonly mistake for these is sentimentality and an intense dread of doing anything that everybody else does not do, or omitting to do anything that everybody else does.*

So next time you are in your doctor's office and you say, "I'm worried about the safety of vaccination," and you are told, "You don't understand, you're not a doctor . . ." remember that, if you are a doctor and say, "I'm worried about the safety of vaccination," you will be told, "We're charging you with serious professional misconduct . . ."

Dr. Jayne L. M. Donegan, MBBS, DRCOG, DFFP, DCH, MRCGP, MFHom
13 June 2013, London, UK
jaynelmdonegan@yahoo.com
www.jayne-donegan.co.uk

Authors' Introduction

Roman Bystrianyk

My journey began many years ago with the birth of my children. I always wanted to make sure they had the best I could provide: healthy food, a secure place to live, lots of toys, and plenty of caring, laughing, and love. When it came time to have them vaccinated I had assumed, like most parents, that it was a good idea. It had to be—governments, medical professionals, and just about everyone agreed that vaccines were one of the greatest medical discoveries of all time. Measles, whooping cough, smallpox, and all sorts of other horrible infectious diseases were nowhere to be seen, thanks to vaccines.

I'm by nature an inquisitive and questioning person, and something didn't sit right with me about vaccination. A nagging inner voice kept telling me that I should know more about these injections going into my family. Somehow I knew I shouldn't completely and blindly accept that vaccines were safe and effective. At this point, I knew almost nothing about vaccines, but as I began to do some reading I found some disturbing bits of information that built upon my baseline apprehension.

But because of the amount of pressure from doctors and my wife at the time, my children had received some vaccines. In the past, I felt enormously guilty after agreeing to allow my sons to be injected, and I hoped no terrible side effects would occur. I remember staying up at night, feeling distraught after agreeing to give them an injection and hoping nothing major would happen to them. I was overwhelmed with worry, wondering if I had done the right thing by succumbing to the pressure to have them vaccinated. Nothing overt appeared to happen, and they seemed to emerge basically unscathed. Despite being told that vaccines were harmless, I was still left with a feeling that maybe I had done the wrong thing.

I started keeping files with the information I was finding in an attempt to make sense of it all. Eventually, I ran across a book by Neil Z. Miller. In it, Miller showed a graph of deaths from measles that had declined by 95 percent before the measles vaccine was put into general use. I couldn't believe it! Wasn't the decline of deaths from disease the claim to fame for vaccines? Wasn't this the main reason for vaccinating? Could this graph be correct?

That graph left me with an irksome, yet simple, question: Were vaccines really responsible for the decline in mortality from infectious diseases and the eradication of certain diseases? It was important to me to remain objective. My goal was to get to the truth. It seemed that this obvious question should be easy to answer. After all, vaccines have been around for more than one hundred years. Surely the CDC or some medical organization would have a large database of mortality and disease rates available. I was amazed that this wasn't the case. Data that I sought wasn't that easy to find. I thought it was strange that the data wasn't on public display for the world to see, especially if vaccines had defeated the deadly infectious diseases of the past. Where was the proof?

I continued to research vaccination and spent countless hours at the Yale Medical Library as well as other research libraries. I located some mortality data and started gathering statistics from different sources and entered it all into a computer spreadsheet program. Few medical journals referenced historic mortality data, and those that did made no mention of something that now became clear to me. Looking at the data from the United States starting from 1900, the measles mortality rate had declined by more than 98 percent before the introduction of the vaccine! Even more shocking was that the same data revealed that whooping cough mortality had declined by more than 90 percent before the DTP vaccine was introduced! I was stunned that no one I knew, including my sons' doctors, had carefully examined this fundamental belief that vaccines were responsible for the massive decline in deaths from measles and whooping cough.

I now realized that the belief that vaccines were essential in eliminating the threat of at least these two diseases was based on a myth. There must have been other factors that led to such a dramatic decline in mortality before vaccine introduction.

I presented a great deal of information to the mother of my children. Even though she was an educated nurse, she found it impossible to accept what I showed her. On a weekend not long after, I noticed that all three of my children were very sick. I examined them more closely and saw that they all had high fevers and extremely red eyes. I couldn't imagine why they were all so sick. I called their mother and found out that they had, without my knowledge or consent, gotten the DTP, MMR, and polio shots all in one visit. A rush of emotions swept over me. I was angry, upset, worried, and devastated. One of the most important health decisions involving my children had been stripped away from me. The children were very ill all weekend. One of my boys kept having sporadic shooting pains in one eye that recurred intermittently for a couple of months and ultimately seemed to resolve.

By this time, I had accumulated a vast amount of information and hard data. It seemed more likely that we had been misled to believe that vaccination was responsible for eliminating the notorious diseases and devastation of the past. I wondered how statistics and information from medical journals were completely disregarded. That brought me to an understanding of how easily people can be ensnared in a faulty belief system. Assurances from medical authorities that, out of love and responsibility, parents should vaccinate their children were all most people needed to hear. I gained clarity that there was an underlying societal belief in vaccines that was not based on history or evidence. That belief is maintained by a public that remains foundationally subservient and obedient to governmental and medical hierarchies that may not deserve their trust.

Several years after my children had that vaccine reaction, one of them collapsed. Subsequent EEG (electroencephalogram) tracings reflected abnormal brain waves consistent with seizures. From my research, I couldn't help but suspect that the vaccines had caused neurological damage. The neurologist told me that nothing nutritionally could be done to help with the seizures. Unwilling to accept this, I did my own research and found studies in medical journals that showed certain nutrients could make a significant difference. I put my son on a protocol of omega-3 fatty acids, B-complex, magnesium, and other nutrients and an organic diet. Happily, after a few months, the EEG revealed no seizure activity! Not only was I thrilled that my son's condition had improved, but the experience had again shown me the power of belief systems. In this case, the belief that nutrients and diet had no effect on brain health was absolutely wrong. Conventional medical journals contained the information on using nutrients to stop seizures, but shockingly, the information just was not being used by the medical profession.

Each one of these experiences propelled me to continue my research. I obtained data from many sources that led me to solidify and round out my hypothesis that vaccines were not responsible for the decline in deaths from infectious diseases. Now I was left with new questions. What did cause the decline of infectious diseases? Why was there such a rock-solid belief that vaccines were responsible? What was the true history?

I continued to pour through hundreds of medical journals and long-overlooked books, magazines, and newspapers from the 1800s and early 1900s. I found thousands of pages that painted a new picture. I was astonished that an amazing and exciting history had all been tossed in the basements of libraries and possibly lost forever. This new information revealed to me a radically different view of life in the 1800s.

I also discovered how science can go horribly wrong. We can easily become captured by a belief system that is built on a shaky and flawed foundation. How often do we believe in something, not because we have done in-depth research on it, but because authority figures tell us it is the truth? What if what we believe is just an illusion?

I hope that you find the information in this book—graphs, quote-filled chapters, and more—an interesting addition to what you believe. I think the pages of each chapter will provide a unique insight and shine a different light on what really is a hidden past. For some of you, this might be a starting point to begin questioning what you may have innocently accepted as the truth. For others, the information might fill in large gaps and answer questions you may have had but never knew where to look. For me, it has been a rewarding process of dissolving illusions that I'd like to share with you.

Suzanne Humphries, MD

It may seem odd that a medical doctor with 19 years of experience has passionately turned away from the practice of vaccination. It may seem even stranger that, with a successful career as a nephrologist, she would pack her medical bags and leave the hospital without looking back. At the top of her game, she left a very lucrative practice and a shining reputation behind. Here's what happened:

Like most doctors, I received a cursory summary of the childhood and adult vaccine schedules and was told that vaccines are safe and effective and to give them on schedule. I never questioned the vaccine schedule and was largely agnostic about it.

After nearly two decades of working in the conventional medical system, several things converged to launch me into a new way of thinking. I never would have predicted that the medical establishment would present itself to me as a blatant violator of life or conflict with my moral and spiritual principles . . . but it did.

The most memorable event was during the winter of 2009 when the H1N1 flu vaccine was given as a separate injection from the seasonal flu vaccine. Many doctors were skeptical of the practice of influenza vaccination, and many of my hospital colleagues signed the exemption form and dodged the vaccine for themselves. However, there were trusting patients who did not have the discernment to refuse, and I got to see the potential result of vaccination on their kidneys.

That winter, three patients in close succession were wheeled into the emergency room of my hospital with total kidney shutdown. When I arrived to talk to them, each one volunteered to me, "I was fine until I had that vaccine." All three had normal kidney function at baseline, as per their outpatient records. All three required acute dialysis, two eventually recovered, and one died of complications several months later, supposedly from his other illnesses. After this series of events,

I began to take vaccine histories on each of my patients and was startled at the connections that could be made just by asking, "When was your last vaccine?" In my opinion, many cases of supposedly idiopathic (a medical term for *unknown*) kidney disease are not idiopathic at all.

During the weeks of dialyzing the three kidney-failure patients, I passed the chief of internal medicine in the hallway. He was someone I had always had a good relationship with, and we were on excellent terms. He asked me the usual, "How are you doing? How is the nephrology practice going?" I decided to tell him what was happening and how I thought the flu vaccine was causing problems. After conveying a small bit of my observations, he became stiff, his face tightened, his body language changed, and he asked me why I was blaming the vaccine. "They just got the flu, and the vaccine didn't have time to work," was his curt response. I replied by pointing out the fact that I had never, in my career as a nephrologist and an internist, seen a case of the flu present with kidney failure unless the patient had become severely dehydrated and/or taken copious amounts of ibuprofen, neither of which these patients had done. Even more striking was that the patients under discussion did not have symptoms of influenza prior to developing kidney failure.

The conversation continued. We ended up discussing the meningitis problem in teenagers and college students. I suggested that the drugs, vaccines, lack of rest, and poor diets of these children may make them vulnerable to bacteria they would otherwise have defense against. After all, I knew that meningococcal bacteria were often found in completely healthy people. Something else must be contributing to the situation in those who get sick. He laughed at me and said, "So you think the diet is causing meningitis?" He went on to remind me that "smallpox was eradicated by vaccines, and polio was eradicated in the United States by vaccines." At that time, I was ignorant of the history of smallpox and polio except that, six years prior, I was asked to be vaccinated for smallpox in order to be a first responder. These first responders would be ready in the case of a terrorist attack or if a person developed smallpox from the vaccine.

As for polio, the images of crippled children, iron lungs, and the terrible days of the vicious poliovirus attacks were branded into my consciousness like most other people's. I thought Jonas Salk was a great American hero. Funny how the events of 1954 were programmed into me, since I was born in 1964. I wouldn't have been able to even think about polio until 1969 at the earliest. So when this doctor made his final comments to me, I was speechless and unable to respond. I felt lambasted.

Later, several patients were admitted with normal kidneys and had their health decline within 24 hours of vaccination. Even these well-defined and documented cases were denied as vaccine-induced by most of my colleagues. There was the rare doctor who would concur with me in private or the nurse who would come and thank me and agree with me while nobody was listening.

Over the following months, I first made it my business to find out everything I could about safety trials for vaccines in kidney patients. I was shocked to find that there were no trials on these types of patients. I was told they could tolerate vaccines because they are "safe and effective." On seeing that safety of vaccines in acutely ill (active heart failure, sepsis, cancer, autoimmune disease) and chronic nephrology patients was a myth, I decided to research the chief of internal medicine's assumptions about the flu vaccine, smallpox, and polio history. What I encountered threw me into a tailspin that ultimately led me to become a full time researcher on the immune system and vaccination.

I came to realize that the guidelines, evidence, and opinions of the leaders were unsound and were NOT leading the herds to authentic health. What was most puzzling to me was how I was treated when I tried to protect my own kidney-failure patients from being vaccinated—especially when they were ill.

After an attempt to get the hospital to defer vaccinating for pneumonia and influenza until the day of hospital discharge instead of admission, I was told not to interfere with the vaccination protocol. Even more outrageously, I was continuously told that if I wanted credibility for my views I should conduct my own study to prove that the vaccines were causing kidney failure. The burden of proof was somehow placed upon me to obtain IRB (Institutional Review Board) approval and funding and conduct a statistically significant study that those who doubted my evidence of harm would believe. Shouldn't the burden of proof rest upon vaccine manufacturers and those who tout their safety? After all, there was no data to support the belief that vaccines did not cause kidney failure and there was plenty of reason to believe they could. To me, it was obvious that nobody was looking, and thus the connections were not made.

This was the first time in my career that my opinion regarding kidney failure was not respected. Any other time I suggested that a drug was responsible for kidney damage, that drug was immediately discontinued—no questions asked. This happens routinely with certain blood pressure drugs, antibiotics, pain killers, etc. Sometimes kidneys can react to drugs in an allergic fashion—to any drug at any time—and that drug would have been stopped. Some drugs cause direct toxicity to the kidneys, and in the past if I suggested to stop or avoid them, they were always avoided. But now I was unable to protect my own kidney-failure patients from vaccinations given in the hospital.

Questioning the vaccines seemed to open an entire Pandora's box that apparently had yellow tape over the lock, along with the message, "Do not cross." I was met with doublespeak—permitted to write an order to stop a vaccine that was to be given if I got there in time, but I was also told that I was doing it too often and that I should not interfere with the hospital's vaccination policy.

When I pointed out the connection between vaccines and worsening or new-onset kidney failure to a couple of open-minded colleagues, they understood, started taking vaccine histories, and saw what was happening. Yet they remained silent. Most doctors continue to practice with comfortable indifference. Some see the errors, damage, and limits of their practices but still walk lockstep with the herd and protect the brotherhood. I don't know what it will take to get these doctors to resist the dictates who rule over them. I've had far more success reasoning with parents and intelligent people who are not attached to traditions that are damaging, unscientific, and not even supported by our own medical literature. This book is for those who want to read what I have discovered, after years of research, to be a much more accurate depiction of vaccination history.

Terminology

Inoculation: The act of introducing an antigenic substance (stimulates the production of antibodies) into the body to produce an immune system reaction to a specific disease.

Variolation: A procedure that entails inoculating a susceptible person with material taken from a vesicle (a blister formed in or beneath the skin) of someone who has smallpox (orthopox variola virus), to try to prevent smallpox in the susceptible person.

Vaccination:

> a) From *vacca*, the Latin word for cow: Inoculation of cowpox virus (orthopox vaccinia virus) with the intention of protecting against smallpox virus. Also known as *cowpoxing*.

> b) Today the term has been used to describe many other types of inoculations: A preparation of a weakened or killed pathogen, such as a bacterium or a virus, or of a portion of the pathogen's structure that, upon administration, stimulates antibody production or humoral immunity against the pathogen.

Immunization: A process that induces an immune response to a specific disease by exposing the individual to a natural or laboratory-derived antigen. The goal of the process is to raise antibodies to a specific antigen.

You can be vaccinated, but if there is no immunity, you are not immunized. You can be unvaccinated, but if you have had the disease and have protection, you are immune; therefore you are immunized.

DTP: Diphtheria, Tetanus, Pertussis vaccine that used the whole bacterial cell after it was killed. This was the original version of the pertussis vaccine that was highly antigenic but more problematic from a safety standpoint. This vaccine is often termed the *whole cell* vaccine. It is still used in developing countries.

DTaP: Diphtheria, Tetanus, acellular Pertussis vaccine. The pertussis portion of these vaccines does not use the whole cell but contains the pertussis toxin either alone or in combination with pieces of other virulence factors from the cell. These are the vaccines used in the United States, the United Kingdom, and most of Europe today. They are thought to be much safer but are far less antigenic. They are also more expensive.

~ 1 ~

THE NOT SO GOOD OL' DAYS

*As we passed along the reeking banks of the sewer the sun shone upon
a narrow slip of the water. In the bright light it appeared the colour
of strong green tea, and positively looked as solid as black marble in
the shadow—indeed it was more like watery mud than muddy water;
and yet we were assured this was the only water the wretched inhabitants had to drink. As we gazed in horror at it, we saw drains and
sewers emptying their filthy contents into it; we saw a whole tier of
doorless privies in the open road, common to men and women, built
over it; we heard bucket after bucket of filth splash into it ...*

– Henry Mayhew (1812–1887), September 24, 1849

*Passing along a rough bank, among stakes and washing lines,
one penetrates into this chaos of small one-storied, one-roomed
huts, in most of which there is no artificial floor; kitchen, living,
and sleeping-room all in one ... Everywhere before the doors
residue and offal [waste]; that any sort of pavement lay underneath
could not be seen but only felt, here and there, with the feet.*

– Friedrich Engels (1820–1895), 1844

Many of us have a picture of the 1800s colored by a myriad of filters
that impart a nostalgic and romantic view of that era. You may
picture a time when gentleman callers arrived to meet a well-
dressed lady in a finely furnished parlor. A time where people
leisurely drifted down a river on a paddlewheel riverboat while sip-
ping mint juleps. A time of more elegant travel aboard a steam train
passing through the beautiful countryside, or a stylish woman
dressed in a long, flowing gown, descending from a sleek horse-
drawn carriage with the aid of a dapper companion in a top hat. You

may think of those times where life was simple and ordered—a seeming utopia, free of the many woes that plague modern society.

But if those filters are removed and a more objective light is cast upon that time, a different picture emerges. Instead, imagine a world where workplaces had no health, safety, or minimum-wage laws. The 1800s was a century when people put in 12 to 16 hours a day at the most tedious menial labor. Imagine bands of children roaming the streets out of control because their parents were laboring long days. Children were also involved in dangerous and demoralizing work. Picture the city of New York surrounded not by suburbs but by rings of smoldering garbage dumps and shantytowns. Cities where hogs, horses, and dogs and their refuse were commonplace in the streets. Many infectious diseases were rampant throughout the world, particularly in the larger cities. This is not a description of the Third World, but a large portion of what the United States and other civilized Western countries used to be only a century or so ago.

Photo 1.1: Syracuse, NY—Shanties Back to an Open Sewer. (1901)

*The "good old days," when everything, in particularly human health, was supposedly better than it is today, are a myth. **The*** *documented history of Western civilization describes an endless and unromantic struggle with sickness and death, tragically high infant mortality, and the premature death of young adults. Death-dealing epidemics attacked helpless communities nearly as often as summer and winter came to pass, and were followed every few years by major catastrophes. In Victorian England, the average age of death among the urban poor was 15 to 16 years.*[1]

During the 1800s, the number of factories grew along with a rapidly increasing population, which resulted in a flood of people from the countryside into the towns and cities looking for work. The population of the city of London, England, increased by almost ninefold during the 19th century. Industrialization rapidly multiplied threats to health because of the enormous simultaneous growth of towns.

In 1750, about 15 per cent of the population lived in towns; by 1880 a staggering 80 per cent was urban. In 1801 one in five workers was employed in manufacturing and linked occupations; by 1871 that had climbed to two in three. The largest city in the Western world, London had about 800,000 inhabitants in 1801; by 1841 its population had grown by a further million, and at the death of Queen Victoria in 1901 the heart of the empire [London] contained seven million inhabitants.[2]

Hazardous housing

Housing could not accommodate the population explosion, which resulted in overcrowding and a remarkable buildup of human and animal waste. In some cases, large buildings, originally built for breweries or sugar refineries, were later divided into numerous

---

[1] Velv W. Greene, PhD, MPH, "Personal Hygiene and Life Expectancy Improvements Since 1850: Historic and Epidemiologic Associations," *American Journal of Infection Control*, August 2001, p. 203.
[2] Roy Porter, *The Greatest Benefit to Mankind*, Harper Collins, New York, 1997, p. 398.

small, dark rooms for families to live in.[3] These conditions contributed to high disease and death rates.

> The stenches from the "horribly foul cellars" with their "infernal system of sewerage" must needs poison the tenants all the way up to the fifth story . . . **the well-worn rut of the dead-wagon and the ambulance to the gate, for the tenants died there like flies in all seasons**, and a tenth of its population was always in hospital.[4]

> The Tenement House Commission long afterward called the worst of the barracks "infant slaughter houses," and showed, by reference to the mortality lists, that they killed one in every five babies born in them.[5]

Photo 1.2: Jefferson Street. The shed barn at right contains three horses. The barn next in view contains six horses and two goats. The house in the center of the picture is full of Italian families and presents no redeeming feature. On the left are other tenements full of families. (1911)

> If there is an open space between them [tenements], it is never more than a slit a foot or so wide, and gets to be the receptacle of garbage and filth of every kind; so that any opening made for the purposes of ventilation becomes a source of greater danger than if there were none.[6]

---

[3] Henry E. Sigerist, *Civilization and Disease,* Cornell University Press, New York, 1943, pp. 38–39.
[4] Jacob A. Riis, *The Battle with the Slum*, Macmillan, New York, 1902, pp. 23–25.
[5] Ibid., pp. 36–37.
[6] Ibid., p. 115.

Although advances had been made by the early 1900s, many still lived in abysmal sanitary conditions. Some tenements were furnished with indoor facilities, but they were often shared by multiple families. Tales of despair and suffering were commonplace among the working poor. Struggle for survival was a daily affair. People were often close to financial and physical collapse.[7]

Photo 1.3: A so-called room of a three-room tenement, but it is merely a large size closet with a slanting ceiling, located under the main entrance stairs of the building. Here, in a three-quarter bed, sleep the father and mother and a little child. The rest of the family sleep in the front room and kitchen. This "room" has absolutely no light or ventilation. (1916)

Poor planning with the ever-increasing number of businesses and population led to haphazard city organization. Businesses of all types, including any of their hazardous environmental by-products, were built alongside crowded living quarters. The lack of health regulations and zoning rules resulted in a dangerous and demoralizing environment for the working-class people. An 1861 article on US cities and parks in the *Atlantic Monthly* described the situation in cities.

> *Narrow and crooked streets, want of proper sewerage and ventilation, the absence of forethought in providing open spaces for the recreation of the people, the allowance of intramural [within the walls of a building] burials, and of fetid nuisances, such as slaughter-houses and manufactories of offensive stuffs, have converted cities into pestilential enclosures,*

---

[7] Andrew Mearns, *'Light and Shade', A Sequel to 'The Bitter Cry of Outcast London,'* 1885, p. 7.

and kept Jefferson's saying—"Great cities are great sores"—
true in the most literal and mortifying sense.[8]

Large numbers of families dwelled within poorly constructed
houses. There was no running water and no toilet. An entire street
would share an outdoor pump and a couple of outside privy vaults or
outhouses.

In 1934 Professor Arthur Cole described how some inhabitants of New York and Boston in the 1850s lived in dark cellars overrun with vermin.

Photo 1.4: The general insanitary conditions which surround the houses on both sides of the alley. The first house on the right is a small dilapidated frame house. Beyond it are three larger tenements. The outbuildings at the left are all dilapidated, and contain privies which are in a foul condition. There are not enough garbage boxes to supply the needs, and the ones provided are so seldom cleaned that the families dump their slops and garbage in the alley. (1901)

While the larger cities
possessed handsome res-
idential districts in which
the streets were paved
and kept clean and the
sewage was properly
cared for, there was also
crowded foreign quar-
ters, veritable hives of
humanity lacking ordi-
nary comforts and often
even necessities. New
York in 1850 had 8,141
cellars sheltering 18,456
persons. There, as in Bos-
ton, about a twentieth of
the population lived in
damp, dark, ill-ventilated, vermin-infested underground rooms.
By the end of the war [US Civil War] fifteen thousand tenement

---

[8] Henry W. Bellows, "Cities and Parks: With Special Reference to the New York Central Park," *Atlantic Monthly*, vol. VII, April 1861, p. 416.

houses had been built in New York, many of them hardly more than "fever nests."[9]

The working classes inhabited the most deplorable housing, which was described by Friedrich Engels in 1844. Engels visited the slums while in Manchester, England, and noted the horrors he observed. He described the people he encountered in London and other towns in England.

> *... these pale, lank, narrow-chested hollow-eyed ghosts, whom one passes at every step, these languid flabby faces, incapable of the slightest energetic expression, I have seen in such startling numbers.*[10]

Hordes of people crowded beneath smoldering, water-rotted roofs, or burrowed among the rats of clammy cellars.[11] Roy Porter, a British historian noted for his work on the history of medicine, wrote about the plight of millions of people in the newly industrialized cities.

Photo 1.5: The conditions of the filth-strewn alleys, of courts and yards littered with rubbish, of ill-smelling stables and manure boxes find their climax and in part their cause in the accumulation of garbage. (1901)

> *For millions, entire lives—albeit often very short ones—were passed in new industrial cities of dreadful night with an all too typical socio-pathology: **foul housing, often in flooded cellars, gross overcrowding, atmospheric and water-supply***

---

[9] Arthur Charles Cole, *The Irrepressible Conflict 1850–1865, A History of American Life Volume VII*, Macmillan, New York, 1934, p. 181.

[10] Friedrich Engels, *The Condition of the Working-Class in England in 1844*, Otto Wigand, Leipzig, p. 98.

[11] Jacob A. Riis, *The Battle with the Slum*, Macmillan, New York, 1902, p. 13.

pollution, overflowing cesspools, contaminated pumps, poverty, hunger, fatigue and abjection everywhere. Such conditions, comparable to today's Third World shanty town or refugee camps, bred rampant sickness of every kind. Appalling neo-natal, infant and child mortality accompanied the abomination of child labour in mines and factories; life expectations were exceedingly low—often under twenty years among the working classes—and everywhere sickness precipitated family breakdown, pauperization and social crisis. [12]

Contemporary writers of the time tried to call attention to the plight of the wretched poor and their terrible living conditions. Andrew Mearns and William C. Preston wrote about the poor in their 1883 book *The Bitter Cry of Outcast London: An Inquiry into the Condition of the Abject Poor.*

Few who will read these pages have any conception of what these pestilential human rookeries are, where tens of thousands are crowded together amidst horrors which call to mind what we have heard of the middle passage of the slave ship. To get to them you have to penetrate courts reeking with poisonous gases arising from accumulation of sewage and refuse scattered in all directions and often flowing beneath your feet; courts, many of them which the sun never penetrates, which are never visited by a breath of fresh air, and which rarely know the virtues of a drop of cleansing water. You have to ascend rotten staircases, which threaten to give way beneath every step, leaving gaps that imperil the limbs and lives of the unwary. You have to grope your way along dark and filthy passages swarming with vermin. Then, if you are not driven back by the intolerable stench, you may gain admittance to the dens

---

[12] Roy Porter, *The Greatest Benefit to Mankind*, Harper Collins, New York, 1997, p. 399.

in which these thousands of beings who belong, as much as you, to the race for whom Christ died, herd together.[13]

The extremely stressful conditions rapidly aged the poor working-class people. Those who escaped death from disease or disability at an early age often only lived into their thirties or forties.

Among the laboring classes, life expectation remained everywhere low—little more than thirty years—and from the 1830s photographs show working people looking old by their thirties and forties, as poor nutrition, illness, bad living conditions and gross overwork took their toll.[14]

Water and sewage and everything offal

Clean water, proper sewage treatment, and fresh air did not exist in these areas. Without any sanitary infrastructure, human and animal waste would flow into the streets, ending up in the local streams and rivers, which happened to also be the people's primary water supply. Sanitary facilities designed for smaller populations failed. Cesspools overflowed and seeped into the local water supplies.

The manner in which the great multitude of the poor is treated by society to-day is revolting. They are drawn into the large cities where

Photo 1.6: Water-closet used by fourteen families. (1916)

---

[13] Andrew Mearns and William C. Preston, *The Bitter Cry of Outcast London: An Inquiry into the Condition of the Abject Poor*, James Clarke & Co., London, 1883, p. 4.

[14] Ibid., p. 425.

they breathe a poorer atmosphere than in the country; they are relegated to districts which, by reason of the method of construction, are worse ventilated than any others; **they are deprived of all means of cleanliness, of water itself, since pipes are laid only when paid for, and the rivers so polluted that they are useless for such purposes; they are obliged to throw all offal and garbage, all dirty water, often all disgusting drainage and excrement into the streets, being without other means of disposing them**; *they are thus compelled to infect the region of their own dwellings.*[15]

In the mid-1800s, public water supplies in McLean County, Illinois, and Chicago were described as being contaminated with human and animal waste. The Chicago Medical Society frequently criticized the city's water supply, which after 1853 was drawn from Lake Michigan by means of a crude wooden inlet 600 feet long, close to where the sewage-filled Chicago River emptied.[16]

Photo 1.7: Public hall and sink. Sink supported only by string and flimsy wooden props. Hall floor covered with fecal matter and sewage. (1903)

Before the 1870s, all kinds of garbage and human and animal waste had been thrown into what

---

[15] Friedrich Engels, *The Condition of the Working-Class in England in 1844*, Otto Wigand, Leipzig, p. 97.

[16] Thomas Neville Bonner, *Medicine in Chicago 1850–1950: A Chapter in the Social and Scientific Development of a City*, American History Research Center, Madison, Wisconsin, 1957, p. 179.

> *became known as the "North and South Sloughs," originally small streams running into Sugar Creek. Over the years the Sloughs "became a . . . sodden pool of stench that was the breeding places for disease . . . because it drained sewage into the community's primary water source, Sugar Creek."[17]*

Poor waste management continued in Paris even after World War I, with many of the city's cesspools still in use.

> *Unlike Londoners, most Parisians were still getting their water in 1870 from fountains or water-sellers, and disposing of waste in court pits. Paris was a city of 85,000 cesspools; many remained until after the First World War.[18]*

Edwin Chadwick, an English social reformer who worked to improve sanitary conditions and public health, believed that sickness bred poverty. He enlisted the aid of three doctors who were sympathetic to sanitary reforms—Neil Arnott, James Phillip Kay-Shuttleworth, and Thomas Southwood Smith. Their 1838 report revealed the squalor in London.

> *"The room of a fever patient, in a small and heated apartment in London, with no perflation [blowing] of fresh air, is perfectly analogous to the stagnant pool in Ethiopia full of the bodies of dead locusts," declared Southwood Smith. "The poison generated in both cases is the same; the difference is merely in the degree of its potency."[19]*

---

[17] Lucinda McCray, *A Matter of Life and Death: Health, Illness and Medicine in McLean County, 1830–1995*, Bloomington Offset Process, Inc., 1996, pp. 54–55.

[18] Roy Porter, *The Greatest Benefit to Mankind*, Harper Collins, New York, 1997, p. 416.

[19] Ibid., p. 410.

Animals: Dead and live, dangerous and diseased

Because there were no environmental laws, industries simply discharged their waste into the air and water. In 1850s London, the environment was filled with dirt that spewed from factories. If human and animal waste in the city streets was not revolting enough, the people withstood an even worse addition to the loathsome scenario—putrefying corpses of animals.

> *In manufacturing towns, factory chimneys spewed soot, and everything was covered with dirt and grime. Smoke was a major ingredient of the famous London fog, which not only reduced visibility, but posed serious health risks. Refuse, including the rotting corpses of dogs and horses, littered city streets. In 1858, the stench from sewage and other rot in London was so putrid that the British House of Commons was forced to suspend its sessions.*[20]

Animals were found in great numbers in the cities, either roaming freely or in slaughterhouses. The *Annual Report of the Metropolitan Board of Health* in 1866 describes slaughterhouses that were intermingled with tenement housing.

> *The suffering caused to animals by the present system of slaughtering is a source of pain and annoyance to all persons living near these establishments. The animals are seldom fed from the time they arrive until they are killed, and constantly give expression to their suffering. Many slaughter-houses are located in the centre of blocks of high tenement-houses, and the business of slaughtering, as viewed from the adjacent*

---

[20] Thomas F. X. Noble, Barry Straus, Duane J. Osheim, Kristen B. Neuschel, Elinor A. Accampo, David D. Roberts, and William B. Choen, *Western Civilization: Beyond Boundaries,* volume II, 6th ed., Wadsworth, Boston, Massachusetts, 2010, p. 579.

windows, is in the highest degree demoralizing in its effects upon the young.[21]

People threw their garbage out onto the city streets, where it was consumed by scavenging pigs, dogs, and rats. The filth in New York City streets had amassed to a depth of two to three feet in the winter. Household refuse and animal waste from horses and the other animals mixed with the muddy streets.

> *. . . nearly every city—from the national capital to some budding Western porkopolis—had its hog nuisance or some equivalent. The streets, squares and parks amounted to public pens, hog holes offending the eye and nose at every turn . . . In the fall of 1853 porkers were more numerous on the streets of Springfield [Illinois] than in the pens at the state fairgrounds. The near-by town of Urbana had a record of more hogs than people, and they had at least equal rights with citizens upon the streets.*[22]

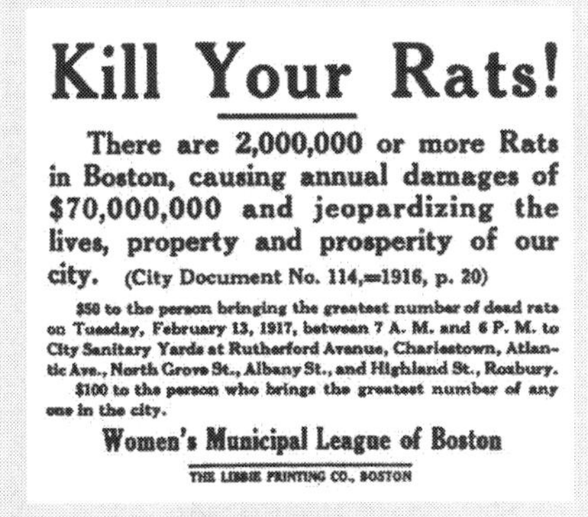

Kill Your Rats!

There are 2,000,000 or more Rats in Boston, causing annual damages of $70,000,000 and jeopardizing the lives, property and prosperity of our city. (City Document No. 114,—1916, p. 20)

$50 to the person bringing the greatest number of dead rats on Tuesday, February 13, 1917, between 7 A. M. and 6 P. M. to City Sanitary Yards at Rutherford Avenue, Charlestown, Atlantic Ave., North Grove St., Albany St., and Highland St., Roxbury.

$100 to the person who brings the greatest number of any one in the city.

Women's Municipal League of Boston

THE LIBBIE PRINTING CO., BOSTON

Photo 1.8: Kill Rats Poster. (1917)

With the accumulation of garbage came the inevitable increase in vermin such as rats, which became an accepted part of city life. Disease-spreading insects of all types, including cockroaches, were commonplace in tenements.

Prisons, dock-yards, and wharves have been celebrated for the multitude and magnitude of the

---

[21] *Annual Report of the Metropolitan Board of Health, 1866,* C.S. Wescott & Co.'s Printing House, New York, 1987, p. 34.
[22] Arthur Charles Cole, *The Irrepressible Conflict 1850–1865: A History of American Life Volume VII,* Macmillan, New York, 1934, pp. 179–180.

rats which infest them, and the cruelty of their voracious attacks upon the inmates of these receptacles of vermin.[23]

In 1916 the cities of New York and Boston were infested with millions of rats, causing a huge amount of destruction.

> *It is estimated by the bacteriological department of the Boston board of health that $72,000,000 in damage is done yearly by the **2,000,000 rats that infest Boston**. About $91,250,000 in damage is done yearly by rodents in New York City.*[24]

During the mid-1800s, hospitals were unsanitary and overcrowded. The American public looked upon them with little regard, considering them a place where the sick and poor went to die. An 1860 article entitled "Rats in the Hospital" published in *Harper's Weekly*, a leading journal of that time, exposed the horrific conditions at Bellevue Hospital in New York. The article was inspired by an incident of a baby who was eaten by rats at that hospital.

> *This day, the inquest held on the body of the infant that was eaten by rats in Bellevue Hospital, New York, was concluded. The evidence of Mary O'Connor, the mother of the child, and that of numerous other witnesses, was taken . . . and recommended that proper means be taken to rid the hospital of the rats that now infest the institution.*[25]

Diseased food

The limited sources of food consumed by the population were often of poor quality or contaminated. A lack of laws or unenforced laws and a systemically corrupt food supply chain led to an abysmal health situation for those eating diseased food. Attempts to improve the situation were almost always opposed by the individuals and businesses engaged in the offenses because it impacted their bottom

---

[23] *The American Medical Gazette*, vol. XI, Hall, Clayton & Co. Printers, New York, 1859, p. 387.

[24] *The Women's Municipal League of Boston Bulletin*, May 1916, p. 20.

[25] *Vincent's Semi-Annual United States Register*, 1860, p. 346.

line. In Chicago and New York City, milk was of such poor quality that it caused the deaths of thousands of children each year.

> *. . . milk sold in Chicago came from cows "fed on whiskey slops with their bodies covered with sores and tails all eat off," a circumstance which enabled the editorial critic to explain "Why so many children die in Chicago." New York's milk supply was also largely a by-product of the local distilleries and **the milk dealers were charged with the serious offense of murdering annually eight thousand children.**[26]*

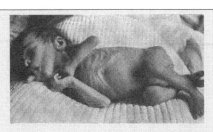

Photo 1.9: A case of Acute Milk Poisoning Having Vomiting, Diarrhoea, Mucous and Bloody Stools, General Emaciation, Acute Cholera Infantum, and Dysentery. (1914)

> *[Cows] shut up, without proper exercise or pure air, the milk is necessarily diseased, and is the cause of extensive mortality among young children and infants. Besides the unhealthy slops, decayed vegetables, and the sour and putrid offals and remnants of kitchens, are gathered up for food of these animals; the consequence of which is, that they become diseased . . .[27]*

In 1860s England, city inspectors attempted to control the sale and use of diseased meats. To avoid financial losses, diseased meat was made into sausages, pickled and cured for ham and bacon, to be sold to an unsuspecting public. Meat that was too diseased for even sausage was fed to the pigs, which would later be eaten by humans.

---

[26] Arthur Charles Cole, *The Irrepressible Conflict 1850–1865: A History of American Life Volume VII*, Macmillan, New York, 1934, p. 181.
[27] Jonathan Pereira, MD, "Milk as Affected by the Diet and Regimen of Cows," *A Treatise on Food and Diet*, J. & H. G. Langley, New York, 1843, p. 287.

The dead-meat markets are contaminated by the carcasses of diseased animals from all sources . . . in the City markets alone his inspectors seize from one to two tons of diseased meat every week; and similar seizures, but to a less extent, are made in butchers' shops and slaughter-houses outside the City by Medical Officers of Health and their assistants. In Edinburgh [England], Mr. Gamgee tells us that 100 to 200 diseased cattle are sold in the dead-meat market every week, carcasses being smuggled in by night even from adjoining piggeries. In this way the best butchers, in ignorance "may and do serve diseased meat to the wealthiest in the land." . . . **Pigs are largely fed upon diseased meat which is too far gone even for the sausage-maker, and this is saying a great deal; and as an universal rule, disease pigs are pickled and cured for bacon, ham, etc.**[28]

People often consumed nutrient-deficient diets and contaminated food that left them weak and susceptible to disease. This 1865 report talks about the deplorable state of food in the city of New York. Decayed and diseased foods were often sold to the working classes, which left them in a weakened physical condition.

The quality of the food sold at the corner and butchers' shops in this neighborhood deserves a more extended notice than it can receive here. A casual examination shows much of it to be unfit for human sustenance. Unwholesome meat, particularly slunk veal [flesh from the fetus of a calf, found during the slaughter of its mother], is constantly vended and consumed. Piles of pickled herrings are exposed to the air till the mass approaches a condition of putridity; and this slimy food, with wilted and decayed vegetables, sausages not above suspicion, and horrible pies, composed of stale and unripe fruits, whose digestion no human stomach can accomplish, all find ready

---

[28] *The British and Foreign Medico-Chirurgical Review, Quarterly Journal of Practical Medicine and Surgery*, vol. XXXV, John Churchill & Sons, London, January–April 1865, pp. 32, 33.

*purchasers. These **decaying animals and vegetable remains are daily entombed in the protuberant stomachs of thousands of children, whose pallid, expressionless faces and shrunken limbs are the familiar attributes of childhood** in these localities.*[29]

The glimpse we have just taken of the underside of Western culture in the 1800s to the 1900s is never discussed in terms of the medical issues and diseases of that notoriously sickened era. Yet those were the most important aspects of susceptibility and spread of illness.

It was not only the adults who suffered these awful conditions. Frequently, children lived an unthinkable existence too. Their lives were often beset not only with pitiful living conditions and diseased, rotten food, but also with long hours of arduous and demoralizing labor, all of which took an enormous toll on their immunity.

---

[29] *Report of the Council of Hygiene and Public Health of the Citizens' Association of New York*, 1865, p. 59.

~ 2 ~

SUFFER THE LITTLE CHILDREN

*I have been working below three years on my father's account:
he takes me down at two in the morning, and I am up at two the
next afternoon. I go to bed at six at night, to be ready for work the
next morning. I have to bear my burthen [burden] four traps or
ladders before I get to the main road, which leads to the pit bottom.
My task is four or five tubs; each tub holds 4 ½ cwt [1 cwt. or
hundredweight = 112 pounds]. I fill five tubs in twenty journeys.
Am very glad when my task is wrought, as it sore fatigues.*

– Ellison Jack, 11-year-old girl, coal bearer, 1840s

*But the young, young children, O my brothers!
They are weeping bitterly.
They are weeping in the play-time of the others
In the country of the free.
"For oh!" say the children, "we are weary,
And we cannot run or leap.
If we cared for any meadows, it were merely
To drop in them and sleep."
They look up with their pale and sunken faces,
And their look is dread to see.*

– Elizabeth Barrett Browning (1806–1861),
"Cry of the Children," 1842

In the Western world, many children enjoy what we have come to
define as a normal childhood. They generally get up in the morning
and have a reasonable breakfast, and then, during the majority of the
year, attend school. In public and private schools, they are educated
in math, science, languages, and other areas of study. While in school,
they are fed, and all their basic needs are usually met. They often

have a chance to experience art, music, and physical education and to play games at recess. During the balance of the day, they may interact with their friends, play games, enjoy sports, watch television, play with their pets, or engage in an entire host of other leisure activities. At night they sleep in a relatively safe environment. In the summer months, they often enjoy long, leisurely days playing and may even take vacations with their family.

Although this life is not enjoyed by all and may not be perfect, it is far more common in the developed world than it used to be. During the 1800s and into the 1900s, life for many children in the United States and England was that of long and brutal hours of hard labor and poverty. Their lives were not filled with joy and laughter, but often with suffering and crushing misery.

From the late 1700s into the 1800s, machines frequently replaced manual labor for the production of most manufactured goods. With the large number of factories, the owners needed sources of cheap labor, which was often found in the form of children. Many machines did not need adult strength to operate, so children could be hired more inexpensively than adults. Factory work for children was abusive and demoralizing.

> *Children from seven years of age upward, were engaged by hundreds from London and other large cities, and set to work in the cotton spinning factories of the north. Since there were no other facilities for boarding them, "apprentice houses" were built for them, in the vicinity of the factories, where they were placed under the care of the superintendents or matrons . . . They were remotely situated, apart from the observation of the community, left to the burdens of unrelieved labor under the harshness of small masters or foremen. Their hours of labor were excessive.* **When the demands of the trade were active they were often arranged in two shifts, each shift working twelve hours, one in the day and another in the night, so that it was a common saying in the north that "their beds never got cold," one set climbing into bed as the other got**

out. When there was no night work the day work was the longer. They were driven at their work and often abused.[30]

The 1816 report of the Select Committee on the state of children employed in manufacturing detailed the distress that children endured. They labored long hours to the point of exhaustion. Those who lived suffered physical breakdown from the harsh conditions they endured.

Photo 2.1: Boy coal miners. (1914)

> *Children of all ages, down to three and four, were found in the hardest and most painful labor, while babes of six were commonly found in large numbers in many factories. Labor from twelve to thirteen and often sixteen hours a day was the rule. Children had not a moment free, save to snatch a hasty meal or sleep as best as they could. From earliest youth they worked to a point of extreme exhaustion, without open-air exercise, or any enjoyment whatever, but grew up, if they survived at all, weak, bloodless, miserable, and in many cases deformed cripples, and victims of almost every disease.*[31]

Some children began work at the age of four. An 1843 report by John W. Parker detailed the ages of the children employed to work.

> *That instances occur in which **Children are taken into the mines to work as early as four years of age, sometimes at five,** and between five and six, not unfrequently between six*

---

[30] Edward P. Cheyney, *An Introduction to the Industrial and Social History of England*, Macmillan, New York, 1920, p. 233.

[31] William Franklin Willoughby and Mary Clare de Graffenried, *Child Labor*, American Economic Association, Guggenheimer, Weil, & Co., Baltimore, March 1890, p. 16.

and seven, and often from seven to eight, while from eight to nine is the ordinary age at which employment in these mines commences. That a very large portion of the persons employed in carrying on the work of these mines is under thirteen years of age; and a still larger portion between thirteen and eighteen. That in several districts female Children begin to work in the mines at the same early age as the males. [32]

By the mid-1800s, child labor had been recognized as a major problem. In England, a commission was appointed in 1840 to investigate.

*This lad is a pitiable specimen of a much enduring class of colliery [underground mine] boys, whose subsistence depends on their own exertions, often prematurely stimulated, either from being deprived of their fathers by death, or laboring under the curse of drunken, dissolute, and unfeeling parents, who would apathetically see their children enslave themselves, rather than contribute to their comfort by a single act of self-denial. These neglected beings turn out in the morning, taking with them a scanty bag of provisions, to be eaten in the bowels of the earth, where **they toil out their daily dole of eight or ten hours; then return to a comfortless home, taking their chance of good meal, a bad one, or none at all. For a bed they are content with an old coal-sack laid upon straw,** or occupy whatever portion they can secure of a family bed, which must suffice for three or four other inmates.* [33]

A public investigation exposed distressing situations termed by some as *mine slavery*. [34]

---

[32] John W. Parker, *Physical and Moral Condition of the Children and Young Persons Employed in Mines and Manufactures*, William Clowes and Sons, London, 1843, p. 1.
[33] Ibid., p. 30.
[34] *The Universalist Union*, vol. VII, August 13, 1842, p. 615.

Children began their life in the coal mines at five, six, or seven years of age. Girls and women worked like boys and men; they were less than half clothed, and worked alongside men who were stark naked. There were from twelve to fourteen working hours in the twenty-four, and these were often at night. Little girls of six or eight years of age made ten to twelve trips a day up steep ladders to the surface, carrying half a hundred weight of coal in wooden buckets on their backs at each journey. Young women appeared before the commissioners when summoned from their work, dressed merely in a pair of trousers, dripping wet from the water of the mine, and already weary with the labor of the day scarcely more than begun. *A common form of labor consisted of drawing on hands and knees over the inequalities of a passageway not more than two feet or twenty-eight inches high a car or tub filled with three or four hundred weight of coal, attached by a chain and hooked to a leather band around the waist.*[35]

Fig. 13.

Fig. 14.

Photo 2.2: Girl and older girl using a creel to move coal. (1842)

---

[35] Edward P. Cheyney, *An Introduction to the Industrial and Social History of England*, Macmillan, New York, 1920, pp. 243–244.

The testimony of a young girl named Ellison Jack illustrated the hardship of her life as a mine worker. She would descend a pit ladder with a basket-like device, or creel, on her back that allowed the lumps of coal to rest on her back and shoulders. With this device, she could fill four or five tubs of coal during her day's work. Each tub holding roughly 500 pounds meant she moved between 2,000 and 2,500 pounds of coal a day. Since each tub took her four trips, each load she carried was about 125 pounds.

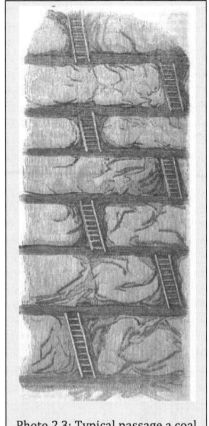

Photo 2.3: Typical passage a coal bearer traversed. (1842)

Large lumps of coal are then placed on the neck, and then she commences her journey to the pit bottom, first hanging her lamp to the cloth crossing her forehead. In this girl's case she has first to travel fourteen fathom, eighty-four feet, from the wall face to the first ladder; this ladder is eighteen feet high. From this ladder she proceeds along the main road, that is probably from three feet six inches to four feet six inches high, and so on to the second ladder, which is eighteen feet high, and so to the third and fourth ladders, until she reaches the pit bottom, where she casts her load.[36]

---

[36] *The Universalist Union*, vol. VII, August 13, 1842, p. 615.

Injuries and disease were commonplace. Many children died of diseases such as typhus, and women also had stillbirths due to the stressful conditions.[37]

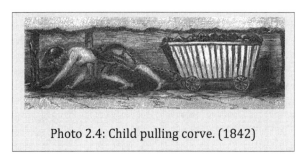

Photo 2.4: Child pulling corve. (1842)

Other mine jobs, although not as labor intensive, were also dull and dreary. One job for boys was to wait all day long to open and close the gates for the wooden sleds, or corves, which were used for hauling coal.

*The trappers sit in a little hole scooped out for them in the side of the gates behind each door, where they sit with a string in their hands attached to the door, and pull it open the moment they hear the corves at hand; and the moment it passes they let the door fall to, which it does of its own weight . . . They have nothing else to do but as their office must be performed from the passing of the first to the passing of the last corve during the day, they are in the pit during the whole time it is worked, frequently above twelve hours a day. **It is a most painful thing to contemplate the dull dungeon-like life these little creatures are doomed to spend—a life, for the most part, spent in solitude, damp, and darkness.** They are allowed no light—but sometimes a good-natured collier will bestow a bit of candle upon them as a treat.*[38]

---

[37] *Parliamentary Papers: Volume 15, Reports from Commissioners—Children Employment (Mines),* February 3–August 12, 1842, p. 93.

[38] *The Universalist Union,* vol. VII, August 13, 1842, p. 615.

In the early 1900s, children were still being employed by the mining industry. Even though children younger than 14 were officially prohibited from working, some as young as 9 or 10 could be found employed in the mines. Due to improved machinery, boys were principally employed as

Photo 2.5: The Lonely Trapper Boy. (1914)

coal breakers, picking out slate from coal as it was dumped into the mine cars. In the breakers where coal was dried, the coal dust was so dense that, even on bright days, light would not penetrate. Breaker boys needed to wear mine lamps on their caps to allow them to see the coal at their feet. Although safety precautions were taken, children sometimes suffered horrific deaths.

> *It is true we occasionally hear of a little boy in the mine run over by a coal car, or kicked to death by a mule, or fatally injured by a piece of falling slate. And **in the coal breakers little boys are sometimes ground in large crushers that break the coal, caught in the wheels or other machinery, or buried in a stream of coal**—the death suffered recently by the little boy in Pittston [Pennsylvania].*[39]

In the 1800s, children employed in glass manufacturing worked long hours in extremely challenging conditions. They suffered from a wide variety of physical problems.

> *In the manufacture of glass . . . the hard labour, the irregularity of the hours, the frequent night-work, and especially the great heat of the working place (100 to 190 Fahrenheit), engender in children general debility and disease, stunted growth, and especially affections of the eye, bowel*

---

[39] Owen R. Lovejoy, *Child Labor in the Coal Mines, Child Labor—A Menace to Industry, Education, and Good Citizenship*, Academy of Political and Social Science, 1906, p. 38.

complaints, and rheumatic, and bronchial affections. **Many of the children are pale, have red eyes, often blind for weeks at a time, suffer from violent nausea, vomiting, coughs, colds, and rheumatism . . . The glass-blowers usually die young of debility or chest infections.**[40]

A 1906 article by Owen R. Lovejoy spoke about child labor in the manufacturing of glass. Boys worked near the blistering heat of the furnace and performed many jobs. Because glass manufacturing could continuously operate, boys were also employed to work at night. After laboring long hours in excessive heat, they were sent home early in the morning.

Photo 2.6: Boys in the manufacturing of medicine bottles. (1914)

It is significant that in many glass-houses one hardly finds the child of a glass-blower. **One worker who spent his life in the glass-house when asked the reason replied: "I would rather send my boys straight to hell than send them by way of the glass-house."** *A young friend, whose character and family are well known, said recently that of the 175 boys with whom he worked in an Indiana factory two years ago there were only ten at the end of the fire who were not confirmed drinkers of intoxicants.*[41]

---

[40] Roy Porter, *The Greatest Benefit to Mankind*, Harper Collins, New York, 1997, p. 401.

[41] Owen R. Lovejoy, *Child Labor in the Glass Industry, Child Labor—A Menace to Industry, Education, and Good Citizenship*, Academy of Political and Social Science, 1906, p. 44.

In the early 1900s in the state of New York, children worked in the cannery industry for endless hours. The housing supplied for these seasonal workers was inadequate and unsanitary. As many as eight people were found living in a small room. The outhouses were unspeakably filthy. There were no screens covering the openings of the windows, permitting swarms of flies to travel from the filth of the outhouses to the

Photo 2.7: Children snipping beans in Maryland. (1913)

small rooms that contained exposed food. The canners blamed God for the terrible plight of the children and women.

"It's the Lord's fault; we cannot control the ripening of the crops," that canners gave in 1912, as in previous years, as their excuse for beginning the work of 12 year old boys at 3 A. M., for working 10 year old girls 14½ hours a day, for working women as many as 100 hours a week.[42]

Photo 2.8: At a Dangerous Capping Machine. (1913)

Eight-year-old girls capped cans. They placed a small tin disk that was soldered to the cover on the filled cans of fruits and vegetables, capping 40 cans a minute. A child was hard pressed to keep up with that rate.

In other industries, the difficult and dirty working

---

[42] *The Child Labor Bulletin*, vol. 1, no. 4, February 1913, pp. 22–23.

conditions, long hours, and exposure to toxins such as lead created a variety of physical disabilities in many.

> *... women and children in lacemaking were often kept at work during the busy season till nine, ten, and even twelve o'clock at night; that the girls in dye-houses who carried wet goods on their backs into drying rooms at as high a temperature as 110, and then out on to the grass fields, were often summoned to work at four or five o'clock in the morning; that there were* **more than 2,000 children under ten years of age at work in the Birmingham hardware industry, one-fourth of them under eight; and that weak-sight, blindness, and lead poisoning were prevalent in the potteries and other industries, which were carried on under shockingly unsanitary conditions.**[43]

An 1890 book on child labor describes the manufacture of paper boxes. Like other factory work, it involved long, endless hours of mind-numbing work.

> *The ceilings were low and begrimed, the light not unfrequently inadequate. Each worker is then provided with an oil-lamp whose smoke and fumes combine with the odors of the glue-pot and neglected water-closets to make the close room more hurtful. Piles of inflammable paper and stacks of boxes await but a spark to kindle a fire*

Photo 2.9: A child employed as a doffer. (1914)

> *that would sweep the building before the dazed inmates could*

---

[43] Edward P. Cheyney, *An Introduction to the Industrial and Social History of England*, Macmillan, New York, 1920, p. 276.

rush to the dark and dangerous stairs, only to find the way barred by packing-cases. In such death-traps thousands of children labor. The lame and humpbacked choose box-making as light work permitting them to sit. Their distorted figures and pain-marked features stand out sadly in the dim light behind long tables piled grotesquely with box-shapes.[44]

A 1913 article in *Good Housekeeping* details the labor of children in the cotton mills.

. . . a majority of the workers in the cotton mills are under 16, and that the ages of them run down to 6 and 7. The girls are used as "spinners" and for the most part—walking up and down between the spinning frames and knotting threads that break; and the boys are employed as "doffers"—for the replacement of the empty bobbins with full ones. The hours that these children work is

Photo 2.10: Children 6, 8, and two of 12 years making hose supporters by lamplight. (1913)

*well nigh incredible. Either they toil from six in the morning until six at night, or from six at night until six in the morning . . . **It is also the truth that the day-shift is frequently asked to work two and three nights a week, so that there are days when the child works for seventeen hours at a stretch.***[45]

---

[44] William Franklin Willoughby and Mary Clare de Graffenried. *Child Labor*, American Economic Association, Guggenheimer, Weil, & Co., Baltimore, March 1890, p. 90.

[45] Judge Benjamin B. Lindsey and George Creel, "Children in Bondage: The Sacrifice of Golden Boys and Girls," *Good Housekeeping*, July 1913, pp. 17–18.

Children could also be employed at home, doing tedious work in what was known as tenement industries. This work involved the production of clothing or other products that factories hired out to be done at home. A 1913 Massachusetts Child Labor Committee report describes the difficult working conditions and the effects on children.

> *It [work] is done in close, poorly-ventilated rooms, often in dirty kitchens and in unhygienic houses . . . The children work long hours and often late at night by lamplight. Small children of five, seven, and nine years of age work in a bending position until nine or ten o'clock. This is bad for the eyes, causes nervous strain, interferes with the child's schooling.* **The anemic, tired, nervous, overworked children are driven until they cry out against the abuse . . . A girl seven years old had worked sitting in the hot sun while she was sick with measles. The lack of care at that time was followed by her death** *. . .*[46]

The breakdown of healthy family systems and the resultant infant neglect was a large contributor to disease in the past 200 years. Women and girls were often forced to work in order to survive. According to the 1901 English census, of the 13 million females older than 10, 4 million were working. The difficult working conditions often resulted in physical breakdown, leaving a population of children who were frequently neglected.

> *Mothers employed in factories are, save during the dinner hours, absent from home all day long, and the care of their infants during their absence is entrusted to young children, hired nurse-girls, sometimes not more than eight or ten years of age . . .*[47]

---

[46] *Child Labor in Massachusetts Tenements, Annual Report of the Massachusetts Child Labor Committee,* January 1, 1913, pp. 5–6.
[47] Sir George Newman, *Infant Mortality: A Continuing Social Problem,* Methueun & Co., London, 1906, p. 95.

Lack of knowledge regarding proper child care, combined with poverty, stressful working conditions, meager nutrition, improper hygiene, and poor sanitation, led to a large number of child deaths.

*Few facts receive more unanimous support from those in intimate touch with this question than the ignorance and carelessness of mothers in respect of infant management. Such ignorance shows itself not only in bad methods of artificial feeding, but in the exposure of the child to all sorts of injurious influences, and to uncleanly management and negligence. **Death in infancy is probably more due to such ignorances and negligence than to almost any other cause, as becomes evident with we remember that epidemic diarrhoea, convulsions, debility, and atrophy, which are the most common causes of death, are brought about in large measure owing to improper feeding or ill-timed weaning; bronchitis and pneumonia are due not infrequently to careless exposure;** and death from measles and whooping-cough is largely caused by mismanagement of nursing.*[48]

Photo 2.11: Massachusetts Mill Workers. (1914)

Due to the extreme working conditions—long hours, revolting environments, little rest, poor nutrition—the resulting health of children was deplorable. Their weakened constitutions left them extremely susceptible to diseases of all types.

---

[48] Sir George Newman, *Infant Mortality: A Continuing Social Problem,* Methueun & Co., London, 1906, p. 262.

*The medical witnesses state that the general health is greatly deteriorated; that the **Children are pale, thin, delicate, feeble, stunted in growth, more than usually susceptible to certain formidable diseases, and much less able than common to resist the ordinary causes of disease.** The prevailing complaints are general weakness, often amounting to fainting, pains in the head, side, back, and loins, palpitations, sickness, vomiting, and loss of appetite, curvature of the spine, scrofula, and consumption. The female health, in particular appears to be constantly and grievously disturbed.*[49]

Children who began work so early in life were subjected to such long hours of labor did not grow so rapidly, nor reach their full stature, nor retain their vigor so late in life, as did the population outside of the factories.[50]

In regard to health, also, there is no occupation which a child can pursue all day and every day without injury . . . As a matter of fact there are a considerable percentage

Photo 2.12: Child factory workers. (1913)

*of accidents in the mills, and a high death rate from tuberculosis. But, we repeat, these incidental dangers might all be done away without affecting the fact that the mental strain involved in the noise of the mill, and the sheer muscular strain of any simple motion repeated past the point of fatigue do seriously weaken the growing child. **Even where there is no immedi-***

---

[49] John W. Parker, *Physical and Moral Condition of the Children and Young Persons Employed in Mines and Manufactures*, William Clowes and Sons, London, 1843, pp. 132–133.

[50] Edward P. Cheyney, *An Introduction to the Industrial and Social History of England*, Macmillan, New York, 1920, p. 240.

ate traceable injury, there is always an indirect effect whereby the child is made more susceptible to infection.[51]

Children in industries were also exposed to a number of poisonous materials that impacted their health and immune systems.

. . . crouching down out of sight behind bales of paper where arsenic is used; exposed to the poison of lead, mercury, phosphorus, copper, and other toxic influences; and the ills of the artificial humidity essential to the spinning of cotton, flax, wool, and silk. The difficulty is to "catch them at it," to discover them really at work, and then to prove that they are under the age required by law, for, as these little people say themselves "It is easy to fix the Board of Health certificate if you only know how." **Lead poisoning, or plumbism, causes loosening and dropping out of teeth,**

Photo 2.13: Only a box for a house, and railroad yard for a playground. (1919)

frightful colic, blindness, paralysis, and sometimes death in convulsions. Phosphorous ulcerates the gums, causes decay of bone, terrible disfigurements, blindness, and paralysis of the wrists, and often death. Mercury gives rise to anemia, or bloodlessness, to spongy gums, loosened teeth, and paresis [impaired movement] of the limbs. *Nitric acid, used for cleaning, may cause instant death. The germs of lockjaw reside in hides, wool, and fur.*[52]

Into the early 1900s, many children of the working poor lived in crowded tenements with no yards. When they had free time, their

---

[51] *The Child Labor Bulletin*, vol.1, no. 4, February 1913, pp. 93–94.
[52] *The American Journal of Nursing*, vol. III, no. 8, May 1903, p. 664.

playgrounds were the city streets or worse. A 1920 article in *Good Housekeeping* stated that 250,000 children died each year in the United States due to poverty.

> There is no escape from the conclusion that **the United States, the richest nation in the world, is allowing every year a quarter of a million of her own children to be killed by poverty.** All other causes come back, in the last analysis, to that one.[53]

The world we enjoy today is built in part on the ceaseless labors of children of the past. The conditions they worked and lived in were just as horrifying as they were for the adults of the time. Extreme working conditions, poor nutrition, and lack of sanitation and hygiene left many children in a terrible state of health. Unfortunately, many children elsewhere in the world today are subject to similar working conditions and poverty.

---

[53] Rose Wilder Lane, "Mother No. 22,999," *Good Housekeeping*, vol. 70, March 1920, p. 112.

DISEASE—A WAY OF LIFE

*Like beasts, like maniacs, the people fell on them ... There is no
more dreadful sight than such popular anger thirsting for blood
and throttling its defenseless victims ... In the Rue Vaugirard, where
two men were killed ... I saw one of these unfortunates when he
was still breathing and the old hags were just pulling the wooden
shoes from their feet and beating him on the head with them till
he was dead. He was quite naked and bloody and mashed; they had
torn off not only his clothes but his hair, his sex, and his nose, and one
ruffian tied a rope to the feet of the corpse and dragging it through
the streets, shouting constantly, "Voilà le Cholera-morbus!"*

– Heinrich Hein (1797–1856), 1832 Paris cholera epidemic

*... the cupidity [extreme greed] of landlords had tempted them to
build up narrow alleys with small wooden tenements, which, costing
but little, and being let to numerous families, yield immense profits.
The alley is often not more than six feet wide, paved with round stones
and with very insufficient means for draining off the water. It is not
uncommon in such situations to find one or two apartments in each
house entirely under ground. Can we wonder if in such a state of things
we find moral as well as physical disease, vice as well as sickness? Can
we expect men who live thus to be sober and orderly, or women to
be cleanly and domestic? In such situations, during the summer
months, diarrhoea and dysentery are rife, and among children fatal.*

– New York physician Benjamin McCready (1813–1892), 1837

Infectious diseases were a constant terror during the 1800s. With
increasingly dense populations, wars, and abject poverty, diseases of
all varieties exacted a horrendous toll. The poverty-stricken masses
carried the brunt of the relentless assaults of these diseases, yet no

class was spared. Periodic epidemics and pandemics swept across the globe, wreaking havoc and killing millions, rivaling the horrors of war. Abysmal sanitation, hygiene, nutrition, and working and living conditions, combined with a sense of utter hopelessness, laid the foundation for the devastation.

Sanitation was not a new concept. In the time of the Old Testament, there were clear-cut biblical rules laid out governing the management and disposal of dangerous human waste and rubbish outside the cities and away from water sources. Greece and Rome also perfected well-regulated public health systems. During the Dark Ages, these ideas simply dropped out of the collective memory in many areas of the world.

In the United Kingdom, as a result of the Enclosures Act that pushed people off common land and the Industrial Revolution, dispossessed people suddenly massed into cities. People lived waist deep in their own midden heaps in overcrowded hovels, drinking filthy polluted water and eating terrible food. These living conditions were the single common factor that led to rampant disease epidemics.

Dr. French noted the influences of living conditions on disease in an article published in 1888.

> **The depressing influences of extreme poverty, filth in all its forms, and the overcrowding of large cities, are great promoters of contagion, resulting in epidemics, plagues, and pestilences; while strict cleanliness, fresh air, pure water, and hygienic living; tend greatly to restrict its spread and prevent these results** . . . The death-rate among infants and young children is especially influenced by the five principal acute contagious or infectious diseases—namely, measles, scarlet fever, small-pox, diphtheria, and whooping-cough.[54]

---

[54] J. M. French, MD, "Infant Mortality and the Environment," *Popular Science*, vol. 34, no. 10, December 1888, p. 228.

The gastrointestinal tract is known to contain around 70 percent of a person's immunity. With insults to a healthy digestive system from toxins, infections, and parasites in water and food, it is easy to see how myriad diseases were able to take hold.

Typhoid fever

Typhoid fever is caused by food or water that's contaminated with *Salmonella typhi* bacteria. Symptoms of typhoid fever include fever, general ill feeling, and abdominal pain. As the disease progresses, the person experiences a high fever with severe diarrhea. Like cholera and dysentery, typhoid fever was a disease that evolved out of improper sanitation and defective civilization.[55]

> *But while it is true both historically and as a fact of to-day, that typhoid fever is a disease of civilization, it ought to be clearly understood that it is only a disease of defective civilization, for it has gradually become notorious that the widespread or frequent occurrence of **typhoid fever in any community must be due, somehow, to defective sanitation; and defective sanitation means defective civilization.**[56]*

Like other diseases of poor sanitation, typhoid fever killed thousands. In the late 1800s to the early 1900s, it was estimated that 40,000 to 50,000 people died from the disease in the United States every year.[57]

> *From January, 1907, to October, 1911, there occurred in Russia 283,684 cases of Asiatic cholera. This included the appalling epidemic of 1910. According to a conservative estimate there occurred in the United States during the same period one million and a quarter cases of typhoid fever, or more than four*

---

[55] H. Curschmann, MD, *Typhoid Fever and Typhus Fever*, W.B. Saunders & Company, 1902, p. 42.

[56] George Chandler Whipple, *Typhoid Fever: Its Causation, Transmission, and Prevention*, John Wiley & Sons, London, 1908, pp. xxiii–xxiv.

[57] *Typhoid Fever: Causation and Prevention*, Seventh Biennial Report of the Board of Health of the State of Iowa, 1893, p. 58.

*cases of typhoid fever in the United States for every case of cholera in Russia. We heard a great deal of the ravages of cholera in Italy in 1910-11, yet in these two years there occurred in Italy about 16,000 cases of cholera and about 6,000 deaths and in **the United States in the same period we had more than a half million cases of typhoid fever and 50,000 deaths.**[58]*

The disease wreaked havoc on the military and was the major killer of US soldiers during the Spanish-American War. It was epidemic in the national encampments, accounting for 86.8 percent of the total deaths from disease during the war.[59] The Civil War was also plagued by typhoid.

Although typhoid had a high mortality rate (36.9 percent) in the Civil War, diarrhea and dysentery—nicknamed the "Tennessee quickstep"—caused more disability and death among Union and Confederate soldiers than any other disease. *Records from Chimborazo Hospital in Richmond, Virginia, and from Confederate army surgeons suggest that at least 90 percent of the soldiers had diarrhea, and that throughout the conflict few ever experienced a normal bowel movement. Speaking for the Union, Walt Whitman noted that the war had been "about nine hundred and ninety-nine parts diarrhea to one part glory." As most soldiers realized early, "Good guts were more important to good soldiering than good brains."[60]*

Tainted food was also a source of disease epidemics. In July 1879, in a canton of Zurich, Switzerland, a large number of people came down

---

[58] *Sewage Pollution of Interstate and International Waters with Special Reference to the Spread of Typhoid Fever*, no. 83, Hygienic Laboratory, March 1912, p. 18.

[59] Vincent J. Cirillo, *Bullets and Bacilli: The Spanish-American War and Military Medicine*, 2004, p. 33.

[60] Ibid.

with what was considered to be typhoid fever, referred to by some as *sausage poisoning.*

> *513 persons of all ages sat down to a cold collation of veal and ham, both of inferior quality. Of that number, 421 were subsequently seized with an acute febrile disease which was at the time looked upon as typhoid. Thirty-four other persons who had obtained meat from the same butcher were also attacked with similar symptoms; and subsequently, a further number of eleven of fifteen who had also been supplied by the same butcher. These cases appear to have ushered an epidemic of what was described as typhoid fever. The symptoms were those of severe gastro-intestinal irritation, with high fever, delirium, stupor, congestion of the lungs, and great prostration . . . With reference to this epidemic, the significant remark occurs—"But great doubts have been expressed as to whether it was really typhoid fever, or a form of poisoning resembling sausage-poisoning."[61]*

Cholera

Cholera is a disease of poor sanitation and crowding. It is a bacterial infection of the small intestine that results in copious watery diarrhea and vomiting and leads to death with agonizing cramps and dehydration. Infants, children, and adults were all its victims during pandemics that resulted in enormous numbers of sick and dead.

The increased commercial trade and travel, combined with atrocious hygienic conditions worldwide, brought forth six cholera pandemics in the 1800s. The first pandemic started in 1816, and the last ended in 1926 (Graph 3.1).

---

[61] Surgeon-General C. A. Gordon, "Remarks on Certain Assigned Causes of Fever," *Medical Times and Gazette*, vol. II, J & A Churchill, London, October 1, 1881, p. 409.

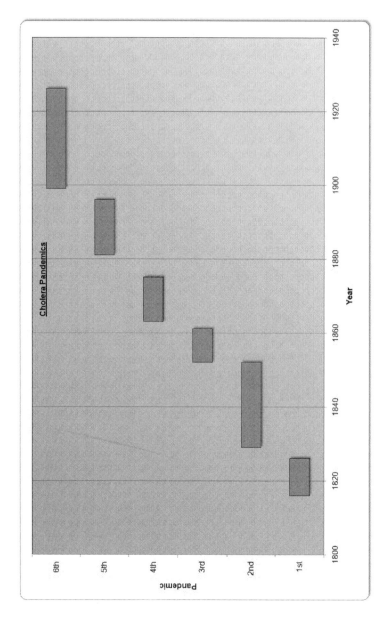

Graph 3.1: Six cholera pandemics. The first pandemic started in 1816, and the last ended in 1926.

More than 15 million cholera deaths in India are esti-
mated to have occurred between 1817 and 1860 . . . *The*
disease reaches Russia, causing Cholera Riots in the streets of
major urban centers . . . *In 1849, a second cholera wave oc-*
curred in Paris and London. It was the worst outbreak in Lon-
don's history, claiming 14,137 lives, more than twice as many
as the 1832 outbreak. The 1849 cholera outbreak in Ireland is
estimated to have killed as many people as died during the
Irish Famine. Cholera also followed along with the settlers
heading to the California gold rush, with 6,000 to 12,000 dying
in 1849. Russia was affected early in this cholera pandemic
(3rd pandemic), with more than 1 million deaths . . . *In North*
America, 3,500 people (5.5% of Chicago's population) died of
cholera in 1854, with up to 150,000 Americans dying of chol-
era between 1832 and 1860 . . . *London's epidemic in 1852-*
1854 killed 10,738 . . . *By 1866, the outbreak reached North*
America, causing up to 50,000 deaths . . . *The 1883-1887 epi-*
demic claimed 250,000 lives in Europe and, in spreading, killed
at least 50,000 in America, 267,890 in Russia, 120,000 in Spain,
90,000 in Japan, 60,000 in Persia, and more than 58,000 in
Egypt . . . *The major Russian cities reported more than*
500,000 cholera deaths during the first quarter of the
20th century.[62]

In 1832 cholera prevailed in France, and within the year
caused 120,000 deaths, 7,000 of which occurred in Paris in the
space of eighteen days.[63]

Cholera struck the United States in 1849, leaving a wide path of devastation. The disease appeared in the South in early spring and
spread quickly throughout the country, causing scores of deaths in
many towns and villages. In an attempt to stop the epidemic and

---

[62] David L. Streiner, Douglas W. MacPherson, and Brian D. Gushulak, *PDQ Public Health*, 2010, p. 198.
[63] Alfred Stillé, MD, *Cholera: Its Origin, History, Causation, Symptoms, Lesions, Prevention, and Treatment*, Lea Brothers & Co., Philadelphia, 1885, p. 19.

purify the atmosphere, huge piles of wood were burned. The smoke hung low in the heavy midsummer air.

> *Thousands fled panic-stricken before the scourge, while days of fasting, humiliation, and prayer were appointed in view of its probable advent... The streets were empty except for the doctors rushing from victim to victim, and the coffin makers and undertakers following closely on their heels.*[64]

Human and animal waste continuously emptied into the only source of water for the people. Lack of knowledge in basic hygiene and primitive or nonexistent sanitation fueled these almost unbroken pandemics of cholera during the 1800s and into the early 1900s.[65] People were under siege from chemicals and toxins that left their battered immune systems at a huge disadvantage.

> *... drinking water presented a growing problem. **The spill-off from the slaughterhouses and the glue factories, the chemicals of the commercial manufacturers, and all of Chicago's raw sewage had begun to contaminate the drinking water.** Chicagoans had endured the cholera epidemic of 1848, an epidemic caused by polluted water; nearby Lake Michigan was far more contaminated in the 1850s.*[66]

Dysentery

Dysentery is an inflammation of the intestine caused by bacteria or an ameba. It is characterized by severe diarrhea with blood and mucus in the feces. Like cholera, dysentery is spread by fecal contamination of food and water, usually in impoverished areas with

---

[64] Arthur Charles Cole, *The Irrepressible Conflict 1850–1865: A History of American Life Volume VII*, Macmillan, New York, 1934, p. 183.
[65] William Buckingham Canfield, MD, *Hygiene of the Sick-Room*, P. Blakiston, Son & Co., Philadelphia,1892, pp. 87–88.
[66] Jane Byrne, *My Chicago*, Northwestern University Press, Evanston, Illinois, 1992, p. 32.

poor sanitation. These diseases of poor sanitation resulted in a monstrous loss of life.

> **The Union army in the Civil War (1861-65) lost 186,216 men to disease, twice the number killed in action;** *nearly half were claimed by typhoid and dysentery.*[67]

During the US Civil War, life within the prison stockades was frightful. Those who died were often buried without coffins in mass graves. Conditions for the sick prisoners were appalling, with "hospitals" supplying little comfort or any hope of help.

> *The hospital itself was a group of worn-out tents, many of them leaky and some of them without sides. There were no bunks and but little straw. Hundreds of patients lay upon the bare ground. Their food differed little from that of the prisoners within the stockade though the surgeon in charge was able to obtain small quantities of flour and arrowroot.* **The prevalent diseases were scurvy, diarrhea, dysentery, and hospital gangrene.**[68]

Typhus fever

Typhus fever is different than typhoid fever and is caused by a rickettsial bacterium most commonly transmitted by the bite of the body louse, which feeds on the blood of humans as it spreads disease. It is considered a filth disease and occurs where there is poor hygiene and sanitation. The vitality of the germs increases in direct proportion to overcrowding and inadequate ventilation.[69] Typhus was another disease that killed enormous numbers of people at different times and places in history.

---

[67] Roy Porter, *The Greatest Benefit to Mankind*, Harper Collins, New York, 1997, p. 399.

[68] Francis Miller and Robert Lanier, *The Photographic History of the Civil War: Prisons and Hospitals*, Review of Reviews Co., New York, 1911, p. 82.

[69] H. Curschmann, MD, *Typhoid Fever and Typhus Fever*, W. B. Saunders & Company, 1902, p. 499.

Like the war itself, typhus began in Serbia, with 10,000 cases as early as November 1914; within six months, deaths had leapt to 150,000. With the revolution of 1917 and the civil war, **typhus ran riot in Russia: between 1917 and 1921 Russia had 25 million cases with up to 3 million deaths.**[70]

. . . Henry P. Davison, Chairman of the League of Red Cross Association, who declared there were 230,000 cases of typhus fever in Poland . . . According to information sent by Colonel E. R. Gilchrist, head of the United States Medical Unit in Poland, **95 per cent of the population has been or is now suffering with typhus.** *The mortality has run from 15 to 60 per cent.*[71]

Sir David Henderson, Director General of the newly created League of Red Cross Societies, with headquarters in Geneva, Switzerland, said last night that the league, at the beginning of its organization was confronted with one of the most serious scourges since the Middle Ages—the typhus epidemic in Eastern Europe . . . There were more than 120,000 cases in Poland alone in July, and conditions are growing worse. We are approaching the worst season for typhus now. **Typhus goes with dirt, and our chief difficulty is in keeping the people clean.** *We sent soap, but then there was no coal to heat the water. We have sent fresh clothes, but we have been unable to supply enough. There is a great lack of materials, hospitals are unequipped, and there is only one doctor to every 10,000.*[72]

---

[70] Roy Porter, *The Greatest Benefit to Mankind*, Harper Collins, New York, 1997, p. 399.

[71] "All Poland Ravaged by Typhus Epidemic, American Medical Experts Report 95 Per Cent. of the People Victims of Disease," *New York Times*, March 25, 1920.

[72] "Typhus in Europe a World Problem, Director of Red Cross League Admits Inability to Cope with It Alone, Worst Since Middle Ages," *New York Times*, November 11, 1919.

Diphtheria

Diphtheria is a term used to describe a particular type of upper-respiratory illness. The determinant of clinical diphtherial disease is not the bacteria *Corynebacterium diphtheriae*, but rather a toxigenic virus (bacteriophage) that infects some of the bacteria. The vast majority of diphtheria bacteria are actually never invaded by a bacteriophage. However when the bacteria are invaded, there is a possibility of serious clinical disease. The virus switches on bacterial toxin genes, which lead to symptoms such as the leathery thick parchment-like secretion that can cover the back of the throat and obstruct breathing and swallowing.

In severe cases, the toxin is distributed to distant organs by the circulatory system and can cause paralysis and congestive heart failure. In the era of slum living and poor nutrition, as with other infectious diseases, considerable numbers of people died with diphtheria.

> *Diphtheria cases are averaging sixty a day, according to statistics to the Department of Health. Health Commissioner Royal S. Copeland said yesterday that an epidemic stage is being approached. Since the beginning of the year there have been 2,773 cases of the disease and 274 deaths . . .* **"A death from diphtheria should be condemned just as severely as a death from typhoid fever," said the statement. "Both are entirely unnecessary and represent what is in effect a sanitary crime . . ."**[73]

> *An infectious disease, dreaded in childhood, but also affecting adults, is diphtheria.* **The number of deaths, caused by it [diphtheria] among the ten million inhabitants of the larger towns in Germany during the ten years 1882-1891 amounted to 111,021 and of every thousand deaths 45 are**

---

[73] "Reports 60 Cases of Diphtheria Daily, Dr. Copeland Plans Campaign Against Disease Approaching Epidemic Stage, 274 Deaths This Year," *New York Times*, February 25, 1920.

due to the disease. In 1892 the death-rate from diphtheria was 12,361 or 41 per 1,000.[74]

Seldom has a community been so alarmed as are the country people along the line of Berks and Lehigh Counties, where two counties join and where diphtheria rages in such a violent epidemic form. Nothing like it has ever affected a similar stretch of country in this section with such fatal results. Many families have lost their children. An estimate made to-day of the number of funerals held places the deaths within the confines of 10 square miles at not less than 60 and probably more.[75]

Pertussis

Pertussis, commonly called whooping cough, is a toxin-mediated bacterial disease that can cause uncontrollable and violent coughing, which is far worse in the undernourished. Whooping cough begins like a common cold, with hoarseness; watering eyes and nose; a short, dry cough; and fever. The fever gives way, and the short, dry cough can be followed by a whoop-sounding cough that often, though not always, characterizes this disease.

Whooping cough is epidemic in every portion of Philadelphia, and tens of thousands of little children are suffering from the disease. It is in the homes of both rich and poor, and as soon as one child in a square is attacked all the children on the same street become affected. Pneumonia and bronchitis often follow in its train, and in severe cases which have been neglected the lungs are so weakened that the patient offers fruitful ground for the seeds of consumption [tuberculosis].[76]

---

[74] *Hygiene and Sanitation: A Popular Manual to Hygiene*, Imperial Board of Health, Berlin, 1904, p. 199.
[75] "Ravages by Diphtheria, A Large Number of Deaths in Berks and Lehigh Counties," *New York Times*, January 5, 1889.
[76] "Whooping Cough in Philadelphia," *New York Times*, July 24, 1893.

Significant figures concerning children's diseases were given by Dr. Royal S. Haynes ... "Whooping cough," said Dr. Haynes, "kills more babies under one year of age than any other contagious disease. There are almost as many deaths from whooping cough as from typhoid." He gave startling statistics showing the "harmless" diseases. The deaths in New York in 1910 from measles were 785; scarlet fever, 953; whooping cough, 461; diphtheria, 1,715; and smallpox only 5 ... In the same year the dreaded typhoid caused only 558 deaths.[77]

Scarlet fever

Scarlet fever is another toxin-mediated bacterial disease. The bacteria involved are Streptococcus pyogenes, also known as group A strep. The disease got its name from the red rash that appears on the skin, mostly on the chest and abdomen, which can then spread to the entire body. In susceptible individuals, symptoms are caused by toxins that the bacteria produce as a result of a specific bacteriophage (virus) that can integrate into the Streptococcal genome, instructing the bacteria to produce the toxin.

In some people, serious complications such as heart and kidney disease can arise. These complications are actually the result of an autoimmune reaction from the antibody produced in response to the infection. Antibodies are thought to be good, but in reality they can cause problems whether induced by a vaccine or an infection.

The idea that antibiotics have eliminated the disease is a fallacy. Scarlet fever still exists, yet the mortality is nothing like it used to be and declined long before antibiotics. In fact, antibiotics actually seem to increase the toxin release from the bacteria.[78] In the 1800s and

---

[77] "Beware of Whooping Cough, Kills More Babies Than Any Other Disease, Says Dr. Haynes," *New York Times*, February 16, 1912.

[78] M. Tanaka, T. Hasegawa, A. Okamoto, K. Torii, and M. Ohta, "Effect of Antibiotics on Group A Streptococcus Exoprotein Production Analyzed by Two-Dimensional Gel Electrophoresis," *Antimicrobial Agents and Chemotherapy*, vol. 49, no. 1, January 2005, pp. 88–96.

early 1900s, when people were undernourished and sickly, scarlet fever resulted in a great many deaths.

> During the fifteen years **1847-1861 inclusive, the deaths from scarlatina and diphtheria in England and Wales amounted to 262,429, and in London alone to 38,890. In other words, one out of every twenty-three deaths occurring in London was due to scarlatina** . . . The reader whose own family has been visited by the fell destroyer, can figure to himself the vast amount of human misery which these figures imply. Although not uncommonly the disease runs such a mild course that medical treatment is almost unnecessary, it is, on the other hand, but too true, that very many cases are amenable to no treatment whatever.[79]

> Hempstead, Long Island, Nov. 20, 1884—Scarlet fever is raging in Smithville South and vicinity to such an extent that the schools have been closed on that account. Three deaths from the disease have occurred . . . [80]

> Canandaigua, N.Y., April 29, 1884—There have been 16 deaths from scarlet fever in this village within eight days. The Board of Health has issued an order prohibiting public funerals and commending the adoption of other sanitary regulations as the epidemic continues.[81]

Measles

Unlike the diseases discussed so far, measles is a *viral* infection. Initial symptoms include runny nose, hacking cough, high fever, and aches and pains. Measles is characterized by small red, irregularly shaped spots with white centers that appear on the skin. Like other diseases, measles epidemics resulted in many deaths.

---

[79] "Scarlatina Epidemics," *British Medical Journal*, September 12, 1863, pp. 285–286.
[80] "Scarlet Fever on Long Island," *New York Times*, November 21, 1884.
[81] "A Scarlet Fever Epidemic," *New York Times*, April 30, 1884.

The startling mortality among children from the little-regarded ailment of measles was indicated to-day by a statement issued by the State Department of Health, showing that in 1906 there were 1,463 deaths from it, 1,240 being of children under 5 years of age. In December alone 2,807 cases of the disease were reported, and a search of the records shows that it kills 2½ times more children than does scarlet fever.[82]

Thousands of natives of Herschel Island are along the Arctic coast are dying of measles . . . They are dying off like rabbits, and there seems to be nothing to check the death rate. The march of civilization has increased the death rate from Nome north. Two years ago the devastation began, and it has continued since. **When the natives began to wear civilized man's clothing, and drink white man's whisky, then began their decline. Pneumonia, rheumatism, grip, and every conceivable malady made their appearance among them and spread along the coast with appalling results.**[83]

Yellow fever

Yellow fever is an acute viral disease transmitted by infected mosquitoes. In 1855 yellow fever devastated the towns of Norfolk, Portsmouth, and Gosport, Virginia, and the surrounding areas. The plague was unrelenting, killing thousands and leaving cities with the highest mortality rates nearly deserted.

. . . the main business street of the city was utterly silent. Not a store was open; only two druggists' shops gave evidence of life. Thoroughfares lately vocal with the bustle of Trade, are now silent as midnight, their stillness broken only by the footfalls of nurses hurrying to the apothecary for medicines. A very few weeks have sufficed to turn a population of a least Twenty

---

[82] "Measles Kills1,463, And 1,240 Were Children Under 5 Years—Pennsylvania's 1906 Record," *New York Times*, January 19, 1908.
[83] "Thousands Die from Measles—The Disease Reported to Be Carrying Off Arctic Coast Natives at Rapid Rate," *New York Times*, November 4, 1902.

Thousand, lately residing in Norfolk and its suburbs, scarcely Three Thousand remains . . . A common spectacle in the streets is a cart laden with coffins, which are deposited at some convenient street-corner, and removed hence by the undertakers as occasion demands. Three or four of these coffins often stand together. The dead are immediately taken out of the houses and placed upon the sidewalks: a strip or parchment inscribed with the name, age and date of the decease of the victim, being nailed upon the lid of each coffin . . . The deaths here have been recently numbered fifty, sixty, seventy—aye, very nearly eighty per day in our remnant of a population of about six thousand, at most, seven thousand! The rich, the poor—old and young, white and colored, all have been indiscriminately leveled down by the disease which now holds fearful sway in our once happy city, throughout whose streets, avenues and squares there reign a silence and a desolation that are sickening and oppressive beyond description.[84]

The article in the *New York Times* describes a scene of swarming insects covering coffins, which reads more like a modern-day horror novel than a news report.

Soon after the attack, the skin of the white patient takes on a yellowish tinge, similar to that of a lemon or orange. Black patients undergo a similar metamorphosis—their hue changes to bronze. In all cases, the progress of the fever is very rapid and very often fatal . . . Since the fatal epidemic has prevailed in our city, a most singular looking fly has made its appearance . . . its body is about the size of the common fly, of a yellowish color . . . They fly together in swarms, and may be seen in large numbers on the fig trees—but their great point of attraction seems to be the coffins in which repose the ill-fated victims of "Yellow Jack." We took a stroll out to that Golgotha of burial grounds, Potters Field, yesterday, and was intensely horrified

---

[84] "Yellow Fever—Fearful Progress of the Disease at Norfolk," *New York Times*, September 11, 1855.

at the seeing many of the coffins that lay on the ground, scattered around, awaiting internment, literally black with these loathsome little insects, that squirmed themselves upon one another so thick as to exclude the coffin entirely from sight.[85]

Cities in the southern United States were accustomed to frequent epidemics and were sometimes stricken with multiple illnesses at the same time, causing widespread panic.

Memphis in 1873 was attacked from three quarters at once—by yellow fever, smallpox and cholera. The people fled in a panic, leaving half the houses vacant.[86]

Consumption

Many other diseases plagued the people of the 1800s and the early 1900s. Tuberculosis is a bacterial infection that affects the lungs. It was once known as "consumption" because it wasted away, or consumed, its victims.

One of the most potent factors in the production of consumption, and especially in tenements, is overcrowding and consequent foulness of the air. "The respiration of impure air," says one great authority on tuberculosis, "directly debilitates the vital powers, enfeebles the nervous system, depresses the appetite, deranges the secretions, and leads to the retention of effete matters in the blood."[87]

Together, pneumonia and tuberculosis were by far the biggest killers of the time.

. . . tuberculosis and pneumonia are in the lead, causing, respectively, death-rates of 1.16 and 1.02 per 1,000 living, with

---

[85] "Yellow Fever—Fearful Progress of the Disease at Norfolk," *New York Times*, September 11, 1855.
[86] Allan Nevins, *The Emergence of Modern America 1865–1878: A History of American Life Volume VIII*, Macmillan, New York, 1927, p. 323.
[87] Arthur R. Guerard, MD, *The Relation of Tuberculosis to the Tenement House Problem*, Macmillan, New York, 1903, p. 462.

deaths by violence, heart disease, and carcinoma in the next places . . . **Consumption and pneumonia are far in the lead, causing together about one-fifth of the total deaths.**[88]

The bare statements that no less than 700,000 men and women of working age in this country are afflicted by a preventable and curable disease and more than 92,000 of them die annually from the disease, sound startling. This is the case, and tuberculosis is the disease. Yet the 92,000 or more workers who die from tuberculosis are only 70 per cent of the total death toll from this disease. **During the past year 132,000 persons of all ages died from tuberculosis in the United States.**[89]

Although these infectious diseases are often considered as separate illnesses, they could strike together or shortly after each other.

Diphtheria, when epidemic, also frequently complicates measles. Much of the mortality from measles in this city, since the year 1858, was due to this cause.[90]

At the Eurana Schwab Home near Huguenot, S. I., at first known as St. Joseph's-by-the-Sea, an epidemic of measles with scarlet fever and pneumonia, has existed among the 300 young children, during which twenty have died of more than 150 who have been affected . . . "The children that come to us, you should remember, are the unwelcome children of the world," said she [Sister Teresa]. "They do not get proper care. They are

---

[88] *Publications of the American Statistical Association*, vol. 9, nos. 65–72, 1904–1905, pp. 260, 261.

[89] "Increasing Output by Preventing Tuberculosis," *The American Contractor*, October 29, 1921, p. 30.

[90] J. Lewis Smith, MD, *A Treatise on the Diseases of Infancy and Childhood*, Lea Brothers & Co., Philadelphia, 1886, p. 193.

always weak and frail when we get them. It is not strange that when disease breaks out, 20 out of 150 should perish."[91]

... one of the most serious combinations is that of measles with diphtheria. I cannot escape the impression that the organism attacked by measles off less resistance to the intoxication and infection from diphtheria ... when measles follows diphtheria with an almost simultaneous infection, both diseases may influence each other in a very ominous manner. A strong boy aged seven years, in good circumstances, taken ill upon February 18th, from diphtheria, which rapidly assumed dimensions in the pharynx. On February 20th he received 600 antitoxin units, and on February 21st, after I visited him for the first time, he at once received 1,500 more ... Upon March 2d an eruption of measles appeared, at once severe apathy and high graded asthenia [loss of strength] occurred; gallop rhythm ... During the night, from March 8th to 9th, death occurred. In this case the periods of infection with the contagium of measles and diphtheria were close together.[92]

Puerperal fever

One of the ugliest, most tragic, and most avoidable chapters in the history of medicine is that of puerperal fever. Puerperal fever is the name given to a deadly infection that affected many mothers in the immediate post-partum period. Severe pain, pelvic abscesses, sepsis, high fever, and agonizing death were brought about by an ascending infection introduced by the contaminated hands of doctors and un-sterile medical instruments. There is no single type of microorganism responsible, though the most common bacteria isolated after the germ theory was developed was *Beta haemolytic streptococcus,* Lancefield Group A.

---

[91] "Many City Waifs Die in St. Joseph's Home, Scarlet Fever, Measles, and Pneumonia Affect 143 of the 300 Inmates, Twenty Fail to Recover," *New York Times*, July 6, 1911.

[92] J. C. Wilson, MD, *Infectious Disease*, D. Appleton and Company, New York, 1911, pp. 338, 339.

In the United States, Europe, New Zealand, Sweden, and wherever conventional midwifery was abandoned and taken over by the new male midwives known as obstetricians and medical students, puerperal fever followed.

> *Man-midwifery was an uncertain but increasingly fashionable and sometimes quite lucrative area of practice for physicians; it may, for this reason, have been a field in which ideas about theory and practice were particularly strongly contested. Midwifery, formerly the preserve of women, was receiving increasing attention from medical men—both physicians and surgeons—during the eighteenth century. Prominent within this area of practice were the surgeons, for whom midwifery was seen as a natural extension of their activities. Surgeons had traditionally been called in to difficult births by midwives, usually when there was a need to extract an already dead foetus from the womb in order to save a mother's life. During the eighteenth century, surgeons were increasingly finding ways to extend their practice into the area of normal childbirth. Men-midwives, although recognized by society as holding respectable positions and possessing expertise, found their status limited by the "hands-on" nature of their work. Nevertheless, within broader social terms, man-midwifery could be seen as a field of financial and career opportunity. These ambiguities and uncertainties within the status of men-midwives may have contributed to the intensity and competitiveness of the debates which can be found in their writings.*[93]

Puerperal fever, also known as childbed fever, was a disease mediated by doctor arrogance. Dr. Oliver Wendell Holmes of the United States and Dr. Ignaz Semmelweis of Austria were prominent, long-suffering advocates for women, who tried to get the medical

---

[93] Christine Hallett, PhD, "The Attempt to Understand Puerperal Fever in the Eighteenth and Early Nineteenth Centuries: The Influence of Inflammation Theory," *Medical History*, vol. 49, no. 1, January 1, 2005, pp. 1–28.

profession to wash their hands and practice more like the traditional midwives did. Both were ignored and even professionally attacked for their views. After years of mental anguish, watching women die needlessly, they left the field of medicine in disgust. Dr. Holmes became a writer. In 1865 Dr. Semmelweis was deceived into entering an insane asylum and when he tried to escape, he was severely beaten by guards. A gangrenous wound to his hand, probably caused by the beating, led to his untimely death two weeks later.

The reason it is important to never forget the history of puerperal fever is because the massive loss of maternal life impacted husbands, surviving infants, older surviving children, the family unit, society . . . and the statistics on life expectancy. Yet we rarely hear the words "puerperal fever" mentioned or discussed.

The epidemic of women and babies dying is documented from records as early as 1746, where more than 50 percent of mothers who gave birth in a Paris hospital died.[94] However, the best and most comprehensive writing on the problem came from Dr. Ignaz Semmelweis in his book, *Etiology, Concept, and Prophylaxis of Childbed Fever*. After noting that the mothers who were tended by medical doctors had more than three times the rate of death than those who were tended by midwives, and that those who were not internally examined lived, he suspected a contagious agent. Doctors often went from touching infected corpses in the cadaver dissection lab, to the maternity ward, where they examined women and delivered babies without handwashing.

Dr. Semmelweis directed the doctors of his hospital to use a chlorinated lime solution on their hands prior to touching women. When doctors and medical students complied, the maternal mortality rate went from a high of 32 percent down to zero. Using a similar

---

[94] Christine Hallett, PhD, "The Attempt to Understand Puerperal Fever in the Eighteenth and Early Nineteenth Centuries: The Influence of Inflammation Theory," *Medical History*, vol. 49, no. 1, January 1, 2005, pp. 1–28.

antiseptic technique, Dr. Breisky of Prague reported in 1882 that he delivered 1,100 women in succession without a single death.[95]

Dr. Semmelweis held several sequential staff positions, and wherever his hygiene method was followed, maternal mortality rates dropped. But most of his contemporaries ignored such outrageous and offensive "nonsense."

Doctors were insulted at the suggestion that their hands were dirty[96], and many had the arrogance to continue to ignore factual evidence showing that they were the cause of maternal suffering and death up until the 1940s when antibiotics were invented.

After the invention of antibiotics, puerperal fever dropped significantly, but Semmelweis' and Breisky's records proved that doctors could have stopped almost all the puerperal fever deaths from occurring in the 1700s if they had only washed their hands and their instruments and stopped using unnecessarily invasive birthing techniques.

> *Another example, from Britain, was the widespread use of chloroform and forceps by general practitioners in uncomplicated deliveries between 1870 and the 1940s. This was described by one observer as a tendency a "little short of murder" and accounted for many unnecessary deaths.*[97]

Considering that one-fifth of the population consisted of women of childbearing age and that a higher than 30 percent maternal mortality rate was not uncommon, the impact on society, life expectancy statistics, and the infectious disease rate (infants whose mothers died around childbirth had a four times higher risk of dying,

---

[95] Frederick C. Irving, MD, "Oliver Wendell Holmes and Puerperal Fever," *New England Journal of Medicine*, vol. 229, no. 4, July 22, 1943, pp. 133–137.

[96] Richard W. Wertz and Dorothy C. Weritz, *Lying-In: A History of Childbirth in America*, Yale University Press, 1989, p. 122.

[97] Irvine Loudon, "Maternal Mortality in the Past and Its Relevance to Developing Countries Today,"*American Journal of Clinical Nutrition,* vol. 72, suppl. 1, July 2000, pp. 241S–246S.

most commonly from infections) was enormous. Yet vaccine enthusiasts never mention this tragedy in their assessment of history and infectious disease. Instead, vaccines are lauded as the great gift to humanity when, in fact, **had doctors simply washed their hands, they would have prevented countless millions of deaths and raised the life expectancy curve markedly.**

The end result of puerperal fever was millions of motherless children relegated to die, or to live a life of malnutrition and disease, often forced to work in mines, factories, and sweat shops. Puerperal fever fueled a social bonfire that left enormous damage in its path. If those infants had mothers to breastfeed them and love them and the older siblings had a mother at home to tend to their needs, the disease and misery of the 1700s to 1900s would have been far less prominent. Doctors today believe that vaccines would have reduced those diseases, while they ignore the fact that their own predecessors created one of the situations which resulted in high disease rates and low life expectancy.

Preventable medical error is well documented all throughout the world and is the third leading cause of death in the United States (225,000 deaths per year*), with similar numbers wherever the same medical paradigms are implemented.

Yet every time an unvaccinated person enters their office, zealously pro-vaccine doctors arrogantly overlook the truth that a person's risk of dying or being maimed from accepted medical practice they offer, is far, far higher than any possible death or maiming from a supposedly vaccine-preventable disease.

*Barbara Starfield, MD, MPH, "Is US Health Really the Best in the World?" *Journal of the American Medical Association,* vol. 284, no. 4, July 26, 2000, pp. 483–485.

There are numerous reputable sources that clearly demonstrate how improved living conditions, more nutritious food, better obstetric care, and other non-vaccine elements were responsible for the decline in infectious disease death rates. Despite this clear evidence, today's vaccine proponents continuously and falsely claim that vaccines are the principal reason for the increase in life expectancy we enjoy today.

In the pages that follow, you will be able to decide for yourself what makes more sense. Was it the vaccines? Or were there other factors that corresponded with the timing of decline in death rates? If so, are *they* to thank for our longer life expectancy? If the answer is that it was not the vaccines, should the World Health Organization (WHO) be working in a different direction today, in poor countries that mirror the conditions of our past?

SMALLPOX AND THE FIRST VACCINE

. . . they lye on their hard matts, the poxe breaking and mattering,
and running one into another, their skin cleaving to the matts
they lye on; they turne them, a whole side will flea off at once.

– William Bradford (1590–1657), 1634

Fresh vesicles subsequently formed around the vaccination pocks coalescing with them and causing them to spread. They developed also on the face, head, body, and in the mouth, the later prevented the child from suckling, and it died exhausted on the 45th day after vaccination.

– Case of a healthy child after vaccination, March 13, 1891

Try re-vaccination—It never will hurt you,
For re-vaccination has this one great virtue:
Should it injure or kill you whenever you receive it,
We all stand prepared to refuse to believe it.

– From a circular signed "The Doctors," 1876

Human smallpox, also known as *Orthopox variola,* was a notorious infectious viral entity that served up a febrile illness and painful, oozing skin lesions (pox) to its victims. The disease not only disfigured but often led to death.

> *The most deadly feature of the new towns was the close proximity of human beings to each other. For example, the report of a health officer for Darlington in the 1850s found six children, aged between 2 and 17, suffering from smallpox in a one-roomed dwelling shared with their parents, and elder brother and an uncle. **They all slept together on rags on the floor, with no bed. Millions of similar cases could be cited,***

with conditions getting even worse as disease victims died and their corpses remained rotting among families in single-roomed accommodations for days, as the family scraped together the pennies to bury them.[98]

Smallpox completely disappeared from the United States by 1949, and worldwide by 1980. Most people today believe that the infectious menace was vanquished by the power of a vaccine.

Battling the speckled monster

The first endeavor aimed at preventing smallpox in the Western world began with Lady Mary Wortley Montagu in 1717. She returned from the Ottoman Empire with knowledge of a practice called *variolation*, which entailed taking a small amount of material from a human smallpox lesion and scratching it into the skin of another person.[99] If all went well, the recipient would suffer a mild attack of smallpox and then become immune to the disease. The hope behind infecting people with smallpox at a time and in a setting of their choosing was that, in a controlled environment while at optimal health, they would fare better against the disease than leaving infection to chance.

Two problems with variolation were that it could result in death and the procedure spread disease into surrounding communities.

*The ensuing and protecting attack of smallpox was by no means always a mild one; it has been reckoned that two or three persons died out of every hundred inoculated. Further, many people rightly suspected that **inoculation, even though it might protect the individual by a mild attack, spread the disease more widely by multiplying the foci of infection.***

---

[98] Dorothy Porter, *Health, Civilization, and the State—A History of Public Health from Ancient to Modern Times*, Routledge, Oxfordshire, England, 1999, p. 113.

[99] William Douglass, MA, *A Summary, Historical and Political, of the First Planting, Progressive Improvements and Present State of the British Settlements of North-America*, London, 1760, p. 407.

For these reasons inoculation fell into general disrepute in Europe after 1728.[100]

James Kirkpatrick arrived in London from Charleston, South Carolina, and described the 1738 epidemic, stressing that inoculation was outstandingly successful. Because of his enthusiasm, inoculation regained favor throughout Europe:

> *In London, after the revival of Kirkpatrick's influences in 1743,* **inoculation became a lucrative branch of surgical practice . . . almost exclusively among the well-to-do.** *The operation was by no means so simple as it looked. It required the combined wits of a physician, surgeon, and an apothecary; while the preparation of the patient to receive the matter was an affair of weeks and much physicking and regimen. The inoculation was for a long time the privilege of those who could afford to pay for it.*[101]

During a 1752 epidemic of smallpox in Boston, some figures showed that more people died when exposed to natural smallpox than when they contracted smallpox through inoculation. This indicated that inoculation could possibly be helpful, particularly for whites.

> *The small-pox in cold countries is more fatal to blacks than whites. In Boston small-pox of 1752, there died whites in the natural way about one in eleven, by inoculation one in eighty; blacks in the natural way one in eight, by inoculation one in twenty.*[102]

Success of variolation was dependent on operator and technique, as well as a host of other factors that could not always be controlled.

---

[100] Frederick F. Cartwright, *Disease and History*, Rupert-Hart-Davis, London, 1972, p. 124.

[101] Victor C. Vaughan, MD, *Epidemiology and Public Health*, C.V. Mosby Company, St. Louis, 1922, p. 189.

[102] William Douglass, MA, *A Summary, Historical and Political, of the First Planting, Progressive Improvements and Present State of the British Settlements of North-America*, London, 1760, p. 398.

A 1764 article made it clear that the unintended result of inoculation was an increased death rate from smallpox.

> *It does not follow Inoculation is a practice favourable to life . . . It is incontestably like the plague a contagious disease, what tends to stop the progress of the infection tends to lessen the danger that attends it; what tends to spread the contagion, tends to increase that danger;* **the practice of Inoculation manifestly tends to spread the contagion, for a contagious disease is produced by Inoculation where it would not otherwise have been produced***; the place where it is thus produced becomes a center of contagion, whence it spreads not less fatally or widely than it would spread from a center where the disease should happen in a natural way; these centers of contagion are manifestly multiplied very greatly by Inoculation . . .*[103]

According to the author, in the 38 years preceding the start of inoculation in 1721, deaths from smallpox relative to the number born was 90 per 1,000, and relative to the number of burials 64 per 1,000. **In the 38 years after the start of inoculation, deaths from smallpox relative to the number born increased to 127 per 1,000 (a 41 percent increase) and relative to the number of burials 81 per 1,000 (a 27 percent increase).**

The medically sanctioned operation was as likely to start an epidemic as to stop one.[104]

From the nipple of the cow

It was rumored among milkmaids that infection with cowpox could protect one from smallpox. In 1774 a farmer named Benjamin Jesty made scratches on his wife and two sons using a darning needle, then rubbed material from the pock of an infected cow into them.

---

[103] "The Practice of Inoculation Truly Stated," *The Gentleman's Magazine and Historical Chronicle*, vol. 34, 1764, p. 333.
[104] Elizabeth A. Fenn, "The Great Smallpox Epidemic of 1775–82," *History Today*, July 20, 2003, p. 12.

Allegedly, when Jesty's sons were later deliberately exposed to smallpox, they did not come down with the disease.

In 1796, believing these stories, Edward Jenner subjected an eight-year-old boy named James Phipps to an experiment. He took disease matter that he believed to be cowpox from lesions on the hands of dairymaid Sarah Nelmes and vaccinated James with it. The child was later deliberately exposed to smallpox in order to test the protective property of the cowpox inoculation. When the boy did not contract clinical smallpox, it was assumed that the cowpox vaccination was successful and that it would also provide lifelong protection against smallpox.

Immunology was so crude that knowledge of preexisting immunity or subclinical infection was not part of Jenner's experimental design. Even though his claims were based on a sample of one and no scientific method, it fueled the belief that once a person was exposed to cowpox, lifelong protection from smallpox was possible.

Jenner's claim was later replaced with varying estimates from 10 years to as little as 1 year.

A 1908 article[105] concluded that some limited immunity lasted only around three years.

> ... it is observed that all un-revaccinated children over one and a-half years of age, or thereabouts, and all re-vaccinated persons whose re-vaccinations are more than three years old, i.e., the vast majority of the entire population—are unprotected.[106]

Another practitioner named Dr. Olesen claimed that revaccination should be done annually.

---

[105] F. Smith, MRCVS, "For How Long Does Vaccination Confer Immunity from Small-Pox?" *Transactions of the Sanitary Institute,* vol. 13, p. 116.
[106] J. W. Hodge, MD, "State-Inflicted Disease in Our Public Schools," *Medical Century,* vol. XVI, no. 10, October 1908, pp. 308–314.

Recent successful vaccination is an absolute protection against smallpox. Protection lasts from six months to twelve months and often much longer. Revaccination is advisable once a year.[107]

Dr. Creighton published a book in 1889 that was highly critical of Edward Jenner and vaccination. He observed that people who had been exposed to cowpox virus had often previously received an inoculation of smallpox. Due to the anecdotal nature of his experiments, Jenner could arrive at whatever conclusion fit his predetermined outcome. Dr. Creighton summarizes:

The only real experiment in the paper on cowpox, as originally offered to the Royal Society, was the inoculation of James Phipps; the results of it, as we have seen, were recorded with a brevity which enabled Jenner to suppress the true and suggest the false. **It is absurd to claim the dozen old cases of cowpoxed milkers, who were subsequently inoculated with smallpox, as experiments; there were many cowpoxed milkers . . . who submitted to inoculation along with others, whenever a general inoculation was afoot; and Jenner's cases were only a few, favourable to his contention** *. . . he himself stands for the man who "peremptorily decides on the truth or falsehood of a theory, on the supposed authority of a few solitary instances."*[108]

Since the late 1700s, the medical profession has supported vaccination, even though there was never a trial where one group was vaccinated and compared to another group of the same size that was not vaccinated.[109]

---

[107] Dr. Olesen, "Vaccination in the Philippine Islands," *Medical Sentinel*, vol. 19, no. 4, April 1911, p. 255.

[108] Charles Creighton, *Jenner and Vaccination*, 1889, p. 59.

[109] *MMWR*, vol. 50, no. RR-10, Centers for Disease Control, June 22, 2001, pp. 1–25.

The CDC admits that, even now, the level of antibody that protects against smallpox infection is unknown.[110] When the authors of *Dissolving Illusions* were growing up in the United States, children were considered vaccinated and immune simply by revealing the scar of vaccination years after the procedure.

Vaccinia: The man-made mystery virus

There is confusion over the origin of the virus termed vaccinia. Jenner named his product after the Latin name for cow, *vacca*, but he believed that genuine cowpox disease originated from a condition in horses called the *grease*. Some practitioners used vaccine lymph from other animals, such as goats. The following 1829 excerpt from the *Lancet* is interesting:

> *The lymph which Dr. Jenner then used, and which he had kept in circulation three or four years about Berkeley, had been taken by him, not from the cow, but the horse, and never subsequently passed through the constitution. In fact, the disease is an equine, not a vaccine [cow] pox, as he decisively ascertained before he died, obtained from the vesicles which arise upon the skin of the horse's legs, in consequence of an erysipelatous affection excited by the matter of grease . . . I have extracted an account from some country of a goat pox, which so resembled the vaccine, that the doctors inoculated with it, and found it an equal preservative. However, this equine lymph of Dr. Jenner produced a vesicle, which, he declared precisely resembled the natural cow-pox vesicle on the teat of the cow . . .[111]*

After years of mixing different animal viruses and passing them through humans and back into cows again, an 1834 article cast doubt on how much vaccine virus even came from cows. Because of

---

[110] *MMWR*, vol. 50, no. RR-10, Centers for Disease Control, June 22, 2001, pp. 1–25.
[111] "Observations by Mr. Fosbroke," *The Lancet*, vol. II, 1829, pp. 583–584.

the confusion regarding what was in the vaccines, the material used for vaccination was sometimes referred to as "vaccine virus."

> *Three opinions exist as to the origin of the vaccine virus. 1st. That of Jenner, who supposed that it proceeded from a malady of the horse, called the Grease, which was contagious, and gave to cows that form of complaint denominated cow-pox. 2nd. That of Dr. Robert of Marseilles, who thought that the vaccine virus was nothing less than the small-pox poison communicated to cows, and modified by transition. 3rd. The opinion that this complaint is as natural to cows as rot to sheep, the small-pox, measles, or scarlatina to man ... Dr. Fiard expresses, as his opinion, that the cow-pox is a malady peculiar to cows; that it is very rare in England, in these animals; and that, in France, there is no evidence to prove that it has ever been produced.*[112]

Because using pox material directly from cows was initially disagreeable to people, Jenner developed "humanized cowpox vaccine." This method still first utilized disease material from an animal, inoculating the raw pus into humans.[113] The vaccination procedure then consisted of rubbing pox pustular lymph from the pock of an inoculated

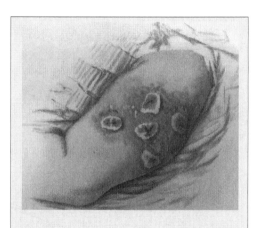

Photo 4.1: Multiple site vaccination of 1898, showing a 'typically good arm.'

human to a cut in the arm of the next human recipient and was termed "arm-to-arm vaccination." Another method of inoculation was to place numerous human pox scabs into a jar, fill it with water,

---

[112] Dr. Fiard, "Experiments upon the Communication and Origin of Vaccine Virus," *London Medical and Surgical Journal*, vol. 4, 1834, p. 796.

[113] Frederick F. Cartwright, *Disease and History*, Rupert-Hart-Davis, London, 1972, p. 127.

and shake. The resultant pus was used as vaccine material for one town.

People were considered vaccinated and immune simply by revealing the scar of vaccination after developing a blister at the site of inoculation. Often multiple sites were used in an attempt to try and ensure maximum protection.[114] Successful vaccination was thought to have occurred by a "good take" after wounding up to four parts of the arm at one sitting. This practice of vaccinating more than one site continued in various parts of the world until 1975.

Obviously, many other diseases from the vaccinated were spread by this route, but arm-to-arm vaccination was used for about 100 years, until it was outlawed in 1898. In 1939 Dr. A. W. Downie showed that although vaccinia virus is immunologically related to cowpox and smallpox, it had distinct immunological differences, which he attributed to the process mentioned above.[115]

> . . . the white variant **on repeated artificial propagation of cowpox virus on the skin of calves or sheep in the preparation of vaccine lymph or in the human skin on arm-to-arm vaccination** which was practiced during last century. Such conditions may have provided an opportunity for the appearance of vaccinia strains as we know them today from a cowpox variant such as that described here.[116]

The standardization and purity of smallpox vaccines was lackluster even after the eradication of smallpox from the United States. Dr. Beddow Bayly's 1952 statements should leave everyone wondering how such a vaccine could have possibly been responsible for eradication of any disease:

---

[114] Derrick Baxby, "Smallpox Vaccination Techniques; from Knives and Forks to Needles and Pins," *Vaccine*, vol. 20, no. 16, May 15, 2002, p. 2142.
[115] A. W. Downie, "Jenner's Cowpox Inoculation," *British Medical Journal*, vol. 2, no. 4726, August 4, 1951, pp. 251–256.
[116] A. W. Downie, "A Variant of Cowpox Virus," *The Lancet*, vol. 1, no. 6717, May 24, 1952, pp. 1049–1050.

*When we recall that **vaccine lymph is derived, in the first place, either from a smallpox corpse, the ulcerated udder of a cow, or the running sores of a sick horse's heels**, the choice depending upon the country of its origin and the firm which manufactures it, it is hardly to be wondered at that it has far-reaching ill effects on the human constitution. Years ago, the **Lancet declared that "no practitioner knows whether the lymph he employs is derived from smallpox, rabbit-pox, ass-pox, or mule-pox."**[117] Our own Ministry of Health has long confessed to complete ignorance of the ultimate source of its own supply of lymph; but last year Dr. A. Downie stated in the British Medical Journal that "the strain of vaccinia virus used for the routine preparation of lymph in this country [England] is believed to have been derived from a case of small-pox in Cologne during the last century." That, of course, disposes of the whole theory of cow-pox vaccination.*[118]

Even modern smallpox vaccines do not actually contain cowpox or smallpox virus but a human/animal hybrid agent that never existed in nature until the era of vaccination. It has been cultivated over time by passing pox material back and forth between animals and humans. Now vaccinia can infect wild animals such as water buffalo,[119] as well as humans.

Some of the animals that have been used to passage today's vaccine virus include rabbits, mice, goats, cows, horses, sheep, and humans.

Dryvax, patented by the company that later became Wyeth, is the oldest smallpox vaccine and has been used since the late 1800s. The methods used to propagate Dryvax resulted in mixtures of

---

[117] "Studies in Vaccinia," *The Lancet,* vol. 199, no. 5150, May 13, 1922, pp. 957–958.

[118] M. Beddow Bayly, MRCS, LRCP, "Inoculation Dangers to Travelers," apeech at the Caxton Hall Westminster, October 2, 1952. Published by the London and Provincial Anti-Vivisection Society.

[119] L. Qin, C. Upton, B. Hazes, and D. H. Evans, "Genomic Analysis of the Vaccinia Virus Strain Variants Found in Dryvax Vaccine," *Journal of Virology,* vol. 85, no. 24, December 2011, pp. 13049–13060.

viruses commonly called "quasispecies." In 2011, Qin et al. geneti-cally characterized the modern Dryvax and stated that all brands of smallpox vaccines prior to the late 1990s were rarely subjected to clonal purification. They concluded that Dryvax was of horse and human viral origin, describing the vaccine as a "molecular fossil":

> *These observations raise intriguing questions about the degree of genome diversity that can be found in old smallpox vaccines. In this communication, we have taken advantage of recent advances in DNA-sequencing technologies to explore this question in greater detail. Our results illustrate the remarkable complexity of the quasispecies that characterize stocks of old, unpurified smallpox vaccines and suggest that **the viruses that have been isolated to date represent only a small fraction of the diversity of viruses in these preparations.**[120]*

Who, then, knows what the "larger fraction" of "old, impure" vac-cines was made from? To say that there is and always has been a great deal of confusion as to what viruses were in smallpox vaccines is a gross understatement.

In 2008, after more than 100 years of use, the Centers for Disease Control (CDC) called for quarantine and destruction of all remaining Dryvax.[121]

Belief eclipses reality

When Jenner published his paper in 1798 claiming lifelong immunity to smallpox and promoting his technique, many doctors who had seen smallpox follow cowpox challenged his doctrine at a meeting of the Medico-Convivial Society.

---

[120] L. Qin, C. Upton, B. Hazes, and D. H. Evans, "Genomic Analysis of the Vaccinia Virus Strain Variants Found in Dryvax Vaccine," *Journal of Virology*, vol. 85, no. 24, December 2011, pp. 13049–13060.
[121] "Notice to Readers: Newly Licensed Smallpox Vaccine to Replace Old Smallpox Vaccine," *MMWR*, vol. 57, no. 8, February 29, 2008, pp. 207–208.

But he [Jenner] no sooner mentioned it than they laughed at it. **The cow doctors could have told him of hundreds of cases where small-pox had followed cow-pox** . . .[122]

In 1799 Dr. Drake, a surgeon from Stroud, England, conducted an experiment to test Jenner's new preventive using vaccine obtained directly from Edward Jenner. The children were then challenged with a smallpox inoculation to see if the cowpox procedure had been effective.

In three of them, a lad aged seventeen and two of the Colborne children (one four years, the other fifteen months), the cowpox vesicles came to early maturity and were scabbed under the usual time. **The lad was inoculated with smallpox on the 20th December, being the eight day from his vaccination, and the two children on the 21st, being again the eight day. They all developed smallpox,** *both the local pustules and the general eruption with fever.*[123]

Dr. Hughes, another doctor from Stroud, reported that the children subsequently developed smallpox and suggested that the vaccination technique failed. Jenner received the report but decided to ignore the results.

Later in 1799, Dr. Woodville, director of the Smallpox Inoculation Hospital in London, began extensive use of cowpox inoculation. He obtained his vaccine material from a cow belonging to a dairy on Gray's Inn Lane in London and vaccinated seven people. Just five days later, using those seven people, he performed the arm-to-arm cowpox vaccination technique on hundreds of others. Dr. Woodville acknowledged that there were serious problems associated with this procedure.

---

[122] Walter Hadwen, MD, *The Case Against Vaccination*, Goddard's Assembly Rooms, Gloucester, January 25, 1896, p. 12.
[123] Charles Creighton, *Jenner and Vaccination*, 1889, pp. 95–96.

*. . . in several instances, the cowpox has proved a very severe
disease. In three or four cases out of 500, the patient has been
in considerable danger, and one child actually died.*[124]

The medical community continued to embrace Jenner's vaccine despite many accounts that refuted its benefits, all describing numerous cases that had natural cowpox or were vaccinated and still died
of smallpox.

By the year 1801, an estimated 100,000 people were vaccinated in
England.

In 1809 the *Medical Observer* reported a series of patients demonstrating the failure of natural cowpox or vaccination to protect from
smallpox:

*1. A Child was vaccinated by Mr. Robinson, surgeon and apoth-
ecary, at Rotherham, towards the end of the year 1799. A
month later it was inoculated with small-pox matter without
effect, and a few months subsequently took confluent small-pox
and died. 2. A woman-servant to Mr. Gamble, of Bungay, in Suf-
folk, had cow-pox in the casual way from milking. Seven years
afterwards she became nurse to Yarmouth Hospital, where she
caught small-pox, and died. 3 and 4. Elizabeth and John
Nicholson, three years of age, were vaccinated at Battersea in
the summer of 1804. Both contracted small-pox in May, 1805
and died . . . 13. The child of Mr. R died of small-pox in October
1805. The patient had been vaccinated, and the parents were
assured of its security. The vaccinator's name was concealed.
14. The child of Mr. Hindsley at Mr. Adam's office . . . died of
small-pox a year after vaccination.*[125]

---

[124] Frederick F. Cartwright, *Disease and History*, Rupert-Hart-Davis, London,
1972, p. 130.
[125] William Scott Tebb, MD, *A Century of Vaccination and What It Teaches*,
Swan Sonnenschein & Co., London, 1898, p. 126.

Medical article after medical article pointed out clearly that exposure to cowpox providing lifelong immunity to smallpox was an unproven theory.

> *The Medical Observer for 1810 contains particulars of **535 cases of small-pox after vaccination, 97 fatal cases, 150 cases of vaccine injuries**, with the addresses of ten medical men, including two professors of anatomy, who had suffered in their own families from vaccination.*[126]

An article in the 1817 *London Medical Repository Monthly Journal and Review* showed yet again that a great many people who had undergone vaccination were still suffering from smallpox.

> *Variola, above all, continues and spreads a devastating contagion. However painful, yet it is a duty we owe to the public and the profession, to apprize them, that **the number of all ranks suffering under Small Pox, who have previously undergone Vaccination by the most skilful practitioners, is at present alarmingly great**. This subject is so serious, and so deeply involves the dearest interests of humanity, as well as those of the medical character, that we shall not fail in directing our utmost attention to it.*[127]

In 1818 Thomas Brown, a surgeon with 30 years of experience in Musselburgh, Scotland, described how no one in the medical profession "could outstrip me in zeal for promoting vaccine practice." But after vaccinating 1,200 people and discovering that many still contracted and even died from smallpox, his conscience could no longer support vaccination.

> *Experience has also shewn [shown], that the natural small-pox have made their appearance, when the vaccine puncture had previously existed, surrounded with the areola of the most*

---

[126] "Vaccination by Act of Parliament," *Westminster Review*, vol. 131, 1889, p. 101.
[127] "Observations on Prevailing Diseases," *The London Medical Repository Monthly Journal and Review*, vol. VIII, July–December 1817, p. 95.

perfect appearance for more than two days, and not in the least modified, but in the highest degree confluent, and followed by death. Small-pox pustules, too, existed within the very areola of the vaccine puncture . . . **The accounts from all quarters of the world, wherever vaccination has been introduced . . . the cases of failures are now increased to an alarming proportion;** *and from a fair and impartial examination appears, where the small-pox contagion has access to operate upon vaccinated cases of upwards of six years standing, and the contagion applied in a concentrated and lasting form, nearly the whole of such cases will yield to the influence of the small-pox contagion.*[128]

Numerous other medical journals detailed how smallpox could still infect those who previously had smallpox and that those who were vaccinated could also be infected.

. . . during the years 1820, 1, and, 2 [1820–1822] there was a great hubbub about the small-pox. It broke out with the great epidemic to the north . . . It pressed close to home to Dr. Jenner himself . . . **It attacked many who had had small-pox before, and often severely; almost to death; and of those who had been vaccinated, it left some alone, but fell upon great numbers.**[129]

Surgeons and doctors were paid well to perform vaccination and embraced it as a new form of income. It is therefore quite significant that so many doctors wrote to medical journals about their experiences. However, just like today, the believers ignored the voices of the medical dissenters, which led to ordinary people speaking out in the lay media.

---

[128] Thomas Brown, Surgeon Musselburgh, "On the Present State of Vaccination," *The Edinburgh Medical and Surgical Journal*, vol. 15, 1819, p. 67.
[129] "Observations by Mr. Fosbroke," *The Lancet*, vol. II, 1829, p. 583.

In 1829 William Cobbett, a farmer, journalist, and English pamphleteer, wrote about the failure of vaccination to protect people from smallpox. Cobbett considered vaccination to be an unproven and a fraudulent medical practice. His reference to 20,000 pounds no doubt refers to the monetary amount the British government had advanced to Edward Jenner in 1822 for further smallpox vaccine experimentation.

> *In the midst of all this mad work, to which the doctors, after having found it in vain to resist, had yielded, the real small-pox, in its worst form, broke out in the town of Ringwood, in Hampshire, and carried off, I believe, more than a hundred persons, young and old, every one of whom had had the cow-pox "so nicely!" And what was now said? Was the quackery exploded, and the granters of the twenty thousand pounds ashamed of what they had done? Not at all: the failure was imputed to unskillful operators; to the staleness of the matter; to its not being of genuine quality . . . what do we know now? Why, that in* **hundreds of instances, persons cow-poxed by JENNER HIMSELF [William Cobbett's capital emphasis], have taken the real small-pox afterwards, and have either died from the disorder, or narrowly escaped with their lives!**[130]

Vaccination makes for milder disease?

When it was clear that the smallpox vaccine was not able to prevent disease, the medical profession tried to justify vaccination by changing the goalposts from lifelong "perfect" immunity to "milder disease." Similar dogma is repeated in 2013 to justify the fact that pertussis and influenza vaccines don't protect recipients either. But did smallpox vaccination really decrease the death rate and make for a milder disease?

---

[130] William Cobbett, *Advice to Young Men and (Incidentally) to Young Women*, London, 1829, pp. 224–225.

In the 1844 smallpox epidemic, about one-third of the vaccinated contracted a mild form of smallpox, but roughly 8 percent of those vaccinated still died, and nearly two-thirds had severe disease.[131]

A letter to a newspaper in 1850 claimed there were more admissions to the London Small-Pox Hospital in 1844 than during the smallpox epidemic of 1781 before vaccination began. The author also noted that one-third of the deaths from smallpox were in people who had previously been vaccinated.

> *Daily experience now unhappily shows an altered state of things: small pox, in spite of vaccination, is rapidly on the increase . . . **There were more admissions to the London Small-Pox Hospital in 1844 than in the celebrated small-pox epidemic of 1781 before vaccination was introduced.** I shall also select the Registrar's returns of one of the country districts (Bradford) to show how little protection vaccination afforded in the last quarter of that year, 1844: 118 [181?] deaths from small-pox were recorded, 60, or nearly one-third, of which had been vaccinated.*[132]

Newspapers constantly reported deaths from smallpox in properly vaccinated citizens, as well as deaths from other conditions after vaccination. For example, a skin condition called *erysipelas* was a particularly prolonged and painful way to die.

> *. . . a boy from Somers-town, aged 5 years, "small-pox conflu-ent, unmodified (9 days)." He had been vaccinated at the age of 4 months; one cicatrix . . . the wife of a labourer, from Lambeth, aged 22 years, "small-pox confluent, unmodified (8 days)." Vaccinated in infancy in Suffolk; two good cicatrices . . . the son of a mariner, aged 10 weeks, and the son of a sugar baker,*

[131] George Gregory, MD, "Brief Notices of the Variolous Epidemic of 1844," *Royal Medical and Chirurgical Society*, January 28, 1845, p. 163.

[132] "Small Pox and Vaccination," *Hampshire Telegraph and Sussex Chronicle*, March 2, 1850.

aged 13 weeks, died of "general erysipelas after vaccination, effusion of the brain."[133]

A girl, aged 4 months, died from erysipelas after vaccination.[134]

8 deaths were tabulated under small-pox, of which two attributed to "erysipelas after vaccination," and one to "effects of vaccination."[135]

Two children, both of the age of six months, died from erysipelas after vaccination. In one case the erysipelas commenced a fortnight after the operation.[136]

Deaths as a result of vaccination were often not reported because of an allegiance to the practice. Often a vaccinated person was recorded as having died from another condition such as chicken pox or erroneously listed as unvaccinated, which must have had a considerable impact on the validity of the statistics of the day.

*... **deaths from vaccination and re-vaccination are hushed up** ... Mr. Henry May, writing to the Birmingham Medical Review, January, 1874, on "Certificates of Death," says "As instances of cases which may tell against the medical man himself, I will mention erysipelas from vaccination and puerperal fever. A death from the first cause occurred not long ago in my practice, and although I had not vaccinated the child, yet in my desire to preserve vaccination from reproach I omitted all mention of it from my certificate of death."[137]*

One child, Elizabeth Sabin, 4 years of age, with six good marks of successful vaccination, caught small-pox and three weeks and three days after being vaccinated, and died. Her case was excluded from the list of the vaccinated in Dr. Bond's statistics.

---

[133] *The Morning Chronicle*, April 12, 1854.
[134] *Lloyd's Weekly Newspaper*, June 10, 1860.
[135] *Glasgow Herald*, December 14, 1870.
[136] *The Morning Chronicle*, October 23, 1861.
[137] *The Ipswich Journal*, November 7, 1876.

Statistics cooked in that way could not be accepted as accurate. He remembered a case in Birmingham where a man named William Wood Warner died of malignant small-pox in eight days, and was classified by the doctor of the hospital as unvaccinated. By the merest of chance he found out from the man's widow and sister that the latter had seen him vaccinated.[138]

In 1898 Dr. Wilder also noted that during the 1871–1872 pandemic, the vaccinated often contracted severe smallpox more rapidly than the nonvaccinated.

Never, however, did the faith in vaccination receive so rude a shock as in the Great Small-Pox Epidemic of 1871 and 1872. Every country in Europe was invaded with a severity greater than had ever been witnessed during the three preceding centuries. In England, the number of deaths from the disease was increased from 2,620 in 1870 to 23,126 in 1871 and 19,064 in 1872, falling again to 2,634 in 1873. Upon the Continent, particularly in France and Germany, the visitation was even more severe. In Bavaria, for example, with a population vaccinated more than any other country of Northern Europe, except Sweden, which experienced the greatest that had ever been known. What was even more significant, **many vaccinated persons in almost every place were attacked by small-pox before any unvaccinated persons took the disease.**[139]

Compulsory vaccination and subsequent pandemics

In 1840, as doctors and citizens realized that vaccination was not what it was promised to be, vaccine refusals increased. Governments passed various laws to force people to be vaccinated. Vaccination

---

[138] Noel A. Humphries, "English Vaccination and Small-Pox Statistics, with Special Reference to the Report of the Royal Commission, and to Recent Small-Pox Epidemics," *Journal of the Royal Statistical Society*, September 1897, p. 545.

[139] Alexander Wilder, MD, "The Fallacy of Vaccination," *The Metaphysical Magazine*, vol. III, no. 2, May 1898, p. 88.

was made compulsory in England in 1853, with stricter laws passed in 1867. In the United States, Massachusetts created a set of comprehensive vaccination laws in 1855.

> . . . *in 1855 Massachusetts took the most advanced stand ever taken by any of the states and enacted a law which required parents or guardians to cause the vaccination of all children before they were two years old, and forbade the admission of all children to the public schools of any child who had not been duly vaccinated.* The selectmen of towns, mayors and aldermen of cities were to "enforce the vaccination of all the inhabitants" and to require re-vaccination whenever they judged the public health to require it; all employees of manufacturing companies, all inmates of almshouses, reform schools, lunatic asylums, and other places where the poor and the sick are received, or houses of correction, jails, prisons, of all institutions supported wholly or partly by the state were to furnish the means of vaccination to such persons as were unable to pay.[140]

Lemuel Shattuck emphasized the need for vaccination and pushed for house-to-house vaccination to be enforced by the authority of the City of Boston in an 1856 report.

> Is there an effectual remedy which can be applied for the removal of this great evil [smallpox]? In the judgment of the undersigned there is; and that remedy is compulsory vaccination. *The City has already provided that no unvaccinated child shall be admitted into the public schools*; and for the class of persons interested it is a most excellent regulation. It has also provided for the gratuitous vaccination of such persons as may apply to the City Physician for that purpose.[141]

---

[140] Susan Wade Peabody, "Historical Study of Legislation Regarding Public Health in the State of New York and Massachusetts," *The Journal of Infectious Diseases*, suppl. no. 4, February 1909, pp. 50–51.

[141] *Memorial in Relation to the Small Pox*, no. 30, City of Boston, 1856, p. 10.

Compulsory vaccination laws did nothing to curb the problem of smallpox. Boston data begins in 1811 and shows that, starting around 1837, there were periodic smallpox epidemics (Graph 4.1). Following the 1855 mandates, there were smallpox epidemics in 1859–1860, 1864–1865, and 1867, culminating with the infamous epidemic in 1872–1873. These repeat smallpox epidemics showed that the strict vaccination laws instituted by Massachusetts had no beneficial effect (Graph 4.2).

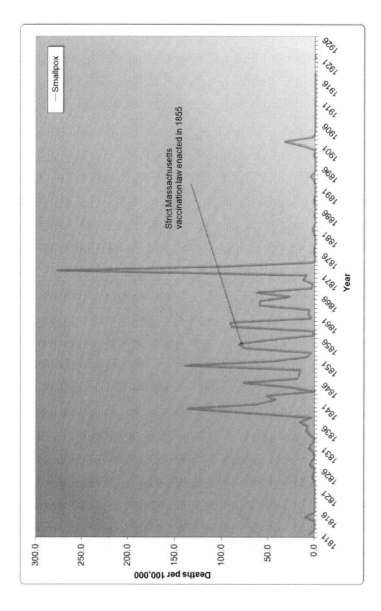

Graph 4.1: Boston smallpox mortality rate from 1811 to 1926.

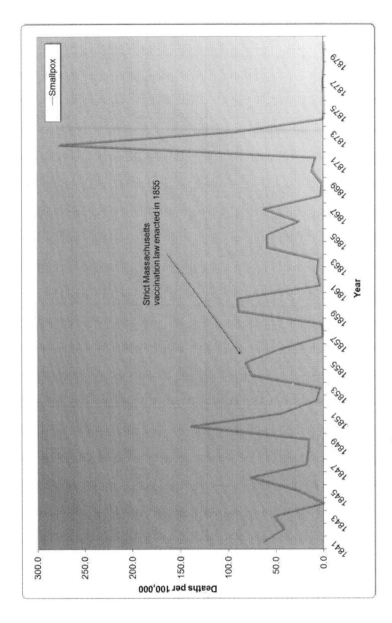

Graph 4.2: Boston smallpox mortality rate from 1841 to 1880.

In fact, more people died from smallpox in the 20 years after the strict compulsory laws than in the 20 years prior.

> ... small-pox, after having almost wholly disappeared from our community during the thirty or forty years which followed the introduction of vaccination in 1800, gradually regained its foothold in Boston, where it continued to prevail almost uninterruptedly, although with varying intensity, from 1839, when the disease for the first time assumed the form of a distinct epidemic, up to 1873. During this period of thirty-five years the course of small-pox has been marked by a succession of epidemic paroxysms, generally by intervals of several years, during which a varying number of sporadic cases has testified to the more or less constant presence of the disease. **The latest epidemic that of 1872-1873, having proved fatal to 1040 persons, was the most severe that has been experienced in Boston since the introduction of vaccination.**[142]

The same pattern of more severe epidemics was to be repeated throughout highly vaccinated populations in the Western world.

> ... Bavaria [Germany] in 1871 of 30,742 cases 29,429 were in vaccinated persons, or 95.7 per cent, and 1313 in the unvaccinated, or 4.3 per cent. In some of the small local outbreaks of recent years the victims have been nearly all vaccinated (e.g., at Bromley [England] in 1881, a total of 43 cases, including sixteen confluent, all vaccinated).[143]

By the end of 1868, more than 95 percent of the inhabitants of Chicago had been vaccinated. After the Great Fire of 1871 that leveled the city, vaccination was made a condition of receiving relief supplies.[144] Despite the passing of strict vaccination laws, Chicago

---

[142] "Small-Pox and Revaccination," *Boston Medical and Surgical Journal*, vol. CIV, no. 6, February 10, 1881, p. 137.

[143] *Encyclopaedia Britannica*, vol. 24, Philadelphia, 1890, p. 29.

[144] Thomas Neville Bonner, *Medicine in Chicago 1850–1950: A Chapter in the Social and Scientific Development of a City*, American History Research Center, Madison, Wisconsin, 1957, pp. 181–182.

was hit with a devastating smallpox epidemic in 1872. The idea of vaccinating most of the population (which would later be termed *herd immunity*) did not protect the population from the scourge of smallpox.

> *But despite these measures, the death rate rose ominously in the aftermath of the fire.* **Over two thousand persons contracted smallpox in 1872, and more than a fourth of these died.** *The fatality among children under five was the highest ever recorded.*[145]

The desecration of the vaccinated people in France, Germany, and England was graphically illustrated in a 1900 medical article:

> *Every recruit that enters the French army is vaccinated. During the Franco-Prussian war there were twenty-three thousand four hundred and sixty-nine cases of small-pox in that army.*
>
> *The London Lancet of July 15, 1871, said:* **Of nine thousand three hundred and ninety-two small-pox patients in London hospitals, six thousand eight hundred and fifty-four had been vaccinated. Seventeen and one-half per cent of those attacked died.**
>
> *In the whole country more than one hundred and twenty-two thousand vaccinated persons have suffered from small-pox* ... **Official returns from Germany show that between 1870 and 1885 one million vaccinated persons died from small-pox.**[146]

---

[145] Thomas Neville Bonner, *Medicine in Chicago 1850–1950: A Chapter in the Social and Scientific Development of a City*, American History Research Center, Madison, Wisconsin, 1957, p. 182.

[146] G. W. Harman, MD, "A Physician's Argument Against the Efficacy of Virus Inoculation," *Medical Brief: A Monthly Journal of Scientific Medicine and Surgery*, vol. 28, no. 1, 1900, p. 84.

In 1899 Dr. Ruata reported on devastating smallpox deaths in over-vaccinated Italy.

> *Among the great number of little epidemics which produced the 18,110 deaths mentioned, I will only note the following: Badolato, with a population of 3,800, had 1,200 cases of small-pox; Guardavalle had 2,300 cases with a population of 3,500; St. Caterina del Jonio had 1,200 cases (population 2,700); Capistrano had 450 cases (population 2,500). All these villages are in Calabria. In Sardinia the little village of Laerru had 150 cases of small-pox in one month (population, 800); Perfugas, too, in one month had 541 cases (population, 1,400); Ottana had 79 deaths from small-pox (population, 1,000), and the deaths were 51 at Lei (population, 414). In Sicily 440 deaths were registered at Noto (population, 18,100), 200 at Ferla (population, 4,500), 570 at Sortino (population, 9,000), 135 at San Cono (population, 1,600), and 2,100 deaths at Vittoria (population, 2,600)!* **Can you cite anything worse before the invention of vaccination? And, the population of these villages is perfectly vaccinated,** *as I have proved already, not only, but I obtained from the local authorities a declaration that vaccination has been performed twice a year in the most satisfactory manner for many years past.*[147]

Dr. Charles Creighton's 1888 critical review of vaccination in the *Encyclopedia Britannica* described the high mortality rate in the 1870–1873 Prussian smallpox pandemic, noting that approximately 60,000 people died from smallpox despite their strict adherence to vaccination.

> *The practice of re-vaccination was first recommended in England by G. Gregory, and in Germany for the army by Heim (1829). It has been more or less the law in Prussia since 1835; "re-vaccination of school pupils at the age of twelve is an*

---

[147] Charles Ruata, MD, "Vaccination in Italy," *The New York Medical Journal*, July 22, 1899, pp. 188–189.

integral part of the vaccination law." Notwithstanding the fact that **Prussia was the best revaccinated country in Europe, its mortality from smallpox in the epidemic of 1871 was higher (59,839) than in any other northern state.**[148]

The Eastern world did not fare much better. Compulsory vaccination began in Japan in 1872 with stricter laws in 1885 requiring compulsory revaccination every five to seven years. From 1885 to 1892, there were more than 25,000,000 recorded vaccinations and revaccinations, yet smallpox epidemics still wreaked havoc upon the Japanese.

> *. . .* **the official records show that during the seven years mentioned [1885–1892] they had 156,175 cases of smallpox and 39,979 deaths.** *By a compulsory law, every infant in Japan had to be vaccinated within the first year of its birth and in case it did not take the first time, three additional vaccinations had to follow within the year, and every year to seven years after.* *In the event of an outbreak of smallpox the Japanese authorities rigidly enforced general vaccination. Now in spite of these precautions the official records show that* **from 1892 to 1897, Japan had 142,032 cases of smallpox and 39,536 deaths.** *Another act passed in 1896 made repetition* **of vaccination every five years compulsory on every subject regardless of station; yet in the very next year, 1897, they had 41,946 cases of smallpox and 12,276 deaths—a mortality rate of 32 per cent,** *nearly twice that from smallpox previous to the vaccination period.*[149]

---

[148] *Encyclopedia Britannica*, 1888.
[149] Simon L. Katzoff, MD, "The Compulsory Vaccination Crime," *Machinists' Monthly Journal*, vol. 32, no. 3, March 1920, p. 261.

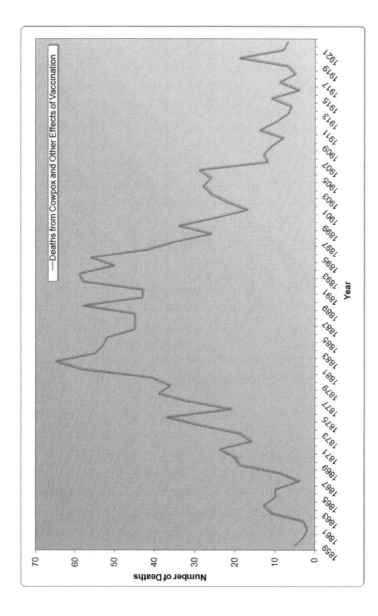

Graph 4.3: England and Wales total deaths from cowpox and other effects of vaccination from 1859 to 1922.

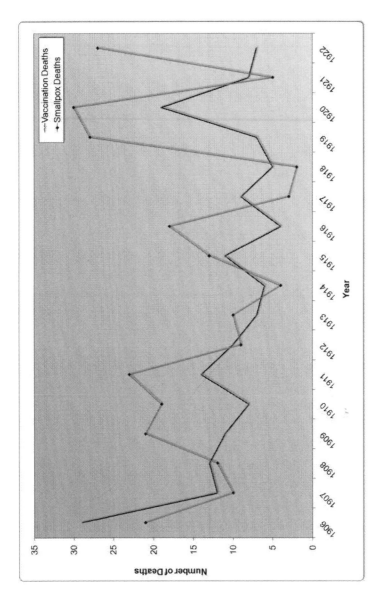

Graph 4.4: England and Wales smallpox deaths vs. smallpox vaccination deaths from 1906 to 1922.

Vaccination-induced deaths and diseases

From 1859 to 1922, official deaths related to vaccination totaled more than 1,600 in England (Graph 4.3). Yet from 1906 to 1922, the number of deaths recorded from vaccination and from smallpox were approximately the same (Graph 4.4).

Official medical pronouncements always heralded vaccination as a very safe procedure done with "pure lymph." Examples of deaths from "cowpox and other effects of vaccination"[150] were common and often resulted from a very serious, often fatal bacterial phage-mediated toxin disease called *erysipelas*.

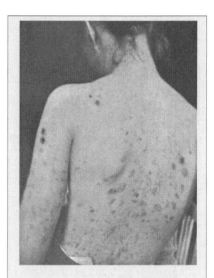

Photo 4.2: Mrs. L. H. age 27 lesions appeared 2 weeks after vaccination. (1904)

George Banford had a child born in 1868. It was vaccinated and after the operation the child was covered with sores, and it was some considerable time before it was able to leave the house. Again Mr. Banford complied with the law in 1870. The child was vaccinated by Dr. Sloanne in the belief that by going to him they would get pure matter. In that case erysipelas set in, and the child was on a bed of sickness for some time. In the third case the child was born in 1872, and **soon after vaccination erysipelas set in and it took such a bad course that at the expiration of 14 days the child died.**[151]

---

[150] "Vaccination," *Encyclopædia Britannica*, The Henry G. Allen Company, New York, vol. XXIV, 1890, pp. 23–30.
[151] Stanley Williamson, "Anti-Vaccination Leagues," *Archives of Disease in Childhood*, vol. 59, 1984, p. 1195.

It is quite certain that in foundling hospitals, such as that of St. Petersburg, **the erysipelas of vaccination has been the starting point of disastrous epidemics of erysipelas** *affecting the inmates generally.*[152]

This is not surprising. Life in the 1800s was such that poverty and lack of sanitation and running water in the slums of London guaranteed at the very least, malnutrition, with its huge impact on the immune system. People with immune deficiency, scurvy, skin ulceration, fungal infections, and impaired lymphatic drainage are at increased risk of superinfection from *Streptococcus pyogenes*, the bacteria that caused erysipelas (and scarlet fever) by means of its toxin.

Jaundice is the yellowish staining of the skin and the whites of the eyes caused by hyperbilirubinemia (an excess of bilirubin in the blood). This usually develops when there is some obstructive process or intrinsic liver disease, but it has been noted in relation to vaccination. One representational case series occurred among revaccinated adults at a large naval shipyard in Bremen, Germany, from October 1883 to April 1884.

Owing to an alarm of smallpox, 1289 workmen were re-vaccinated between the 13th August and 1st September with the same humanized lymph preserved in glycerin; of these 191 had jaundice at various intervals down to the month of April following. Circumstantial evidence (agreement and difference) clearly traced the epidemic to the vaccination.[153]

---

[152] *Encyclopaedia Britannica*, vol. 24, Philadelphia, 1890, p. 26.
[153] *Encyclopaedia Britannica*, vol. 24, Philadelphia, 1890, p. 26.

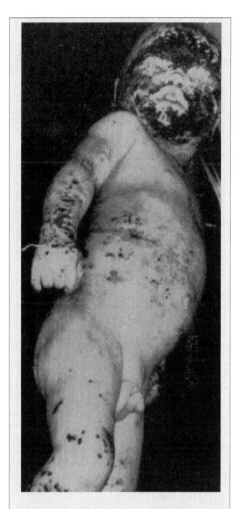

Photo 4.3: Post-mortem photograph of child described in Case 1. Areas of gangrene are secondarily infected with Pseudomonas aeroginosa, Micrococcus pyogenes and beta enterococcus. (1958)

In these cases, it is highly likely that acute infectious hepatitis was a result of contamination of human lymph-derived vaccine. Other infectious diseases attributed to vaccination include tuberculosis and syphilis. In 1863 Dr. Ricord spoke before the Academy at Paris.

*First I rejected the idea that syphilis could be transplanted by vaccination. But facts accumulated more and more, and now **I must concede the possibility of the transfer of syphilis by means of the vaccine**. I do this very reluctantly. At present I do not hesitate longer to acknowledge and proclaim the reality of the fact.*[154]

In 1948, there were an estimated 200 to 300 deaths[155] as the result of smallpox vaccination, while during the same time there had only been 1 smallpox death.[156]

A study in 1958 detailed the cases of 9 children in which 2 died of a skin condition due to vaccina-

[154] "Vaccination," *New York Times*, September 26, 1869.
[155] *The Yale Journal of Biology and Medicine*, vol. 41, 1968, p. 10.
[156] David Koplow, *Smallpox: The Right to Eradicate a Global Scourge*, University of California Press, 2004, p.21.

tion, now being termed *eczema vaccinatum*. The occurrence of this disease was estimated by the authors to be between 1 in 20,000 to 1 in 100,000, with a fatality rate of 4–40 percent. However, they acknowledged that most cases were not reported, and there was no accurate accounting on this consequence of vaccination. The first case discussed was a 15-month-old boy who died after suffering for 13 days (Photo 4.3) from eczema vaccinatum.

Because of poor surveillance and vaccine reaction under-reporting, the authors of a 1970 study suspected that the number of smallpox vaccine-related deaths was higher than the reports reflected. This study only examined deaths from 1959 to 1968 in the United States. If the deaths were this high in a country with a modern health-care system, what was the total number of deaths from smallpox vaccination from 1800 to the present across the entire world?

*The data presented here as well as findings from other studies indicate that **the risks of smallpox vaccination as currently practiced in the United States are considerable. Surveillance of the complications of smallpox vaccination is poor, and the extent of underreporting is unknown.** The observation that several deaths from diseases other than vaccinial complications were misclassified or erroneously reported as deaths from vaccinia raises the possibility that vaccinial complications may also be misdiagnosed or misclassified with other disease entities. **Some patients die of residual effects of central nervous system damage caused by postvaccinial encephalitis.** Their death certificates may mention only the immediate causes which developed during institutional care and not the under-lying cause of death. In our studies of vaccination complications occurring in 1963, three of seven deaths definitely related to vaccination did not appear in our search of death certificates. The actual number of deaths caused by smallpox* *vaccination complications may be higher than the seven per year indicated by this review.*[157]

The death rate for smallpox declined after 1872, but there is no evidence that vaccination had anything at all to do with it. In the early 1900s, death from smallpox all but vanished from England (Graph 4.5). Interestingly, the pattern of smallpox deaths mirrored almost perfectly a much bigger killer—scarlet fever, a bacterial toxin-mediated disease. There was a scarlet fever toxin vaccine, which was never widely used because it had severe consequences to many of its recipients. A marked decline in scarlet fever death occurred long before any antibiotic was used.

Some may look at the graphs and think that the vaccine just needed longer to have its effect. But after 1872, vaccination coverage rates slowly declined from a high of nearly 90 percent. Coverage rates plummeted to only 40 percent by 1909 (Graph 4.6). Despite declining vaccination rates, smallpox deaths remained low, vanishing to near zero after 1906. Smallpox vaccination has always correlated positively to epidemics in the countries that collected data in the vain hope of proving the vaccine's worth.

---

[157] J. Michael Lane, MD, MPH; Frederick L. Ruben, MD; Elias Abrutyn, MD; and J. Donald Millar, MD, DTPH, "Deaths Attributable to Smallpox Vaccination, 1959 to 1966, and 1968," *Journal of the American Medical Association*, vol. 212, no. 2, April 20, 1970, p. 444.

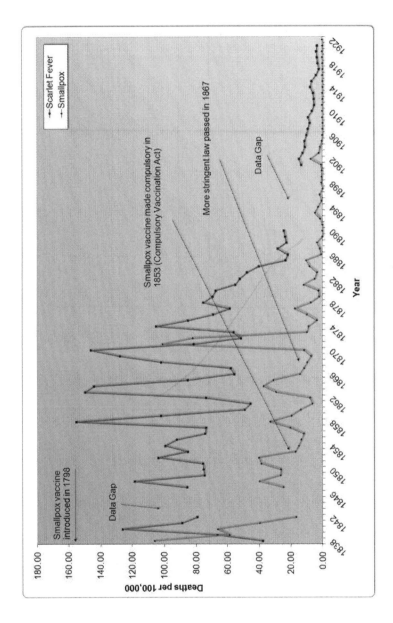

Graph 4.5: England and Wales smallpox and scarlet fever mortality rates from 1838 to 1922.

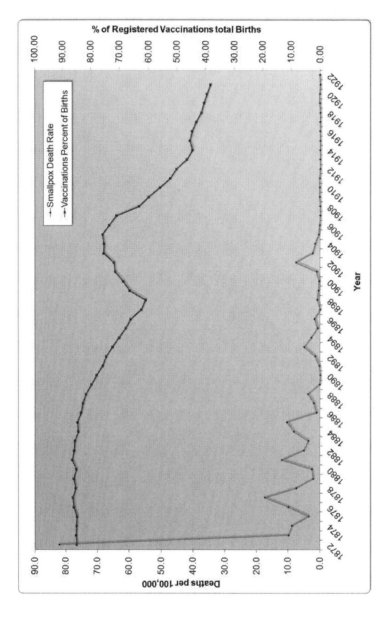

Graph 4.6: England and Wales smallpox mortality rate vs. smallpox vaccine coverage rates from 1872 to 1922.

Dr. Del Campo undertook a five-year investigation into numerous physiologic responses to different vaccinations. His published report from 1967 concluded that vaccination is a trauma of considerable intensity, of which the most serious alterations occur with live viral vaccines.[158] Imagine what the impact of vaccination could have been one hundred years earlier in conditions far worse than 1967.

After the 1872 pandemic, even more people lost confidence in vaccination. They began asking the question as to whether better sanitation, hygiene, improved housing, nutrition, and isolation of cases were the best ways to deal with smallpox. These ideas, which clashed with the medical profession and governmental laws, culminated in a large demonstration in 1885 against compulsory vaccination in the small manufacturing town of Leicester, England. People had had enough. The tide was about to turn against both the medical profession and the law.

---

[158] A. Del Campo, "Physiological Changes of the Vaccinated Organism: A Basis for the Interpretation of the Clinical Complications Due to Prophylactic Vaccines," 1967, pp. 280–284.

~ 5 ~

CONTAMINATED VACCINES

Consequences are unpitying.

– George Elliot (1819–1880)

The fact that man knows right from wrong proves his intellectual superiority to the other creatures; but the fact that he can do wrong proves his moral inferiority to any creatures that cannot.

– Mark Twain (1835–1910)

Smallpox vaccines have always been an unknown broth of hundreds of thousands of non-cowpox microbes. The purity was not guaranteed even when smallpox vaccines were advertised as "pure lymph." Dr. Bayly discusses the terminology:

> *Presumably it is called "pure" because, under the Therapeutic Substances Act (**1943**) it must not contain more **than 20,000 extraneous micro-organisms per cubic centimeter** . . . according to the British Medical Journal (November 4th, 1950)[159] that "With the best of care, **heavy bacterial contamination of vaccine lymph is inevitable during its preparation**, and as many as **500 million organisms per ml. may be present**, particularly in the tropics. They belong mostly to the cocci group, but may include also **Bacillus subtilis, Bact. Coli, Pseudomones pyocyanea, yeasts and fungi; anaerobic organisms** may also be occasional contaminants."[160]*

---

[159] V. N. Krishnamurthy, "Effects of Penicillin and Streptomycin on Vaccine Lymph," *BMJ*, vol. 2, no. 4687, November 4, 1950, pp. 1035–1047.

[160] M. Beddow Bayly, MRCS, LRCP, "Inoculation Dangers to Travelers," speech at the Caxton Hall Westminster, October 2, 1952. Published by the London and Provincial Anti-Vivisection Society.

Dr. Bayly was speaking in 1952, after viral and bacterial identification were possible. Vaccine contamination was not addressed in the 19th century and a lab analysis of the smallpox vaccine was not done until the germ theory was widely accepted.

Serious infections and deaths occurred after the inception of smallpox vaccines. In the late 1700s, there was no such thing as cold-chain refrigeration. Needles were reused from person to person, and there was little to no consciousness of sterility. Ampules and containers that held the vaccine material were not sealed the way they are today.

Vaccination was introduced at the end of the 18th century into a relatively dirty age, using the methods already established for smallpox inoculation (variolation). Vaccine was either inserted without any skin preparation, or perhaps the skin was wiped with a non-too-clean cloth, possibly soaked in equally-dirty water or perhaps spirit.[161]

What really contaminated the early vaccines is anyone's guess. However, there are many documents and reports of serious health problems after vaccination.

Foot-and-mouth disease

Foot-and-mouth disease is an acute and highly contagious viral disease that chiefly affects cloven-hoofed animals. It is characterized by eruptions of blisters on the mucous membranes of the mouth and on the skin between the toes and above the hooves. This disease has been a major concern because it attacks cattle, pigs, and sheep, which have been domesticated by humans.

Because of the high rate of infectivity and because the virus can be transmitted before clinical signs occur, foot-and-mouth disease was one of the most feared reportable diseases in North American mam-

---

[161] Derrick Baxby, "Smallpox Vaccination Techniques 2. Accessories and After-care," *Vaccine*, vol. 24, nos. 13–14, March 28, 2003, pp. 1382–1383.

mals. Epidemics have resulted in the slaughter of millions of infected and uninfected animals to prevent the virus from spreading. The financial loss to farmers was substantial. Trade restrictions based on disease outbreaks have had major impacts on both local and national economies.

Although the United States has not had a foot-and-mouth outbreak since 1929, it is still regarded as a grave threat. The disease is spread with the movement of infected animals, such as pigs and cattle, as well as contaminated objects or people. In 1870, 1880, and 1884, the first three outbreaks occurred and were relatively minor.

Epidemics in 1902 and 1908 were serious, with an even more serious one in 1914. Interestingly, the **epidemics of 1902 and 1908 were initiated during the process of vaccine manufacture. At that time, the only vaccine being manufactured was for use against smallpox.**

> In November 1902, the malady was discovered in Massachusetts and Rhode Island and later involved New Hampshire and Vermont. **The source of the infection probably was imported cowpox vaccine virus contaminated with the virus of foot-and-mouth disease** . . . The disease next appeared early in November, 1908, in cattle near Danville, Pa. It was traced to the stockyards in East Buffalo, N. Y., and to Detroit, Mich., and extended to other points in Michigan, New York, and Pennsylvania, and to Maryland. Investigation demonstrated that the **outbreak started in calves used to propagate vaccine virus** at an establishment near Detroit and that the **source of the infection was contaminated Japanese vaccine virus.**[162]

Animals that contracted the disease suffered morbidly, and some died.

---

[162] *Yearbook of the United States Department of Agriculture, 1915,* Washington Government Printing Office, 1916, pp. 20–21.

As soon as the disease has become well established the patient evinces pain when attempting to eat; in fact the appetite is often so seriously affected that all food is refused and the animal uneasily opens and shuts its mouth with a characteristic smacking sound, while strings of cohesive, ropy saliva hang suspended from the lips. With the advance of the disease the vesicles have widened and extended until they may reach a diameter ranging from that of a dime to that of a silver dollar. These rupture soon after their appearance . . . The

Photo 5.1: Head of cow affected with foot-and-mouth disease. (1914)

attack upon the feet of an animal is frequently manifested in all four feet at once . . . As the feet become sensitive and sore the animal lies down persistently, and it has been found that bed sores develop with amazing rapidity in all such cases and wholly baffle all attempts at treatment until after the patient has regained its feet. The disease may attack some of the internal organs before it appears upon any external tissues. These cases are very liable to prove quickly fatal. The animal dies from paralysis of the heart, due to the formation of poisonous principles within the system, or it may suffocate by reasons of the action of these same poisons upon the tissues of the lungs, or it may choke to death as a result of paralysis of the throat.[163]

The mortality rate was about 3 percent in mild cases but could be as high as 30–40 percent in malignant cases.

---

[163] John R. Mohler, VMD, "Foot-and-Mouth Disease," *United States Department of Agriculture Farmer's Bulletin*, no. 666, April 22, 1915, pp. 8–10.

The 1902 epidemic lasted six months and infected 244 herds, including 4,712 cattle. Vigorous measures were put into effect, and the disease was finally contained. Animals were killed, and their bodies were burned or buried.

Of these, 205 herds with 3,872 cattle as well as 360 hogs and 220 sheep and goats, were slaughtered. The cattle infected but not slaughtered were those that either died or completely recovered before slaughtering could be carried out . . . "Method of slaughtering and burying cattle." The trench is deep enough to allow carcasses to be covered with at least 5 feet of dirt. Animals are led to trench and there killed, usually by shooting. Hides are slashed to prevent anyone from exhuming carcasses in order to get the hides, and carcasses are cut open and covered with quicklime.[164]

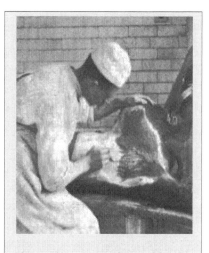

Photo 5.2: From the stable the calf is led to the operating room and strapped on the operating table. The shaved abdomen and thighs are again washed and then scarified with superficial linear incisions made with a surgeon's knife. Into the bleeding incisions made by the knife, vaccine (cowpox) virus is carefully smeared with an ivory or metal instrument. (1901)

During a 1908 epidemic, inspectors made more than one hundred thousand visits to farms, stockyards, and other locations, inspecting and reinspecting approximately a million and a half

---

[164] John R. Mohler, VMD, "Foot-and-Mouth Disease," *United States Department of Agriculture Farmer's Bulletin,* no. 666, April 22, 1915, pp. 5–6, 14.

animals. Again, severe measures were put into place, and the epidemic was eliminated in about five months.

> *One hundred and fifty-seven premises were found infected, and 3,636 animals (2,025 cattle, 1,329 hogs, and 282 sheep and goats), valued at $90,033.18, were slaughtered.*[165]

The source of this epidemic was carefully researched to determine that it was from the manufacturing of vaccine virus. Vaccine virus was produced on a living calf or heifer. The animal was bound to a table where its belly was shaved. Then, multiple scratches or cuts were made, into which the seed virus was placed to grow. The animal was released, and the cowpox infections were allowed to incubate. After about a week, infectious pus was extracted from the wounds to be used in smallpox vaccines for humans. The diseased animal was released and allowed to mix back with the herd. Finally, it was slaughtered, and its meat and carcasses were either used or destroyed.

> *. . . the outbreaks of foot-and-mouth disease in 1902 and 1903 were quite closely associated with the vaccinated cattle of the New England Vaccine Company's establishment and Dr. E. E. Tyzzer's experimental work with vaccine at a farm at Wakefield Mass. . . . the place where it was thought to have originated was the farm of Mr. Owen Clark, who had a contract with Doctor C., of the New England Vaccine Company, to rent calves for the propagation of vaccine virus. These calves were later returned to Mr. Clark after the vaccine virus had been secured.*[166]

> *. . . the vaccine virus propagated by Manufacturer B in April and May, 1908, was contaminated with the virus of*

---

[165] John R. Mohler, VMD, "Foot-and-Mouth Disease," *United States Department of Agriculture Farmer's Bulletin,* no. 666, April 22, 1915, p. 7.
[166] John R. Mohler, VMD, and Milton J. Rosenau, MD, "The Origin of the Recent Outbreak of Foot-and-Mouth Disease in the United States," US Department of Agriculture, Bureau of Animal Industry, Circular 147, 1909, p. 11.

foot-and-mouth. The history of this particular vaccine shows that it was a Japanese strain, imported for the purpose of improving the standard vaccine produced by that company. The fact that the foot-and-mouth infection was present in the vaccine virus of Manufacturer B for so long a period, but was not transmitted to outside cattle, was doubtless due in part to this firm's practice of killing its calves after taking the vaccine virus. Manufacturer A, on the other hand, rented his calves and placed them again on the market a short time after the vaccine material was taken.[167]

Although no connection was ever officially made between the 1870, 1880, and 1884 outbreaks of foot-and-mouth disease and vaccine production, the fact of the matter is that the start of these epidemics coincided with vaccine production that began in the United States in 1870.

Calf lymph began to be used in the United States in 1870; the original lymph was obtained from France and inoculated into a herd of cows on a farm near Boston, Massachusetts.[168]

The suspected route of the 1870 outbreak was infected cattle from Canada.

An extensive outbreak in 1870 was introduced by way of Canada, where the infection was brought by an importation of cattle from Scotland. It spread into the New England States and New York and appears to have been arrested within a few months.[169]

---

[167] John R. Mohler, VMD, and Milton J. Rosenau, MD, "The Origin of the Recent Outbreak of Foot-and-Mouth Disease in the United States," US Department of Agriculture, Bureau of Animal Industry, Circular 147, 1909, p. 25.

[168] Frederick F. Cartwright, *Disease and History*, Rupert-Hart-Davis, London, 1972, p. 130.

[169] A. D. Melvin, "Special Report on Diseases of Cattle," US Department of Agriculture, Bureau of Animal Industry, 1916, p. 384.

The origin of the 1902 epidemic was first thought to be foreign shipping, and only after an in-depth investigation was the smallpox vaccine virus production determined to be the actual source. Detailed investigations of the pre-1902 foot-and-mouth outbreaks were never conducted. Although not proven, it seems likely that these previous foot-and-mouth disease epidemics could certainly have been a result of vaccine production.

> *Dr. Peters concludes that as foot-and-mouth disease prevails extensively in France, Austria, Italy, and Switzerland, and also in less degree, in other European countries, it seems not impossible that the disease was imported from Europe in **some fresh virus brought over to some vaccine establishment in the United States to renovate a product that was losing its vitality.**[170]*

One of the strains of vaccine virus that caused two epidemics of foot-and-mouth disease originated in Japan, which had contaminated vaccines for years. Even though there was vaccine contamination, it was assumed that contaminant viruses would not be a risk for infection to humans because vaccine was only introduced through cutaneous [skin] inoculation.

> *It is doubtful whether the disease can be transmitted to man by cutaneous or subcutaneous inoculation, though it is probable that the infection may be communicated if the virus directly enters the blood through wounds of any kind.[171]*

> *. . . no instance of the transmission of foot-and-mouth disease to man through vaccine virus has been recorded, and it is doubtful, in view of the evidence submitted, if it is possible to*

---

[170] John T. Bowen, MD, Boston, "Acute Infectious Pemphigus in a Butcher, During an Epizotic of Foot and Mouth Disease, with a Consideration of the Possible Relationship of the Two Affections," *Journal of Cutaneous Diseases Including Syphilis*, vol. XXII, no. 6, June 1904, p. 263.

[171] *Farmers' Bulletin*, no. 666, April 22, 1915, United States Department of Agriculture, Washington, DC, p. 15.

reproduce the disease in him by the cutaneous inoculation commonly used in the process of vaccination.[172]

This made no sense, especially knowing that cowpox causes at least a subclinical infection. So why wouldn't other viruses have the ability to do the same? Even a cursory understanding of anatomy should have revealed that blood circulates constantly via capillaries through the skin.

Human beings have historically been infected by the natural route with foot-and-mouth disease, but it was rare, even with close exposure to infected animals. The human disease, when it occurred, was seldom fatal and usually manifested with mild symptoms. However, more serious cases are documented:

The symptoms in man resemble those observed in animals. There is fever, sometimes vomiting, painful swallowing, heat and dryness of the mouth, followed by an eruption of vesicles on the buccal mucous membrane and very rarely by similar ones on the fingers. The vesicles appear on the lips, gums, cheek, and edge of the tongue, and are about the size of a pea.[173]

Natural exposure to animals and their viruses does not manifest the same as direct injection of animal viruses during the process of vaccination. Doctors noticed that cases of foot-and-mouth disease were transmitted to humans through smallpox vaccination, and in those cases the disease was not so mild. A speech by Senator Money of Mississippi on February 25, 1909, in the debate concerning the foot-and-mouth disease epidemic in 1908 affirms this truth.

This is an important question with respect to cattle, but it is very much more important to the human beings of this country. These vaccine points are the things with which we vaccinate the children of this country against smallpox. It has

---

[172] John R. Mohler, VMD, and Milton J. Rosenau, MD, "The Origin of the Recent Outbreak of Foot-and-Mouth Disease in the United States," US Department of Agriculture, Bureau of Animal Industry, Circular 147, 1909, p. 28.
[173] Ibid., p. 8.

been found that it sometimes makes them immune from small-pox, but gives them the foot-and-mouth disease, which is just about as bad.[174]

At a meeting of the American Dermatological Association in 1902, Dr. James Howe of Boston presented 10 cases of a serious skin condition that occurred between July 1, 1901, and July 1, 1902. During this time, the City Board of Health administered approximately 230,000 vaccinations.

> *... while the wave of vaccination, as we might term it, was at its full height, there were received into the Boston City Hospital for treatment a remarkable series of cases of Bullous [fluid filled vesicles] Dermatitis. All of these cases appeared in persons who had been recently vaccinated, with the exception of one additional case not included in the above mentioned cases ... All of them were of a severe type, several proving fatal, and I am in a great doubt as to how to properly classify them ... **In the 10 cases which followed vaccination there were six deaths, a most extraordinary mortality.**[175]*

The 10 cases were described in detail by Dr. Howe. "Case 1" was a 43-year-old man:

> *Two weeks after vaccination his left arm became rather sore, and two large reddish areas appeared on the site of the vaccination. A day or two later these reddened areas were each covered with a bleb the size of a ten-cent piece ... a little more than four weeks after he was vaccinated, all soreness in the arms having in the meantime disappeared, crops of bullæ [blisters], varying from a split pea to a quarter of a dollar, began to appear on the face and scalp, also in the axillæ [armpit], the inner aspects of the thighs, and on the back and abdominal*

---

[174] *Congressional Record*, February 25, 1909.
[175] *Transactions of the American Dermatological Association at Its Twenty-Sixth Meeting Held in Boston, Massachusetts, September 18–20, 1902*, P. F. Pettibone & Co., Chicago,1903, pp. 23, 35.

walls . . . The scalp is covered with bloody crusts, both eyes are closed, swollen and crusted, and a purulent secretion bathes the lids. There was no pain or itching. There were discrete bullæ, varying in size from a quarter to a half dollar, scattered here and there over the lower extremities. The temperature was at this time 103° . . . On the 22ⁿᵈ [day] . . . His breathing was rapid and difficult, and, as he was unable to swallow even liquids, nutrient enemata [provided rectally] were given. Death occurred suddenly at eleven P.M.[176]

Dr. Howe detailed nine other similar cases—some who recovered after a long illness and some who died. He asked if this could be the result of vaccination or infectious material introduced at the time of vaccination or some other cause. He would not have known about the vaccines that were contaminated with foot-and-mouth disease virus, because they were not definitively identified in the vaccines until several years after the date of this lecture.

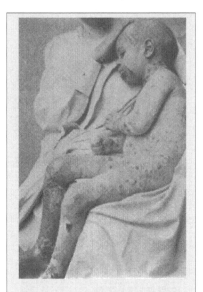

Photo 5.3: Bullous dermatitis closely allied to acute pemphigus. (1908)

So far as could be learned, animal lymph was used in all these cases, and it undoubtedly came from a trustworthy source, and with possibly one or two exceptions the vaccination was done by physicians appointed by the Boston Board of Health.[177]

---

[176] *Transactions of the American Dermatological Association at Its Twenty-Sixth Meeting Held in Boston, Massachusetts, September 18–20, 1902*, P. F. Pettibone & Co., Chicago,1903, pp. 24–25.

[177] Ibid., p. 36.

Dr. Bowen reported more cases of bullous dermatitis in children following vaccination. He noted in one case that the "type of the disease in the case is severe, having persisted for five years."[178] During the discussion, Dr. Stelwagon raised his suspicion of a connection between the disease seen in people who handled animal products and the cases being described by Dr. Howe.

> *I recently saw an article by Bulloch and Pernet, in the British Journal of Dermatology, in which the writers reported a number of cases of acute pemphigus in persons who handled animal products, and it occurs to me that in the cases described by Dr. Howe the infecting material might have been accidentally obtained from the animals from which the vaccine was procured.*[179]

In another paper, Dr. Bowen examined the case of a skin disease that appeared in a butcher in the form of large blisters during the 1902 foot-and-mouth epidemic. It was labeled as *pemphigus*. Pemphigus is known today as an autoimmune disease[180] of unknown cause. This wholesale meat cutter received several cuts on his hand that became swollen and infected. Three weeks later, he entered Massachusetts General Hospital.

> *. . . the lesions appeared on the hand, he began to have an affection of the nose, which was generally swollen and crusted, so that the nostrils were completely occluded. About eight days ago, there appeared, at first on the head and ears, multiple yellowish "blisters," which had steadily extended over the body*

---

[178] *Transactions of the American Dermatological Association at Its Twenty-Sixth Meeting Held in Boston, Massachusetts, September 18–20, 1902*, P. F. Pettibone & Co., Chicago,1903, p. 39.

[179] Ibid., p. 40.

[180] Normally, the immune system produces antibodies that attack viruses and harmful bacteria. In people with pemphigus, however, the immune system mistakenly attacks the cells in the epidermis, or top layer of the skin, and the mucous membranes. Antibodies are produced against proteins in the skin known as desmogleins, which when attacked, cause skin to separate and fluid to collect between the layers of skin, forming blisters that do not heal.

up to the present time . . . was covered with large and small bullæ on an uninflamed base, often sharply raised and very tense, distributed over the trunk, extremities, neck and scalp. Upon the scalp many of the lesions had dried into crusts, which were often hemorrhagic [profuse bleeding]. Upon both ears there where hemorrhagic crusts of considerable size, besides purely bullous lesions. On the sides of the neck, abdomen, back and thighs, there were numerous bullæ from half an inch to an inch in diameter.[181]

The butcher slowly improved and recovered and was discharged from the hospital three weeks after arriving. In his paper, Dr. Bowen made the link between the foot-and-mouth disease epidemic of 1902, the vaccine, and *pemphigus*. He noted that just before the 1902 outbreak, people who were recently vaccinated developed this serious and sometimes fatal skin condition.

Dr. Tyzzer proves conclusively that foot-and-mouth disease may be disseminated by means of vaccination, and that this actually occurred in the summer of 1903. We know of a well defined bullous affection which occurs in butchers and people who have to do with animal products, and which is very often fatal. **We know that another series of cases with similar symptoms occurred in Boston from January to June, 1902, just before the outbreak of foot-and-mouth disease, in people of varying occupations, but who had all been vaccinated . . . It would seem that there is sufficient resemblance between foot-and-mouth disease and acute pemphigus to warrant a belief that they belong in the same group of affections,** *and that they may possibly be allied.*[182]

---

[181] John T. Bowen, MD, "Acute Infectious Pemphigus in a Butcher, During an Epizotic of Foot and Mouth Disease, with a Consideration of the Possible Relationship of the Two Affections," *Journal of Cutaneous Diseases Including Syphilis*, vol. XXII, no. 6, June 1904, p. 254.
[182] Ibid., pp. 263–264.

Dr. Bowen describes a number of similar cases in people with different occupations, including butcher, tanner, blacksmith, and farmer. All had contact with animals or animal products. Most had wounds on their fingers or hands. Some recovered after a long illness, and some died.

Ongoing reports of acute *pemphigus* following vaccination appeared in various medical journals. These cases were severe and sometimes even fatal.

> *In New Orleans there had been a recent outbreak of smallpox, and following the necessarily extensive vaccination there had been numerous vaccination eruptions. The first eruption of this kind that had come to his notice was in a little child . . . The lesions were for the most part bullous. A few days later, he found the spots had become hemorrhagic. After several days in the hospital the child became almost comatose . . . The case had been under observation for two years . . . He had seen three other cases of this kind . . .*[183]

> *While most of these cases run a relatively benign course, **I saw a fatal termination in a case of bullous eruption of the acute pemphigus type. This occurred in a girl of five years, the eruption beginning two weeks after vaccination.** I have also seen four other cases of generalized bullous eruption of the type described above, occurring shortly after vaccination.*[184]

> *A negro carpenter, age 60, was vaccinated . . . on June 9, 1910 . . . That night patient had some headache, and the following morning, four weeks after his vaccination, a bullous eruption appeared on his left arm . . . At first the blebs varied in*

---

[183] "The Relation of Dermatitis Hepertiformis to Erythema Multiforme and to Pemphigus," *Transactions of the American Dermatological Association*, September 1896, p. 39.
[184] Jay Frank Schamberg, MD, *Diseases of the Skin and the Eruptive Fevers*, W.B. Saunders Company, 1908, p. 439.

*size from a pea to others having a base about the size of a dime. They increased rapidly in size, many becoming as large as a walnut, or even larger. By the second day the bullæ had appeared on the legs and trunk, especially in the left axilla. During the third and fourth day the entire body became covered with these bullæ, varying in size from a pea to a walnut... Toward the end of the first week **several blebs developed in the mouth**, one small one on the tongue, and one large one on the side of the pharynx. The latter, when it burst, "nearly drowned him," according to his wife ... For two days, while the bullæ were in his throat and mouth, he was able to take only liquid nourishment. His temperature varied from 96° F. to 99.8° F ... Between two and three weeks after the disappearance of the first crop of bullæ, they began to recur over the same areas and the back was covered with a second crop of bullæ, large and small, some confluent as before ... September 9.—The patient steadily improved under treatment ... A few more bullæ appeared upon the left arm, back, and buttocks. These were smaller than before and ran a similar course ... the disease may, however, be due to an infection is shown by the fact that Pernet and Bulloch report three cases of acute pemphigus in butchers, all whom had wounds which continued to suppurate [form pus] up to the time of the outbreak of pemphigus.*[185]

Vaccine production, utilizing animals that were also used for food, was the genesis of at least two epidemics of foot-and-mouth disease in the United States and possibly the source of other epidemics. The infected animals inflicted disease upon an unknown number of butchers, tanners, blacksmiths, and others who worked with animal products.

---

[185] Reynolds Hayden, "Acute Pemphigus Following Vaccination," *United States Naval Medical Bulletin*, October 1911, pp. 482–485.

Contaminated vaccines were also used to vaccinate untallied masses of people. This resulted in the unintended consequence of pain and suffering and sometimes even death. The following figure shows the connection from vaccine to animals to humans.

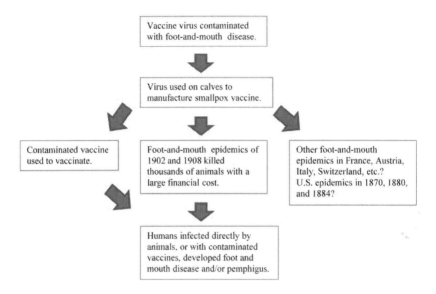

Figure 5.1: Connection between vaccines and foot-and-mouth disease.

Unfortunately, it is difficult to determine how many other foot-and-mouth epidemics may have occurred in the world due to contaminated strains of vaccine. If butchers and animal handlers developed foot-and-mouth disease simply from touching or breathing the air in the midst of these animals, what kind of fallout could have gone uncalculated after the injection of this contaminant along with smallpox vaccines? We know there were high numbers of people with vaccine sickness and vaccine-related deaths. How many deaths were due to this particular adulteration?

The most puzzling thing of all is that this vaccine has long been credited with the only eradication of a disease from the planet. Knowing the process of vaccine production and what was in them, is it really possible that *this* vaccine eradicated any disease?

Numerous well-documented incidents of vaccine contamination have occurred. Even today, a contaminant cannot be screened for unless the scientists suspect it is there, have designed a specific test, and perform the test adequately. Occult infections (infections first recognized by secondary manifestations) are known to exist inside various vaccines in present times.[186] The SV-40 virus was a known contaminant of polio vaccines grown on monkey kidney cells up through the 1980s.

As long as animals and animal cells are used for vaccine manufacture, the potential for infection will exist. There is no proposed end to the use of animals in vaccine production.

---

[186] In 2009, a porcine (pig) virus was discovered in both brands of the infant rotavirus vaccine manufactured from monkey-gut viruses. PCV-2 (porcine circovirus 2) came from a commonly used protease extracted from pigs, called trypsin. This virus is a known cause of wasting-disease and immunosuppression in pigs.

~ 6 ~

THE GREAT DEMONSTRATION

Decorous and admissible language fails me, in alluding to that which might have seemed incredible thirty years ago—the commanding of vaccination on a second child of a family, when vaccination has killed the first; and then sending the father to prison for refusal.

– Emeritus Professor F. W. Newman (1805–1897), October 26, 1874

Those who would give up essential Liberty to purchase a little temporary safety, deserve neither Liberty nor Safety.

– Benjamin Franklin (1706–1790)

Freedom is never voluntarily given by the oppressor; it must be demanded by the oppressed.

– Martin Luther King Jr. (1929–1968)

It was March 23, 1885, and after a long, harsh winter, the manufacturing town of Leicester, England, enjoyed one of the first beautiful spring days. Thousands from the vicinity and surrounding towns gathered to protest what they felt was an unjust law forced upon them by the British government.

Although vaccination for smallpox had been used since the year 1800, the government did not begin to enforce it until the first acts in 1840 and 1853. The 1853 law set the governmental machinery in place to require every child to be vaccinated within three months of birth.

Through a series of legal acts over the years, the British government had, by the time of the protest in Leicester, made refusing smallpox vaccination a crime punishable by fines or imprisonment. The following was reported in March 1884 in the *Leicester Mercury*.

> *Edward Irons was summoned for neglecting to comply with an order for the vaccination of his son, aged two years. He said he had a conscientious objection to conforming to the Vaccination Act, and he was also acting under the advice of his doctor, who stated that vaccination was not conducive to the child's health, nor would it benefit him. One of his children had been vaccinated, and she had suffered considerably from the effects of it, and he could not allow the boy to undertake the same risk. He then gave the opinions of several medical gentlemen on the evils of vaccination, and said he thought it would be inadvisable for the Bench to enforce the law upon a conscientious objection. The Chairman said there were few questions which had given rise to more varied opinions than the subject of vaccination. It had been proved beyond doubt that vaccination had caused smallpox to show itself in a much milder form. The Bench were unanimous in their opinions upon the question. They acted upon public grounds, and decided that the order should be enforced within a fortnight. If the order were not complied with, defendant would be liable to a penalty of twenty shillings. That course would be taken with all cases that came before them.*[187]

The 1867 Vaccination Act consolidated existing laws regarding vaccination and instituted a fine for parents who did not present their children for vaccination within three months of birth.

> *The next landmark in the history of vaccinal legislation is the law of 1867, and this is to this day the law under which all*

---

[187] Stanley Williamson, "Anti-Vaccination Leagues," *Archives of Disease in Childhood*, vol. 59, 1984, p. 1195.

> *penalties are exacted against* **unbelievers**. *This is the vaccination law of England [in 1897]* . . .[188]

Despite the actions taken by the government to ensure a very high vaccination rate, a massive smallpox epidemic hit not only Leicester but all of England and other parts of the world in the early 1870s. The epidemic in Leicester resulted in thousands of cases of smallpox and hundreds of deaths, shaking to its core many people's belief in the protective powers of vaccination.

> *. . . as the years continued more parents heard of, saw, or experienced a growing list of complications attributed to vaccination. The 1871-72 smallpox epidemic gave a vivid example to the townspeople, in that although they had complied with the law* **some 3,000 cases occurred and of these 358 died, some of them vaccinated according to the law.**[189]

A letter appearing in the July 1884 issue of the *Leicester Mercury* reflected the feelings of those who had lost faith in vaccination.

> *It must strike the reflective observer as rather singular that all* **the recent smallpox outbreaks have made their appearance among populations where the laws enforcing vaccination have been rigorously and systematically carried out.** *96% of births in London are protected by vaccination. May I venture to ask whether medical men who have defended and fostered a system of medical procedure which eighty years' experience has demonstrated a disastrous and humiliating failure ought not to feel honourably bound on public grounds to retrace their steps and confess that vaccination,*

---

[188] Alfred Milnes, MA, "Statistics of Small-Pox and Vaccination, with Special Reference to Age-Incidence, Sex-Incidence, and Sanitation," *Journal of the Royal Statistical Society*, September 1897, p. 557.

[189] Stuart M. F. Fraser, "Leicester and Smallpox: The Leicester Method," *Medical History*, 1980, vol. 24, p. 330.

like other once popular prescriptions of inoculation, bleeding and mecurization, is a serious and mischievous blunder.[190]

A swelling wave was developing. Laws were initially passed after people refused the vaccine when they noticed the negative complications. Later, they submitted because of the new laws and still were stricken with deadly smallpox epidemics. Then, even more people rebelled.

Although incongruous with logic, the government took steps to further increase the rate of vaccination by using vaccination officers to prosecute parents who refused to have their children vaccinated.

After the serious smallpox epidemic of 1870-1, part of the pandemic which swept over Europe, the appointment of vaccination officers was made compulsory, and the authorities in Leicester, as elsewhere, attempted to enforce vaccination more rigorously. Prosecutions in the town increased from two in 1869 to over 1,100 in 1881, the total for the twelve years being over 6,000. Of these, 64 had involved imprisonment and 193 distraints [seizure of property to obtain money owed] upon goods, the latter often being effected with much difficulty owing to popular sympathy with the defendants. All classes of the community were represented—among those who set the law at defiance, and those who were prosecuted were regarded as martyrs.[191]

Even from the earliest days of vaccination, many people were moved to oppose the law because so many children suffered serious health problems and death following the procedure.

Primarily it was due to the serious after-effects and injury to health of which many people had had personal experience in their own families, or believed that they had had, and which

---

[190] *Leicester Mercury*, July 3, 1884.

[191] C. Killick Millard, MD, DSc, "The End of Compulsory Vaccination," *British Medical Journal*, December 18, 1948, p. 1073.

undoubtedly were much more common in those days of arm-to-arm vaccination, when the importance of asepsis [the state of being free of pathogenic microorganisms] was unknown or little understood . . . To be compelled to have a healthy and beloved child vaccinated when it was sincerely believed that injury to health might follow seemed to many parents to constitute an intolerable interference with individual liberty.[192]

The penalties fell disproportionately on the poor who, if they could not afford to pay the fine for noncompliance with the vaccination law, would have the settlement forcibly offset by seizure and sale of their furniture. From the *Leicester Mercury*, January 1884:

A man named Arthur Ward had two children injured through vaccination and refused to submit another one to the operation. A fine was imposed and on 24th November two police officers called for the penalty, or in default to ticket the goods. The husband was out at the market, and the poor woman had no money to pay. The goods downstairs were considered insufficient to cover the amount, and the officers demanded to go upstairs. The woman refused to allow this, and an altercation took place, and harsh language was used by the officers, who threatened to take her husband to prison, terrifying Mrs. Ward. At that time she was pregnant, and the shock to the system, and the fright, were of such a character that symptoms ensued which ultimately led to a premature confinement, and on 26th December she gave birth to a still-born child. She never recovered and last week she expired. The doctor who had attended Mrs. Ward said that although he believed in vaccination he did not think it was the duty of any professional man to carry out the laws in the outrageous and brutal manner in which they were enforced.[193]

---

[192] C. Killick Millard, MD, DSc, "The End of Compulsory Vaccination," *British Medical Journal*, December 18, 1948, p. 1073.
[193] Stanley Williamson, "Anti-Vaccination Leagues," *Archives of Disease in Childhood*, vol. 59, 1984, pp. 1195–1196.

Because of the serious and sometimes fatal results of the procedure, and the government's steadfast support of forced vaccination through fines and imprisonment, the people were motivated to revolt. In great numbers, they took to the streets of Leicester to protest. At the time of the demonstration, thousands of prosecutions were being brought against parents who refused vaccination for their children.

> *The widespread opposition to the enforcement of the compulsory clauses of the Vaccination Acts which exists in Leicester culminated yesterday in a great demonstration, which was carried out very successfully. The position which the inhabitants of the town have assumed with regard to this question is due to a variety of causes. At the present moment there are over 5,000 persons being summoned for refusing to comply with the law. . . . summonses issued in the year 1884 only reached seven, or a little over one summons in every two months, while at the present moment forty-five summonses are being heard and disposed of every week. But even the disposal of forty-five defendants every week is not sufficient to meet the requirements of the case, and the defaulters and the objectors increase faster than the cases can be dealt with.*[194]

The crowd gathered in Leicester from a number of different counties in England and included people of all professions.

> *The demonstration . . . drew delegates from all parts of the country, while many letters of sympathy were received not only from England, Scotland, and Ireland, but from Jersey, France, Switzerland, Belgium, Germany, and America. Most of the large towns in the kingdom sent special banners, the Yorkshire, Irish, and Scotch being very prominent. The anti-vaccinationists in Jersey sent a very elaborate banner setting forth that the Acts had been four times defeated there, while the Belgium banner had this inscription in French—"Neither fines nor*

---

[194] "Anti-Vaccination Demonstration at Leicester," *The Times*, March 24, 1885.

imprisonment will prevent vaccine being a poison nor the vaccination laws an infamy."[195]

It was a festive atmosphere with music playing and hundreds of flags and banners displayed with sayings such as "Liberty is our birthright, and liberty we demand," "Oppressive laws make discontented peoples," "The mothers of England demand repeal," "The Three Pillars of Vaccination—Fraud, Force, and Folly," and "We no longer beg but demand the control of our children."

The mayor of the city received the procession, and a member of the municipal council presided. An effigy of Jenner [considered the father of vaccination] was hung from the gallows and given the "long drop" at intervals as the procession advanced. Those men who had suffered the extreme penalty of imprisonment made a prominent figure, and others, whose goods had been seized, displayed samples of the otherwise rather commonplace utensils to admiring eyes. The obnoxious parliamentary acts were enthusiastically burned. A wagon carrying unvaccinated children bore the motto: "They that are whole need not a physician."[196]

The most important feature was a large number of men who had undergone the extreme process of imprisonment rather than submit to the law. Next came a larger detachment, consisting of men who had their household goods seized and sold by public auction, samples of the goods which had been seized and sold being conveyed in wagons. The next detachment consisted of a conveyance filled with unvaccinated children . . . This was followed by a large number of delegates, many of whom were from London, Leeds, Manchester, Halifax, Blackburn, Keighley, Bedford, Birmingham, Lincoln, and Norwich. Among other features in the procession were a horse

---

[195] "Anti-Vaccination Demonstration at Leicester," *The Times*, March 24, 1885.
[196] "A Demonstration Against Vaccination," *Boston Medical and Surgical Journal*, April 16, 1885, p. 380.

and cow, drawn in wagons and exhibited as sources of vaccination.[197]

Both the devices and mottoes were of the most profuse order. One of the devices was an effigy of Dr. Jenner inscribed "child-slayer;" a second was a complete funeral cortège, consisting of a coffin on open bier, mourners, etc., and inscribed "another victim of vaccination"...[198]

The large two-mile-long procession marched around the town for about two hours, receiving enthusiastic cheering at various points along the route. The townspeople showed their support by waving streamers with flags and sayings along the route. The procession continued to marketplace.

... a goodly number of anti-vaccinators were present, and an escort was formed, preceded by a banner, to accompany a young mother and two men, all of whom had resolved to give themselves up to the police and undergo imprisonment in preference to having their children vaccinated. The utmost sympathy was expressed for the poor woman, who bore up bravely, and although seeming to feel her position expressed her determination to go to prison again and again rather than give her child over to the "tender mercies" of a public vaccinator. The three were attended by a numerous crowd and in Gallowtreegate three hearty cheers were given for them, which were renewed with increased vigour as they entered the doors of the police cells.[199]

Organizers of the event estimated the number at attendance to have been between 80,000 and 100,000. Mr. Councillor Butcher of

---

[197] "Anti-Vaccination Demonstration at Leicester," *The Times*, March 24, 1885.
[198] "Anti-Vaccination Demonstration at Leicester," *The Leeds Mercury*, March 24, 1885.
[199] Stanley Williamson, "Anti-Vaccination Leagues," *Archives of Disease in Childhood*, vol. 59, 1984, p. 1195.

Leicester presided and congratulated the crowd on the magnificent and elaborate display. He said:

> *. . . the exemplary conduct of the many thousands of people who had attended the demonstration showed that they were determined only to use fair and constitutional means to bring about a repeal of the Acts.*[200]

He addressed the audience:

> *Many present had been sufferers under the Acts, and all they asked was that in the future they and their children might be let alone. They lived for something else in this world than to be experimented upon for the stamping out of a particular disease. **A large and increasing portion of the public were of opinion that the best way to get rid of smallpox and similar diseases was to use plenty of water, eat good food, live in light and airy houses**, and see that the Corporation kept the streets clean and the drains in order. If such details were attended to, there was no need to fear smallpox, or any of its kindred; and if they were neglected, neither vaccination nor any other prescription by Act of Parliament could save them.*[201]

The crowd cheered. Mr. William Young, secretary of the London Society, followed with a resolution:

> *That the principle of the Compulsory Vaccination Acts is subversive of that personal liberty which is the birthright of every free-born Briton; that they are destructive of parental rights, tyrannical and unjust in operation, and ought therefore to be resisted by every constitutional means.*[202]

After the demonstration, an evening meeting took place in Temperance Hall under the presidency of Rev. J. Page Hopps. The hall was decorated with flags and sayings denouncing the practice of

---

[200] "Anti-Vaccination Demonstration at Leicester," *The Times*, March 24, 1885.
[201] J.T. Biggs, *Leicester: Sanitation Versus Vaccination*, 1912, p. 117.
[202] Ibid.

vaccination. **There were delegates from more than 60 towns on the platform.** Mr. W. Stanyon presented a resolution that passed unanimously.

> *That the Compulsory Vaccination Acts, which make loving and conscientious parents criminals, subjecting them to fines, loss of goods, and imprisonment, propagate disease and inflict death, and under which five thousand of our fellow-townsmen are now being prosecuted, are a disgrace to the Statute Book, and ought to be abolished forthwith.*[203]

The demonstration was considered a wonderful success by the people in attendance. Dr. Spencer T. Hall, a 73-year-old resident of Blackpool, was overcome with emotion when speaking of the events of the day. He said his tears were tears of joy at having lived to see vaccination being so challenged.

> **He had been vaccinated at two years of age, and very seriously injured; but at fourteen he had a severe attack of small-pox, which was followed by improved health.** *Far rather would he have small-pox than be vaccinated. He had paid fines for all his children.* **In his long and wide experience he had never seen such evil results from small-pox as he had seen from vaccination.**[204]

These fearless people wanted to be able to make their own decisions for their health and the health of their children and thus fought for self-determination.

> *The fearful mortality from small-pox in completely vaccinated and presumably well "protected" Leicester during the years 1871-2 had the effect of destroying the people's faith in "protective" vaccination. The result was that* **poor and rich alike, the toilers, the aristocrats, and the municipal authorities, began to refuse vaccination for their children**

---

[203] J.T. Biggs, *Leicester: Sanitation Versus Vaccination*, 1912, p.120.
[204] Ibid., pp. 125–126.

> **and themselves**. *This refusal continued until 1890, when, instead of ninety-five per cent the vaccination reached only about five per cent of the total births.*[205]

Thousands of brave people set off a historical rebellion that successfully countered a prevailing medical belief and heavy-handed government rule. The medical profession proclaimed that the Leicester residents would suffer greatly for their decision to turn their backs on vaccination. They prognosticated that this unvaccinated town with its "highly flammable material"[206] would suffer with the "dread disease"[207] that would spread like "wild-fire on a prairie"[208] and decimate the population.

But the leaders of Leicester held steadfast to what they knew was right and successfully implemented their plan of sanitation, hygiene, and isolation—instead of vaccination. Their grand experiment would test the very notions of freedom of choice, self-determination, and the heart of a flawed medical belief.

---

[205] J. W. Hodge, MD, "How Small-Pox Was Banished from Leicester," *Twentieth Century Magazine*, vol. III, no. 16, January 1911, p. 337.
[206] Ibid.
[207] "A Demonstration Against Vaccination," *Boston Medical and Surgical Journal*, April 16, 1885, p. 380.
[208] B. O. Flower, "Fallacious Assumptions Advanced by Advocates of National and State Medical Legislation," *Twentieth Century Magazine*, vol. IV, no. 24, September 1911, p. 537.

~ 7 ~

THE REBEL EXPERIMENT

*You may just as well try and stop a small-pox epidemic by
vaccination as to prevent a thunderstorm with an umbrella.*

– Dr. Druitt, late 1800s

*What an act of insanity it would be to implant the infective
products of undefined disease into the bodies of eight thousand
healthy children in order to prevent the possible development of a very
few mild cases of small-pox! Could absurdity go further than this?*

– Dr. J. W. Hodge, 1911

*Any intelligent fool can make things bigger and
more complex . . . It takes a touch of genius—and a lot
of courage—to move in the opposite direction.*

– Albert Einstein (1879–1955)

Concerns over vaccine safety, effectiveness, and governmental infringement on personal liberty and freedom through compulsory vaccination stoked the fires of the anti-vaccination movement. People began to resist the government and chose to pay fines. Some even accepted imprisonment rather than allowing vaccination for themselves or their children. The public backlash culminated in the Great Demonstration in Leicester, England, in 1885.

That same year, Leicester's government, which had pushed for vaccination through the use of fines and jail time, was replaced with a new government that was opposed to compulsory vaccination. By 1887 the vaccination coverage rates had dropped to 10 percent.

Since 1885, there had been no prosecution, and last year (1887), he believed, the number of vaccinations in Leicester amounted to only 11 and 12 per cent of births.[209]

The "Leicester Method" relied on quarantine of smallpox patients and thorough disinfection of their homes. They believed this was a cheap and effective means to eliminate the need for vaccination.

The last decade has witnessed an extraordinary decrease in vaccination, but, nevertheless, the town has enjoyed an almost entire immunity from small-pox, *there never having been more than two or three cases in the town at one time. A new method for which great practical utility is claimed has been enforced by the sanitary committee of the Corporation for the stamping out of small-pox is one of the least troublesome diseases with which they have to deal. The method of treatment, in a word, is this:—As soon as small-pox breaks out, the medical man and the householder are compelled under penalty to at once report the outbreak to the Corporation. The small-pox van is at once ordered by telephone to make all arrangements, and thus, within a few hours, the sufferer is safely in the hospital. The family and inmates of the house are placed in quarantine in comfortable quarters, and the house thoroughly disinfected.* **The result is that in every instance the disease has been promptly and completely stamped out at a paltry expense.** *Under such a system the Corporation have expressed their opinion that vaccination is unnecessary, as they claim to deal with the disease in a more direct and much more efficacious manner. This, and a widespread belief that* **death and disease have resulted from the operation of vaccination,** *may be said to be the foundation upon which the existing opposition to the Acts rests.*[210]

---

[209] *The Parliamentary Debates*, vol. CCCXXVI, June 1, 1888, p. 933.
[210] "Anti-Vaccination Demonstration at Leicester," *The Times*, March 24, 1885.

Even though it was clear that the Leicester Method was superior to vaccination, those who strongly endorsed vaccination believed that the immunity enjoyed by the town of Leicester was temporary and that sooner or later the town would suffer a large smallpox epidemic. They were convinced that a great tragedy was inevitable and there would be tremendous suffering for the unfortunates who followed the leaders into what they felt was a misguided adventure. They thought that the "gigantic experiment" would result in a terrible "massacre," especially in the "unprotected" children.

> *Sir Duminie Corrigan, M.D. when acting as one of the committee in 1871, on the Vaccination Act, said: "An unvaccinated child is like a bag of gunpowder which might blow up the whole school, and ought not, therefore to be admitted to a school unless he is vaccinated."*[211]

> *One cannot help feeling that whenever the remarkable immunity which Leicester is said to have enjoyed for some eight years from this dread disease shall be broken . . . The corporation having thrown over vaccination are disposed to place their whole confidence upon prompt notification and isolation of every case that occurs . . . It is the unprotected children upon whom the scourge will fall heaviest, and the surrounding country will suffer from an epidemic . . .*[212]

> *Let them remove the cordon of protected persons about the cases, and their boasted arrangements will prove a delusion; the sick will be without nurses, and the very industry of Leicester will be molested by a plague which will stagger the radical authorities of the borough, and bring the thousands of*

---

[211] J. W. Hodge, MD, "How Small-Pox Was Banished from Leicester," *Twentieth Century Magazine*, vol. III, no. 16, January 1911, p. 340.
[212] "A Demonstration Against Vaccination," *Boston Medical and Surgical Journal*, April 16, 1885, p. 380.

unvaccinated and unrevaccinated inhabitants to cry for the blessings discovered by Jenner.[213]

The antivaccinators of Leicester . . . having to a great extent thrown off the armour of vaccination, are waging a desperate and gallant, though misguided, conflict against the enemy . . . But in Leicester, when its time arrives, we shall not fail to see a repetition of last century's experiences, and certainly there will afterwards be fewer children left to die from diarrhoea. It is to be hoped that, when the catastrophe does come, the Government will see that its teachings are duly studied and recorded.[214]

Despite such prophesies of doom from the medical profession, the majority of the town's residents remained steadfast because their experience reinforced their belief that vaccination did not control smallpox. The prophecy that the Leicester residents would eventually be plagued with disaster never did come to pass.

Leicester enjoyed better success against smallpox than other towns in England that were highly vaccinated. In the 1893 smallpox outbreak, the well-vaccinated district of Mold in Flintshire, England, had a death rate about 32 times higher than Leicester.

Not only may well-vaccinated towns be affected with smallpox, but the most thorough vaccination of a population that is possible to imagine may be followed by an extensive outbreak of the disease. This happened in the mining and agricultural district of Mold, in Flintshire . . . **Leicester, with a population under ten years of age practically unvaccinated, had a small-pox death-rate of 144 per million; whereas Mold,**

---

[213] "Leicester, and Its Immunity from Small-Pox," *The Lancet*, June 5, 1886, p. 1091.
[214] C. Killick Millard, MD, DSc, "The End of Compulsory Vaccination," *British Medical Journal*, December 18, 1948, p. 1073.

with all the births vaccinated for eighteen years previous to the epidemic, had one of 3,614 per million.[215]

In the 1891–1894 smallpox outbreak described by Dr. J. W. Hodge, the highly vaccinated town of Birmingham had 63 smallpox cases and 5 deaths per 10,000 of population, compared with Leicester at 19 cases and 1 death per 10,000.

> . . . **Leicester had less than one-third the cases of small-pox and less than one-fourth the deaths in proportion to population than well-vaccinated Birmingham;** so that both the alleged protection from attacks of the disease and the mitigation of its severity when it does attack, are shown not only to be absolutely untrue, in this case, to the absence of vaccination.[216]

The death rate from smallpox per hundred thousand in Leicester during the 1892–1894 outbreak was 5.7. In Birmingham it was 8.0, Warrington was 10.0, and Middlesbrough was 14.4. Over the years, Leicester's death rate from smallpox declined even more. In the 1902–1903 outbreak the death rate was 5.3, and by the 1903–1904 outbreak it was down to 1.2.

> Leicester's small-pox history, and her successful vindication of sanitation as a small-pox prophylactic, will bear the closest scrutiny. **Each successive epidemic since vaccination has decreased, with a larger proportion of unvaccinated population, furnishes a still lower death-rate.**[217]

In 1904 C. Killick Millard, MD, who was at the time minister of health in Leicester, reported his observations of smallpox and vaccination. He formerly believed that vaccination provided the individual

---

[215] William Scott Tebb, MD, *A Century of Vaccination and What It Teaches*, Swan Sonnenschein & Co., London, 1898, pp. 93, 94.

[216] J. W. Hodge, MD, "Prophylaxis to be Realized Through the Attainment of Health, Not by the Propagation of Disease," *The St. Louis Medical and Surgical Journal*, vol. LXXXIII, July 1902, p. 15.

[217] J. T. Biggs, *Leicester: Sanitation Versus Vaccination*, 1912, pp. 459–460.

complete, although temporary, protection against smallpox. But following the events of Leicester, Dr. Millard had a philosophical turnaround and had to re-examine the relationship between vaccination and protection.

> ... the fact that these prophecies, which were first made nearly twenty years ago, have, as yet, been unfulfilled, is one of the strongest reasons for re-examining the question of the influences of the vaccinal condition of a community in determining small-pox incidence.[218]

After his experience and understanding of smallpox deepened, Dr. Millard refuted the myth that unvaccinated people were at greater risk of contracting smallpox in an epidemic. Importantly, he noted that unvaccinated children were not highly susceptible to smallpox. He also observed that children in general were commonly infected by adults who had been vaccinated.

> *The Danger of Unvaccinated Persons Contracting Small-Pox.—Moreover, the experience of Leicester during the recent epidemic, as in the previous epidemic (1892-93) ten years ago, seems to show that where modern measures are carried out, unvaccinated persons run less risk of contracting small-pox, even in the presence of an epidemic, than is usually supposed. It was predicted that once the disease got amongst the unvaccinated children of Leicester it would "spread like wildfire." I certainly expected this myself when I first came to Leicester, and it caused me much anxiety all through the epidemic. Yet although, during the ten months the epidemic lasted, 136 children (under fifteen years) were attacked, inflicted largely by once-vaccinated adults, it cannot be said that the disease ever showed any tendency to "catch on" amongst the entirely unvaccinated child population . . . I have said enough*

---

[218] J. T. Biggs, *Leicester: Sanitation Versus Vaccination*, 1912, p. 507.

> *to show that the "Leicester Method" in Leicester succeeded bet-*
> *ter than was anticipated.*[219]

In addition, Dr. Millard noted that vaccination was not the harmless procedure it was often touted to be. He made the extremely important observation that, even if vaccination did reduce the severity of smallpox, it still couldn't stop the spread of the disease, because both severe and mild forms were contagious.

> *I would say here that from what I have myself seen of vaccina-*
> *tion in Leicester, I cannot quite regard it as the trifling opera-*
> *tion so many medical men appear to think it. It constitutes a*
> *very definite, though usually only temporary, interference with*
> *health, and occasionally it is responsible for much more serious*
> *ill effects . . . If it only mitigates, then **since the mildest small-***
> ***pox is admittedly as contagious as the most severe, vac-***
> ***cinated small-pox is no less dangerous to the community***
> ***than unvaccinated;** therefore there is no reason, and there-*
> *fore no right, to enforce vaccination by law.*[220]

Six years later in 1910, Dr. Millard concluded that infantile vaccination played a much smaller part in limiting the spread of smallpox than was generally predicted and that unvaccinated people were not a danger to the community. Therefore compulsory vaccination was not justified.

> *Another year has passed without any case of small-pox having*
> *occurred in Leicester. It is now four years since the small-pox*
> *hospital was last used, or five years if the single case in 1906 be*
> *excluded. As I have pointed out before, the experience of Leices-*
> *ter proves that the danger of unvaccinated persons contract-*
> *ing small-pox, even in the presence of an epidemic—provided*
> *modern methods of dealing with the disease are efficiently*
> *carried out—has been somewhat overrated; whilst the danger*
> *of vaccinated persons spreading the disease—through the*

---

[219] J. T. Biggs, *Leicester: Sanitation Versus Vaccination*, 1912, pp. 510–511.
[220] Ibid., pp. 513, 514.

occurrence of highly modified cases which are so apt to be "missed"—has not hitherto been sufficiently emphasised. It is very doubtful, therefore, whether it is any longer legitimate to justify vaccination being made compulsory, on the ground—at one time so much insisted upon—that "unvaccinated persons are a danger to the community."[221]

Even after 30 years of Leicester's successful experiment, there were those who still believed disaster would eventually befall the "unprotected fools" who favored not vaccinating. An article in the 1914 *New York Times* stated:

. . . a very large unprotected population has grown up, nearly equal to or even outnumbering the protected, as in Leicester where 75 per cent are said to be unvaccinated. So far there has been no great disaster, but from the experience of Canada, which was grievously scourged a generation ago because it allowed a large unprotected population to grow up, we can safely predict a dreadful reckoning in England. It may be all right to assert that this is Nature's way of eliminating the fools who haven't sense enough to live in modern crowds, but among the dead will be many who have been deceived by men who were considered experts worthy of belief. Those who openly oppose vaccination or who tell everybody to wait until they come to the bridge of danger before crossing it, are taking a heavy responsibility on their souls.[222]

Most infants in Leicester remained unvaccinated. Although some school children developed smallpox, there were no major outbreaks. How could the medical experts have been so wrong? In 1893,

---

[221] J. T. Biggs, *Leicester: Sanitation Versus Vaccination*, 1912, pp. 406–407.
[222] "Urges Necessity for Vaccination, Commissioner Goldwater's Contention Indorsed by *American Medicine*, Canada's Scourge Warns, England's Neglect May Result in a Smallpox Disaster, Germany Keeps It Down," *New York Times*, April 5, 1914.

Professor E. M. Crookshank,[223] author of *History and Pathology of Vaccination* and Professor of Comparative Pathology in King's College, London, expressed his views on vaccination.

> *Unfortunately, a belief in the efficacy of vaccination has been so enforced in the education of the medical practitioner that it is hardly probable that the futility of the practice will be generally acknowledged in our generation, though nothing would more redound [contribute] to the credit of the profession and give evidence of the advance in pathology and sanitary science. It is more probable that when, by means of notification and isolation, small-pox is kept under control, vaccination will disappear from practice, and will retain only an historical interest.[224]*

In hindsight, Dr. Crookshank was an optimist to think that the futility of the practice of vaccination would be acknowledged in any generation. Smallpox vaccination was discontinued nearly one hundred years later, but the fact that the practice was unnecessary and had caused needless suffering and death was never recognized or acknowledged. In fact, despite all the serious problems with it and the lack of evidence of effectiveness, it is still upheld as the exemplary vaccine to promote vaccine faith today.

The year 1948 brought an end to compulsory vaccination in England. By that point, the experiment in Leicester, which had been going on for more than 60 years, proved to be a great success. In 1948 Dr. Millard stated:

---

[223] Edgar March Crookshank, M.B. Lond. (Honours in Obst.) 1884, M.R.C.S. Eng. 1881 (King's Coll.); Exhib. and Gold Medallist in Anat. 1st M.B. Lond. 1879; Fell. King's Coll.; Mem. Roy. Micros. Soc. and Path. Soc.; Prof. of Comp. Path, and Bacteriol. King's Coll.; late House Surg. King's Coll. Hosp., and Civil Surg. Med. Staff Egyptian Campaign (Medal and Clasp, Tel-el-Kebir, and Khedive's Star); Director of the Bacteriological Laboratory, King's College, London.

[224] Edgar March Crookshank, *History and Pathology of Vaccination Volume 1: A Critical Inquiry*, 1889, London, pp. 465-466

. . . in Leicester during the 62 years since infant vaccination was abandoned there have been only 53 deaths from smallpox, and in the past 40 years only two deaths. Moreover, the experience in Leicester is confirmed, and strongly confirmed, by that of the whole country. **Vaccination has been steadily declining ever since the "conscience clause" was introduced, until now nearly two-thirds of the children born are not vaccinated. Yet smallpox mortality has also declined until now quite negligible.** *In the fourteen years 1933-1946 there were only 28 deaths in a population of some 40 million, and among those 28 there was not a single death of an infant under 1 year of age.*[225]

In a 1980 *Medical History* article, Stuart M. Fraser commented on the success of the Leicester Method.

Leicester stands as an example, probably the first, where measures other than total reliance on vaccination were introduced successfully to eradicate the disease from the community . . . **A system of immediate notification, isolation, and quarantine of contacts is one which has proved particularly effective in containing and limiting smallpox.**[226]

Forty-two years after his 1904 report, Dr. Millard, who had been the minister of health in Leicester from 1901 to 1935, explained why he believed medical experts of the day were wrong. At the core was a set of self-reinforcing beliefs in vaccination.

Looking back it is interesting to consider why medical experts were so mistaken in their prophecies of disaster to come if universal vaccination of infants was abandoned. It was probably due to the belief, then so strongly held, that it was infant

---

[225] C. Killick Millard, MD, DSc, "The End of Compulsory Vaccination," *British Medical Journal*, December 18, 1948, p. 1074.
[226] Stuart M. Fraser, "Leicester and Smallpox: The Leicester Method," *Medical History*, vol. 24, 1980, p. 324.

vaccination, and that alone, which had brought about the great diminution of smallpox mortality that followed upon an introduction of vaccination. That this was clearly a case of cause and effect was reiterated in every textbook and in every course of lectures on public health. It was hailed, indeed, as the outstanding triumph of preventative medicine. No wonder that medical students accepted it as an incontrovertible scientific fact.[227]

Medical authorities often used diagrams to show that vaccination enforcement was tied to a decrease in smallpox deaths. Such diagrams were designed to illustrate an apparent correlation between the rate of infant vaccination and smallpox mortality. But those diagrams were flawed. Again, Dr. Millard commented.

*We now know that the apparent correlation must have been a coincidence, because **smallpox mortality continued to decrease even after vaccination was decreasing also, and this had now gone on for 60 years.** Obviously there must have been other causes at work which brought about the dramatic fall in smallpox mortality since the beginning of the nineteenth century, and to the extent vaccination has for so many years been receiving more credit—perhaps much more—than it was entitled to.*[228]

After the 1872 epidemic in Leicester, both vaccination rates and deaths from smallpox declined (Graph 7.1). **In contrast to what vaccine enthusiasts say today, overall child mortality declined after 1885 while vaccination rates plummeted** (Graph 7.2). It's important to note that the death rate for children of all ages did not begin to change until about 1880. **Decades of strict vaccination laws did absolutely nothing to improve the overall life expectancy of children in all age groups.**

---

[227] C. Killick Millard, MD, DSc, "The End of Compulsory Vaccination," *British Medical Journal*, December 18, 1948, p. 1074.
[228] Ibid.

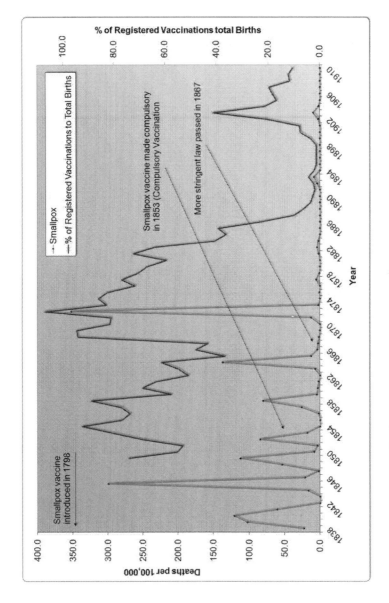

Graph 7.1: Leicester, England, smallpox mortality rate vs. smallpox vaccination coverage from 1838 to 1910.

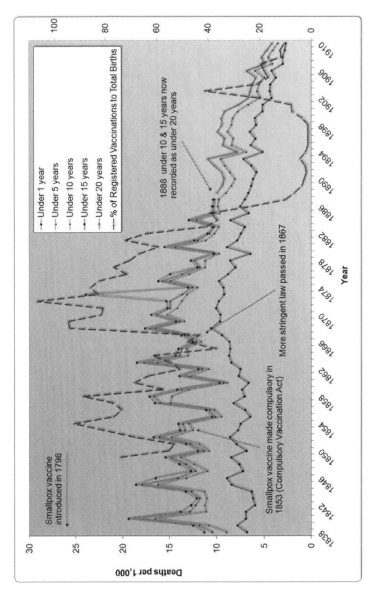

Graph 7.2: Leicester, England, mortality rates for various age groups vs. smallpox vaccination coverage from 1838 to 1910.

The principles pioneered in Leicester were instrumental in the decline of this historically horrific disease.

> **Contrary to popular belief smallpox was not eradicated by mass vaccination.** *Though tried initially it proved difficult to implement in many countries and was abandoned in favour of surveillance-containment. This involved trained workers searching for cases, with rewards for those who found them. Cases and their contacts were then isolated; contacts were vaccinated.*[229]

The experiment of 60+ years not only showed that the method was successful, it also demonstrated that established scientific thinking could be mistaken. Despite Leicester's success and the change of smallpox expression to that of a mild disease, governments elsewhere continued to use heavy-handed measures backed by the force of law to compel people to be vaccinated.

In 1902 Alderman Thomas Windley read a paper at the annual meeting of the Royal Institute of Public Health in Exeter, England. Windley was the chairman of a sanitary committee for 47 years, and in his speech he challenged the medical profession to recognize the success in Leicester.

> *. . . [if] the evils which they conscientiously believe would follow by the absence of vaccination in a great manufacturing town like Leicester have not been experienced? They may fairly be asked to consider whether the time has not arrived when they can give a little credit to Leicester for what they have done in stamping out repeated outbreaks of small-pox, and for being the first to set an example of the most successful methods in dealing with this loathsome and terrible infectious disease,*

---

[229] Derrick Baxby, "The End of Smallpox," *History Today*, March 1999, p. 16.

which has since been followed by nearly all the great towns of the country.[230]

In 1911 Dr. J. W. Hodge published a paper on how smallpox was controlled in Leicester. By this time, the rebel experiment had been successful for decades.

*The experience of unvaccinated Leicester is an eye-opener to the people and an eye-sore to the pro-vaccinists the world over. Here is a great manufacturing town having a population of nearly a quarter of a million, which has demonstrated by a crucial test of an experience extending over a period of more than a quarter of a century, that **an unvaccinated population has been far less susceptible to small-pox and far less afflicted by that disease since it abandoned vaccination than it was at a time when ninety-five per cent of its births were vaccinated and its adult population well re-vaccinated.***[231]

Yugoslavia February 16–April 11, 1972

The WHO was forced to implement a version of the Leicester Method in the latter stages of their smallpox campaigns, when it became plain to them that vaccination didn't reliably protect.

Yugoslavia experienced a smallpox epidemic beginning in February 1972. The index case was a recently vaccinated Yugoslavian haji pilgrim who picked up the disease while traveling through Iraq. He had been vaccinated in December 1971 at a public health clinic.

By the time the epidemic was controlled in April of 1972, there were 175 cases and 35 deaths. Of note was that the older portion of the population was highly vaccinated, and the third wave of cases was

---

[230] Thomas Windley, *Leicester and Smallpox: Thirty Years' Experience: A Paper Read at the Annual Meeting of the Royal Institute of Public Health, Held at Exeter*, August 1902.

[231] J. W. Hodge, MD, "How Small-Pox Was Banished from Leicester," *Twentieth Century Magazine*, vol. III, no. 16, January 1911, p. 342.

almost all in people who were previously vaccinated. The WHO's own report states:

> *In the age group 20 and over, 92 patients had previously been vaccinated while 21 were unvaccinated. The relatively large number of previously vaccinated cases among those over seven years of age indicates a substantial decrease in post-vaccinal immunity following primary vaccination, as well as a lack of successful revaccination when they were seven and 14 years old.*[232]

The first death was on March 10, and the health officials had no idea the cause was smallpox. The autopsy report said the cause of death was penicillin anaphylaxis. Vaccination did not begin until March 16.

Even though they knew that vaccination was ineffective, the Yugoslavian Federal Epidemiologic Commission went ahead and vaccinated 18 million citizens. Vaccination had to continue through the end of April because so many of the vaccinations were considered unsuccessful and had to be repeated. An obvious question is, just how many smallpox vaccines in the previous 200 years didn't "take" either? Yet no one knew . . . In the meantime, the Leicester Method was also carried out, and all cases were quickly quarantined.

> *Contacts were placed in special quarantine facilities (e.g. in the Djakovica hospital and in a motel near Belgrade). There were also quarantine facilities set up in individual houses, as well as in whole villiages, as was the case with Danjane and Ratkovac and some other villiages.*[233]

---

[232] S. Litvinjenko, B. Arsic, and S. Borjanovic, "Epidemiologic Aspects of Smallpox in Yugoslavia in 1972," World Health Organization Report, Belgrade, Yugoslavia, May 10, 1973, http://whqlibdoc.who.int/smallpox/WHO_SE_73.57.pdf, accessed June 18, 2013.

[233] S. Litvinjenko, B. Arsic, and S. Borjanovic, "Epidemiologic Aspects of Smallpox in Yugoslavia in 1972," World Health Organization Report, Belgrade, Yugoslavia, May 10, 1973, http://whqlibdoc.who.int/smallpox/WHO_SE_73.57.pdf, accessed June 18, 2013.

The epidemic was rapidly extinguished.

Vaccination, although known to be ineffective, had to be implemented if the history of vaccine success was to be upheld. But what really stopped the epidemic was use of the Leicester Method.

~ 8 ~

THE POWER OF THE STATE

No man is good enough to govern another man
without that other's consent.

– Abraham Lincoln (1809–1865)

I assert that it is beyond the functions of law to dictate
a medical procedure, or enforce any scientific theory.

– Emeritus Professor F. W. Newman (1805–1897), October 26, 1874

By the mid-1800s and into the 1900s, governmental support of vaccination as the only means of controlling smallpox was firmly entrenched. As seen in England in the late 1800s, despite a parent's belief that a vaccine had caused a child's injury or death and despite dissenting medical opinions, governments and courts were unified in their decree that vaccination had to be enforced. Fines, seizure of personal property, and imprisonment were instituted to compel the population into compliance of the law based upon the dominant medical paradigm. Punishments were carried out for not vaccinating.

England, August 1869:

> *In August [1869] Mrs. Anne Sipple was committed for seven days' hard labor—an illegal sentence—and confined in a stone cell with an infant of eighteen months, the child deprived of shoes and socks, and a diet of bread and water only for both.*[234]

---

[234] Noel A. Humphries, "English Vaccination and Small-Pox Statistics, with Special Reference to the Report of the Royal Commission, and to Recent Small-Pox Epidemics," *Journal of the Royal Statistical Society*, September 1897, p. 558.

Atlanta, Georgia, December 17, 1897:

> *Miss L. Miller a modiste [one that produces, designs, or deals in women's fashions] of 91 Crew Street, was fined $25.75 [estimated value of $680 in 2009 dollars] by Recorder Calhoun to-day for refusing to be vaccinated. She was unable to pay the amount, and was ordered to serve twenty-five days in the city prison. After having been in prison for three hours Miss Miller said she would allow her family physician to vaccinate her. She was subsequently vaccinated and released.*[235]

Boston, Massachusetts, January 26, 1902:

> *In order to stamp out smallpox, which is semi-epidemic here, the Board of Health started compulsory vaccination to-day. The work was begun in East Boston, where 125 surgeons, each accompanied by a policeman, made a house-to-house canvass, vaccinating all who had not been recently inoculated. Those who refused to allow the operating will be hauled into court.*[236]

Asheville, North Carolina, March 18, 1903:

> *Prof. A. T. Weaver, at the head of a leading educational institution, has been sent to jail because he refused to be vaccinated and also because of his refusal to pay a fine of $25 for the same. The vaccination was ordered as a precaution against smallpox. Prof. Weaver, it is said, may institute legal proceedings against the authorities and may take his case before the Supreme Court of North Carolina.*[237]

With its orders to force vaccination, personal choice and freedom were disregarded by the state. Where vaccines were resisted, police

---

[235] "Vaccination Before Prison, Atlanta Woman Submits Rather Than Spend 25 Days in Jail," *New York Times*, December 18, 1897.
[236] "Fighting Smallpox in Boston, 125 Surgeons, Accompanied by Policemen, Vaccinated 15,000 Persons Yesterday," *New York Times*, January 27, 1902.
[237] "A Professor Sent to Jail," *New York Times*, March 19, 1903.

sometimes accompanied health officers, using heavy-handed tactics to carry out their goal of vaccinating.

Passaic, New Jersey, April 11, 1901:

> *There was a lively time in the works of the American Tobacco Company this afternoon, when the 350 girls employed objected to being vaccinated by the physicians sent there by the health officers . . . When the health officers went to the factory the girls were informed that every one of them would have to be vaccinated. Some of them fainted, others became hysterical, and there was a general rebellion. About 200 of them, led by Florence Haskell, attempted to get out of the works, but they found all the exits locked. The police were called and the work of vaccination began. Some of the girls fought the officers and were led up to the physicians screaming, struggling, and kicking. The greatest excitement prevailed and all work had to be suspended. At one time some of the girls threatened to destroy the factory if they were not allowed to go out, but all were finally vaccinated.*[238]

Lead, South Dakota, April 24, 1902:

> *There was some excitement in this city and Deadwood last night when several hundred miners were forcibly vaccinated. So many cases of smallpox has occurred in the two cities that an order was issued compelling vaccination. The miners refused. Last night the Sheriff, five deputies, and four policemen accompanied the City Physician and four assistants in a round-up of the saloons, theatres, and gambling dens . . . Several fights occurred, but the miners were overawed . . . At first the miners were disposed to be ugly, but finally turned it*

---

[238] "Factory Girl's Resistance, American Tobacco Company's Employees' Fight Against Compulsory Vaccination," *New York Times*, April 12, 1901.

off in merriment but for some time last night it appeared a riot would ensue.[239]

Montreal, Canada, September 28, 1885:

> *The by-law passed by the Provincial Board of Health making vaccination compulsory having appeared in the Official Gazette increased the excitement among the French Canadians to such an extent that a riot broke out in the east end this morning, and before the crowd dispersed they smashed many of the windows of the East End Health Office . . . some 50 police had meantime arrived and drove the mob down the street, but they immediately gathered on the Champ de Mars in the rear, where a lively hand-to-hand conflict took place, but the rioters, when dispersed at one place, immediately met at another and renewed the stone throwing, and several of the police were wounded . . . the mob returned to the house of Dr. Laporte, public vaccinator, and set fire to it . . . the rioters proceeded once more to the East End Health Office, and easily overpowered the five policemen who were on guard. The whole front of the office was torn out and the smallpox placards and sulphur for disinfecting houses were piled up in the middle of the street and set fire to . . . The police then charged the crowd and drove them out to the city limits. The clubs were plied with vigor and many of the rioters were badly cut about the head.*[240]

No profession was exempt from the tyrannical legal rulings. A judge, in a decision that forced vaccination on a teacher, stated that any teacher was essentially a slave to the Board of Education and therefore had no right to resist.

---

[239] "Miners Resist Vaccination, Sheriff and Party of Officers Aid Physicians in Enforcing the Law in South Dakota," *New York Times*, April 25, 1902.
[240] "French Against English, A Riot in Montreal Caused by Compulsory Vaccination," *New York Times*, September 29, 1885.

Philadelphia, Pennsylvania, November 14, 1901:

> *The advocates of compulsory vaccination won a victory to-day when Judge Arnold handed down a decision denying the injunction asked for by Miss Mary Helen Lyndall of the Girls' High School against the Board of Education, which suspended her for refusing to comply with its order to procure a certificate of successful vaccination within the last five years or else submit to an inoculation. In addition to refusing to the injunction asked for, the Judge discourages insubordination by announcing that the relation of a teacher to the Board of Education is that of a servant to a master.*[241]

One way to enforce vaccination was to require all school-age children to attend school and then require them to be vaccinated. Parents who tried to avoid vaccination by keeping their children home soon found themselves subject to fines and imprisonment.

Derby, Connecticut, April 26, 1902:

> *Because he has decided to oppose to the last resort compulsory vaccination for his children, John McGuigan, a resident of this city, has received hundreds of letters from all parts of the country, and many of the missives contain offers of aid, pecuniary and otherwise. McGuigan was informed that he must have his two children vaccinated. He refused on the ground that one of the children, by a previous vaccination, had suffered serious complications. School regulations forbade the presence of children not vaccinated and McGuigan kept his children home. He was arrested on a charge alleging violation of the law providing for the proper schooling of children, and was fined in the*

---

[241] "Teacher Must Be Vaccinated, Court Sustains Philadelphia Board in Suspending Woman Who Refused," *New York Times*, November 15, 1901.

police court. He appealed to the Superior Court, and the case awaits assignment for trial.[242]

Personal experiences of vaccine failure or serious damage from previous vaccination did not stop the state from pursuing their oppressive methods.

Passaic, New Jersey, March 8, 1912:

> *Health Commissioner George Michels of this city will be arraigned in the police court to-morrow on a technical charge of disorderly conduct. The complaint is brought by the Board of Education, which accuses Mr. Michels of refusing to allow his daughter, Dorothy, a school girl, to be vaccinated. Mr. Michels was placed under arrest to-day. "I would move out of the State rather than be compelled to vaccinate my child," said Mr. Michels to-day.* **"My father died of smallpox after being vaccinated and my sister was crippled through being vaccinated, and there are many cases on record in and out of the city of great harm and even death caused by vaccination."** *Two weeks ago Dorothy Michels was sent home from School 9 because she was not vaccinated. She is 11 years old.*[243]

Hammonton, New Jersey, November 9, 1922:

> *The State Board of Education has denied the appeal of James Adams, Luke Bales and George Ware of Berlin Township that the decision of State Commissioner of Education Enright, to the effect that the children of the men named must be vaccinated before they can attend the public schools of Berlin Township, be set aside. The children were refused entrance to the schools of the township in March last, because they were not vaccinated. The parents were arrested and fined $10 and costs, sentence being suspended in the hope they would reconsider*

---

[242] "Fights the Vaccination Law, Man Opposes School Regulations for His Children and Gets Offers of Aid," *New York Times*, April 27, 1902.
[243] "Fights Vaccination Law, Passaic Health Commissioner Arrested for Refusing to Obey It," *New York Times*, March 8, 1912.

their determination. This hope failed, and they were taken before Justice Walker and fined $100 each, the defendants to be jailed until the fines were paid. They served but a day or so when the Court ordered their release pending an appeal. One of the fathers is said to have threatened to shoot any doctor who attempted to vaccinate his child on an official order to do so.[244]

Despite attempts to assert personal free choice, in the case *Zeucht v. King* the US Supreme Court decided that states have the right to exert "police power" to enforce vaccination. The court stated that protection of "public health" overrode any consideration of personal choice or liberty.[245]

Vaccinations continued to be forced on the people in spite of objections by physicians, a large disruption of the school system, and many people becoming seriously ill.

Patterson, New Jersey, March 27, 1906:

*By this order every pupil and teacher in the public and parochial schools, about 30,000 persons in all, was to submit to vaccination. Many of the pupils' and teachers' physicians refused to permit their patients to be vaccinated, and this resulted in the suspension of twenty teachers and several hundred pupils. To add to the discomfiture of the Educational Commission, **many of those vaccinated have become seriously ill. Before the work is over physicians estimate that over 150 will be incapacitated.**[246]*

Violent clashes sometimes resulted when a person refused to be vaccinated. In this tragic case, not only was a police officer killed but,

---

[244] "Lose Vaccination Appeal, New Jersey Fathers Were Jailed Under School Law," *New York Times*, March 28, 1906.

[245] "Compulsory Vaccination," *The Mississippi Law Review*, vol. 1, no. 4, March 1923, p. 79.

[246] "Won't Be Vaccinated, 20 Teachers and Hundreds of Pupils Suspended from Paterson Schools," *New York Times*, March 28, 1906.

ironically, the person to be "protected" by vaccination was hunted down and shot and, most likely, died.

Macon, Georgia, December 23, 1904:

> *Refusing to submit to vaccination at Sandersville, Boss Garrett shot and killed special officer Gideon Mathews to-day. Garrett escaped, but a strong posse of citizens immediately started in pursuit. The fleeing man was overtaken one mile north of town. He attempted further flight, and was shot through the thigh by Deputy Marshall Wilson, arrested and lodged in county jail. Garrett also suffered a serious wound in the right side, inflicted by special officer Matthews. It is thought he will not live.*[247]

The old penalties for refusing to be vaccinated are shocking. It's not possible to know from a *New York Times* article whether this soldier objected to being vaccinated because of his belief in free choice, health concerns, or other reasons. It is clear that he paid an extremely heavy price of 15 years in a military prison at Fort Leavenworth where he probably endured hard labor. With such a severe sentence, the state was obviously making an example of this unfortunate man.

Camp Dodge, Iowa, May 1, 1918:

> *Elmer N. Olson of Goodrich, Minn., a soldier in training here, refused to submit to vaccination. He was tried by general court-martial and sentenced to fifteen years in the disciplinary barracks at Fort Leavenworth.*[248]

---

[247] "Murder over Vaccination, Man Kills an Officer and Is Shot, Perhaps Fatally," *New York Times*, December 24, 1904.
[248] "Refused Vaccination, Got 15 Years," *New York Times*, May 2, 1918.

Eugenics and vaccination

Eugenicists believed that society could be improved through controlling the population's genetic composition through the elimination of the "dysgenic," or the undesirable elements.

The development of medical and social services resulted in the preservation of hundreds of thousands of dysgenic individuals who in former centuries would have succumbed in the struggle of life. At the same time millions of physically best equipped young men are killed off periodically in wars. This amounts to a negative selection and must ultimately result in the deterioration of the race. ***Eugenics was a direct outcome of Darwinian theories.***[249]

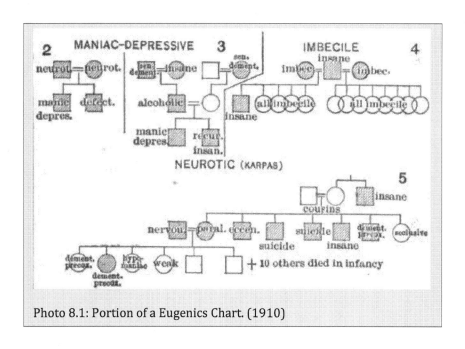

Photo 8.1: Portion of a Eugenics Chart. (1910)

It was believed by some that eugenics-based forced sterilization was similar to compulsory vaccination in that it upheld a belief that

---

[249] Henry E. Sigerist, *Civilization and Disease,* Cornell University Press, New York, 1943, p. 104.

societal "good" overrode any personal liberty or choice. In 1928 Dr. Suren H. Babington wrote in *California and Western Medicine*:

> *The sterilization of the mentally diseased makes it possible to curtail their ever-increasing number. Considering both scientific and humanitarian points of view, **sterilization is one of the most valuable means for not only improving the human race** and protecting its welfare, but also decreasing the number of unfortunates to be born to suffer intensely all their lives for faults not their own.*[250]

If individuals who were considered "imbeciles" could reproduce, the government intervened using forced sterilization. The science of the time held that mental "defects" were undesirable and therefore the state had a duty to take any action to prevent propagation of those defective genes. Forced sterilization was justified because of the belief that the "human race" could actually be improved by way of deleting so-called defective genes. This was all wrapped with a cloak of supposed scientific legitimacy.

The concept of preventing "unfit" individuals from having children originated in psychiatry.

> *In 1886, August Forel, the Swiss psychiatrist, sterilized a woman who was suffering from a sexual neurosis. In 1892 he castrated individuals for purely eugenic reasons.*[251]

In 1922 Dr. Harold Gosline stated in the *American Journal of Psychiatry* that he believed eugenics would be key in eliminating mental disease and positively impact poverty, delinquency, and crime.

> *I would reiterate that we may reasonably expect from routine laboratory work to be able to prevent mental disease and*

---

[250] Suren H. Babington, MD, "Human Sexual Sterilization: A Contribution to the Study of the Problem," *California and Western Medicine*, vol. 29, no. 6, 1928, p. 369.

[251] Henry E. Sigerist, *Civilization and Disease,* Cornell University Press, New York, 1943, pp. 104–105.

defect. Laboratories in state hospitals are the most tangible tools yet placed in the hands of mental hygiene for this purpose and in time they will render the same service that general hospital and research laboratories have rendered public health of which mental hygiene is but a branch. I believe that public health measures and eugenics measures will go far toward eradicating mental disease and defect, and their related branches of poverty, crime and delinquency . . .[252]

Dr. Suren H. Babington considered from a psychiatric point of view that "mental defectives" were "insane." He saw them as a threat to "race betterment" because, left unchecked, they would continue to have mentally defective children.

*We hope that the time will come when we shall sterilize also those **mental defectives** . . . **From the point of view of the psychiatrist, they, too, are "insane," and are a menace to race betterment**, because they go on propagating their own kind in large numbers.*[253]

In 1910 C. B. Davenport of the Carnegie Institution of Washington and director of Experimental Evolution published *Eugenics: The Science of Human Improvement by Better Breeding.* He stated:

Two imbecile parents, whether related or not, have only imbecile offspring . . . I am aware, no case on record where two imbecile parents have produced a normal child. So definite and certain is the result of the marriage of two imbeciles, and so disastrous is reproduction by an imbecile under any conditions that it is a disgrace of the first magnitude that thousands of children are annually born in this country of imbecile parents to replace and probably more than replace the deaths in the

[252] Harold I. Gosline, MD, "The Laboratory Service in State Hospitals for Mental Diseases," *The American Journal of Psychiatry*, vol. 1, The Johns Hopkins Press, Baltimore, 1921–1922, p. 419.

[253] Suren H. Babington, MD, "Human Sexual Sterilization: A Contribution to the Study of the Problem," *California and Western Medicine*, vol. 29, no. 6, 1928, p. 369.

army of about 150,000 mental defectives which this country *supports.* **The country owes it to itself as a matter of self-** **preservation that every imbecile of reproductive age** **should be held in such restraint that reproduction is out of** **the question. If it proves to be impracticable then sterili-** **zation is necessary—where the life of the state is threat-** **ened extreme measures may and must be taken.**[254]

Eugenicists believed that eugenics was a lofty form of patriotism and a tool to improve the human race by genetically selecting out the "delinquents" and "defectives." In 1922 Dr. Harry H. Laughlin, eugenics associate in the Psychopathic Laboratory of the Municipal Court of Chicago and eugenics director of the Carnegie Institution of Washington, wrote *Eugenical Sterilization in the United States.* He stated:

Photo 8.2: Feeble-Minded at Vineland Colony in New Jersey. "They have the bodies of adults but the minds of children. It is not to the interest of the state that they should be allowed to mingle with the normal population; and it is quite as little to their own interest, for they are not capable of competing with people who are normal mentally." (1918)

Eugenics stands against **the forces which work** **for racial deterioration,** **and for improvement** **and vigor, intelligence** **and moral fiber of the** **human race.** *It repre-* *sents the highest form of* *patriotism and humani-* *tarianism, while at the* *same time it offers imme-* *diate advantages to ourselves and to our children. By eugenic* *measures, for instance, our burden of taxes can be reduced by*

---

[254] C. B. Davenport, *Eugenics, The Science of Human Improvement by Better Breeding*, Carnegie Institution of Washington, Director, Department of Experimental Evolution, Cold Spring Harbor, New York; Secretary, Committee on Eugenics, American Breeders Association; Henry Holt and Company, New York, 1910, pp. 14–16.

decreasing the number of degenerates, delinquents and defectives supported in public institutions; such measures will also increase safeguards against crimes committed against our persons or our property.[255]

In a landmark 1926 case, *Buck v. Bell*, the Supreme Court of the United States, in an 8 to 1 decision, legitimized Virginia's sterilization laws. This ruling supported the argument that the interest of the states in a "pure" gene pool outweighed the interest of an individual. In his opinion on sterilization laws, Justice Oliver Wendell Holmes Jr. invoked compulsory vaccination to justify the verdict.

It is better for all the world if instead of waiting to execute degenerate offspring for crime or let them starve for their imbecility, society can prevent those who are manifestly unfit from continuing their kind. **The principle that sustains compulsory vaccination is broad enough to cover cutting the Fallopian tubes.**[256]

Eugenicists used compulsory vaccination as the precedent for their argument on sterilization to "protect" the public. They believed vaccination protected individuals and the public from disease and eugenical sterilization protected society from "racial degeneracy."

Compulsory Vaccination is analogous to compulsory eugenical sterilization to the extent that both are non-punitive and that both involve the seizure of the individual and subjecting him or her to surgical treatment . . . Vaccination protects the individual from a serious and loathsome disease in the more

---

[255] Harry Hamilton Laughlin, *Eugenical Sterilization in the United States*, Psychopathic Laboratory of the Municipal Court of Chicago, 1922, p. v.
[256] Henry E. Sigerist, *Civilization and Disease*, Cornell University Press, New York, 1943, p. 105.

immediate future; eugenical sterilization protects society from racial degeneracy in the more remote future.[257]

Tens of thousands of people believed by the US government to be unfit were sterilized, mostly in the state of California.

The California Sterilization Law was adopted in 1909. The total number of operations performed to May, 1927, was somewhat in excess of five thousand, which is four times the number performed in all the rest of the world, as far as we know, for eugenical reasons in state governmental institution.[258]

Before 1933 a number of countries had the legal power to prevent manifestly unfit individuals from procreating offspring, but sterilization was applied on a very small scale. **In the United States by January 1, 1937, only 25,403 persons had been sterilized, most of them in California.**[259]

Eugenicists promoted and pushed for laws to sterilize anyone they viewed as the genetic defectives in society. State governments established medical boards to decide who was to be sterilized. That board determined if a person was likely to have children who could inherit idiocy, insanity, or feeblemindedness or be predisposed to criminality.[260]

New Jersey passed a law in April 1911 which, like other laws, called for creation of a medical board to determine who should be sterilized.

... herby created the **"Board of Examiners of Feeble-minded (including idiots, imbeciles and morons), Epileptics and**

---

[257] Harry Hamilton Laughlin, DSc, *Eugenical Sterilization in the United States*, Psychopathic Laboratory of the Municipal Court of Chicago, December 1922, p. 339.

[258] Ibid., p. 369.

[259] Henry E. Sigerist, *Civilization and Disease,* Cornell University Press, New York, 1943, p. 106.

[260] Laughlin, pp. 19–20.

other Defectives," whose duty it shall be to examine into the mental and physical condition of the feeble-minded, epileptic, certain criminals and other defective inmates . . .[261]

Harry Hamilton Laughlin was a major advocate of sterilization for eugenics reasons. He was secretary of a committee appointed by the Eugenics Section of the American Breeders' Association. His assignment was "to Study and to Report on the Best Practical Means for Cutting Off the Defective Germ-Plasm in the American Population." In 1932 he and other leading eugenicists attended the Third International Congress of Eugenics, which was held in New York City. The exhibits were intended to show that eugenics was a "pure and applied science." Major Leonard Darwin, the son of Charles Darwin, also presented his views at the meeting. *The New York Times* reported on the event.

*Eugenists from all over the world will attend the Third International Congress of Eugenics today and tomorrow at the American Museum of Natural History. At general and sectional meetings they will discuss advances in the study for the physical and mental improvement of the human race . . . It [the exhibit] will seek to emphasize the fact that eugenics is concerned primarily with racial and family-stock, quality in the turn-over of population from generation to generation. "As a pure science," the announcement says, "**eugenics tries to understand the forces which govern this turn-over, while as an applied science it strives to use these forces in the improvement of family-stocks and races.**"*[262]

Absolute governmental power was taken to an even greater extreme with the rise of Nazi power in the early 1900s. It is estimated that, in

---

[261] Harry Hamilton Laughlin, DSc, *Eugenical Sterilization in the United States*, Psychopathic Laboratory of the Municipal Court of Chicago, December 1922, p. 24.

[262] "Eugenics Congress Opens Here Today, Scientists of Many Nations to Attend Sessions at the American Museum, Osborn to Give Address, He Will Discuss 'Birth Selection Versus Birth Control,' Son of Darwin to Send Message," *New York Times*, August 21, 1932.

the first years of the Nazi regime, approximately a quarter million people were forced to be sterilized to improve the "human race." Sterilization was performed because of hereditary feeblemindedness, schizophrenia, manic-depressive psychosis, epilepsy, Huntington's chorea, and hereditary deafness and blindness, as well as genetically transmitted bodily malformations. Who would be sterilized was determined by so-called Hereditary Health Courts.

The Germans bestowed an honorary doctorate to Harry Laughlin in 1936 for his eugenics sterilization work. Although the Germans implemented sterilization on a larger scale, the idea of sterilization of unfit individuals had its roots in Scandinavian countries and the United States, **whose ruling bodies used forced vaccination as a precedent.**

Unbeknownst to many today, Margaret Sanger, the founder of Planned Parenthood, believed that personal reproductive choice was vital for "racial betterment."

> *Before Eugenists and others who are laboring for racial betterment can succeed, they must first clear the way for Birth Control . . . While I personally believe in the sterilization of the feebleminded, the insane and the syphilectic, I have not been able to discover that these measures are more than superficial deterrents when applied to the constantly growing stream of the unfit . . . **Only upon a free, self-determining motherhood can rest any unshakable structure of racial betterment.***[263]

Eugenics was applied to immigrants. From 1892 to 1954, more than 12 million people entered the United States through the gateway of Ellis Island in New York Harbor. At first, the emphasis was on detecting infectious diseases such as typhoid and smallpox in immigrants, but over time the identification of what were considered mental defects grew in significance.

---

[263] Margaret Sanger, "Birth Control and Racial Betterment," *The Birth Control Review*, February 1919, pp. 11–12.

. . . mental abnormality assumed growing importance, as eugenics came into fashion. In such selection processes, ethnic prejudices inevitably operated. **Mediterranean types and eastern European Jews were widely regarded as inferior stock***: "Steerage passengers from a Naples boat show a distressing frequency of low foreheads, open mouths, weak chins, poor features, skew faces, small or knobby crania, and backless heads," commented the distinguished sociologist, E. A. Ross, in 1914.*[264]

Due to hardening racial prejudices, in 1924 the United States passed the Johnson Reed Act to introduce immigration quotas. Supporters of eugenics and the racial hygiene theory were strong supporters of the Act. Calvin Coolidge, the 30th president of the United States, declared:

America must be kept American. Biologic laws show . . . that Nordics deteriorate when mixed with other races.[265]

In 1922 Harry Olson, Chief Justice of the Municipal Court of Chicago, discussed his legal opinion on the constitutionality of eugenics sterilization. He was fully supportive of the model eugenics legislation that was proposed all over the United States. He believed that as long as hearings were held and the "due process of law" was being followed, the courts would uphold these laws as constitutional. His conviction in the "science" of eugenics was steadfast.

If the science of eugenics has so far advanced, as seems to be the fact, that it can be determined that certain individuals are afflicted with physical, nervous, and mental disorders that are hereditary and will reappear in the next or later generation, and threaten the safety of society . . . then there can be no question but that legislation contemplated by the model act will be an effective protection to future generations . . . **Not only must**

---

[264] Roy Porter, *The Greatest Benefit to Mankind*, Harper Collins, New York, 1997, p. 424.
[265] Ibid.

nations defend their future against racial degeneration from within, but they must limit immigration of defective stocks from all other lands . . . "The Rising Tide of Color," by Lothrop Stoddard, warns us of danger to the white race, but this book of yours [Harry Laughlin] warns humanity of the menace to all races—to the entire human race—of racial degeneracy.[266]

Even though the Nazi approach was considered extreme, the premise of using government power to protect greater society from "imbeciles" and other genetic defects continued to be defended. Historian and author Henry E. Sigerist wrote in 1943:

I think it would be a great mistake to indentify eugenic sterilization solely with the Nazi ideology and to dismiss the problem simply because we dislike the present German regime and its methods. The pioneering steps were, after all, taken by the United States and Switzerland, and the Scandinavian laws are just as stringent as the German. The problem is serious and acute, and we shall have to be forced to pay attention to it sooner or later.[267]

State governments implemented laws that endowed enormous power to a small group of medical "experts" who determined if a person was, in their opinion, genetically "fit."

The German Nazi regime took the idea of sterilization of the "dysgenic"[268] to an appalling conclusion. The horrific impact of the visual and mass media coverage of the Nazi Holocaust camps at the end of World War II finally dislodged eugenics as an accepted practice.

---

[266] Harry Hamilton Laughlin, DSc, *Eugenical Sterilization in the United States*, Psychopathic Laboratory of the Municipal Court of Chicago, December 1922, p. 322.

[267] Henry E. Sigerist, *Civilization and Disease*, Cornell University Press, New York, 1943, pp. 106–107.

[268] Ibid., p.104.

In the United States, eugenics eventually lost scientific acceptance and public support. New scientific discoveries led to the rejection of eugenic research results. Moreover, events in Nazi Germany during the 1930s, and the close cooperation between American and German eugenicists, seriously damaged the standing of the American eugenics movement, and the revelation of Nazi crimes in the 1940s discredited eugenic theories.[269]

Severe state control faded from governments, but only after many had been terrorized for decades. After the atrocities of World War II came to light, eugenics and oppressive actions taken by the government for the "public good" lost popular support, and its history quickly vanished from the collective public memory. Compulsory vaccination unceremoniously ended in England in 1948 shortly after the end of World War II.

The year 1948 will ever be memorable in the history of vaccination in this country as seeing the end of compulsory vaccination of infants, a measure which has been the subject of such acute and bitter controversy for so many years. Having regard to the great importance attached to universal vaccination of infants as our "first line of defense," and to the firm belief that only by compulsion could this be secured, it is rather surprising that the proposal to abolish compulsion did not arouse more opposition. In the event the opposition was almost negligible.[270]

Conclusion

The success of Leicester has to this day been ignored by the medical community and governments. They prefer to persist not only in their

---

[269] Henry Friedlander, *The Origins of Nazi Genocide: From Euthanasia to the Final Solution*, University of North Carolina Press, Chapel Hill, 1995, p. 9.
[270] C. Killick Millard, MD, DSc, "The End of Compulsory Vaccination," *British Medical Journal*, December 18, 1948, p. 1073.

belief in vaccination but in the need to force people to be vaccinated regardless of the valid arguments over personal safety or liberty.

Perhaps the most important reason to learn history is so that the worst things are never repeated. The ability to choose what is injected into our bodies is now being removed by states and workplaces. Loss of religious exemptions once seemed impossible, but the stridency of the pro-vaccine and their civic religion is effectively working to remove all but the most specific medical vaccine exemptions.

What will come after that?

~ 9 ~

THE CASE OF ARTHUR SMITH JR.

First Do No Harm.

– Medical Dictum

The road to hell is paved with good intentions.

– Proverb

Majorities are never a proof of the truth.

– Dr. Walter R. Hadwen (1854–1932), 1896

The year was 1914. Arthur Smith Jr. was a normal, healthy 11-year-old boy living in his home at 8 John Street in New Windsor, New York, with his father, Arthur Smith; his mother, Hilda; and his two sisters, Annie and Jennie. Although not at the head of his class, he did well in school.

At the opening of the fall school term, a letter was sent to every school in the state of New York. The letter, by Dr. Finnegan of the State Department of Education, called upon the board of education, including every school trustee, to enforce the compulsory vaccination law. The letter stated that if a child was not vaccinated, he or she could not attend school. If kept home for that reason, the parents would ultimately be arrested and sent to prison.

> *Among the documents being sent out to schools throughout the State by Dr. John H. Finley as Commissioner of Education, is a notification to officers of public, parochial, and private schools that no pupil shall be admitted for attendance unless he or she has been vaccinated, as required by law. Attorney General Carmody has rendered an opinion, in which he says: "Children*

in parochial schools should be vaccinated, as are children in the schools supported at public expense . . . The purpose of the statute being so plain, good citizens will not question its application, but in recognition of the declaration of a policy will accede thereto.[271]

In the fall of 1914, the New Windsor School Board's principal informed the children that they would all be vaccinated. They were told that if they didn't comply, they would be prohibited from attending school and their fathers would be arrested and fined. This coercive dilemma was faced by Arthur Smith's family.

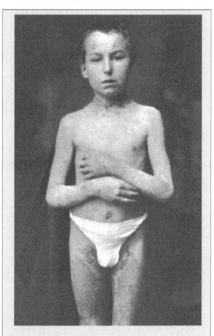

From continually telling the children to notify their parents they could not attend school if not vaccinated, they so intimidated the mother and I, that thinking we could not successfully fight the order, at last we consented to have our children vaccinated by a physician of our own choice.[272]

At that point, the Smiths had all three of their children vaccinated. Two of them, Annie and Jennie, suffered some discomfort and recovered. However, a short time after being vaccinated, Arthur began to experience serious complications. Within a week, his

Photo 9.1: Arthur Smith, Jr. August 1915 (approximately 1 year after vaccination)

---

[271] "Vaccination Act Sweeping, Includes Parochial as Well as Public Schools, Carmody Holds," *New York Times*, August 24, 1914.
[272] "Little Smith Boy Is Slowly Dying of Blood Poison, Child Suffers Untold Agony as a Result of Vaccination," *Newburgh Daily News*, March 12, 1915.

hands, arms, feet, and legs had swollen to twice their normal size. Blisters covered his entire body, and when they broke yellow pus was discharged and turned into sores. Six months later, his parents feared he was dying.

> *Now he is dying. His body is a mass of running sores. He cannot wear any clothing. His hair is falling out. He is suffering untold torments. Instead of attending school or playing with children of his own age he has to sit by the stove in the house, swathed in ointment-soaked bandages and suffer untold agony. All because he was vaccinated.*[273]

The sad truth was that the school trustees, including the school principal, were actually opposed to the compulsory vaccination law. They refused to do more than have Dr. Finnegan's letter read to the children. Numerous boards of education and school trustees throughout the state of New York actually ignored the state demand for enforcement of the compulsory vaccination law. In New Windsor, nothing more was done except to read the letter.

Many people in the town were angry about what happened to the Smith boy. One man said that the suffering the child endured was "worse torture than the torments of the damned."[274] Another man, a prominent educator who lived in New Windsor, said

> *If the Smith boy dies, he will be a victim of the State law. I am willing to put it stronger. He will have been murdered by Dr. Finnegan merely to please a lot of medical fanatics.*[275]

After Arthur began to show negative effects of the vaccine, he remained under the continual care of a physician. The original vaccinating doctor treated Arthur without success. Another doctor was called. For five months, he treated him with ointments and internal medicines, all of which failed to check the unknown disease.

---

[273] "Little Smith Boy Is Slowly Dying of Blood Poison, Child Suffers Untold Agony as a Result of Vaccination," *Newburgh Daily News*, March 12, 1915.
[274] Ibid.
[275] Ibid.

In May of 1915, Arthur's father took him to Albany, New York, to see Dr. Curtis, a blood specialist. After examination, he determined that Arthur was suffering from a case of pemphigus and noted that he had only seen one other case in a 50-year-old man who died of the condition. Coincidentally, and unknown to the Smith family, it had recently been determined through a 1915 investigation that vaccines were contaminated with foot-and-mouth disease. Finally, after three years, in December of 1918, Arthur recovered almost completely.

> *I wish to say that my boy at the present time is in fairly good health, and there are no eruptions on his body and with each succeeding year the effect seems to be gradually dying away. The summer of 1917 he broke out in eruption quite bad, especially his legs, being most severe on the thighs, and also in the summer of 1918, but not near so bad as in the preceding summer. He is free of any eruption at the present time, but the upper part of his body and especially his arms are covered with a large amount of brown spots on the skin where the eruptions have completely died away, but I think that with each succeeding year, as he grows stronger, the effects will entirely disappear, with the exception of the brown spots on the skin, which I suppose will always remain and for which there can be no remedy.[276]*

Arthur Smith survived his long ordeal, although it was impossible to tell if the spots he had on his skin at the age of 14 ever cleared. We also don't know what residual health problems he may have been left with prior to his death in 1983.

Mr. Smith was not the only child who suffered as a result of Dr. Finnegan's compulsory vaccination order. The daughter of Michael Rossin of New Windsor was vaccinated in the New Windsor School in October of 1914.

---

[276] Charles M. Higgins, *Horrors of Vaccination Exposed and Illustrated*, Brooklyn, New York, 1920, p. 122.

A week later, her body broke out in sores, blisters, and boils. She suffered for two months before the eruptions ceased to appear on her body. As a result of the vaccination her mentality has suffered and, although she is back in school today, her health and brains have been so seriously affected that she is unable to keep up with those of her own age in her school work.[277]

Mary McCurry was also vaccinated at the New Windsor School in October of 1914.

Within a week she developed a nervous disorder which soon showed all the symptoms of the disease known as St. Vitus' dance [a disorder affecting children and characterized by jerky, uncontrollable movements]. Her condition became such that within three weeks from the time she was vaccinated, she had to be taken from school. She has not returned since. The vaccination scar is an ugly black mark on her body. Prior to being vaccinated, Mary had never received a medical treatment. Her nervous system showed no signs of a breakdown and she was unusually bright. She weighed the day she was vaccinated 94 pounds. Now the child is little more than a nervous wreck, she weighs less than 70 pounds and she has no control over her muscles which twitch and turn.[278]

Years earlier, Mary's brother Thomas McCurry also suffered a severe reaction to vaccination. He was seven years old when he was vaccinated at the Washington Street School in Newburgh. Shortly after being vaccinated, sores began to appear all over his body. He was taken out of school and did not return.

Careful treatment and assiduous nursing succeeded in overcoming the breaking out. Then the boy began to complain of dizzy spells and while under medical care for these, he

---

[277] "Little Smith Boy Is Slowly Dying of Blood Poison, Child Suffers Untold Agony as a Result of Vaccination," *Newburgh Daily News*, March 12, 1915.
[278] Ibid.

developed blindness. He was totally blind for more than a year. Hardly had he recovered his sight than he was stricken with paralysis and the spine began to twist. He became helpless. Two years ago he lost the power of speech and now all he can do is utter gutturals which are unintelligible. His eyes are all that remain alive now and the way he talks with his eyes is too pitiable and heartrending to be described . . . Mr. and Mrs. McCurry candidly place the blame for the suffering of Mary and Thomas on vaccination. They say their other children never will be allowed to run chances of suffering the way these two have.[279]

Despite the suffering of these and an unknown number of other children and adults, officials maintained their steadfast support of compulsory vaccination. These reports, which were in contrast to the official belief that vaccination was a harmless procedure, faded from societal memory. What remained was the myth and illusion of vaccination safety, necessity, and effectiveness.

---

[279] "Little Smith Boy Is Slowly Dying of Blood Poison, Child Suffers Untold Agony as a Result of Vaccination," *Newburgh Daily News*, March 12, 1915.

THE HEALTH REVOLUTION

Slovenliness is no part of religion.
Cleanliness is indeed next to Godliness.

– John Wesley (1703–1791)

May we be and beseech your proteckshion and power. We are Sur, as it
may be, livin in Wilderness, so far as the rest of London knows any-
thing of us, or as the rich and great people care about. We live in muck
and filth. We aint got no priviz, no dust bins, no drains, no water-splies,
and no drain or suer in the hole place. The Suer Company, in Greek St.
Soho Square, all great rich powerfool men take no notice watsomdever
of our complaints. The Stenche of Gulley-hole is disgustin. We all of us
suffer, and the number are ill, and if the Cholera comes Lord help us.

– A letter in *The Times*, 1849

It is not strange that health improves when the population
gives up using diluted sewage as the principle beverage.

– Dr. Thurman Rice, 1932

By the mid-1800s, slums had become commonplace settlements in
the Western world. New York City had 100,000 slum dwellers living
in 20,000 tenement buildings. They were a crowded and vile predic-
ament. Throughout these unsanitary slums, death was ever present.
Cholera, typhoid, scarlet fever, smallpox, typhus, and other infectious
diseases were never idle.

But during this time, the seeds of change were sowed and slowly
took root. It was the beginning of the Sanitation Revolution. A new
understanding that filth contributed to human illness had come to
light. It was also known that poverty was often a result of such

illness and not just the cause. Based on this awareness, projects for the supply of clean water and removal of human and other waste gradually began to be implemented.

> *Twenty per cent of pauperism was due to fever, and the blame fell on overcrowding, negligent waste disposal, dirty water and bad diet. Poverty could not be abolished, but poverty due to preventable disease could be: The primary and most important measures, and at the same time the most practicable, and within the recognized province of administration, are drainage, the removal of all refuse from habitations, streets and roads, and the improvement of the supplies of water.*[280]

To address public health concerns, local government began setting standards for the protection of human health. Social reformers, activists, doctors, and others pushed for changes to improve the general well-being of the population. Governments began to focus on removal of waste, supplying the population with clean water, and a whole host of other issues dealing with health.

> *... to relieve the suffering of the laboring classes in England, an improbable coalition of social activists, prison reformers, physicians, clergy, and scientists started advocating sanitary reform in the early 1800s. They maintained that both illness and poverty resulted from "insanitary" conditions and practices that could be remedied. **This "sanitary movement" was instrumental in getting legislation passed in Great Britain during the 1850s and 1860s to create public health authorities with the power to regulate sewage collection, water supply, environmental nuisances, and a***

---

[280] Roy Porter, *The Greatest Benefit to Mankind*, Harper Collins, New York, 1997, p. 411.

remarkable list of other relevant matters, such as physician licensing and child labor abuses.[281]

Throughout most of the world during the 1800s, there was a relentless threat from cholera, which resulted in millions of deaths. The former notion that there was a spontaneous generation of disease arising from mysterious gases called *miasma* was changing toward a biological understanding of the microbial aspect of these diseases.

In 1854 English physician John Snow determined that the source of the cholera epidemic in London was contaminated water supplied by a street pump. Snow noticed that all the people who were being affected by cholera drew water from that particular pump. He used scientific evidence to convince the city council to ban the polluted water supply. The city ordered the pump closed, and the epidemic subsided, demonstrating that the source of the disease was something in the water.[282]

Through citizen initiatives, governments added on the responsibility of maintaining public health. These efforts transformed cities from human and animal waste cesspools into clean and hygienic places where people could thrive. The modern city was taking shape bit by bit.

*Following the last cholera epidemic in Stockholm in 1853, which left 3000 dead, public opinion for improved sanitation resulted in the establishment of a new sanitation office, which was charged with managing excreta disposal efficiently and cleaning streets and yards belonging to the city . . . Through changes made in **the 30 years leading up to the early 1890s, excreta disposal in Stockholm was developed from an***

---

[281] Velv W. Greene, PhD, MPH, "Personal Hygiene and Life Expectancy Improvements Since 1850: Historic and Epidemiologic Associations," *American Journal of Infection Control*, August 2001, p. 205.

[282] David L. Streiner, Douglas W. MacPherson, and Brian D. Gushulak, *PDQ Public Health*, 2010, p. 198.

almost medieval system to a hygienic standard acceptable for the 20th century.[283]

In 1898 Dr. T. W. Huntington commented on the improvements in saving lives through the use of sanitary science.

*Looking over the time since we have anything like history, we find that the great loss of life has been through epidemics. **Deaths from wounds, accident, etc. have been insignificant when compared with the enormous loss of life which have occurred through epidemics.** I recently had occasion to call attention to the epidemic of cholera at Hamburg. There were about 18,000 cases, of which more than one half died. At Altoona, which derived its water supply from the same source, the Elbe, but filtered it before use, there were comparatively few cases.*[284]

A new public health movement began in England, where great efforts were made to improve sanitary conditions. Construction of the London sewage system began in 1859. Work carried on for six years until the system was completed in 1865. Various acts of Parliament, such as the Sewage Utilization Act in 1865 and the Sanitary Act in 1866, gave the government authority to maintain the sewage system, regulate the water supply, and make overcrowding of residences illegal. England set an example that was quickly followed by other countries. However, these positive changes were often met with resistance by those who were profiting from the slums.

Great blocks of slums are owned by men who resisted all sanitary improvements by securing from the Tammany-ridden city health department appointments as "health officers" in a system of sanitary police provided for in 1860. In protest "citizen's

---

[283] Bo Burström, MD, PhD; Gloria Macassa, MD; Lisa Öberg, PhD; Eva Bernhardt, PhD; and Lars Smedman, MD, PhD, "The Impact of Improved Water and Sanitation on Inequalities in Child Mortality in Stockholm, 1878 to 1925," *Public Health Now and Then*, vol. 95, no. 2, February 2005, p. 209.

[284] "Sacramento Society for Medical Improvement Regular Meeting," *Occidental Medical Times*, vol. 12. no. 1, June 21, 1898, p. 376.

committee" appealed to the state authorities at Albany and secured an investigation that led to some relief. It is not surprising that New York had the highest death rate of all American cities.[285]

Into the later 1800s, larger sanitary infrastructures were put in place. These projects transformed the landscape of London from a city of filth to one where basic sewage and clean water were part of city life.

Metropolitan Board of Works empowered its chief engineer, Joseph Bazalgette, to create an ambitious scheme for main drainage, which was completed in 1875. London's water was increasingly drawn from the higher reaches of the Thames and from the Lea Valley, and filter beds were developed. The new sanitary infrastructure was a triumph of civil engineering.[286]

By the early 1900s, the infectious nature of the water supply was also addressed through the use of chlorination, which virtually eliminated waterborne diseases such as cholera, typhoid, and dysentery.

To solve the problems of pure water and sewage disposal, which were always acute in overgrown cities, bacteriology and chemistry continued to lend aid. An important advance was achieved with the chlorination of water, first introduced in America in 1908 and rapidly adopted after 1913. This method proved superior to water filtration as a protection against water-borne diseases.[287]

Over time this safer water was piped directly to homes and businesses. The innovation of the water closet—a term used to describe a room with a toilet—allowed for proper disposal of human waste.

---

[285] Arthur Charles Cole, *The Irrepressible Conflict 1850–1865: A History of American Life Volume VII*, Macmillan, New York, 1934, pp. 181–182.

[286] Roy Porter, *The Greatest Benefit to Mankind*, Harper Collins, New York, 1997, p. 413.

[287] Harold Underwood Faulkner, *A History of American Life Volume XI—The Quest for Social Justice 1898–1914*, Macmillan, New York, 1931, p. 239.

Thus, excrement no longer had to be disposed of into the streets where it would eventually end up in the population's drinking water.

> In the 1850s, wastewater was discharged into open ditches, some covered with planks or stones ... In 1895, there were only 40 premises with water closets. By 1904, this number had increased to 1506, and in 1909 the city decided to grant permission to connect water closets to the municipal sewerage system. In 1909, a second sewerage plan was launched, and a first water waste treatment plant was constructed.[288]

> As twenty-five years have passed away since medical officers of health were appointed to the metropolitan districts, it may be useful to take a cursory glance at the progress made. The works carried out by the Metropolitan Board of Works ... those who were familiar with London thirty years ago that ought to be a much healthy place of residence now than it was then, even although its bounds have been very greatly extended, and the population increased. Not only have numerous uninhabitable dwellings been removed, and in many cases replaced by better built habitation, which are less overcrowded, but many of the streets have been widened, and new streets made through densely crowded poor neighborhoods. A very large number of cesspools have been emptied and filled up, and replaced by water-closets connected with the sewers; the yards behind the houses of the poor have been in most instances properly drained; the houses themselves frequently white-washed; and other sanitary works performed.[289]

The push for changes in human hygiene had to overcome the societal thinking of the day. The general belief was that bathing was not necessary for either health or appearance, and body odor was

---

[288] Harold Underwood Faulkner, *A History of American Life Volume XI—The Quest for Social Justice 1898–1914*, Macmillan, 1931, p. 210.

[289] John W. Tripe, MD, "The Sanitary Condition and Laws of Medieval and Modern London," *Medical Times and Gazette*, vol. II, J & A Churchill, London, November 19, 1881, p. 595.

acceptable. Those who advocated hygiene needed to instill new standards into the population.

> *Cleanliness became the chief postulate of the hygienic movement of the 19th and 20th centuries. It had to overcome many obstacles, notably the resistance of people who claimed that the frequent use of soap was harmful to the skin . . .*[290]

These fundamental changes in hygiene were well under way before the germ theory of disease was generally accepted. Even by the early 1900s, many in the medical profession, health officers, and the public still believed that filth emanated poisonous gases that caused disease.[291] This theory would eventually be dismissed.

> *One of the most important aspects of public health work in a modern city is the assurance of general sanitary conditions, particularly with respect to water supply and the disposal of wastes. The growth of the public health movement in the nineteenth century was largely a matter of spreading the gospel of cleanliness and prophylaxis. **Long before the germ theory was enunciated, sanitarians and health workers sought to convince communities of the preventive value of general cleanliness.***[292]

> *The 1880s had been "the dark, desperate, impossible decade," with widespread malnutrition among the working class. In the 1890s, people had better opportunities for improved nutrition—not only because there was more money for food, but also because women could stay home to cook . . . From the 1890s, the principles for governing the city changed from being purely economic to including concern for the health of*

---

[290] Henry E. Sigerist, *Civilization and Disease,* Cornell University Press, New York, 1943, p. 27.

[291] Charles V. Chapin, MD, "End of Filth Theory of Disease," *Popular Science Monthly,* January 1902, p. 235.

[292] Thomas Neville Bonner, *Medicine in Chicago 1850–1950: A Chapter in the Social and Scientific Development of a City,* American History Research Center, Madison, Wisconsin, 1957, p. 179.

the population. A "sanitary police" department was instituted as part of the new emphasis on improvements in environmental hygiene. This authority was charged with inspecting food and milk and checking adherence to a local ordinance mandating the cleanliness and tidiness of outdoor premises.[293]

There was also a call for improvements in the dreadful housing conditions. Owners were forced to make alterations to unlivable tenements. The worst of housing, particularly vermin-infested cellars, were closed. In 1866 New York City created an efficient municipal board of health to tackle these issues.

Within four years it had closed virtually all the cellars and basements used for foul lodgings. It had completed a survey of the tenements and ordered the owners to effect alterations making them decently habitable.[294]

Governments instituted city planning to remove various polluting businesses away from where people lived. Slaughterhouses, meat-packing plants, glue factories, tanneries, and other manufacturers were targeted. These offending and polluting industries were slowly pushed outside the city limits to improve public health.

The board of 1868 forced the removal of all downtown slaughterhouses, of which there had been twenty-three in a single half-ward, to points above Fortieth Street. At the same time the first collecting sewer to free the pier slips from the accumulation of waste was built, and others rapidly followed.[295]

. . . local medical officers of health, whose duties were to regulate "offensive trades" (slaughtering, tanning, dyeing, etc.)

---

[293] Bo Burström, MD, PhD; Gloria Macassa, MD; Lisa Öberg, PhD; Eva Bernhardt, PhD; and Lars Smedman, MD, PhD, "The Impact of Improved Water and Sanitation on Inequalities in Child Mortality in Stockholm, 1878 to 1925," *Public Health Now and Then*, vol. 95, no. 2, February 2005, p. 210.
[294] Allan Nevins, *The Emergence of Modern America 1865–1878: A History of American Life Volume VIII*, Macmillan, New York, 1927, p. 322.
[295] Ibid., p. 322.

remove "nuisances," regulate houses unfit for human habitation, provide burial grounds, and deal with water supplies, sewers, waste disposal, and other environmental hazards.[296]

In Chicago the meatpacking industry resisted public health policies. Throughout its history, the industry dumped animal carcasses and chemicals into the Chicago River and Lake Michigan. Oscar Coleman DeWolf, a commissioner of health in 1880s Chicago, worked to clean up the meatpacking industry by instituting workplace inspections and attempting to move the slaughterhouses to the outskirts of the city.

Workshop and factory inspection was undertaken for the first time during his [De Wolf] tenure in office; attempts were made to demonstrate the link between mortality rates and unhealthful working and living conditions. His biggest battle was with the packing houses which sought to thwart necessary sanitary regulations by every means at their disposal, fair and foul. The menace to health from the offal dumped in river in lake, quite apart from the working conditions within the plant, was a serious health problem.[297]

In addition to understanding that sources of disease were due to improper handling of waste and contaminated water, it was now being recognized that food contamination was a major problem. Milk in particular was a major cause of illness and death. In 1898 Dr. W. E. Bates commented on the milk supply.

I agree with Dr. Simmons in the idea that next to the water supply, the milk supply is the main source of [typhoid] infection . . . one hundred and fifty cases in six weeks, and they traced every one of them to the one source—the milk supply. It was

---

[296] Roy Porter, *The Greatest Benefit to Mankind*, Harper Collins, New York, 1997, p. 412.
[297] Thomas Neville Bonner, *Medicine in Chicago 1850–1950: A Chapter in the Social and Scientific Development of a City*, American History Research Center, Madison, Wisconsin, 1957, p. 184.

found that the cows drank of very filthy water, which was loaded with typhoid germs. Whether the milk was infected by the cows drinking it, or whether the milkman diluted it with the water is in question.[298]

Interventions included higher standards of cleanliness, improved handling of human waste, increased food inspection and handling, better child feeding practices, and health education emphasizing hygienic practices. These changes were all put into place throughout the Western world at approximately the same time.

Physicians, lawyers, scientists, and engineers, with representatives of charitable organizations, formed an influential body that pressed local policymakers to make improvements conducive to health. They emphasized breastfeeding and the distribution of controlled milk to infants and children when breastfeeding was not possible.[299]

Mothers breastfed almost exclusively until the mid-1800s when poor-quality formulas and powdered milk became available. Breast-feeding became less and less popular into the 1900s and hit an all-time low in the 1940s, with only about 25 percent of infants initially breastfed and then weaned rapidly. This contributed to the disease and general ill health of infants of the time. George Newman, the medical officer of health for Finsbury, England, promoted the idea that breastfeeding and pasteurization of milk would reduce the high infant mortality rate.

Newman pointed out that breastfed infants suffered less from summer diarrhea than infants who were fed artificial formula or cow's milk. He considered the high infant mortality rate to be mainly a problem of motherhood, and he emphasized proper training of mothers and promotion of breastfeeding.

---

[298] "Sacramento Society for Medical Improvement Regular Meeting," *Occidental Medical Times*, vol. 12. no. 1, June 21, 1898, p. 381.

[299] Bo Burström MD, PhD; Gloria Macassa, MD; Lisa Öberg, PhD; Eva Bernhardt, PhD; and Lars Smedman, MD, PhD, "The Impact of Improved Water and Sanitation on Inequalities in Child Mortality in Stockholm, 1878 to 1925," *Public Health Now and Then*, vol. 95, no. 2, February 2005, p. 210.

> *Pasteurization of milk and milk stations were other measures*
> *that he proposed to reduce infant mortality rates.*[300]

Pasteurization of milk became standard. Toxins such as formaldehyde were discovered and eliminated. Through inspections, this dietary staple changed from a dangerous and frequently deadly drink to one that people could trust to be safe.

> *. . . milk pasteurization program which became the basis of*
> *Chicago's compulsory pasteurization ordinance in 1909, the*
> *first such law in the United States. Milk inspection had begun*
> *in 1877, but the search for disease germs was not inaugurated*
> *until 1893. The presence of formaldehyde poison to prevent*
> *souring was first detected in 1900 and soon eliminated.*[301]

> *The one practicable method of destroying bacteria present in*
> *milk is that known as pasteurization, which, when properly*
> *performed, consists in heating milk to a temperature of*
> *approximately 60° C. (140° F.) for some twenty to thirty*
> *minutes. This is sufficient to destroy the germs of tuberculosis,*
> *typhoid fever and diphtheria, and many organisms . . .*[302]

In 1907 Dr. Charles Page noted that it was not necessary to use injections of disease matter to battle diphtheria. Sanitation, hygiene, and changing the standard of living would be used to defeat this and other diseases.

> **It is not by adding disease to disease that the evil of diph-**
> **theria will be combated, but it is by the removal of the**
> **dark, damp, ill-ventilated slums which infest our towns**
> **and cities;** *by letting light and air into the over-crowded and*

---

[300] Richard D. Semba, "Vitamin A as 'Anti-Infective' Therapy, 1920–1940," *American Society for Nutritional Sciences*, 1999, p. 784.
[301] Thomas Neville Bonner, *Medicine in Chicago 1850–1950: A Chapter in the Social and Scientific Development of a City*, American History Research Center, Madison, Wisconsin, 1957, pp. 189–190.
[302] Frederic S. Lee, PhD, *Scientific Features of Modern Medicine*, Columbia University Press, 1911, p. 108.

unsanitary dwellings of the poor, and by the inculcation of les-
sons of cleanliness and hygiene among the people.[303]

By the 1900s, more people had realized that the key to the defeat of human-bred infectious diseases like cholera and typhoid was healthier living. Also, the death and morbidity of diseases when they did occur was not so high when the human constitution was supported. Superintendent of schools F. M. Buckley of Ansonia, Connecticut, proclaimed in 1911 that living a healthy lifestyle eliminated the fear of infectious diseases.

> *Accordingly, the present generation is beginning to learn and will realize more thoroughly as time wears on that the fatalistic idea with regard to contagious and infectious disease is absolutely erroneous and that many so-called unavoidable diseases are positively preventable. It is not true each individual must run the gamut of measles, scarlet fever, whooping cough, diphtheria, tuberculosis and the like if proper precautionary measures be taken at the outset.* **Sunshine, fresh air, wholesome nutrition, exercise, rest and the hygienic mode of living are far more effectual than all the subsequent medication in existence.**[304]

Dr. James Gordon Cumming stated in his 1922 article in the *Journal of the American Medical Association* that sanitation would eliminate the threat of diphtheria. The use of immunizations, serums, laboratory tests, and quarantines were not what was vital. What was needed was shifting the population to acquire an intuitive knowledge of hygiene, sanitation, and basic immune support.

> **The eradication of diphtheria will not come through the serum treatment of patients, by the immunization of the well,** *or through the accurate clinical and laboratory diagnosis*

---

[303] Charles E. Page, MD, "Diphtheria: Is the Prevailing Antitoxin Treatment Only Another Medical Delusion?" *Medical Brief, A Monthly Journal of Scientific Medicine and Surgery*, vol. XXXV, 1907, pp. 482–483.
[304] *Oral Hygiene*, vol. 1, no. 1, January 1911, pp. 183–184.

of the case and the carrier followed by quarantine; rather it will be attained through the mass sanitary protection of the populace subconsciously practiced by the people at all times.[305]

Sanitation and hygiene were not the only elements of society undergoing radical changes. The brutal working conditions also began to improve.

Thousands of women worked long hours earning deplorable wages in shops and factories. With no labor laws or trade unions, they were paid very little and struggled each day to survive.

In New York City alone there were seventy-five thousand women workers who lived on the ragged edge of misery. In the first year of peace [after the Civil War], with prices rising to an unprecedented height, fifteen thousand or more of them, employed in shops and factories, earned only from two dollars and fifty cents to four dollars a week. Yet they were far more fortunate than the wretched stratum of women employed as pieceworkers on cheap garments.[306]

Susan B. Anthony became the head of the Workingwomen's Protective Association. Women's labor organizations fought to make improvements for those caught in a life of virtual slavery in sweat shops. The labor movement was born out of the desperation of the working masses.

Industries such as dressmaking comprised what was known as the "sweated industries." Those who sewed in the workshops of London endured harsh working conditions. For several months a year, workers were expected to work 18 to 20 hours a day. Because of the seasonal nature of the work, women often turned to

---

[305] James Gordon Cumming, MD, "Is the Control of Diphtheria Leading to Eradication?" *Journal of the American Medical Association*, vol. 78, no. 9, March 4, 1922, p. 632.

[306] Allan Nevins, *The Emergence of Modern America 1865–1878: A History of American Life Volume VIII*, Macmillan, New York, 1927, p. 324.

prostitution to survive. Activist groups, unions, and the press slowly forced changes in these working conditions.

> *The Anti-Sweating League, backed by the trade unions, was formed in 1906 and helped to force action by the Liberal government. **A House of Commons Select Committee on "sweating" defined such work in 1888-90 as "work carried on for inadequate wages and for excessive hours in insanitary conditions," and it was mostly done by women.** The work was done in unregulated workrooms as well as in homes. Winston Churchill introduced the Trades Boards Act in 1909 to deal with some of the worst areas. Trades Boards were set up, empowered to regulate pay and conditions in four of the most notorious trades, including tailoring.*[307]

During the 1880s, many women had to work to provide for their families. By the 1930s, there had been a shift, and they only worked to provide for extras rather than for survival.

Over the years, a number of laws were passed in England that slowly decreased the severe working conditions for children. In 1802 the English Health and Morals Apprentices Act limited the laboring of children in cotton mills to 12 hours. The Act in 1833 banned the work of children under 12 years old for more than 8 hours and children from 13 to 18 years old to no more than 12 hours. In 1842 women and children under 10 years of age were prohibited from working underground in mines. By 1874 children younger than 10 years of age were no longer allowed to work in factories.

In 1852 Massachusetts passed laws that required students to attend school. Within the next 50 years, all states had laws on their books to at least get America's children through the elementary school years. However, the quality of these schools improved slowly.

---

[307] Joan Perkin, "Sewing Machines: Liberation or Drudgery for Women?" *History Today*, vol. 52, December 2002, pp. 39–40.

The life conditions of thousands of poor children in tenement houses are hard enough. It is the duty of the city to see to it that their bad environment is not continued in the schools . . . Dr. William T. Armstrong followed, and said to the physicians of New York it made little difference who was responsible for the evils of schools. It was their duty to demonstrate those evils scientifically and uncontradictably until public sentiment demanded a remedy.[308]

Although many improvements had been made by the end of the 1800s, there was still much improvement to be had.

But the general sanitary conditions of the city in the 1890's was still poor by modern standards. In the suburbs and outlying districts, unsanitary pumps and wells were still in service; the city's milk supply was at best adulterated, at worst contaminated; many streets were still unpaved; refuse and garbage were still dumped into alleys in many sections, and rarely was a garbage found to be covered. **The city's water supply, moreover, was frequently impure. The new drainage canal was not opened until 1900; citizens were still pouring sewage into Lake Michigan in the 1890's and then drinking the lake water.**[309]

These transformations occurred over many decades. Changes came about slowly and in many different forms. Under the leadership of Chicago's department of health, regulations were instituted to improve food handling. Basement bakeries that were once common were ordered to be closed. Baby welfare campaigns were started in the early 1900s, with doctors visiting to instruct mothers in the proper care of their infants. Weekly bulletins were issued to the public, providing valuable information on health.

---

[308] "A Disgrace to the City, The Hygienic Condition of the Primary Schools," *New York Times*, February 7, 1891.
[309] Thomas Neville Bonner, *Medicine in Chicago 1850–1950: A Chapter in the Social and Scientific Development of a City*, American History Research Center, Madison, Wisconsin, 1957, p. 187.

Changing public opinion, the labours of medical officers of health, the creation of filtered water supplies and sewage systems, slum clearance, the work of activists promoting the gospel of cleanliness, and myriad other often minor changes—for example the provision of dustbins with lids, to repel flies—combined to create an improving urban environment.[310]

In the United States, the big transformation in personal hygiene started after cities instituted "water works," which piped filtered water directly into the home from a central distribution system. By 1890, 1.4% of the urban population was so served by water works; by 1910, this number had increased to more than 25%. As water became available, sinks, bathtubs, showers, and indoor toilets were installed. The sale of soap and washing machines increased in a parallel fashion. The personal hygiene transformation was on the way, fueled by aesthetics, social pressures, commercial advertising, and even theologic incentives ("Cleanliness is next to Godliness").[311]

A wide variety of technological innovations arrived on the scene. These changes combined to create a vastly improved situation for health. Electricity, refrigeration, transportation, the flush toilet, and other scientific advancements all propelled Western societies to improved vigor and health.

Technology has had an enormous impact upon health. Innovations such as field drainage tiles, the flush toilet, water purification, and pasteurization have undoubtedly saved more lives than antibiotics. Automobiles, while creating a variety of new dangers, have certainly reduced the hazard of widespread animal waste in the streets. Increasingly

---

[310] Roy Porter, *The Greatest Benefit to Mankind*, Harper Collins, New York, 1997, pp. 426–427.

[311] Velv W. Greene, PhD, MPH, "Personal Hygiene and Life Expectancy Improvements Since 1850: Historic and Epidemiologic Associations," *American Journal of Infection Control*, August 2001, p. 205.

effective means of sterilizing baby bottles have decreased infant mortality from diarrheal diseases.[312]

Medicine in general, and vaccines even more so, contributed very little to this phenomenal transformation. Regardless, the medical paradigm became the dominant belief, generally displacing all other vastly important human innovations.

> *. . . compared to medical therapeutics, public health and hygiene have tended to assume the position of the poor relation or ugly sister. Transplant surgeries make headlines, while health education can barely find space in school curricula.*[313]

---

[312] Lucinda McCray, *A Matter of Life and Death: Health, Illness and Medicine in McLean County, 1830–1995*, McLean County Historical Society, p. 46.
[313] Ibid., p. 59.

~ 11 ~

THE AMAZING DECLINE

By the time laboratory medicine came effectively into the picture the job had been carried far toward completion by the humanitarians and social reformers of the nineteenth century . . . When the tide is receding from the beach it is easy to have the illusion that one can empty the ocean by removing the water with a pail.

– René Dubos (1901–1982), Mirage of Health, 1959

There was a continuous decline, equal in each sex, from 1937 onward. Vaccination [for whooping cough], beginning on a small scale in some places around 1948 and on a national scale in 1957, did not affect the rate of decline if it be assumed that one attack usually confers immunity, as in most major communicable diseases of childhood . . . With this pattern well established before 1957, there is no evidence that vaccination played a major role in the decline in incidence and mortality in the trend of events.

– Gordon T. Stewart, 1977

With so many changes occurring due to massive public health initiatives, the dreadful living situation that existed for multitudes dramatically improved by the mid-1800s. Sanitary infrastructure, understanding of hygiene, vastly improved nutrition, labor laws, advances in science, and many other factors coalesced to create a radical shift. Children who were once dying from diarrhea and common infectious diseases were living and thriving in greater numbers within the span of several decades.

The Western world had transitioned from squalor and suffering to what we recognize as our modern world.[314]

The big killer fades away

At the end of the 1800s, smallpox changed its character. After the summer of 1897, the severe type of smallpox with its high death rate, with rare exception, had entirely disappeared from the United States.

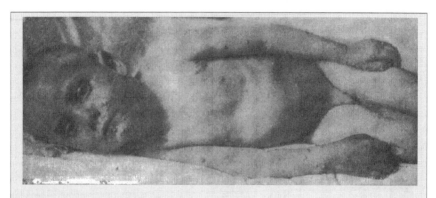

Photo 11.1: Extremely mild case of smallpox, bearing some resemblance to chickenpox. (1901)

Smallpox turned from a disease that killed 1 in 5 of its victims to one that only killed anywhere from 1 in 50 and later to as low as 1 in 380. This disease could still kill, but having become so much milder, it was mistaken for various other pox infections or skin eruptions.

> *During 1896 a very mild type of smallpox began to prevail in the South and later gradually spread over the country.* ***The mortality was very low and it [smallpox] was usually at first mistaken for chicken pox*** *or some new disease called "Cuban itch," "elephant itch," "Spanish measles," "Japanese measles," "bumps," "impetigo," "Porto Rico scratches," "Manila scab," "Porto Rico itch," "army itch," "African itch,"*

---

[314] Velv W. Greene, PhD, MPH, "Personal Hygiene and Life Expectancy Improvements Since 1850: Historic and Epidemiologic Associations," *American Journal of Infection Control*, August 2001, pp. 203–204.

"cedar itch," "Manila itch," "Bean itch," "Dhobie itch," "Filipino itch," "nigger itch," "Kangaroo itch," "Hungarian itch," "Italian itch," "bold hives," "eruptive grip," "beanpox," "waterpox," or "swinepox."[315]

By the early 1900s, there were those who recognized that sanitation had done what vaccination had failed to do—conquer smallpox. Smallpox vaccination was on the decline, and yet smallpox, like other diseases, was disappearing as a major threat. In 1914 Dr. C. Killick Millard wrote in *The Vaccination Question*:

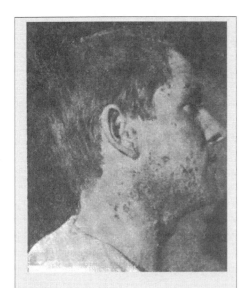

Photo 11.2: Impetigo contagion in an adult. (1901)

For forty years, corresponding roughly with the advent of the "sanitary era," smallpox has gradually but steadily been leaving this country (England). For the past ten years the disease has ceased to have any appreciable effect upon our mortality statistics. For most of that period it has been entirely absent except for a few isolated outbreaks here and there. **It is reasonable to believe that with the perfecting and more general adoption of modern methods of control and with improved sanitation (using the term in the widest sense) smallpox will be completely banished from this country as has been the case with plague, cholera, and typhus fever.** *Accompanying this decline in smallpox there has been a notable diminution during the past decade in the amount of*

---

[315] Charles V. Chapin, "Variation in Type of Infectious Disease as Shown by the History of Smallpox in the United States," *The Journal of Infectious Diseases*, vol. 13, no. 2, September 1913, p. 173.

infantile vaccination. This falling off in vaccination is steadily increasing and is becoming very widespread.[316]

The author of a 1913 article in the *Journal of Infectious Diseases* presented a table showing that, in 1895 and 1896, the smallpox death rate was where it had been historically recorded for decades, around 20 percent. The table also showed that after 1896, the death rate fell off rapidly, down to 6 percent in 1897 to as low as 0.26 percent by 1908.

On the whole the disease seems to have shown a tendency to diminish, somewhat in severity. This tendency is not marked and the somewhat lower case fatality noted in later years may be due to the better recognition of cases, now that the type has become more widely known. **At first fatalities of 1 to 2 per cent and even more were commonly reported, while later fatalities have often been much less. Thus in North Carolina in 1910 there were 3,875 cases with 8 deaths, a fatality of 0.2 per cent, and in 1911 there were 3,294 cases in that state without a single death.**[317]

Something changed to make smallpox a much less lethal and morbid disease with no secondary fever and little, if any, discomfort. The eruptions, as in classic smallpox, were often a dozen or fewer. The redness usually disappeared in three or four weeks and left no permanent marks.[318] In the absence of an epidemic, a case of mild smallpox was likely to be overlooked or mistaken for chicken pox.

. . . chickenpox, is a minor communicable disease of childhood, and is chiefly important because it frequently gives rise to difficulty in

---

[316] Harry Bernhardt Anderson, *State Medicine a Menace to Democracy*, 1920, p. 84.

[317] Charles V. Chapin, "Variation in Type of Infectious Disease as Shown by the History of Smallpox in the United States," *The Journal of Infectious Diseases*, vol. 13, no. 2, September 1913, p. 178.

[318] Ibid., p. 179.

diagnosis in cases of mild smallpox. **Smallpox and chickenpox are sometimes very difficult to differentiate clinically.**[319]

By the 1920s, it was recognized that the new form of smallpox produced little in the way of symptoms, even though few people had been vaccinated.

Photo 11.3: Well marked eruption of chickenpox, showing lesions in varying stages of development. (1901)

*Individual cases, or even epidemics, occur in which, **although there has been no protection by vaccination, the course of the disease is extremely mild**. The lesions are few in number or entirely absent, and the constitutional symptoms mild or insignificant.*[320]

As the classic and deadly variety of smallpox declined, so did the rate of vaccination. This, in turn, sounded alarms in the medical community. The fear was that the milder type of smallpox could at some point revert back to its original and more deadly form.

> *We must prepare for a pandemic of smallpox! . . . It has been two decades since epidemics of any proportions swept over the country and while the war [World War I] resulted in the vaccination of large numbers of young adults the very young are almost unvaccinated, while those of middle life and older have not been revaccinated for many years.*[321]

---

[319] John Gerald Fitzgerald, Peter Gillespie, and Harry Mill Lancaster, *An Introduction to the Practice of Preventive Medicine*, C.V. Mosby Company, 1922, p. 197.
[320] John Price Crozer Griffith, *The Diseases of Infants and Children, Volume 1*, W.B. Saunders Company, 1921, p. 370.
[321] G. Koehler, *Pharmacology and Therapeutics, Preventive Medicine*, The Year Book Publishers, 1921, p. 322.

By the 1920s and into the 1930s, mild smallpox had almost completely replaced the severe form in the United States. There were exceptions, however, with outbreaks in seaports and near the Mexican border. Once the mild type of smallpox became prevalent, there was no evidence that it ever reverted to the older, more virulent, type.

> *Although mild cases of smallpox were known before, they have come practically to replace the severe forms in many extensive areas, such as the whole United States, Brazil, large parts of Africa.*[322]

> **The mild form of smallpox commonly designated by its Portuguese name, alastrim, has prevailed over vast regions of the United States for over 30 years.** *It is estimated that the germ of this disease must have been transmitted from one human being to another more than 800 times and yet it is bred true. Throughout all these "generations" the organism maintains its early characteristics ... Most American health officers and epidemiologists who have experience with the two types of smallpox do not believe that as yet there has been any reversion of the mild strain to the old classic strain.*[323]

The warning in 1921 of an impending smallpox epidemic never materialized despite declining vaccination rates. Had the environment in which smallpox and other infectious diseases existed changed?

By the time the following report was written in 1946, smallpox had all but vanished from England and the Western world.

> *What has been the cause of the rise and fall of smallpox? Its decline in the later decades of the nineteenth century was at one time almost universally attributed to vaccination, but it is*

---

[322] George Dock, MD, "Smallpox and Vaccination," *Journal of the Missouri State Medical Association*, vol. 19, April 1922, p. 168.

[323] Charles V. Chapin and Joseph Smith, "Permanency of the Mild Type of Smallpox," *Journal of Preventive Medicine*, 1932.

doubtful how true this is. Vaccination was never carried out with any degree of completeness, even among infants, and was maintained at a high level for a few decades only. There was therefore always a large proportion of the population unaffected by the vaccination laws. Revaccination affected only a fraction. At the present the population is largely entirely unvaccinated. Members of the public health service now flatter themselves that the cessation of such outbreaks as do occur is due to their efforts. But is this so? The history of the rise, the change in age incidence, and the decline of smallpox rather lead to the conclusion that we may here have to do with a natural cycle of disease like plague, and that smallpox is no longer a natural disease for this country.[324]

Vaccination rates declined from the late 1800s and remained low up until the time compulsory vaccination ended in England in 1948.

Vaccination rates . . . fell to 50 percent in 1914 and 18 percent in 1948.[325]

The practice of vaccination continued from the time of the last smallpox death in the United States in 1948 until 1963. This resulted in an estimated 5,000 unnecessary vaccine-related hospitalizations from generalized rash, secondary infections, and encephalitis.

It was not only smallpox that became less of a threat. Beginning in the mid-to-late 1800s and into the 1900s, the mortality rate for all infectious diseases dropped. The deadly threats that were once so commonplace slowly faded into the past. By the end of the 19th century, it was apparent that sanitation was making a significant impact against the bacterial diseases, typhus and typhoid fever, without any vaccine.

---

[324] *Journal of the Royal Sanitary Institute*, vol. 66, 1946, p. 176.
[325] Arthur Allen, *Vaccine: The Controversial Story of Medicine's Greatest Lifesaver*, 2007, p. 69.

In 1838 in England 1228 persons died of fever, typhus and typhoid, per million of living. Twenty years later the figures were reduced to 918; in 1878 to 306 of typhoid to thirty-six of typhus fever. In 1892 only 137 died of typhoid fever, and only three of typhus per million living. In London the death rate was 307 in 1869; in 1892 it was 102. **Three factors have been concerned in this extraordinary saving of life—the cleansing of towns, the purification of the water supplies, and the introduction of good sewers.**[326]

Typhoid fever

By the early 1940s, deaths from typhoid fever had become exceedingly rare. From 1900 to 1943, the deaths from typhoid and paratyphoid fever, which had already significantly declined during the last part of the 1800s, had declined an additional 98 percent.

Very striking also has been the decline in death rates for diseases such as typhoid and paratyphoid fever. The death rate for these two diseases taken together, decreased from 31.3 per 100,000 population in 1900 to 0.5 in 1943.[327]

Death from scarlet fever, measles, whooping cough, chicken pox, diphtheria, and other diseases that were once considered a tragic part of life abated significantly.

All of the old menaces like **typhoid, smallpox, measles, scarlet fever, whooping cough and diphtheria have become minor causes of death.** *The chance is very remote indeed that any of them will ever again assume sufficient importance in the mortality tables seriously to affect the general death rate.*[328]

---

[326] William Osler, MD, "The Relation of Typhoid Mortality and Sewerage," *Maryland Medical Journal*, vol. XXXVIII, no. 13, January 8, 1898, p. 217.
[327] *Vital Statistics of the United States 1943 Part I*, US Bureau of the Census, 1945.
[328] Dr. Louis Dublin, "Better Economic Conditions Felt in Fewer Deaths," *Berkley Daily Gazette*, December 27, 1935.

The health revolution that commenced in the 1800s so strikingly transformed the Western world that, by the early 1940s, it was expected that the threat of death from these diseases would eventually reach zero—"complete eradication."

> *From the vital statistics of insurance companies, we learn that life for children in this country has been made infinitely safer. We have reduced death from principal communicable diseases of childhood—**measles, scarlet fever, whooping cough, diphtheria—by 31% in a single year to a new record low, a point actually promising complete eradication of these diseases!***[329]

> *Measles, scarlet fever, whooping cough, and diphtheria—the principal communicable diseases of childhood—declined 31 percent in the year, or from 4.2 per 100,000 in 1939 to 2.9 in 1940. Each of these diseases reached a new minimum in 1940, and all except whooping cough had a mortality rate of less than 1 per 100,000. **Only a comparatively few years ago the death toll from this group of diseases was serious, but it has now been reduced to a point where their complete suppression may be expected.** The public-health movement is said to be responsible for the reduction in mortality from diarrhea and enteritis, which in 1930 had a rate of 20.4 per 100,000 and in 1940 had dropped to a rate of 4.6. **Advances in sanitary science, including the Pasteurization of milk, the better refrigeration of foods, and the purification of water supplies, as well as the general rise in the standard of living, are the main reasons for this improvement.***[330]

Scarlet fever

Throughout the 1800s, scarlet fever was a significant killer. This toxin-mediated streptococcal bacterial disease is highly contagious. The bacteria are spread by inhalation or direct skin contact. Scarlet

---

[329] "2 Inches Taller . . . 15 Pounds Heavier," *Life*, June 2, 1941, p. 71.
[330] *Handbook of Labor Statistics, 1941 Edition*, US Department of Labor, pp. 396–397.

fever mortality surpassed that of many other infectious diseases in the 1800s. It was a far bigger killer than smallpox, whooping cough, measles, and diphtheria.

During the Sanitation Revolution from the mid-1800s and into the early 1900s, scarlet fever deaths plummeted. The death rate declined by 100 percent by the mid-1900s (Graph 11.1). Even by the early 1900s, anyone who became ill with scarlet fever had a 95 percent decreased mortality risk compared to the antecedent century. It is noteworthy that the terror of scarlet fever became a distant memory—**long before antibiotics were available to treat it**.

> *A review of the experience of Providence, Rhode Island, with regard to scarlet fever from 1865 to 1924 shows that the death rate of children aged two to four decreased during this period from 691 to 28.3 per 100,000 . . . From 1886 to 1888 one in every five cases died, while from 1923 to 1924 only one in every 114 cases ended fatally. A similar trend has been demonstrated for England and Wales.*[331]

In the case of scarlet fever, nothing was eradicated. Something altered the susceptibility of humans to scarlet fever bacterial toxin. Even today, the organism innocently colonizes 15–20 percent of school children and remains ever present.[332]

Whooping cough and measles

The threat of death from all infectious diseases had faded to insignificance by the mid-1900s (Graph 11.2). By the time a vaccine arrived on the scene for whooping cough, the death rate had declined by more than 99 percent (Graph 11.3).

---

[331] Walter R. Bett, ed., *The History and Conquest of Common Disease*, University of Oklahoma Press, 1954, p. 35.
[332] Stanford T. Shulman, Alan L. Bisno, Herbert W. Clegg, Michael A. Gerber, Edward L. Kaplan, et al., "Clinical Practice Guideline for the Diagnosis and Management of Group A Streptococcal Pharyngitis," *Clinical Infectious Diseases*, 2012, p. 12.

The decline in death rates [from whooping cough] during the early 20th century was rapid, and by World War II the rate was about one-tenth of that at the turn of the century.[333]

Immunization against pertussis, which was introduced at a time when mortality from the disease had been falling steeply for 70 years, made a much less convincing impact . . . the death rate had fallen very substantially before 1957, and there was relatively very little room for improvement.[334]

In the case of measles, the death rate had declined by almost 100 percent (Graph 11.4). You would never know it today, but the dreaded measles was no longer a major issue in the Western world by the time vaccines were deployed.

Before the general nutrition status of European children reached the high level it is today, measles infection was something to be feared. As reviewed by Morely and colleagues, measles accounted for 11% of all deaths in Glasgow in the years 1807-1812 . . . **Even in the absence of a vaccine, by 1960, notification of childhood measles in England and Wales was only 2.4% and mortality fell to 0.030%,** *which is 1:200 of the 1908 Glasgow mortality rate.*[335]

People still came down with these illnesses. However, in the developed world, they were almost always relatively mild childhood diseases.

England began keeping mortality statistics on a national level in 1838. Although these national statistics were not started in the United States until the year 1900, they also show dramatic declines in deaths from infectious diseases. For example, deaths from

---

[333] D. L. Miller, R. Alderslade, and E. M. Ross, "Whooping Cough and Whooping Cough Vaccine: The Risks and Benefits Debate," *Epidemiologic Reviews*, vol. 4, 1982, pp. 2–3.

[334] Ibid., p. 9.

[335] Clive E. West, PhD, "Vitamin A and Measles," *Nutrition Reviews*, vol. 58, no. 2, February 2000, p. S46.

whooping cough had declined by more than 90 percent prior to the introduction of a vaccine in the mid-1940s (Graph 11.5). Deaths from measles had declined by more than 98 percent before the introduction of a vaccine in 1963 (Graph 11.6). The statistics show sharp downward trends at year 1900, but it is highly probable that, just like in the United Kingdom, an even earlier decline had already begun before the United States began to chart its national statistics.

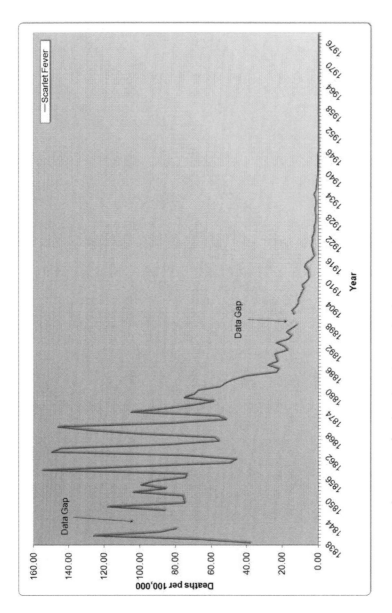

Graph 11.1: England and Wales scarlet fever mortality rate from 1838 to 1978.

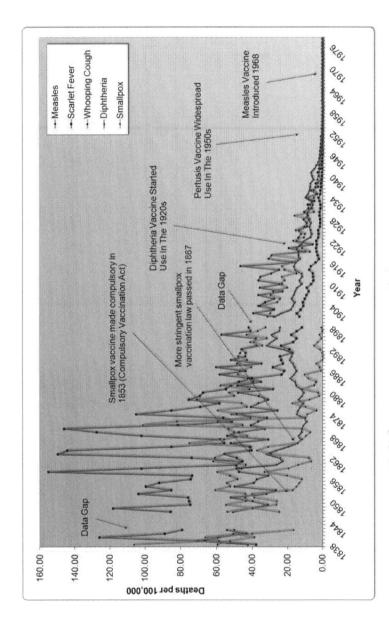

Graph 11.2: England and Wales mortality rates from various infectious diseases from 1838 to 1978.

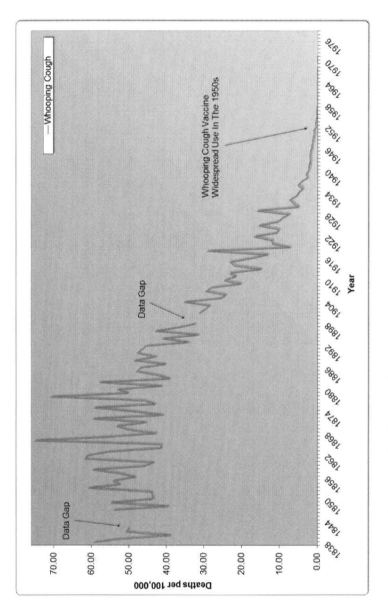

Graph 11.3: England and Wales whooping cough mortality rate from 1838 to 1978.

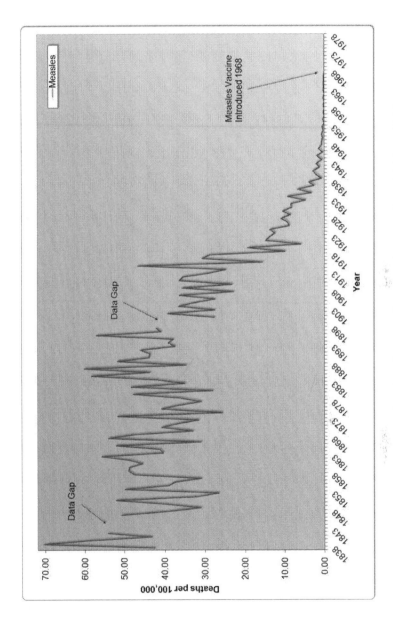

Graph 11.4: England and Wales measles mortality rate from 1838 to 1978.

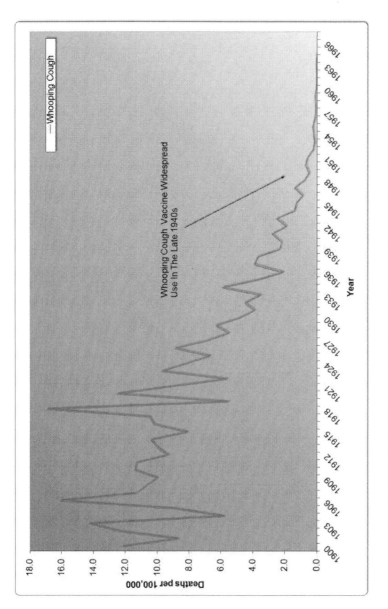

Graph 11.5: United States whooping cough mortality rate from 1900 to 1967.

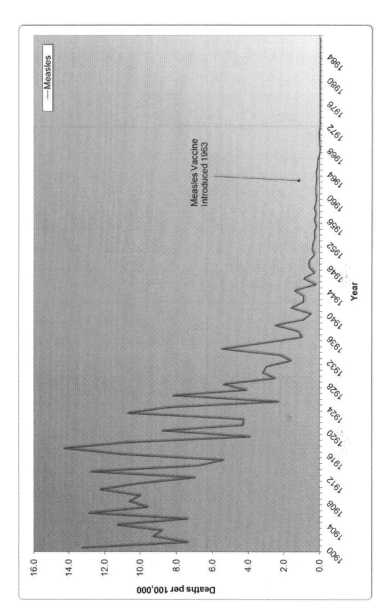

Graph 11.6: United States measles mortality rate from 1900 to 1987.

Diphtheria

There were two types of prophylaxis for diphtheria. The first was the *antitoxin* in 1895, which was a preformed antibody made in a horse after the horse was given the diphtheria toxin. The horse blood product was then injected into humans. This form of protection is passive and very short lived and has a history of serious contaminations. Severe reactions, including fatal forms of serum sickness, were historically problematic and are still listed on the package inserts as cautions. Today horse-serum antitoxin is only considered after known exposure or active infection. It is not really a vaccine in the sense that it does not incite an active immune response to diphtheria on the part of the recipient.

The other type of prophylaxis is what is in today's DPT vaccine, the diphtheria *toxoid*. This is an antigenic form of the bacterial toxin that has been altered so it shouldn't cause active disease but will stimulate the recipient to make antibodies.

Most of the world thinks that diphtheria vaccines are responsible for the low incidence and mortality of the disease today. However, with a careful look at the vital statistics, it is clear that high uptake of diphtheria vaccines has not led to a lowered incidence or severity of disease.

In fact, **the introduction of diphtheria antitoxin in 1895 preceded a large spike in diphtheria mortality**. This is shown in Graph 11.7 of Leicester, England. The rise in deaths was approximately 10 to 15 times higher than it had been for the previous 57 years (1838–1895) and continued for 5 more years (1896–1901).

Neither antitoxin nor toxoid vaccines led to declines in morbidity and mortality. From 1894 to 1920, the death rate in children had dropped by about 87 percent in New York City.

> *That **the drop in diphtheria morbidity and mortality is not wholly due to preventive immunization appears to be indicated by the fact that this decline set in actually in the***

nineteenth century before diphtheria antitoxin began to be used generally, and continued progressively even before preventative immunization became widespread. The death rate among children up to ten years of age in New York City was 785 per 100,000 in 1894, declining to less than 300 in 1900; and in 1920, when active immunization [toxoid] of school children began, it fell below 100.[336]

Although credit has historically been given to the introduction of the antitoxin treatment started in 1895, the decline in deaths also began well before its introduction (Graph 11.8).

Another spike in the mortality came after the introduction of the toxoid vaccine in 1920. In the United States, deaths from diphtheria had declined 98 percent from the year 1900 up to the mid-1940s before the DTP vaccine was introduced (Graph 11.9). Note that the declining mortality rate was actually interrupted temporarily after the vaccine was introduced.

The improvement in living conditions, not vaccines, marked the beginning of an amazing decline in disease mortality. Today, in societies that break down, we see not only life expectancy decline, but diseases erupt in highly vaccinated populations. Russia in the 1990s was a case in point. During that decade, there was significant political and social turmoil. Russian literature points out that the vaccinated develop diphtheria and that mortality is highest in those who are malnourished and alcoholic. **In 1994 male life expectancy dropped from its high of 65 years down to 57 years in Russia.**[337] Belarus data from the 1990s shows that highly vaccinated Russia still had diphtheria.

---

[336] Walter R. Bett, ed., *The History and Conquest of Common Disease*, University of Oklahoma Press, 1954, p. 24.
[337] Professor Boris Prokhorov, *The Crises of Public Health in Russia in the XX Century*, Figure 9.9, p. 29.

The analysis of vaccination history shows that out of 11 cases 7 (63,6%) were vaccinated according to schedule, 4 vaccinated but not according to schedule.[338]

An outbreak in St. Petersburg, Russia, occurred in the 1990s. More than 2,500 cases were in that city. A complete analysis of the vaccination history and disease severity was undertaken. The authors concluded that vaccine immunity is "short lived" and that:

If a wide diphtheria epidemic affects an industrialized country, it would probably not any more be the big killer that it was in Europe and in the United States in the 1950s and 1960s.[339]

Laboratory workers are well aware that many of us carry *Corynebacterium diphtheriae* bacteria as commensals, without the toxin producing virus. Diphtheria bacteria will never be eradicated. Therefore, vaccinationists will always say the vaccine is necessary. Given the lack of proven (by controlled trials) efficacy of the vaccine and the short-lived antibody following vaccination, one must question many of the current assumptions that form the basis of pamphlets read by parents and doctors.

Even though much of the literature from the 1930s showed no effect of vitamin C on diphtheria, the studies were limited by the low dosing of the vitamin. Dr. Klenner used adequate doses and found the survival greater in those treated with vitamin C:

Harde et al. reported that diphtheria toxin is inactivated by vitamin C in vitro and to a lesser extent in vivo. I have confirmed this finding, indeed extended it. Diphtheria can be cured in man by the administration of massive frequent doses of hexuronic acid (vitamin C) given intravenously and/or intramuscularly. To the synthetic drug, by mouth, there is little response, even when 1000 to 2000 mg. is used every two hours.

---

[338] Translated Russian documents in authors' possession.

[339] Asa G. Rakhmanova et al., "Diphtheria Outbreak in St. Petersburg: Clinical Characteristics of 1,860 Adult Patients," *Scandinavian Journal of Infectious Diseases*, no. 28, 1996, pp. 37–40.

This cure in diphtheria is brought about in half the time required to remove the membrane and give negative smears by antitoxin. This membrane is removed by lysis when "C" is given, rather than by sloughing as results with the use of the antitoxin. An advantage of this form of therapy is that the danger of serum reaction is eliminated. The only disadvantage of the ascorbic acid therapy is the inconvenience of the multiple injections. This concept of the action of vitamin C against certain toxins has led to treating other diseases producing exotoxins.[340]

Dr. King showed that dietary vitamin C had a significant impact on severity of diphtheria in guinea pigs which, like humans, also do not make their own vitamin C.

It is evident from the study that there is a wide zone of vitamin C deficiency, without the appearance of scurvy, where physiological processes are subnormal and the animal is more sensitive to injury from bacterial toxin.[341]

Perhaps the best prevention and treatment that exists against all toxin-mediated diseases will never be accepted by conventional medicine, simply because it cannot be patented.

Tuberculosis

Tuberculosis was another big killer in the 1800s. By the late 1930s, the death rate had dropped by 92 percent. By 1970, the decline in mortality had reached more than 99 percent (Graph 11.10).

---

[340] F. R. Klenner, "The Treatment of Poliomyelitis and Other Virus Diseases with Vitamin C," *Southern Medicine and Surgery,* vol. 111, no. 7, July 1949, pp. 209–214.
[341] C. G. King and M. L. Menton, "The Influence of Vitamin C Level upon Resistance to Diphtheria Toxin," *The Journal of Nutrition,* 1935, vol. 10, no. 2, pp. 129–140.

The annual tuberculosis death-rate for every 100,000 popula-
tion was round 450 in Massachusetts in 1857. It dropped
steadily and reached 35.6 in 1938.[342]

Some would argue that the use of streptomycin in 1948 contributed to the decline in tuberculosis. However, bacterial resistance was an immediate issue with streptomycin, which was not reliably bactericidal with single drug therapy. More notably is that the decline in incidence and mortality was already rapidly occurring before the antibiotic.

Tuberculosis, pneumonia, and influenza were far bigger killers than most other infectious diseases of the time. During the 1900s, these three diseases were killing 5 to 16 times more people than typhoid, scarlet fever, whooping cough, measles, or diphtheria (Graph 11.11). Apart from the 1918 flu pandemic, these diseases also declined throughout the 1900s (Graph 11.12). Although deaths from influenza and pneumonia still occurred, after 1950 they did so at a much lower rate.

Between 1850 and 1900, the commonly recurring epidemics of
cholera, smallpox, malaria, and typhoid were gradually
brought under control. During the next 50 years, gratifying
victories over such endemic diseases as tuberculosis, diphthe-
ria, measles, and scarlet fever were witnessed. These diseases
were less dramatic than epidemics, but each was among the
*leading causes of death before 1900. **By the middle of the***
20th century, except for the 1918 influenza pandemic,
death from infectious disease in Western industrialized
countries was no longer a major component of mortality
statistics.[343]

---

[342] Henry E. Sigerist, *Civilization and Disease,* Cornell University Press, New York, 1943, p. 55.
[343] Velv W. Greene, PhD, MPH, "Personal Hygiene and Life Expectancy Improvements Since 1850: Historic and Epidemiologic Associations," *American Journal of Infection Control,* August 2001, p. 204.

It is often asserted that life expectancy dramatically increased during this time due to advances in medicine and vaccination. But there is a salient piece of information that is often left out, and that is that most of the improvement in mortality was in children under one year of age (Graph 11.13). There were certainly improvements in all age groups, but the vast majority in average life span gain had occurred because babies were no longer dying from poverty-driven ailments or diarrhea—and because their mothers stopped dying of puerperal fever (Graph 11.14).

> *Infant mortality rates exceeded 200 per 1,000 in Stockholm until 1900 and declined to 50 per 1000 by 1925. Most of the decline, which occurred in the postnatal (1-11 month) period, was driven by a decline in diarrhea mortality. Other important causes of death included congenital conditions; tuberculosis; meningitis; undernutrition; and other diseases associated with poverty, crowding, and adverse living conditions, which were a major reality for the majority of the rapidly growing urban population in Stockholm.*[344]

---

[344] Bo Burström, MD, PhD; Gloria Macassa, MD; Lisa Öberg, PhD; Eva Bernhardt, PhD; and Lars Smedman, MD, PhD, "The Impact of Improved Water and Sanitation on Inequalities in Child Mortality in Stockholm, 1878 to 1925," *Public Health Now and Then*, vol. 95, no. 2, February 2005, p. 208.

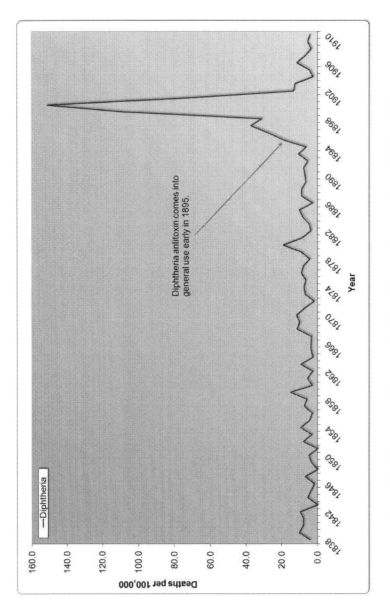

Graph 11.7: Leicester, England, diphtheria mortality rate from 1880 to 1910.

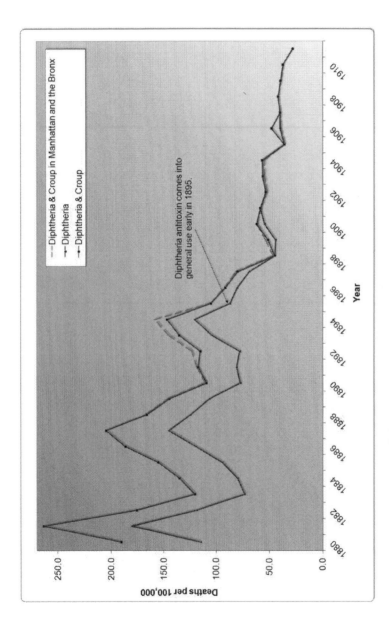

Graph 11.8: New York City diphtheria mortality rates from 1880 to 1911.

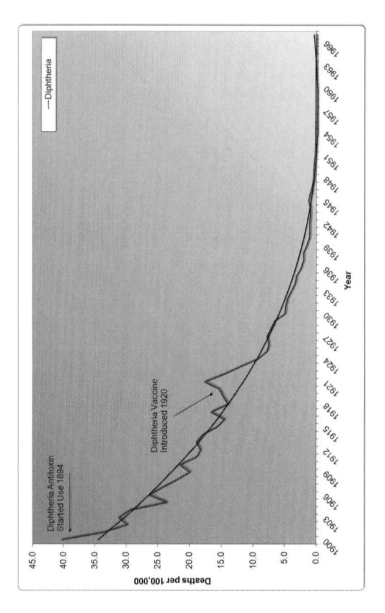

Graph 11.9: United States diphtheria mortality rate from 1900 to 1967.

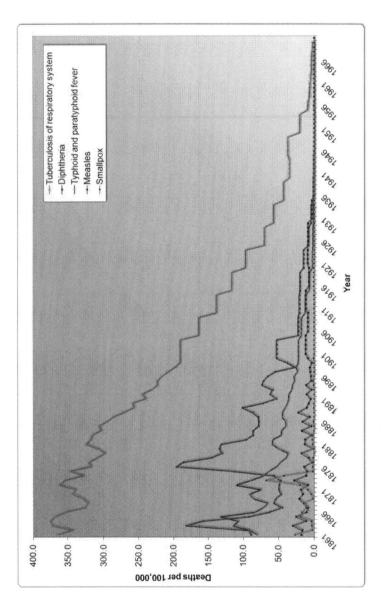

Graph 11.10: Massachusetts tuberculosis, diphtheria, typhoid, measles, and smallpox mortality rates from 1861 to 1970.

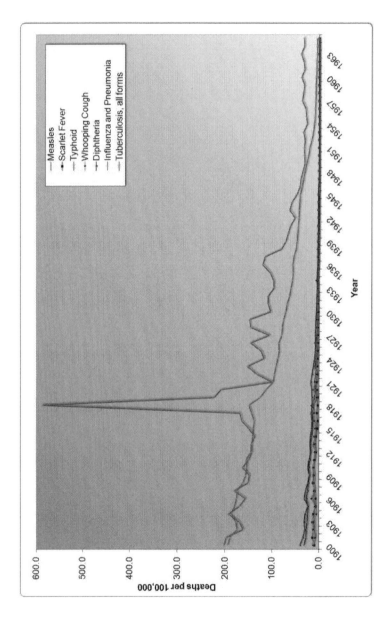

Graph 11.11: United States mortality rates from various infectious diseases from 1900 to 1965.

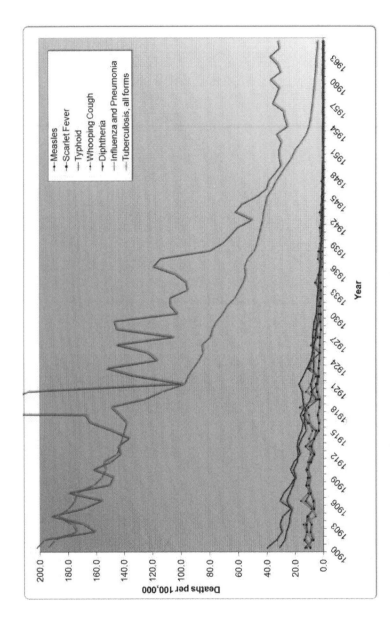

Graph 11.12: United States mortality rates from various infectious diseases from 1900 to 1965 magnified view.

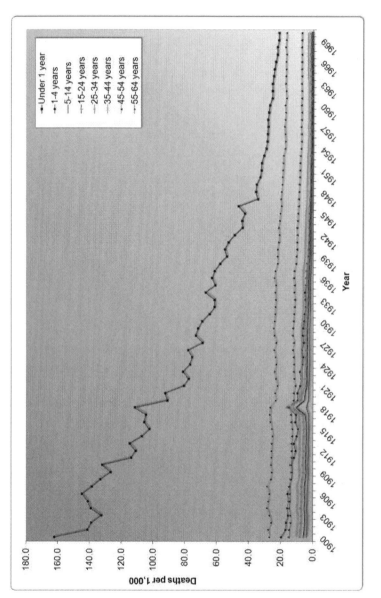

Graph 11.13: United States mortality rates for age groups from 1900 to 1970.

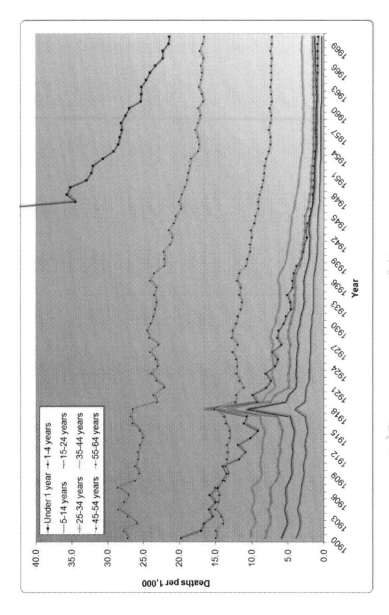

Graph 11.14: United States mortality rates for age groups from 1900 to 1970 magnified view.

Diarrhea

From 1900 to 1943, deaths from diarrhea declined from 143.7 to 9.4 per 100,000—a 93.5 percent decrease. This mortality decline occurred before any antibiotics were in use and probably had little, if anything, to do with vaccination.

> *There were probably many causes of the decline in diarrhea mortality; improvements in the provision of water and sanitation, changes in hygienic perception and behavior, and general socio-economic improvements, including improved nutritional status, are all thought to have been contributing factors.*[345]

By the early 1930s, victory was declared over the problem of infectious diarrhea that had plagued very young children for decades.

> *By the late 1920s the major cause of mortality changed among infants and young children in Europe, Great Britain and the United States.* **The epidemics of summer diarrhea and high infant mortality had virtually disappeared to the point that epidemics of diarrhea was declared defeated in Great Britain by the early 1930s** . . . *the case fatality rates for pneumonia were also dropping during the same period. The case fatality rate for pneumonia had dropped by nearly two thirds . . . Hess's colleagues attributed these changes in diarrheal and respiratory disease to model institutional care, which included unobstructed, sunny infirmaries, large verandas and avoidance of overcrowding or "hospitalism."*[346]

It should be clear that deaths from all diseases were on the decline—even those diseases that still struck at similar rates—prior to the availability of antibiotics. A positive change in the baseline health of

---

[345] Bo Burström, MD, PhD; Gloria Macassa, MD; Lisa Öberg, PhD; Eva Bernhardt, PhD; and Lars Smedman, MD, PhD, "The Impact of Improved Water and Sanitation on Inequalities in Child Mortality in Stockholm, 1878 to 1925," *Public Health Now and Then*, vol. 95, no. 2, February 2005, p. 208.

[346] Richard D. Semba, "Vitamin A as 'Anti-Infective' Therapy, 1920–1940," *The American Society for Nutritional Sciences*, 1999, pp. 785–786.

the population made the biggest difference, and that occurred through changes in the environment and nutrition.

> *An analysis has been made of the evolution in Switzerland of mortality due to the main infectious diseases ever since the causes of death began to be registered.* **Mortality due to tuberculosis, diphtheria, scarlet fever, whooping cough, measles, typhoid, puerperal fever and infant gastroenteritis started to fall long before the introduction of immunization and/or antibiotics.** *The decline was probably due to a great extent to various factors linked to the steady rise in the standard of living: qualitative and quantitative improvements in nutrition; better public and personal hygiene; better housing and working conditions and improvements in education.*[347]

During this time, deaths from scurvy were also decreasing. The nutritional status of the Western world as a whole had undergone a fundamental improvement. The diseased, putrid, and unwholesome food that people had been accustomed to eating was replaced with a more varied and nutritionally superior diet.

> *Incomplete as it is, the evidence for the nineteenth century is at least consistent with the view that diet was the most significant environmental influence in relation to the trend of mortality from tuberculosis . . .* **there is no serious doubt that conditions had improved considerably by 1850, and a notable feature of improvement must have been a better diet.** *The fact that mortality fell rapidly from the time when nutrition improved, and when there is no reason to believe that*

---

[347] E. Gubéran, "Tendances de la mortalité en Suisse," *Schweiz Med Wochenschr*, vol. 110, 1980, p. 574.

exposure to infection was reduced, seems to us to provide good grounds for regarding diet as an important influence.[348]

Hospitals

Before improvements were made in hospital hygiene, hospitals were even more serious sources of infection than they are today. *Hospitalism* was a general term used to describe the negative influences upon infants in hospitals and asylums. During the 1800s, the public often believed that these dirty and overcrowded institutions were a danger to health and well-being. An 1898 book discusses the situation.

> *The town free from infection; the hospital saturated by it, to such an extent as to induce its own surgeons to recommend their patients not to enter it, to compel them to refrain from operating, and, after every attempt that science and humanity could suggest—every hygienic means employed in vain in the fruitless attempt to eradicate the pestilence from the "very fabric" itself—to cause the governors, as a last resource, to decide on the demolition of the building and its complete reconstruction, at great expense, as the only remedy.*[349]

Slowly, institutional care was improved and replaced the old-style hospitals that had been responsible for so many deaths.

A 1977 analysis of the effect of medical intervention on the decline of mortality in the United States since 1900 stated how little medical measures had to do with disease decline.

> *In general, **medical measures (both chemotherapeutic and prophylactic) appear to have contributed little to the overall decline in mortality in the United States since***

---

[348] Thomas McKeown and R. G. Record, "Reasons for the Decline of Mortality in England and Wales During the Nineteenth Century," *Population Studies*, vol. 16, no. 2, November 1962, p. 115.

[349] John Eric Erichsen, "On Hospitalism and the Causes of Death After Operations," *Society of the New York Hospital*, March 1898, p. 98.

about 1900—having in many instances been introduced several decades after a marked decline had already set in and having no detectable influence in most instances. More specifically, with reference to those five conditions (influenza, pneumonia, diphtheria, whooping cough, and poliomyelitis) for which the decline in mortality appears substantial after the point of intervention—and on the unlikely assumption that all of this decline is attributable to the intervention ... *it is estimated that at most 3.5 percent of the total decline in mortality since 1900 could be ascribed to medical measures introduced for the diseases considered here.*[350]

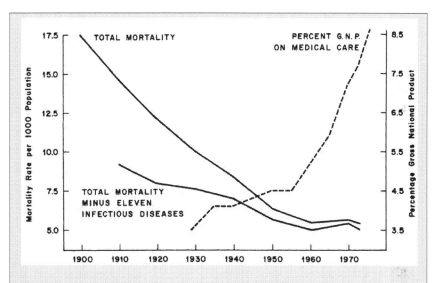

Figure 11.1: Age-and Sex-adjusted Mortality Rates for the United States 1900-1973, Including and Excluding Eleven Major Infectious Diseases, Contrasted with the Proportion of the Gross National Product Expended on Medical Care.

The improvement in hospital safety compared to the 1800s may seem revolutionary. The bad news is that in the year 2000 the

[350] John B. McKinlay and Sonja M. McKinlay, "The Questionable Contribution of Medical Measures to the Decline of Mortality in the United States in the Twentieth Century," *The Milbank Memorial Fund Quarterly, Health and Society*, vol. 55, no. 3, summer 1977, p. 425.

Institute of Medicine released a report showing that hospitals and doctors are the third leading cause of death in the United States, only after cancer and heart disease.

The combined effect of errors and adverse effects that occur because of iatrogenic damage not associated with recognizable error include:

- *12,000 deaths/year from unnecessary surgery*
- *7,000 deaths/year from medication errors in hospitals*
- *20,000 deaths/year from other errors in hospitals*
- *80,000 deaths/year from nosocomial infections in hospitals*
- *106,000 deaths/year from nonerror, adverse effects of medications*[351]

The above numbers are thought to be an underestimate of the actual damage. The modern outpatient setting was also noted to be dangerous in the IOM report.

It concluded that between 4% and 18% of consecutive patients experience adverse effects in outpatient settings, with 116 million extra physician visits, 77 million extra prescriptions, 17 million emergency department visits, 8 million hospitalizations, 3 million long-term admissions, 199,000 additional deaths, and $77 billion in extra costs (equivalent to the aggregate cost of care of patients with diabetes).[352]

Unfortunately, the flawed belief that vaccines and other medical advances were responsible for this amazing decline has dictated how infectious diseases are treated today. Instead of an emphasis on hygiene, nutrition, and appropriate vitamin supplementation, immune system support, and natural remedies, the emphasis is

---

[351] Barbara Starfield, MD, MPH, "Is US Health Really the Best in the World?" *Journal of the American Medical Association,* vol. 284, no. 4, July 26, 2000, pp. 483–485.
[352] Ibid., pp. 483–485.

always on costly antibiotics, vaccinations, and other medical procedures.

These choices have not been without consequences, as they fight the germs instead of supporting the life force. The host cannot rid its surroundings of microorganisms and, in fact, may be best served by cultivating the beneficial ones as they are actually part of the host's defense.

> *The prevailing view of interactions between complex, multicellular hosts and the microbes that surround them is skewed by a historical focus on pathogens. But in our rapidly accelerating exploration of the microbial world around us, there may be advantages to taking the broader view of immunity to pathogens as one aspect of a microbiome management system that regulates interactions with intimately associated microbiota, the great majority of which may be beneficial.*[353]

---

[353] Eric T. Harvill, "Cultivating Our 'Frenemies': Viewing Immunity as Microbiome Management," *Journal of the American Society for Microbiology,* vol. 4, no. 2, March 26, 2013, pp. 1–3.

~ 12 ~

THE "DISAPPEARANCE" OF POLIO

*I also looked at their children and wondered why they got
so sick. This time the answer came rather quickly and
from the mouth of an Aboriginal woman: "Before
the white man came, we had good health and no sickness."*

– Dr. Archie Kalokorinos

*Morris Beale, who for years edited his informative publication,
Capsule News Digest, from Capitol Hill, offered a standing
reward during the years from 1954 to 1960 of $30,000,
which he would pay to anyone who could prove that the
polio vaccine was not a killer and a fraud. There were no takers.*

– Eustace Mullins (1923–2010), *Murder by Injection*

*Live virus vaccines against paralytic poliomyelitis, for example,
may in each instance produce the disease it is intended to
prevent; the live virus vaccines against measles and mumps
may produce such side effects as encephalitis. Both of these
problems are /due to the inherent difficulty of controlling
live viruses in vivo [once they are placed in a live person].*

– Jonas and Darrell Salk, Science, March 4, 1977

The polio story is a haunting one: long, complicated, and ugly. It's not a story you will have read or that the medical profession will be able to tell. Beyond the smoke and mirrors lie sketchy statistics, renaming of diseases, and vaccine-induced paralytic polio caused by both the Salk,[354,355] and the Sabin vaccines. Dr. Albert Sabin's oral polio

---

[354] A. Langmuir, *The Wyeth Problem: An Epidemiological Analysis of the Occurrence of Poliomyelitis in Association with Certain Lots of Wyeth Vaccine,*

vaccine (OPV) continues to cause paralysis in vaccine recipients today.[356,357]

Despite many well-documented historical problems, polio and smallpox vaccines serve as the anchor for vaccination faith today. The subject stirs passion in those who believe their ancestors were affected by the dreaded virus or their children could be crippled by it today.

Many believe that a disease called polio has been eradicated in the Western hemisphere. Most everyone thinks that polio was eliminated by vaccination. But to fully understand where polio went, one must understand what polio was. Then, it becomes clear that it is impossible to eradicate it with a vaccine. However, the vaccine did lend itself to many well-documented—although not well-known—problems.

The term *poliomyelitis* is a description of spinal pathology. The meaning of the word comes from Greek *Polios* (gray), *muelos* (marrow), *itis* (inflammation) and denotes inflammation of the gray matter of the spinal cord. The gray

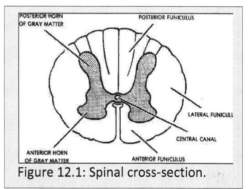

Figure 12.1: Spinal cross-section.

matter is labeled here on the cross section of the spinal cord. Poliomyelitis can occur in the brainstem and the spinal cord.

Polio Surveillance Unit, Epidemiology Branch, Communicable Disease Center, Department of Health, Education, and Welfare, September 6, 1955, p. 19.

[355] N. Nathanson and A. Langmuir, "The Cutter Incident," *American Journal of Hygiene*, 1963, vol. 78, pp. 29–60.

[356] J. F. Modlin, "The Bumpy Road to Polio Eradication," *New England Journal of Medicine*, vol. 362, June 24, 2010, pp. 2346–2349.

[357] A. Shahzad, "Time for a Worldwide Shift from Oral Polio Vaccine to Inactivated Vaccine," *Clinical Infectious Diseases*, vol. 49, October 15, 2009, pp. 1287–1288.

The result of this inflammation, whether chemical or viral, is reflected by certain characteristic muscular symptoms that have been conditioned into the minds of several generations to look like the boy in the picture to the right. The most visible aspects of polio were the braced limbs, iron lungs, deformities of hips and legs, clubbed feet, and scoliosis.

A small number of polio victims were placed on what is locked into our collective memory: iron lung machines. Those images are perhaps the most terrifying because they represent the most serious form of polio called *bulbar poliomyelitis,* where the brain stem is involved and the death rate is highest.

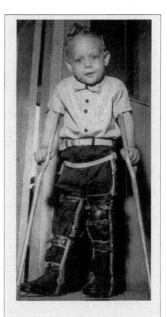

Photo 12.1: George Clark walks on crutches and heavy braces. He had polio attack last April. (1956)

Poliomyelitis was widely believed to be caused by a virus that infects the intestinal tract and moves into the body.

Prevalence of polio, 1912–1969

Since the early 1900s, we have been indoctrinated to believe that polio was a highly prevalent and contagious disease. Graph 12.1 depicts the incidence of various diseases in the United States between 1912 and 1970. Poliomyelitis is the line (with square points) at the bottom and reveals that the incidence was very low when compared to that of other infectious diseases. Polio has also been portrayed as a vicious crippler in the early and mid-1900s when it was habitually diagnosed by doctors who used a very loose definition of the disease. This graph denotes rates of clinical disease, most of which resolved and left no residual paralysis at all.

Given what a low-incidence disease it was, how did polio come to be perceived as such an infamous monster? This is a question worthy of consideration, especially in light of the fact that the rate was far less than other common diseases, some of which declined in incidence to nearly zero with no vaccine at all. Those who still embody a fear of polio may argue that it was a monster because it crippled people, especially children. But it was later revealed, after a vaccine was lauded for the eradication of polio, that much of the crippling was related to factors other than poliovirus, and those factors could not possibly have been affected by any vaccine.

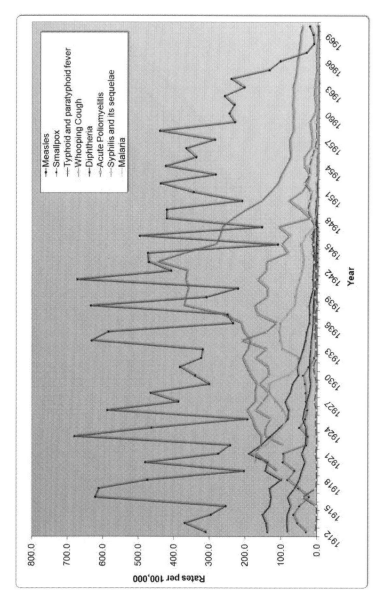

Graph 12.1: United States disease incidence from 1912 to 1970.

Natural (wild) poliovirus

It is easy to assume that poliovirus appeared abruptly or somehow changed in the 1900s to become as problematic as it was alleged to be. Naturally existing poliovirus was a common bowel inhabitant for millennia, always there, continuously circulating through humans, but never causing paralysis until later when something changed. The key question is: What opportunities could have arisen that afforded poliovirus the ability to cause epidemics in the early 20th century?

Under healthy environmental and dietary conditions, certain populations had antibodies to all three types of the virus and did not develop paralysis or have significant symptoms after infection. The remote Brazilian Xavante tribe serves as an example. This tribe was relatively untouched by modern man because they fought encroachments by slaughtering anyone who got close. There was a brief period of time in the 1700s when some of the natives lived among the white men until they realized that doing so brought waves of disease and death upon them. Those who survived fled and moved farther west in an attempt to isolate themselves. Around the 1950s, a few Indian health service members managed to get some cooperation for a study that evaluated the resistance to disease and the immune status of those native people. The results of the pilot study were published in 1964.

Isolated native tribes seem to have had no problem with the infections that were plaguing white men, even though blood results showed that the natives were indeed exposed and infected by many of those very same germs. Dr. Neel found that:

> *The paradox of a virtual absence of paralytic poliomyelitis among such heavily infected groups as this [referring to the Xavante Indians], despite high antibody titers, is well*

known, but the interpretation of the observation remains under discussion.[358]

These isolated people, who had not adopted any of the habits or medical interventions that are now known to increase susceptibility to poliomyelitis, were fully infected and immune! Native Indian populations had evidence of infection with all three strains of poliovirus, but developed no poliomyelitis whatsoever.

> *. . . studies of antibody avidity according to the techniques of Sabin (1957) were made on randomly selected specimens. All specimens were positive for antibodies to all three types of poliomyelitis, providing additional confirmation of the validity of the findings [that the Indians were all immune and none of them paralyzed]. . . . The percentage of positive reactors is striking.*[359]

These people had true herd immunity:

> *. . . all of the 60 persons tested with both techniques have antibodies to type I, 59 [had antibody] (98.3 ± 1.7 per cent) to type II, and 56 [had antibody] (93.3 ± 3.2 per cent) to type III.*[360]

Within Neel's paper, there is ample documentation and reference to the fact that native populations, when left to their natural diet and habitat, can become infected with influenza, salmonella, and measles. But the diseases do not spread clinically within the tribe, and mortality is nonexistent.

> *. . . in this instance, under-reporting hardly can be invoked as an explanation,* **one must conclude that in the Peruvian altiplano most infections are subclinical or give rise to only trivial illness.** *. . . The demographic data make it clear*

---

[358] J. V. Neel et al., "Studies on the Xavante Indians of the Brazilian Mato Grosso," *American Journal of Human Genetics*, vol. 15, March 1964, pp. 52–140.
[359] Ibid.
[360] Ibid.

that the eight persons positive for influenza did experience their disease while in contact with other members of the tribe. Why did the disease not spread?[361]

Dr. Albert Sabin, inventor of the oral polio vaccine, also noted in 1947 that native peoples were infected by poliovirus before the age of five, and yet there was no paralysis among them. There was, however, a significant rate of paralytic poliomyelitis in American servicemen in the same areas. Paralytic disease was common in the colonizing communities but not in natives.

*. . . the most important question: **why did paralytic poliomyelitis become an epidemic disease only a little more than fifty years ago**, and as such why does it seem to be affecting more and more the countries in which sanitation and hygiene, along with the general standard of living, are presumably making the greatest advances, while other large parts of the world, regardless of latitude, are still relatively unaffected?[362]*

Sabin said that the virus was present all over the world and that asymptomatic infection was widespread, even in regions where epidemics were unknown. The incorrect assumption by Dr. Sabin was that polio had anything to do with wealth per se. It probably had more to do with the subtle deterioration of innate immunity due to what wealthy people and American servicemen were spraying in the environment, what doctors were doing to them, and other lifestyle habits.

Dr. Archie Kalokerinos, a medical doctor who spent his career tending to the aboriginal people of Australia, was told repeatedly by the

---

[361] J. V. Neel et al., "Studies on the Xavante Indians of the Brazilian Mato Grosso," *American Journal of Human Genetics*, vol. 15, March 1964, pp. 52–140.

[362] A. Sabin, "The Epidemiology of Poliomyelitis: Problems at Home and Among the Armed Forces Abroad," *Journal of the American Medical Association*, vol. 134, June 28, 1947, pp.749–756.

elders that the tribes had no disease until the white men arrived and that they didn't even have names for these diseases.[363]

Although Dr. Sabin was simply puzzled about the clean and advanced parts of the world getting sick, he failed to connect the rate of paralysis to easily identifiable factors. Examining what changed in the environment and the human diet and how that clearly affected the susceptibility to paralysis in developed areas is key to understanding polio.

The white man's diet of refined and processed foods with the resultant lack of vitamins, the environmental and agricultural poisons, and specific invasive medical procedures all contributed to the rise in susceptibility of people living in industrialized parts of the world. But by the time those connections were made, disease-causing food was well ingrained in the modern palate. Medical advances were met with gratitude even though many of them were dangerous and overused. **Refined sugar, white flour, alcohol, tobacco, tonsillectomies, vaccines, antibiotics, DDT, and arsenic had become financial golden calves that led humanity blindly down a spiral of disease and misery.** Unfortunately, the paralysis was uniformly attributed to poliovirus infections which thus justified and prioritized vaccine research at all costs. **Many thousands of people were needlessly paralyzed because the medical system refused to look at the consequences of these golden calves, gave only lip service to the success of the Sister Kenny treatment of paralysis (discussed later in this chapter), and concentrated solely on vaccine research.**

What polio was and where it is now

Before the vaccine was in widespread use, many distinct diseases were naively grouped under the umbrella of "polio." Only after the vaccine was widely accepted was there an effort to distinguish

---

[363] A. Kalokerinos, *Shaken Baby Syndrome: An Abusive Diagnosis*, April 12, 2008, March 2012, Copyright 2012, Robert Reisinger Memorial Trust. E-book available on beyondconformity.co.nz and vaccinationcouncil.org websites.

poliovirus from other types of paralytic disease. The following list represents a few that could have been categorized and documented as polio prior to 1958.

- Enteroviruses such as Coxsackie and ECHO
- Undiagnosed congenital syphilis
- Arsenic and DDT toxicity
- Transverse myelitis
- Guillain-Barré syndrome
- Provocation of limb paralysis by intramuscular injections of many types, including a variety of vaccines
- Hand, foot, and mouth disease[364]
- Lead poisoning[365]

These are all conditions that still exist today and that a polio vaccine could not prevent.

The face of polio may have changed, but it was mostly due to the power of the pen, advances in diagnostic and life-support technology, removal of certain toxic influences, and advancements in physical therapy.

Specific polio diagnosis was not pursued with laboratory testing before 1958. The diagnostic criteria for polio were very loose prior to the field trials for the vaccine in 1954. Before the vaccine was deployed, health-care professionals were vigilantly programmed to be on the lookout for polio. After the trials, they were vigilantly noting who developed polio—vaccinated or unvaccinated—and made every effort to diagnose a non-polio illness in a vaccinated person. Dr. Bernard Greenberg, head of the department of biostatistics of the University of North Carolina School of Public Health and chairman of

---

[364] W. Xu, C. F. Liu, L. Yan, J. J. Li, L. J. Wang, et al., "Distribution of Enteroviruses in Hospitalized Children with Hand, Foot and Mouth Disease and Relationship Between Pathogens and Nervous System Complications," *Virology Journal*, vol. 9, January 9, 2012, p. 8.

[365] A. F. Braff, D. O. Lynn, and O. A. Wurl, "Fatal Lead Poisoning Simulating Poliomyelitis," *US Armed Forces Medical Journal*, vol. 3, no. 9, September 1952, pp. 1353–1357.

the Committee on Evaluation and Standards of the American Public Health Association, stated in 1960:

> *Prior to 1954 any physician who reported paralytic poliomyelitis was doing his patient a service by way of subsidizing the cost of hospitalization and was being community-minded in reporting a communicable disease. The criterion of diagnosis at that time in most health departments followed the World Health Organization definition: "Spinal paralytic poliomyelitis: signs and symptoms of nonparalytic poliomyelitis with the addition of partial or complete paralysis of one or more muscle groups, detected on two examinations at least 24 hours apart." Note that "two examinations at least 24 hours apart" was all that was required. . . . Laboratory confirmation and presence of residual [longer than 24 hours] was not required.*[366]

The practice among doctors before 1954 was to diagnose all patients who experienced even short-term paralysis (24 hours) with "polio." In 1955, the year the Salk vaccine was released, the diagnostic criteria became much more stringent. If there was no residual paralysis 60 days after onset, the disease was not considered to be paralytic polio. This change made a huge difference in the documented prevalence of paralytic polio because most people who experience paralysis recover prior to 60 days. Dr. Greenberg said:

> **The change in 1955 meant that we were reporting a new disease, namely, paralytic poliomyelitis with a longer-lasting paralysis.** *Furthermore diagnostic procedures have continued to be refined. Coxsackie virus and aseptic meningitis have been distinguished from paralytic poliomyelitis. Prior to 1954 large numbers of these cases were mislabeled as paralytic poliomyelitis.* **Thus, simply by changes in**

---

[366] H. Ratner et al., "The Present Status of Polio Vaccines," *Illinois Medical Journal*, vol. 118, nos. 2, 3, pp. 84–93,160–68. Edited from a transcript of a panel discussion presented before the Section on Preventive Medicine and Public Health at the 120th annual meeting of the Illinois State Medical Society in Chicago, May 26, 1969.

diagnostic criteria, the number of paralytic cases was predetermined to decrease in 1955-1957, whether or not any vaccine was used.[367]

As a case in point on how much paralytic disease thought to be polio was not at all associated with polioviruses, consider the well-documented Michigan epidemic of 1958. This epidemic occurred four years into the Salk vaccine campaign. An in-depth analysis of the diagnosed cases revealed that more than half of them were not poliovirus associated at all (Figure 12.2 and Figure 12.3). There were several other causes of "polio" besides poliovirus.

During an epidemic of poliomyelitis in Michigan in 1958, virological and serologic studies were carried out with specimens from 1,060 patients. Fecal specimens from 869 patients yielded no virus in 401 cases, poliovirus in 292, ECHO (enteric cytopathogenic human orphan) virus in 100, Coxsackie virus in 73, and unidentified virus in 3 cases. Serums from 191 patients from whom no fecal specimens were obtainable showed no antibody changes in 123 cases but did show changes diagnostic for poliovirus in 48, ECHO viruses in 14, and Coxsackie virus in 6. **In a large number of paralytic as well as nonparalytic patients poliovirus was not the cause. Frequency studies showed that there were no obvious clinical differences among infections with Coxsackie, ECHO, and poliomyelitis viruses. Coxsackie and ECHO viruses were responsible for more cases of "nonparalytic poliomyelitis" and "aseptic meningitis" than was poliovirus itself.**[368]

---

[367] H. Ratner et al., "The Present Status of Polio Vaccines," *Illinois Medical Journal*, vol. 118, nos. 2, 3, pp. 84–93,160–68. Edited from a transcript of a panel discussion presented before the Section on Preventive Medicine and Public Health at the 120th annual meeting of the Illinois State Medical Society in Chicago, May 26, 1969.

[368] G. C. Brown, "Laboratory Data on the Detroit Poliomyelitis Epidemic 1958," *Journal of the American Medical Association*, vol. 172, February 20, 1960, pp. 807–812.

After the vaccine, there was a concerted effort to distinguish cases with poliovirus from cases without it. This was not a concern prior to 1958 when many diseases common today hid behind the name *poliomyelitis*. Transverse myelitis, viral or aseptic meningitis, Guillain-Barré syndrome (GBS), chronic fatigue syndrome, spinal meningitis, post-polio syndrome, acute flaccid paralysis (AFP), enteroviral encephalopathy, traumatic neuritis, Reye's syndrome, etc., all could have been diagnosed as polio prior to 1958.

A modern scientific publication has even cast strong doubt on President Franklin Roosevelt's well-publicized polio diagnosis. The conclusion of a team of modern researchers is that he actually had GBS and not polio as was originally believed.[369]

---

[369] Goldman et al., "What Was the Cause of Franklin Delano Roosevelt's Paralytic Illness?" *Journal of Medical Biography*, vol. 11, 2003, pp. 233–240.

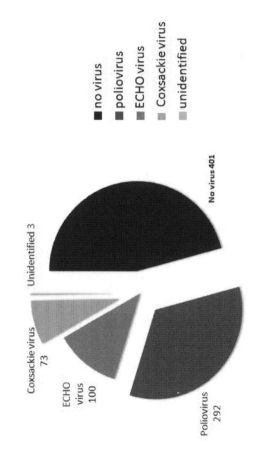

Figure 12.2: Michigan polio 1958 - epidemic virus identification via fecal analysis.

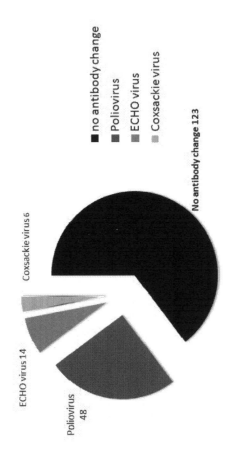

Figure 12.3: Michigan polio 1958 - epidemic viral antibody changes.

If polio is still here, why don't we see it?

Wild poliovirus was never the big killer or paralyzer the public was led to believe it was through the many frightening images shown repeatedly in the 1950s. Dr. Lennette, a well-respected virologist and pioneer of diagnostic virology with the California Department of Health, said in reflection on September 1987:

> *Actually, economically the disease wasn't very important. Secondly, not many cases were seen in this country. There weren't too many people paralyzed from polio in any one neighborhood, so it never made much of an impact.*[370] (See also Graph 12.1.)

The pictographic and cinematic images of polio that were used to rally the public toward vaccine development and acceptance dropped away after the vaccine campaign began. The public gratefully embraced the vaccine that was believed to have removed the frightful disease. To maintain public belief in the vaccine, especially in light of several serious instances of vaccine-induced paralytic polio, the images of polio in the new, highly vaccinated population had to be deleted. Optimism regarding the vaccine prevailed. The March of Dimes campaigns that were once designed to impact human fear and emotion transitioned into what we see today as advertising for "working together for stronger, healthier babies"—funding vaccines for infants and pregnant mothers.

In the 1940s, physical therapy and mobilization were ultimately recognized and developed as an important early intervention for paralysis victims. The cruel and barbaric treatments mentioned in Dr. J. R. Paul's book *A History of Poliomyelitis*,[371] which included tendon cutting and transplantation and other such "salvage operations," early

---

[370] Edwin H. Lennette, "Pioneer of Diagnostic Virology with the California Department of Public Health," an oral history conducted in 1982, 1983, and 1986 by Sally Hughes, Regional Oral History Office, The Bancroft Library, University of California, Berkeley, 1988.

[371] J. R. Paul, *A History of Poliomyelitis,* Yale University Press, New Haven, Connecticut, 1971, pp. 335–339.

and prolonged splinting, surgical straightening, and painful but ineffective electrical treatments, were abandoned.

As a result, images of crying children in plaster casts and splints were not as prevalent. Outcomes in paralysis and deformities improved simply because the disease began to be treated better from the outset. But this change did not happen overnight. It took Sister Elizabeth Kenny, a pioneer of what is now known as physical therapy, 30 years to get the orthodox medical community to accept that they had been incorrectly treating polio and were thus responsible for much of the residual paralyses, deformities, and lingering stiffness.

Dr. John Pohl, one of Sister Kenny's strongest American supporters, reflected on the misery that polio victims endured before the Kenny technique was used in Minnesota, circa 1940:

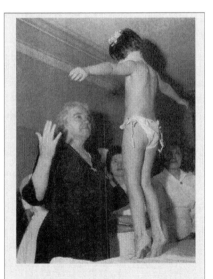

The more she talked, the more it seemed she made sense. Before she came, our city hospital was just crowded with polio. And treatment, in plain language, was just no damned good. If you could have visited the hospital, you would have seen little kids lying stiff and rigid, crying with pain, even though—as she saw—they were not necessarily paralyzed. ***We'd take the children to the operating room in those days, straighten them out***

Photo 12.2: Sister Kenny encourages a polio patient to stand for the first time. (1946)

under anesthetic, and put them in plaster casts. When they woke up, they screamed. The next day they still cried from the pain. That was the accepted and universal

treatment virtually all over the world. I saw it in Boston and New York City and London. She said, "That's all wrong."[372]

Splinting and casting of paralyzed limbs was the primary form of treatment in the first half of the 20th century. Affected limbs were routinely immobilized in casts for three to six months and often as long as two years.

This is a very important link to the story of polio. The manner in which stiff, painful, numb muscles were handled by doctors had a lot to do with the early face of polio and why it looks so different today in countries where paralytic poliomyelitis is treated differently.

The improper treatment of poliomyelitis led to the dysfunction of limbs, regardless of whether the virus was present or not. Dr. Donald Young Solandt and his associates at the University of Toronto reported that completely immobilizing an animal's limb produced similar muscle changes as nerve cutting or nerve removal.[373] Solandt's research demonstrated that immobilization alone was enough to induce flaccidity and apparent paralysis even with completely intact motor and sensory nerve pathways. Later writing by Mead also described how polio victims were treated in hospitals.

Orthopedists . . . believed in the "extreme fragility" of poliomyelitic muscle. Many victims of this disease were cast in plaster for 6 months or so, and their deformities were operated on in due course. Not even massage—much less, vigorous exercise of the affected muscle was countenanced.[374]

Thus the manner in which acutely affected muscles were treated had everything to do with outcome. The expectation among doctors and

---

[372] Victor Cohn, *Sister Kenny: The Woman Who Challenged the Doctors*, University of Minnesota Press, 1975, p. 5. With reference to interview with Dr. John Pohl.

[373] D. Y. Solandt et al., "The Effect of Skeletal Fixation on Skeletal Muscle," *Journal of Neurophysiology*, vol. 6, January 1, 1943, pp. 17–22.

[374] S. Mead, "A Century of the Abuse of Rest," *Journal of the American Medical Association*, vol. 182, October 1962, pp. 344–345.

the public was that poliomyelitis meant a life of corrective surgery and lameness. Sister Kenny proved them wrong.

Today, in Gaza, India, and Nigeria, where poliomyelitis is prevalent and limbs are treated according to the old ways, outcomes are similar to the images of the 1930s and 1940s.[375] Those images of crying children in plaster casts, used to influence the population to accept vaccination, were quite rare when the Kenny method was used. Given the history of successful treatment of paralyzed limbs from poliomyelitis, it does seem strange to revert back to the damaging old ways. How welcome would polio vaccine campaigns be today, if Sister Kenny's method was implemented in Gaza, India, and Nigeria and those unnecessarily deformed and atrophied limbs were nonexistent?

The iron lung and transverse myelitis

We no longer have iron lungs that look like miniature space rockets, the continuous images of which could instill morbid fear in any parent. Instead, we have small boxes with tubes going directly into the airway, called ventilators. So, when a child is admitted to the hospital with compromised respiratory muscles or brain stem afflictions, instead of being put into an iron lung she is connected to a ventilator. Although this is still frightening, it does not elicit the trepidation of the iron lung.

---

[375] Referencing the situation in Nigeria. www.gettyimages.co.nz/detail/news-photo/child-cries-as-his-polio-strickened-legs-are-placed-in-news-photo/52622460. Similar images can be seen in Gaza.

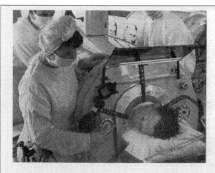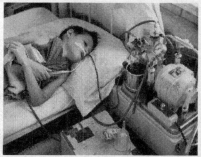

Photo 12.3: Iron lung encases 27-year-old Boyce Rash whose respiratory muscles have been paralyzed. Breathing function is so impaired that a mechanical apparatus is required to force air in and out of the patient's lungs. Seven iron lungs were shipped to Hickory, two of them from Boston. John Bryan, 8, uses oxygen inhalator. It feeds oxygen to nose of patient who has difficulty in breathing normally. Most severe cases involve paralysis of respiratory muscles. Tube extending from mouth collect saliva which boy cannot swallow because of paralyzed throat muscles. (1943)

Dr. Douglas Kerr from Johns Hopkins stated in his foreword to *The Autoimmune Epidemic* published in 2009:

> *Infants as young as five months old can get transverse myelitis, and some are left permanently paralyzed and dependent upon a ventilator to breathe . . . my colleagues at the Johns Hopkins Hospital and I hear about or treat hundreds of new cases every year.*[376]

Does the public have any idea that there are hundreds of cases of something that is now called transverse myelitis that would have historically been called polio and is now leaving children permanently dependent on a modern version of the iron lung?

---

[376] Donna Jackson Nakazawa, *The Autoimmune Epidemic: Bodies Gone Haywire in a World Out of Balance—and the Cutting-Edge Science That Promises Hope*, 2009, p. xv.

Approximately 33,000 people are afflicted by transverse myelitis in the United States, with 1,400 new cases per year. The symptoms of this disease are described by the National Institutes of Health.

. . . loss of spinal cord function over several hours to several weeks. What usually begins as a sudden onset of lower back pain, muscle weakness, or abnormal sensations in the toes and feet can rapidly progress to more severe symptoms, including paralysis, urinary retention, and loss of bowel control. Although some patients recover from transverse myelitis with minor or no residual problems, others suffer permanent impairments that affect their ability to perform ordinary tasks of daily living.[377]

Photo 12.4: Knox Out DDT product advertisement. (1948)

This is but one disease that would have been called polio in the years leading up to 1954. What causes transverse myelitis?

Researchers are uncertain of the exact causes of transverse myelitis. The inflammation that causes such extensive damage to nerve fibers of the spinal cord may result from viral infections or abnormal

---

[377] *Transverse Myelitis Fact Sheet,* National Institutes of Health, www.ninds.nih.gov/disorders/transversemyelitis/detail_transversemyelitis.htm.

*immune reactions. Transverse myelitis also may occur as a complication of syphilis, measles, Lyme disease, and **vaccinations**. Cases in which a cause cannot be identified are called idiopathic.*[378]

DDT poisoning: A cause of polio-like illness

Insects were not just the bane of cattlemen and farmers throughout the world. Flies, in particular, were believed to spread polio outdoors and in the home. In response, fearful parents sprayed DDT on all their windowsills and sprinkled it on sandwiches in their children's lunch boxes. DDT in water was used to rinse clothes, bedding, and mattresses. It was thought to be a safe and effective insecticide—even safe enough to spray at public beaches and directly onto children in an effort to halt the spread of polio. (See DDT advertisement on the previous page. "Only a little fly you say? Yes . . . but what a dangerous monster! He can carry polio, and many other horrible disease germs, right into your home!")

Photo 12.5: Flying and Biting Bugs on Jones Beach Die in a Cloud of DDT, New Insecticide—A truck-mounted for generator squirts the poison, mixed with oil droplets, over a four-mile area of the New York City playground. Spread by Army and Navy planes and by hand sprays, DDT routed dangerous disease-bearing flies and mosquitoes on Pacific islands. DDT has a drawback—it kills many beneficial and harmless insects, but does not kill all insect pests. Birds and fish which eat large numbers of DDT-poisoned insects may be casualties too. (1945)

---

[378] *Transverse Myelitis Fact Sheet,* National Institutes of Health, www.ninds.nih.gov/disorders/transversemyelitis/detail_transversemyelitis.htm.

But science did not support such practices. Most people wrongly thought that DDT was not only nontoxic, but that it was actually good for them.

By the 1960s, there was convincing evidence that polio-virus could live quite happily in pesticide-treated cells, and more-over, that the pesticides led to increased susceptibility of viral invasion.[379] DDT was found to enhance the release and intracellular multiplication of poliovirus.[380] Thus, it likely contributed to creating a monster out of a normally benign gut virus. Unfortunately, this in-formation was not published in the medical literature until a full decade after the polio vaccine was an accepted solution to poliomye-litis. Coincidentally, DDT was phased out of use in the United States and Canada beginning in the 1960s, right around the time that polio was disappearing.

During summer months at the beach, sugared foods were consumed in large volume. Sugar is known to create a toxic environment in the gut, altering the balance of beneficial and toxin-producing bacteria. Together with DDT, sugar would have created the perfect storm to damage the bowel and systemic immune systems.

Diet—in particular, diets high in refined sugar and flour—has a known impact on susceptibility to severe poliovirus infection. The harsh chemicals used in cane sugar refining are thought by some scientists[381] to have contributed to the synergy between an otherwise innocent virus and the sugar. In addition, as Dr. Sandler

---

[379] J. Gabliks, "Responses of Cell Cultures to Insecticides: Altered Susceptibility to Poliovirus and Diphtheria Toxin," *Proceedings of the Society for Experimental Biology and Medicine,* vol. 120, October 1965, pp. 172–175.

[380] J. Gabliks and L. Friedman, "Effects of Insecticides on Mammalian Cells and Virus Infections," *Annals of the New York Academy of Sciences*, vol. 160, 1969, pp. 254–271.

[381] F. Van Meer, "Poliomyelitis: The Role of Diet in the Development of Disease," *Medical Hypotheses*, vol. 3, March 1992, pp. 171–178.

demonstrated,[382] sugar metabolism and post-prandial hypoglycemia increased cellular viral susceptibility.

In the fear-baked summers of polio, many parents were totally unaware that exposure to DDT alone induced symptoms that were completely indistinguishable from poliomyelitis—even in the absence of a virus.[383]

> *Acute gastroenteritis occurs, with nausea, vomiting, abdominal pain, and diarrhea usually associated with extreme tenesmus [the feeling of having to pass stool with inability to do so]. Coryza [head cold], cough and persistent sore throat are common, often followed by a persistent or recurrent feeling of constriction or a "lump" in the throat; occasionally the sensation of constriction extends substernally and to the back and may be associated with severe pain in either arm.* **Pain in the joints, generalized muscle weakness, apprehension and exhausting fatigue are usual; the latter are often so severe in the acute stage as to be described by some patients as "paralysis."**[384]

---

[382] B. Sandler, *Diet Prevents Polio,* Lee Foundation for Nutritional Research, 1951.

[383] M. Biskind, "DDT Poisoning and the Elusive 'Virus X': A New Cause for Gastroenteritis," *American Journal of Digestive Diseases,* vol. 16, no. 3, 1949, pp. 79–84.

[384] Ibid.

Photo 12.6: "The great expectations held for DDT have been realized."
Penn Salt chemicals advertisement. (1947)

The paralysis that the world witnessed in the first part of the 20th century was largely from toxins in the environment like DDT, lead, and arsenic. Those toxins seriously disrupt mucosal immunity, allowing a previously benign virus to bypass the innate immune system and cause paralysis and other clinical symptoms. Where those chemicals are still used today, you will see reports of paralysis, which used to be called polio, but authorities now call it "acute flaccid paralysis."

How could doctors in the 1940s and 1950s possibly have distinguished a case that presented like DDT poisoning from poliomyelitis? They couldn't. After all, most people thought DDT was completely nontoxic and even healthy. These toxicity cases would have been diagnosed as polio and treated as such, often with a crippling outcome. It is not surprising that Dr. Fred Klenner was able to cure 60 out of 60 cases (100 percent) of polio (including bulbar polio) with the detoxifying agent, vitamin C, given in high intravenous doses.[385,386] Doctors were on the lookout for polio but not DDT poisoning.

> *Despite the fact that DDT is a highly lethal poison for all species of animals, the myth has become prevalent among the general population that it is safe for man in virtually any quantity.* *Not only is it used in households with reckless abandon, so that sprays and aerosols are inhaled, the solutions are permitted to contaminate the skin. Bedding and other textiles are saturated. Food and food utensils are contaminated. DDT is also widely used in restaurants and food processing establishments and as an insecticide on crops. Cattle, sheep and other food animals are extensively dusted with it and large areas are indiscriminately sprayed from airplanes for mosquito control. DDT is difficult and usually*

---

[385] Fred R. Klenner, MD, "The Treatment of Poliomyelitis and Other Virus Diseases with Vitamin C," *Southern Medicine & Surgery*, vol. 111, July 1949, pp. 209–214.

[386] R. Landwehr, "The Origin of the 40-Year Stonewall of Vitamin C," *Journal of Orthomolecular Medicine*, vol. 6, no. 2, 1991.

completely impossible to remove from contaminated foods (it is not affected by cooking) and it accumulates in the fat and appears in the milk of animals who feed on sprayed pasture or on contaminated fodder or who lick the DDT from their hides. As DDT is a cumulative poison, it is inevitable that large-scale intoxication of the American population would occur. In 1944, Smith and Stohlman of the National Institutes of Health, after an extensive study of the cumulative toxicity of DDT, pointed out, "The toxicity of DDT combined with its cumulative action and absorbability from the skin places a definite health hazard on its use."[387]

This following diagram reveals the parallel between polio epidemics in the United States and tonnage of pesticide (most of which was DDT) production from 1940 to 1970.

---

[387] M. Biskind, "DDT Poisoning and the Elusive 'Virus X': A New Cause for Gastroenteritis," *American Journal of Digestive Diseases*, vol. 16, no. 3, 1949, pp. 79–84.

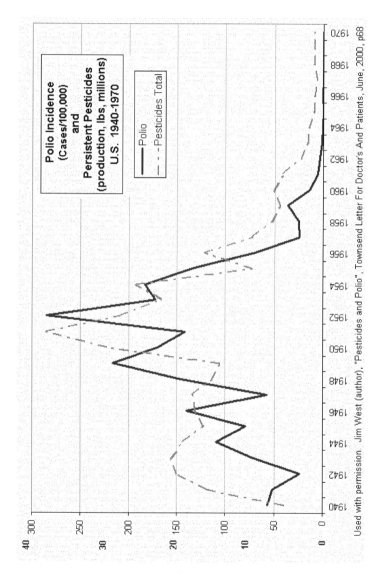

Figure 12.4: Polio incidence and persistent pesticide production.

Used with permission. Jim West (author), "Pesticides and Polio", Townsend Letter For Doctor's And Patients, June, 2000, p68

It's no small wonder that polio appeared to be such a vicious entity from the late 1800s and up until DDT was phased out of use in the United States. But that didn't happen until after a vaccine for polio was fully embraced as a savior of humanity in 1954. The United States was considered free of wild polio as of 1979.

Photo 12.7: Speaking of Pictures . . . These Demonstrate How DDT Paralyzes a Mosquito—In glass case mosquito feels effects of DDT, gives frantic kick, leaps into air. **As DDT enters nervous system and starts to paralyze muscles, mosquito seems to be trying to kick off paralyzing sensation. Paralysis of the nervous system affects the mosquito legs.** The mosquito staggers, falls over, tries to push back onto its legs. It makes one last violent effort to rise but topples back onto its head. On its back and almost completely paralyzed, the mosquito continues to battle against DDT but only succeeds in wiggling convulsively. It took DDT 45 minutes to knock the mosquito out completely. (1946)

Today in India, "polio" is a well-publicized problem, and DDT can be found on shelves just about anywhere. India, one of four countries that still manufactures DDT, remains the chemical's largest consumer and producer.[388] China suffered an epidemic of polio in 2011 and is one of the four countries that has produced and

---

[388] *Report of the Expert Group on the Assessment of the Production and Use of DDT and Its Alternatives for Disease Vector Control,* Third Meeting Geneva, United Nations Environment Programme, November 10–12, 2010.

continues to use DDT.[389] Although breast milk DDT levels in women in the United States is among the lowest in the world after decades of its banning, many other countries are still polluted with the chemical.

Polio by arsenic poisoning

Arsenicals, or compounds containing arsenic, are some of the oldest known causes of poliomyelitis. Yet old texts considered arsenic to be "potent," "effective," and "safe" and claimed that it "generally agrees very well" with children.[390] Doctors prescribed arsenic in cases of lung problems such as asthma, and it was added to tobacco for smoking. It was also used for cholera on the basis that a greater poison would destroy the lesser poison, and dentists used arsenous acid to kill nerve endings in decayed teeth.

Arsenic was used in wallpaper, paper, fabrics, paints, and dyes in the 1700s and 1800s until women's groups responded to the poisonings by bringing in muted colors with vegetable dyes. Paris Green and Scheele's Green were commonly used arsenic-based products that could result in polio symptoms.

After the removal of arsenic-containing pigments, arsenic poisoning resulted from medicines approved by the AMA in the form of supposedly therapeutic injections. Arsenic was used on fruits and vegetables in lead arsenate and calcium arsenate sprays, which resulted in human and animal ingestion. Washing or removing the outside contaminated layers of arsenic-treated produce was rarely recommended. Massive spray programs in the spring and at harvest are among the reasons why polio was once commonly referred to as

---

[389] Henk van den Berg, "Global Status of DDT and Its Alternatives for Use in Vector Control to Prevent Disease," *Environmental Health Perspectives*, vol. 117, no. 11, November 2009, pp. 1656–1663.

[390] Peter Bartrip, "A 'Pennurth of Arsenic for Rat Poison': The Arsenic Act, 1851 and the Prevention of Secret Poisoning," *Medical History*, vol. 36, January 1992, pp. 53–69. Page 55, second paragraph, Bartrip quotes several medical texts of the times.

summer diarrhea. Later, after cold storage for produce was used to extend the shelf life, the programs extended into the winter.

Sister Elizabeth Kenny was a nurse from the Australian outback whose observations led her to treat polio with hot packs and physical therapy. When some of the first "infantile paralysis" epidemics were quietly beginning in remote areas of Australia, she was called to help.

The year was 1912, and she was 23 years old with rudimentary medical training under her belt. In the pages of her autobiography lies evidence that the poliomyelitis she treated was chemical in nature, although at the time she had no idea what might be causing it. Years later, she became quite famous throughout the world for reversing the deformed physical outcomes of polio, which were often caused by accepted orthopedic treatments at the time. In her autobiography, she commented on that fateful night in the Australian outback:

> A very agitated father of seven children came to me with the appalling announcement that his ten-year old son and his four-year-old daughter had been taken with what he called the "cow disease" and neither of them could stand or walk. "They went lame yesterday, just like the cattle have been doing for the past two or three weeks," he explained, "and today they can't move."[391]

Cows are not clinically susceptible to poliovirus-induced poliomyelitis. But they were treated with arsenical dips to rid them of ticks, as noted in another part of Kenny's autobiography.

> On the range itself the cattle had to be moved from time to time for grazing purposes, and periodically "dipped" or run through a narrow canal of water treated with a chemical to kill the ticks which infect the herds with the disease known as

---

[391] E. Kenny, *And They Shall Walk*, Robert Hale Limited, 1951, p. 23.

"red water"—the arch enemy of the North Queensland cattlemen.[392]

Sister Kenny was naive to the significance of these events. But today we know that chemicals can and do produce symptoms of anterior horn spinal motor neuron disease that were, at the time, clinically and pathologically indistinguishable from viral polio and indistinguishable from what we think of as polio.[393,394,395]

Not only could congenital syphilis be mistaken for polio, but the treatment of adult syphilis more than likely contributed to the statistical rise in pre-vaccine polio when copious amounts of arsenic-derived medications were prescribed by medical doctors.

In 1939 the AMA lent its Seal of Acceptance exclusively to drugs approved by Chair Morris Fishbein. One of the heavily endorsed products was the arsenical Tryparsamide, manufactured by Merck under license from the Rockefeller Institute for Medical Research. This drug was used with the hope of countering the symptoms of advanced syphilis, often giving more than 100 injections to a single patient.

Another patient who had previously received thirty-four injections of arsphenamine, twenty-three injections of bismuth and seventy-six mercury rubs had a paretic type of serologic relapse after 104 injections of tryparsamide.[396]

---

[392] E. Kenny, *And They Shall Walk*, Robert Hale Limited, 1951, p. 79.

[393] F. Burgess and G. R. Cameron, "The Toxicity of D.D.T.," *British Medical Journal*, vol. 1, June 23, 1945, pp. 865–871.

[394] M. Biskind, "DDT Poisoning and the Elusive 'Virus X': A New Cause for Gastroenteritis," *American Journal of Digestive Diseases*, vol. 16, no. 3, 1949, pp. 79–84.

[395] Ralph R. Scobey, MD, "The Poison Cause of Poliomyelitis and Obstructions to Its Investigation," *Arch Pediatr*, vol. 69, April 1952, pp. 172–193.

[396] F. E. Cormia, "Tryparsamide in the Treatment of Syphilis of the Central Nervous System," *British Journal of Venereal Diseases*, vol. 10, April 1934, pp. 99–116.

It was widely known that any type of intramuscular injection could precipitate poliomyelitis, especially one with toxic chemicals and irritants.[397] Arsenic, even if swallowed, caused symptoms indistinguishable from poliomyelitis.

> *Dr. Robert W. Lovett of the Massachusetts State Board of Health (1908), describing the epidemic of poliomyelitis in Massachusetts in 1907, and after reviewing the medical literature on experimental poliomyelitis, states: "The injection experiments prove that certain metallic poisons, bacteria and toxins have a selective action on the motor cells of the **anterior cornua** when present in the general circulation; that the paralysis of this type may be largely unilateral; that the posterior limbs are always more affected than the anterior; and that the lesions in the cord in such cases do not differ from those in anterior poliomyelitis." . . . Popow **concluded that arsenic, even in a few hours after its ingestion, may cause acute central myelitis or acute poliomyelitis.**[398]*

Two other arsenic drugs, neoarsphenamine and neosalvarsan, were well known to cause polio-like syndrome, diagnosed as polio. Reports in Germany in 1914 and 1928 on provocation polio by arsenic injections must have been overlooked.[399] The AMA, Merck, and Rockefeller, despite warnings from the inventor of Tryparsamide regarding its danger, continued to distribute the drug,[400] and polio epidemics continued to rise.

---

[397] M. Gromeier et al., "Mechanism of Injury-Provoked Poliomyelitis," *Journal of Virology*, vol. 72, 1998, pp. 5056–5060.

[398] Ralph R. Scobey, MD, "The Poison Cause of Poliomyelitis and Obstructions to Its Investigation," *Arch Pediatr*, vol. 69, April 1952, pp. 172–193.

[399] H. Kern, "Ueber eine anstaltsendemie von Heine-Medizinscher krankheit," *Muen Med Wochen*, vol. 61, 1914, pp. 1053–1055; "Alterthum, Lues congenital and poliomyelitis," *Deut Med Wochen*, vol. 54, 1928, pp. 522–523;
H. Gougerot, "Eveil d'infection neurotrope a virus filtrant a ls suite d'arsenotherapie chez dez syphilitiques," *Bull Soc Derm Syph*, vol. 42, 1935, pp. 794–795.

[400] E. Mullins, *Murder by Injection*, National Council for Medical Research, 1988.

Undiagnosed syphilis

Is it possible that some polio victims could have been undiagnosed syphilitics? (Graph 12.1) Tabes dorsalis, the slow deterioration of nerves and gray matter of the spinal column, is a crippling symptom of syphilis that also affects gray matter of the spinal column. At the time, syphilis was far more prevalent than polio. Infants infected with syphilis at birth may be asymptomatic and may not manifest signs commonly associated with congenital syphilis.

From a case report in 1988:

> *A 54 year old woman was referred for poor balance, leg weakness and pain, recurrent left knee effusions, and a previous history of "polio."*

> *Since her clinical and electrophysiological presentation was incompatible with previous poliomyelitis, we hypothesize that she acquired syphilis congenitally and experienced her first symptoms of tertiary disease at age 7 years.*

> *Infants infected at birth may be asymptomatic and may not manifest signs commonly associated with congenital syphilis. Even though most features of tabes dorsalis do not develop until 10-25 years after primary infection, this latency may be as short as 5 years[401] in children.*

> **Distal weakness and atrophy may be late manifestations of tabes dorsalis, attributed to extension of the syphilitic process to anterior horn** *cells or motor roots.*[402]

Although neurosyphilis usually affects the posterior horns of the spinal cord, here we see that anterior horns can also be affected, just like in poliomyelitis, when there is congenital syphilis. This case of

---

[401] H. H. Merritt, R. D. Adams, and H. C. Solomon, *Neurosyphilis*, Oxford University Press, New York, 1946.

[402] P. Donofrio et al., "Tabes Dorsalis: Electrodiagnostic Features," *Journal of Neurology, Neurosurgery & Psychiatry*, vol. 51, 1988, pp.1097–1099.

syphilis exemplifies how congenital syphilis and polio could have been easily confused.

Morbidity of polio, then and now

The CDC defines polio's statistical paralytic rate and estimates that it is less than 1 in 100 for some sort of permanent paralytic syndrome.

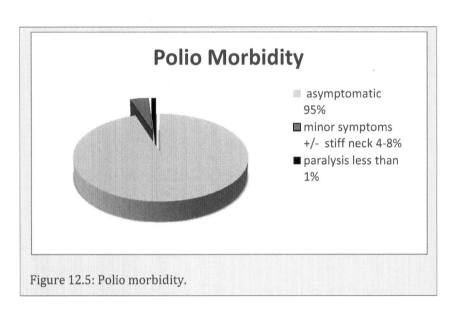

Figure 12.5: Polio morbidity.

Approximately 95% of persons infected with polio will have no symptoms. About 4-8% of infected persons have minor symptoms, such as fever, fatigue, nausea, headache, flu-like symptoms, stiffness in the neck and back, and pain in the limbs, which often resolve completely. Fewer than 1% of polio cases result in permanent paralysis of the limbs (usually the legs). Of those paralyzed, 5-10% [of that 1%] die when the paralysis strikes the respiratory muscles.[403]

---

[403] "Polio Disease In-Short," Centers for Disease Control and Prevention, Department of Health and Human Services, www.cdc.gov/vaccines/vpd-vac/polio/in-short-both.htm, accessed June 17, 2013.

Prior to vaccination, Dr. Maurice Brodie reported that only 1 in 170 children with **no antibody** to polio became ill during epidemics. By these two drastically different risk estimations, you can see that statistics are not set in stone, nor are they necessarily a reliable indicator of risk. The CDC reports a 59 percent higher paralysis rate than was actually measured during a pre-vaccine epidemic.

> It would seem that the lack of antibody is a factor predisposing to the disease inasmuch as over 85 per cent of those under 5, and over 70 per cent of the 6-10 year old group show no antibody or only a small amount of antibody. This does not explain why in an epidemic approximately only 1 of the 170 children under 5 showing no antibody, and about the same proportion of those under 10 develop the disease. This may be due to the individual non-specific variation in the susceptibility of the children . . .[404]

Dr. Brodie seemed clued in to the susceptibility factor, but he didn't proffer it any further—undoubtedly because he was also single-minded in the pursuit of a vaccine. Unfortunately for the dead and paralyzed recipients, Brodie's vaccine was not safe even though it was, in reality, no more dangerous than Dr. Jonas Salk's vaccine was in its 1955 production. Dr. Brodie allegedly committed suicide at the age of 36 in 1939.[405]

The question to ask today is, how much poisoning by chemicals and infection with other viruses was counted as polio in the statistics? According to the CDC, less than 1 percent of infected people develop paralysis, and 5–10 percent of that 1 percent suffer respiratory death. Yet in several polio epidemics, far more than 1 percent were paralyzed and even died.

---

[404] M. Brodie and W. Park, "Active Immunization Against Poliomyelitis," *American Journal of Public Health*, vol. 26, February 1936, pp. 119–125.
[405] J. R. Paul, *A History of Poliomyelitis*, Yale University Press, New Haven, Connecticut, 1971, p. 261.

Sister Elizabeth Kenny in Australia reported that 6 of the 20 children in her district were afflicted by painful or paralytic polio. How could 6 out of 20 children in a thinly populated rural area be stricken with polio (infantile paralysis) if it is a viral illness supposedly asymptomatic in 95 percent of those infected? Was it because all were exposed to chemicals?

> She went on to the house where the brother and sister were stricken. Their symptoms were the same. Within less than a week the inexperienced, self-appointed nurse found herself with a polio epidemic on her hands, affecting six of the twenty children in the thinly settled district.[406]

Dr. Archie Kalokerinos was a doctor in a cotton-growing area of Australia. A prominent feature that he noted were all the drums of toxic cotton field spray, which the children found marvelous to play on when full and in when empty.

Dr. Kalokerinos rapidly became familiar with the paralytic disease called polio.

> As far as I knew no epidemic of polio had been in progress. But the consultant was right—too right. It was the beginning of a big epidemic. In a very short space of time I was to become the "expert". I could almost smell polio from afar.
>
> During emergencies I was sometimes covered with sputum, urine, and faeces. At one stage the domestic staff refused to clean my room. The fear of catching polio was understandable. But I came through it all without a scratch. I guess that God was looking after me.[407]

Perhaps Dr. Kalokerinos and all the regular staff (except one junior surfer doctor who lived life in the fast lane) never caught polio, either because they were naturally immune to poliovirus like most of

---

[406] Victor Cohn, *Sister Kenny: The Woman Who Challenged the Doctors*, University of Minnesota Press, 1975, p. 42.
[407] Personal correspondence in authors' possession.

the population, they were not directly exposed to the agrichemicals, or they were just lucky . . .

David Oshinsky's book *Polio: An American Story* chronicles multiple incidents of more than one family member dying or becoming permanently paralyzed after supposed infection with poliovirus.

> *Polio hit the Iowa farmbelt hard in 1952. They had tested the well water—it was fine—and **used extra DDT** to drive away flies. . . . Nine of the eleven children recovered, two were left paralyzed. . . . It was even worse for a family living near Milwaukee. Four of the six children came down with bulbar polio.*[408]

All four children who were exposed to DDT died after being treated conventionally by medical doctors with oxygen, penicillin, and plasma.

> *Wonder drugs and iron lungs and round-the-clock attention had failed to keep these children alive. In an era without a vaccine, it was a terrifying thought.*[409]

Indeed terrifying. Doctors certainly should have known that penicillin would do nothing for a virus. Furthermore, any injection could be a cause of paralyzing polio (provocation polio) if circulating poliovirus was a factor. Did those doctors unwittingly cause the deaths of the children by inducing bulbar polio—the most serious type of polio that affects the brain stem?

Were those children previously tonsillectomized, a well-documented underlying factor not just in bulbar polio but in poliomyelitis incidence? For poliovirus to cause damage requires access to the inside of the body through "peripheral nerve damage," something which tonsillectomy provides in abundance. The invasive procedure of

---

[408] David M. Oshinsky, *Polio: An American Story*, Oxford University Press, 2005, pp. 163–164.
[409] Ibid.

surgical tonsil removal raised the risk of bulbar polio, as revealed in numerous studies and reports.[410,411,412,413]

Healthy tonsils were removed by surgeons for various financially rewarding but scientifically unsound reasons. Fifty to 80 percent of middle-class and upper-class children in the United States were needlessly subjected to tonsillectomies in the polio epidemic era. Anderson showed in his large group from a 1943 epidemic in Utah that poliomyelitis was more than 2.5 times more prevalent in tonsillectomized children than age-matched non-tonsillectomized children. The incidence of bulbar poliomyelitis was 16 times higher in tonsillectomized children than in the general child population. Forty-six percent of the bulbar polio cases had been preceded by recent tonsillectomy.[414]

Cunning reported in his series of 0- to 10-year-old bulbar poliomyelitis cases that the ratio of tonsillectomized to non-tonsillectomized was 6 to 1.[415,416] In 1971 Dr. Ogra reported in the *New England Journal of Medicine* that post-operatively, previously

---

[410] M. Siegel, M. Greenberg, and M. C. Magee, "Tonsillectomy and Polio-myelitis, II, Frequency of Bulbar Paralysis, 1944–1949," *Journal of Pediatrics*, vol. 38, no. 5, May 1951, pp. 548–558.

[411] Francis Thomas, "Poliomyelitis Following Tonsillectomy in Five Members of a Family," *Journal of the American Medical Association*, vol. 119, no. 17, 1942, pp. 1392–1396.

[412] J. A. Glover, "The Paediatric Approach to Tonsillectomy," *Archives of Disease in Childhood*, vol. 23, 1948, pp. 1–6.

[413] R. V. Southcott, "Studies on a Long Range Association Between Bulbar Poliomyelitis and Previous Tonsillectomy," *Medical Journal of Australia*, vol. 2, no. 8, August 1953, pp. 281–298.

[414] John Anderson, "Poliomyelitis and Recent Tonsillectomy," *Journal of Pediatrics*,1945, pp. 68–70.

[415] D. S. Cunning, "Tonsillectomy-Poliomyelitis Survey, 1947," *Laryngoscope*, vol. 58, no. 6, June 1948, pp. 503–513.

[416] D. S. Cunning, "Tonsilectomy and Poliomyelitis," *Archives of Otolaryngology*, vol. 46, no. 5, November 1947, pp. 575–583.

existing pharyngeal anti-polio antibody titers decreased sixfold to eightfold.[417]

The issue with how doctors treated patients in the epidemic era does not end with what doctors did do, but with what they refused to do. Dr. Klenner had a nearly 100 percent success rate in curing dozens of cases of polio (even bulbar cases) with intravenous infusions of vitamin C. He presented this information at symposia and meetings. He was met mostly with disbelief and ignored. Nonetheless, he continued to cure case after case of polio with vitamin C and published extensively on the details of his experience.[418]

> *In the poliomyelitis epidemic in North Carolina in 1948, 60 cases of this disease came under our care. . . . Two patients in this series of 60 regurgitated fluid through the nose. This was interpreted as representing the dangerous bulbar type. For a patient in this category postural drainage, oxygen administration, in some cases tracheotomy, needs to be instituted, until the vitamin C has had sufficient time to work—in our experience 36 hours. Failure to recognize this factor might sacrifice the chance of recovery. With these precautions taken, every patient of this series recovered uneventfully within three to five days.[419]*

Dr. Klenner was not the only doctor to publish on the successful reversal of severe poliomyelitis cases with high-dose vitamin C.[420,421]

---

[417] P. L. Ogra, "Effect of Tonsillectomy and Adenoidectomy on Nasopharyngeal Antibody Response to Poliovirus," *New England Journal of Medicine*, vol. 284, no. 2, January 14, 1971, pp. 59–64.

[418] Robert Landwehr, "The Origin of the 42-Year Stonewall of Vitamin C," *Journal of Orthomolecular Medicine*, vol. 6, no. 2, 1991.

[419] Fred R. Klenner, MD, "The Treatment of Poliomyelitis and Other Virus Diseases with Vitamin C," *Southern Medicine & Surgery*, vol. 111, July 1949, pp. 209–214.

[420] E. Greer, "Vitamin C in Acute Poliomyelitis," *Medical Times*, vol. 83, November 1955, pp. 1160–1161.

Laboratory and vaccine sources of epidemics

Nowhere else in polio's history was there more panic than during New York City's 1916 epidemic. (Note the large 1916 peak on the polio curve in graph 13.1.) Dr. H. V. Wyatt published a document in 2011 discussing the possibility that a highly virulent laboratory-engineered strain of poliovirus "escaped" from the Rockefeller laboratories, causing the largest epidemic of polio in US history. Just what exactly could have escaped from the lab is unknown.

> The epidemic was thought to have affected 23,000 cases with 5,000 deaths through New England and the Middle Atlantic states, reaching Delaware, Maryland and the District of Columbia with a few cases in Vermont and Canada. It had no apparent connection to lesser epidemics in West Virginia and in Minnesota, Wisconsin and Michigan. These features were never experienced again. Three other aspects were not noted at the time: the number of children age 2 yr affected was the highest ever recorded; the case fatality rate of 25% was the highest ever recorded [certainly higher than natural wild type polio virus which is less than one percent]; the epidemic started in early May, well before the normal summer polio season.[422]

At the time, the epidemic was broadcast to the public as having been started by children who arrived from Italy. But the immigration data does not fit with that hypothesis. Official immigration books show that the epidemic began before those children arrived.

> The 1916 epidemic is featured in many accounts of polio, but details and emphases differ and many are incorrect. The early

---

[421] Claus W. Jungleblut, "Further Observations of Vitamin C Therapy in Experimental Poliomyelitis," *Journal of Experimental Medicine*, September 1937, pp. 470–471.

[422] H. V. Wyatt, "The 1916 New York City Epidemic of Poliomyelitis: Where Did the Virus Come From?" *The Open Vaccine Journal*, vol. 4, 2011, pp. 13–17.

cases in May in Brooklyn had not been reported, but were found at a later date by the USPHS researchers.[423]

The epidemic was unique in that the virus was highly destructive to the nervous system, much like the Rockefeller labs cultivated "MV" strain.

> *Three miles from the epicentre of the outbreak, Simon Flexner and his associates at the Rockefeller Institute at 63rd Street and York Avenue, near Queensborough Bridge on Manhattan Island, had been passaging spinal cord tissue containing poliovirus, from one Rhesus monkey spinal cord to another. These experiments continued with the passage virus which at times was reinforced with newly acquired virus from patients . . . Those doctors had no awareness of what they were handling. . . . By 1916, mutants of the original Rockefeller virus had been selected for replication in monkey motor neurones, but were still capable of high levels of replication in other cells . . . It is a remarkable coincidence that a unique neurotropic strain of poliovirus was developed a few miles from an epidemic caused by a uniquely pathogenic strain of the virus . . . A few blocks from the Rockefeller Institute at Lexington Avenue and 63rd Street the 3rd Avenue elevated line linked at Municipal Building station to the BRT line to Brooklyn over Brooklyn Bridge with a stop at 3rd Street and 5th Avenue where the first case lived. However, almost anywhere in New York was within a few streets of a rail link to the Rockefeller Institute.*[424]

The significance of this epidemic is that it set the stage for the terror to come. Doctors and parents alike, after this aberrantly lethal polio epidemic, were perched for an ominous future and thus ready and willing to do whatever was necessary to eradicate polio.

---

[423] H. V. Wyatt, "The 1916 New York City Epidemic of Poliomyelitis: Where Did the Virus Come From?" *The Open Vaccine Journal*, vol. 4, 2011, pp. 13–17.
[424] Ibid.

Many doctors of the 1940s were aware that the pitchmen of the National Foundation for Infantile Paralysis (NFIP) and March of Dimes were responsible for the expanded terror that swept the nation.[425] Few today are aware of the intimate relationship between the NFIP and the Rockefeller Institute. Nearly all the researchers for the polio vaccine were from Rockefeller. Dr. Thomas Rivers, virologist and director, was an "unpaid consultant" to NFIP and Basil O'Connor (NFIP's founder) and also served as mentor and advisor to Albert Sabin and Thomas Francis.

Sabin developed the live vaccine that is now used in India, and Francis headed the largest public health experiment in history, the Salk vaccine trial of 1954. Rivers was the commandant of the plan to conquer polio in 1938.[426] He is rumored to have had a serious distaste for Sister Kenny, as did AMA's Morris Fishbein and NFIP's Basil O'Connor. NFIP's attempts to buy her and discredit her were, fortunately, futile.

Synthetic poliovirus

Today, laboratory generation of infectious virus in the absence of a natural viral template has been accomplished by scientists. It was funded by the US Defense Advanced Research Project Agency (DARPA). Dr. Eckhard Wimmer, one of the scientists involved in the project, reported:

> *The empirical formula of poliovirus is $C_{332,652}H_{492,388}N_{98,-2450}O_{131,196}P_{7,501}S_{2,340}$ .... Placing the atoms in order, a particle of high symmetry emerges. ... Our experiment has thus overthrown one axiom in biology—namely, that the proliferation of cells or, for that matter, viruses depends on the physical presence of a functional genome to instruct the replication process. It was believed that without parental genomes, no daughter cells or*

---

[425] Victor Cohn, *Sister Kenny: The Woman Who Challenged the Doctors*, University of Minnesota Press, 1975, p. 125.

[426] David M. Oshinsky, *Polio: An American Story*, Oxford University Press, 2005, pp. 60, 170.

*progeny viruses would arise. We have broken this fundamental law of biology by reducing poliovirus to a chemical entity, which can be synthesized on the basis of information stored in the public domain.... **Just like a common chemical, poliovirus has been synthesized in the test tube.**[427]*

Dr. Wimmer also reports that neurovirulence can be manipulated readily in synthetic polioviruses, though he presumes that this capability will be used for attenuation rather than for raising more virulent species. Either one is equally possible.

The Cutter disaster and other vaccine blunders

Most people today don't know about the infamous Cutter disaster. This was a virus-related poliomyelitis epidemic that was initiated by the use of the Salk vaccines just after they were rapidly developed and fast-tracked into licensure by the US Department of Health, Education, and Welfare. This record-breaking approval process took only two hours.[428]

Because of outside pressure, the licensing committee in charge of approving the vaccine did so after deliberating but without first having read the full research, namely the Francis Report on which their approval was to have been based. Dr. Howard Shaughnessy, laboratory director, Illinois Department of Health, testified to this event:

Previously it [the vaccine] had been distributed as an experimental product, not a licensed product . . . the committee was asked to come to a decision very quickly . . . there was discussion of the report that Dr Francis had given, but we were not in a position to discuss it very intensively because we had not seen the report prior to this morning and the report was

---

[427] E. Wimmer, "The Test-Tube Synthesis of a Chemical Called Poliovirus: The Simple Synthesis of a Virus Has Far-Reaching Societal Implications," special issue, *European Molecular Biology Organization Report*, vol. 7, July 20, 2006, pp. S3–S9.

[428] Richard Carter, *Breakthrough: The Saga of Jonas Salk*, Trident Press, New York, 1955, p. 282.

distributed to us after the presentation . . . we were pressured in the sense that we were told that speed was essential, and when we came up toward the 5:00 time, some of us felt we would like to discuss this matter more. We were told that to discuss the matter further it would have to go into the following week, and we would have to go to Washington or Bethesda and most of the members were unwilling to do so. We were in effect pressured into an earlier decision than we ordinarily would have made. . . . It was part of the pressure of events, put it that way.[429]

Dr. Thomas Francis did not issue the final report of his evaluation of the 1954 field trials until April 1957, two years after the licensing of the vaccine.[430] At the time, public health authorities decreed that physicians inject the fast-tracked vaccine before those doctors knew much about the science or the large Francis trial. The consequences of this impulsive action turned out to be significant.

The Salk invention was an injectable, supposedly formaldehyde-inactivated version of poliovirus vaccine. There were serious problems with the viral inactivation process that were known by insiders from the outset of the vaccine's development. Any professional objection by scientists involved during the development of the vaccine was rapidly subdued.[431] Dr. Paul Meier attested to the practice of firing scientists who disagreed with the NFIP's plans.

---

[429] Opening brief of Defendant and Appellant Cutter Laboratories Gottsdanker v. Cutter Laboratories (1960) 182 Cal. App.2d 602 pp. 31–33. Dr Shaughnessy was Director of Laboratories and Head of Department of the Illinois Department of Public Health, University of Chicago, and member of the Ann Arbor Licensing Committee for the Salk vaccine.

[430] T. Francis et al., "Evaluation of the 1954 Field Trial of Poliomyelitis Vaccine: Final Report," Poliomyelitis Vaccine Evaluation Center, University of Michigan, Ann Arbor, April 1957.

[431] H. Eyer et al., *Social Medicine and Hygeine: An Evaluation of the Protective Immunization Against Poliomyelitis, Report of the Scientific Committee, 1956.* This 102-page document with 22 corresponding graphs is a translation of a larger 492-page German report from an article that appeared in the *Munch Med*

Jonas Salk had a paper in which he argued that all the virus was inactivated, and that there was no live virus left. But, the sixth lot was not listed. And so I said that something was wrong. He cut out data in order not to show what happened to some lots. . . . Well, NFIP did form an advisory committee. And they reformed it five or six times. **Each time somebody didn't agree, they dropped them and got somebody who might agree. By the time they were done forming the committee, everybody on it was distinguished, but very agreeable.**[432]

As a result of ignoring the warnings by highly qualified scientists who repeatedly and publicly explained why and how the inactivation process was flawed from the beginning, the vaccine virus needlessly infected, paralyzed, and killed children and their household contacts.

Others Wendell Stanley, Sven Card, Enders, Herdis von Magnus and myself among others disagreed, convinced that the inactivation process did not follow a straight line and it was not permissible to extend the curve below the baseline. . . **And I remember Colin MacLeod raising the question whether this was really the way to go, but that's the way the matter stood, namely, "We'll go ahead and make the vaccine."** *Well, the vaccine was made that way. Then Cutter made several batches of the vaccine,* **which upon inoculation into man produced cases of poliomyelitis,** *some of them with severe paralysis.*[433]

Wochenschr, April 6, 1956. A copy of English translation is in the authors' possession.

[432] H. A. Marks, "Conversation with Paul Meier, Interview by Harry M. Marks," *Clinical Trials*, vol. 1, February 2004, pp. 131–138.

[433] Edwin H. Lennette, "Pioneer of Diagnostic Virology with the California Department of Public Health," an oral history conducted in 1982, 1983, and 1986 by Sally Hughes, Regional Oral History Office, The Bancroft Library, University of California, Berkeley, 1988.

Millionaire vaccine inventor Paul Offit, a supporter of mandatory vaccinations, wrote a book on the Cutter incident. In the book, even he admits:

> ... the disease caused by Cutter's vaccine was worse than the disease caused by natural polio virus.[434]

History books credit Cutter Laboratories for the disaster. The official explanation of the problem was that the live virus particles clumped into cellular debris (monkey kidney tissue from the manufacture) and, as a result, formaldehyde could not penetrate the center of the clump. Although this clumping may have occurred, it was not the major reason for the presence of live virus in the 1955 vaccine.

There is a body of literature that speaks to the real cause of the problem, which was known from the outset of the development of Salk's vaccine.

Dr. Thomas Rivers, the mastermind of Rockefeller's polio vaccine mission, hired all the chairmen of departments of virology. He had enormous clout, and nobody dared argue with him, lest their careers be ruined. Dr. Edwin Lennette had some interesting reflections in the 1980s about Rockefeller, Rivers, and the formalin inactivation curve:

> Well, in those days, as I should point out perhaps, things were quite different from today because a professor in this country, just as in Germany, was a highly respected individual, and you didn't argue with him.[435]

Dr. Lennette, talking about a pre-vaccine trial meeting of the minds in New York City in 1953, said:

---

[434] Paul Offit, MD, *The Cutter Incident*, Yale University Press, 2005, p. 86.
[435] Edwin H. Lennette, "Pioneer of Diagnostic Virology with the California Department of Public Health," an oral history conducted in 1982, 1983, and 1986 by Sally Hughes, Regional Oral History Office, The Bancroft Library, University of California, Berkeley, 1988.

Tom Rivers was there, Tommy Francis, Joe Smadel, and Colin MacLeod, all of whom were deeply involved. These were people to whom you might apply the term "the establishment," . . . These were the "old graybeards" who had been through the mill of medical science . . . The question was raised as to whether the vaccine would be safe at the present level of inactivation with formaldehyde. And I remember distinctly Tom Rivers saying, "If you put any more formaldehyde in, you'll make it so damn safe it won't be any good." That's recorded somewhere in the minutes of that meeting.[436]

Salk and the scientists who remained on the NFIP board interpreted the formaldehyde inactivation curve incorrectly. As a result, live virus remained. Stubbornly, they would not heed the warnings.

Salk's basic hypothesis is false. As early as the poliomyelitis congress in Rome in September 1954, Swedish observations were put forward concerning virus inactivation with formaldehyde which showed that the inactivation curve is not a straight line but shows a continuous curvature. The phenomenon has nothing to do with the presence of aggregates; filtration does not in any way affect the shape of the curve.[437]

There was yet another factor in the virulence of the 1955 vaccine. The vaccine used in the 1954 trial contained Merthiolate, a mercury compound that had a virucidal (virus-killing action) effect. Because Jonas Salk was disappointed in the antibody-stimulating effect that the 1954 field trial demonstrated, the Merthiolate was removed in the 1955 vaccine to induce a faster antibody response in vaccine

---

[436] Edwin H. Lennette, "Pioneer of Diagnostic Virology with the California Department of Public Health," an oral history conducted in 1982, 1983, and 1986 by Sally Hughes, Regional Oral History Office, The Bancroft Library, University of California, Berkeley, 1988.

[437] Sven Gard, "Prophylactic Vaccination Against Poliomyelitis, " *Svenska Läkartidningen (Swedish Physician's Journal),* vol. 53, no. 121(nr3)a, January 1956 (3rd week), translated from Swedish and distributed by the Oak Park Health Department, Oak Park, Illinois. Ref. p. 8.

recipients. Not only was the 1955 vaccine not the same celebrated vaccine that was trialed in 1954, it was also riddled with live viruses of a highly neurovirulent nature—the Mahoney strain.

Between April 17 and June 30, 1955, 260 poliomyelitis cases were documented after inoculation of about 400,000 persons with the Cutter vaccine. Ninety-four cases were among vaccinees, 126 among family contacts, and 40 among community contacts. An estimate of the case-infection ratio is in the range of 1 case per 100 to 600 injected infections.[438]

It is a documented fact that household adult contacts did contract polio—secondarily—from the vaccine,[439] and some became severely paralyzed. Thirteen household contacts required iron lungs, and five died. There were documented cases where infants received the vaccine injection, shed live virulent virus in the stool, and never got sick. But their mothers became very ill, and so did neighbors. A conservative report revealed that 39 friends and neighbors of children who received the Cutter vaccine were paralyzed. Many more were infected to lesser degrees.

The newly formed Polio Surveillance Unit (PSU) did not capture all the cases that developed from the domino effect of this grand mishap. The reason is that they had strict cutoff dates beyond which any reported polio was considered not to be from the vaccine.

Paul Offit summarized the estimate of known damage:

> **In the end, at least 220,000 people were infected with live polio virus contained in Cutter's vaccine; 70,000 developed muscle weakness, 164 were severely paralyzed, 10 were killed.** Seventy five percent of Cutter's victims were paralyzed for the rest of their lives.[440]

---

[438] N. Nathanson and A. Langmuir, "The Cutter Incident," *American Journal of Public Hygiene*, vol. 78, no. 1, 1963, pp. 29–60.

[439] Ibid., pp. 16–81.

[440] Paul Offit, MD, *The Cutter Incident*, Yale University Press, 2005, p. 89.

Anyone infected with live vaccine virus, whether symptomatic or not, was readily contagious and capable of spreading the dangerous Mahoney virus strain in their communities. It is evident that the viral ecosystem was forever altered by the introduction of polio vaccines.

Looking beyond Cutter

Here is some of what Paul Offit left out of his book. Even though Cutter Laboratories took the fall for the 1955 disaster, all manufacturers had difficulty killing the virus in their vaccines before and after the disaster.[441,442] Cutter was not the only manufacturer documented to have produced live virus vaccine that was injected into children and caused paralysis. In 1990, after decades of information concealment, the Freedom of Information Act led to the release of documents that proved Wyeth also produced a paralyzing vaccine.[443,444]

Wyeth and Cutter are thought today to have been the only companies that produced live virus vaccine; however, all the vaccine companies could have released active vaccine virus because the "minimum licensing requirements"[445] set by the US Department of Health, Education, and Welfare were not met by any pharmaceutical company. The initial minimum licensing requirements established in April 12, 1955, stated that "all virus infectivity is destroyed with certainty."[446] According to later documents and courtroom testimonies,

---

[441] L. Scheele and J. Shannon, *Technical Report, Public Health Implications in a Program of Vaccination Against Poliomyelitis,* June 7, 1955, p. 7. Digital copy is in the authors' possession.

[442] Richard Carter, *Breakthrough: The Saga of Jonas Salk,* Trident Press, New York, 1965, p. 324.

[443] H. Ratner, "An Untold Vaccine Story," *Child and Family,* vol. 21, no. 3, 1993, pp. 253–263.

[444] A. Langmuir and N. Nathanson, "The Wyeth Problem," prepared by the Poliomyelitis Surveillance Unit, Epidemiology Branch of the Communicable Disease Center, Department of Health, Education, and Welfare, September 6, 1955.

[445] Minimum requirements involved extra vaccine filtration steps and tests on cortisone-treated primates.

[446] "Minimum Requirements," 1st revision, US Department of Health, Education, and Welfare, Public Health Service, April 12, 1955, p. 2.

this definition was not followed, and manufacturers were never held to such standards. In 1992 Dr. Neil Nathanson stated:

> *Minimum requirements were meant to state the assurance that the final vaccine contained less than 5 tissue culture infectious doses per liter . . . in other words to assure that there would be less than one chance in 100,000 that the vaccine would contain one paralytogenic dose per 1,000 human doses of vaccine.*[447]

Does this sound like insurance that "all infectivity was destroyed with certainty?" A Tissue Culture Infective Dose (TCID) is a mathematical calculation. According to the late virologist Dr. Wendell Stanley, a single TCID contained up to 30 poliovirus particles, and any one of them could have caused poliomyelitis.[448]

There are a couple of problems associated with risk calculation using TCIDs. First, the cutoff choice of less than 5 TCIDs was arbitrary. Second, there is an assumption that all virions (complete, infectious virus particles) would be distributed evenly and necessarily be included in any test sample. Remember the problem with particulate clumping? According to statistician Dr. Paul Meier, if each virion injected did cause a case of paralytic poliomyelitis, the injection of 1 milliliter of vaccine where the batches contain 5 TCIDs per liter could cause up to 500 cases per 100,000 vaccinated.[449]

The reason there was not much more paralysis among the vaccinated was because, as was already known, 80–90 percent of the childhood population at the time was already naturally immune to at least one strain of poliovirus.[450] In his book, Dr. John Paul estimated

---

[447] Neal Nathanson, *Mosley vs. Health and Human Services, Declaration*, p. 8.
[448] Gottsdanker v. Cutter Laboratories (1960) 82 Cal. App. 2d 602 (2869:902870:3; 2871: 14–17) pp. 65–69.
[449] P. Meier, "Safety Testing of Poliomyelitis Vaccine," *Science*, vol. 125, May 31, 1957, pp. 1067–1071.
[450] T. Francis et al., *Evaluation of the 1954 Field Trial of Poliomyelitis Vaccine: Final Report*, Poliomyelitis Vaccine Evaluation Center, University of Michigan, Ann Arbor, April 1957, p. 152.

that 80 percent would have had some pre-vaccine antibody to the poliovirus.[451] Anyone who was immune naturally would also, fortunately, have been immune to the corresponding vaccine virus.

You may be wondering how this information was concealed from the public for nearly fifty years. Congressman Percy Priest ordered and chaired a full investigation of the vaccine controversy. He admitted in 1956 that:

> . . . in the previous year (1955) many responsible persons had felt that the public should be spared the ordeal of "knowledge about controversy." **If word ever got out that the Public Health Service had actually done something damaging to the health of the American people, the consequences would be terrible. . . . We felt that no lasting good could come to science or the public if the Public Health Services were discredited.**[452]

So much for evidence-based medicine and scientific truth. Instead of discrediting the PSU, the decision was made, after some deliberation, to leave Wyeth's paralyzing vaccine on the market, place the whole blame on Cutter, and ignore the ongoing problem with live viruses in the vaccines that persisted even after the revisions for safer manufacture were carried out. Only Cutter's vaccines were recalled. All other manufacturers' vaccines released in the 1950s were sold and injected into America's children. Millions of vaccines were also exported all around the world.

There were other more insidious and unaddressed problems with the Salk vaccine. Once a vaccine passed the minimum requirement tests showing that all the virus was theoretically killed, **the virus was found to have resurrected on the shelves weeks or months later**, even after the new safety standards were put in place in 1956.

---

[451] J. R. Paul, *A History of Poliomyelitis,* Yale University Press, New Haven, Connecticut, 1971, pp. 335–339, 427.
[452] Richard Carter, *Breakthrough: The Saga of Jonas Salk*, Trident Press, New York, 1965, pp. 318–319.

Dr. S Stephen Chapman . . . reported . . . he had centrifuged the vaccine and had obtained live virus, "more than we theoretically ever could have anticipated having . . . this brings up the problem of reactivation of the so called dead vaccine."[453]

The most likely explanation for this apparent resurrection is that the safety testing didn't detect small amounts of live virus, and without Merthiolate in the vaccine the virus was able to replicate. In 1954 Salk's trial vaccine contained a mercury compound patented as Merthiolate, which was used to prevent mold from growing and to prolong the shelf life. When it was obvious that the vaccine was not as antigenic as hoped, a decision was made to remove the mercury compound in the 1955 manufacture. Salk never wanted the mercury in the first place and protested that it ruined the vaccine, making the Mahoney strain less antigenic.

Swedish scientists, after the Cutter disaster in 1955, began to test some of their vaccine that was waiting to be dispensed. They did this in response to the alarming news coming from the United States about vaccine-induced paralysis. Tests were done on batches of vaccine that were previously shown to be free of active virus. Upon repeat testing, 30 percent of the vaccine samples showed the presence of active virus.[454]

The fundamental problem was that, although required safety testing was done with the hope of releasing only safe vaccines, the foundational principles with which the vaccine was manufactured were highly flawed from the beginning. Salk's hypothesis was false. This problem was never fully addressed. According to expert

---

[453] Ratner, Herbert, "A Premature Salk Vaccine, April 19, 1956," *Child and Family*, vol. 20, 1988, pp. 255–263.

[454] H. Eyer et al., *An Evaluation of the Protective Immunization Against Poliomyelitis, Report of the Scientific Committee, Social Medicine and Hygeine,* 1956, p. 13. This 102-page document with 22 corresponding graphs is a translation of a larger 492-page German report from an article that appeared in the *Munch Med. Wochenschr* April 6, 1956. A copy of English translation is in the authors' possession.

virologist Dr. Sven Gard, a fundamental property of the virus that had to do with its structure was overlooked.[455] **Dr. Gard also stated that vaccination in the United States caused as many cases of poliomyelitis as it prevented in 1955.**[456]

According to Dr. Wendell Stanley, the formaldehyde engendered a "tanning" effect upon the outer coating of the virus, but potentially left the infectious internal portion of the virus intact.

> *The outer protein portion of the virus is not infective, and yet it is this portion which produces antibodies. In making a vaccine, the effort is centered on trying to remove the virus activity contained in the nucleic acid core while at the same time keeping the protein unchanged so that it may produce antibody. This is complicated . . . This results in a "tanning" effect as leather is tanned, making it more resistant to anything attempting to pass through it . . . there is an intermediate stage [in the inactivation] which is reversible, so that there is no viral activity shown by any of the safety tests and yet after further chemical treatment, activity can be gained from this same material. . . . Virus can be held for many days, and in fact may years and still be able to be reactivated at a subsequent time . . . formaldehyde comes off the protein. The partially tanned virus may be altered . . . will not give a positive test at the 14th day but would prove infectious at the end of three or four weeks. . . . In addition the virus in a vaccinal suspension is not homogenous but contains viruses which are slightly*

---

[455] Sven Gard, "Prophylactic Vaccination Against Poliomyelitis, translated for and distributed by the Oak Park Health Department, Oak Park, Illinois," *Swedish Physician's Journal*, January 1956. Ref. p. 8 of translation. Provided by Herbert Ratner, MD. Paper in authors' possession.

[456] Sven Gard, "Prophylactic Vaccination Against Poliomyelitis," *Svenska Läkartidningen (Swedish Physician's Journal)*, vol. 53, no. 121(nr3)a, January 1956 (3rd week), translated from Swedish and distributed by the Oak Park Health Department, Oak Park, Illinois. Ref. p. 6 of translation. Courtesy of the estate of Herbert Ratner. Copy in authors' possession.

different in character and have different susceptibility and ability to resist activation.[457]

Safety must be built into the method itself so that it automatically leads to a product of a well-defined quality. Instead of creating a reliably killed vaccine in the 1950s, companies had to rely upon post-manufacture safety tests alone for a vaccine that was known by all involved to consistently have some degree of live virus particles. Dr. Edwin Lennette, director of the California State Department of Health stated that, in general, vaccines could test negative in the lab and in test animals, yet behave differently in humans:

> *You just put in some formaldehyde or whatever and inactivate the virus, and you do a few tests, and if nothing happens in the animal, then you think, well, we've got a vaccine. But you put it into man, who is the ultimate susceptible animal, and then something else goes wrong, and you've got a problem.*[458]

In subsequent years, instead of removing the dangerous Mahoney strain, American manufacturers continued releasing vaccines that were safer but far less antigenic. They tended to the problem, not by addressing the fundamental flaw, but by adding more filtrations of the vaccine. Dr. Gard said:

> ***I am now quite confident that the whole philosophy behind the Salk vaccine . . . is wrong, indeed. When repeated filtrations are applied for removal of "aggregates" one is only hunting ghosts.*** *The effect of filtration is nothing but a gradual removal of virus, live and dead alike. It*

---

[457] Gottsdanker v. Cutter Laboratories (1960) 82 Cal.App.2d 602 (2869:902870:3; 2871: 14–17) .

[458] Edwin H. Lennette, "Pioneer of Diagnostic Virology with the California Department of Public Health," an oral history conducted in 1982, 1983, and 1986 by Sally Hughes, Regional Oral History Office, The Bancroft Library, University of California, Berkeley, 1988.

could just as well be substituted by plain dilution of the vaccine.[459]

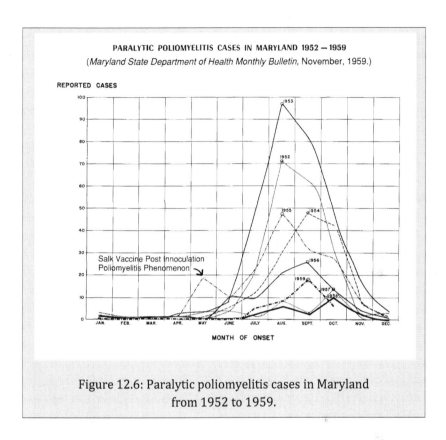

PARALYTIC POLIOMYELITIS CASES IN MARYLAND 1952 – 1959
(*Maryland State Department of Health Monthly Bulletin*, November, 1959.)

REPORTED CASES

Salk Vaccine Post Innoculation
Poliomyelitis Phenomenon

MONTH OF ONSET

Figure 12.6: Paralytic poliomyelitis cases in Maryland from 1952 to 1959.

Even with such effective viral dilution of the vaccine and four revisions to the minimum requirements set forth by the government for producing safe vaccines in 1955, there was ongoing evidence that vaccine-induced infections continued. There were preseason polio (as in vaccine-provoked polio) peaks that were not present before the vaccine years. As you can see in Figure 12.6, 1955 has the largest peak, but 1956–1959 also had preseason increases that were not present in 1954 or earlier. As the years progressed, these peaks were

---

[459] Herbert A. Ratner, "A Premature Salk Vaccine, April 19, 1956," *Child and Family*, vol. 20, 1988, pp. 255–263. Referencing personal letter from Dr. Gard, a copy of which is in the authors' possession.

smaller, due to filtering out both live and inactivated virus, so the vaccines had much lower viral levels.

A lengthy German Scientific Committee report from 1956[460] contains graphs depicting the 1955 preseason peak in Wisconsin, Illinois, Massachusetts, Georgia, Pennsylvania, Colorado, Virginia, Louisiana, Nevada, Oregon, and Idaho.

Not all the vaccine-induced cases were accepted by the Polio Surveillance Unit. Many paralyzed recipients were denied validation and compensation for illness that occurred after the vaccine was given in 1955. The requirements for so-called accepted cases of vaccine-associated polio were more stringent than the requirements for reporting polio in nonvaccinated individuals.[461,462]

For example, only cases that began in the inoculated limb were accepted by the PSU, and only within a very narrow timeframe. The PSU used norms that historically were not so restrictive. Thus, only first-generation infection cases were reported and only if they met the stringent laboratory validation criteria. This would have excluded chain reaction cases that broke out later.

The Salk vaccine was anything but a lifesaver. It was known from the start to be trouble, and trouble it was. Wild poliovirus was never a lone or major cause of poliomyelitis. But even if it was, the Salk vaccine could not possibly have been a solution to ridding the world of polio. Nonetheless, Jonas Salk and his vaccine have been forever cast into heroism in the archives of vaccine mythology.

---

[460] H. Eyer et al., *An Evaluation of the Protective Immunization Against Poliomyelitis,* Report of the Scientific Committee, Social Medicine and Hygiene, 1956. This 102-page document with 22 corresponding graphs is a translation of a larger 492-page German report from an article that appeared in the *Munch Med Wochenschr* April 6, 1956. A copy of English translation is in the authors' possession.

[461] *Poliomyelitis Trends, 1958,* Dominion Bureau of Statistics, Ottawa, Canada, June 29, 1959, p. 1m.

[462] Herbert Ratner, Declaration of Herbert Ratner, Diane Lynn Armbrust Mosley vs. Secretary of the Department of Health and Human Services, October 1, 1992.

Monkey virus contamination

Vaccines manufactured using monkey kidneys up into the 1980s have been definitively noted[463] to contain a carcinogenic monkey virus that some medical researchers believe can result in cancer in a portion of the millions who were given them.[464] Simian virus number 40 (SV40) is a monkey virus that has been found in several types of human cancers, including lung mesotheliomas, several types of brain tumors, and bone, breast, colon, and kidney tumors.[465] Unfortunately, the controversy over the percentage of tumor specimens containing SV40 DNA and proteins has paralyzed the research field. Because of financial and political conflicts of interest, the research necessary to firmly validate the vaccine-virus association will probably never be done.

> *This controversy was magnified by the legal implications of associating the production and distribution of contaminated polio vaccines to the development of human mesotheliomas and brain tumors. Study sections reviewers have been unwilling to support SV40 research citing the need to first address the "controversy," yet without funding it is impossible to conduct studies to address controversial findings.*[466]

SV40 is known to exist in cancerous tissue, but not in surrounding healthy tissue,[467] to cause extensive genetic damage in vitro (cell

---

[463] Rochelle Cutrone, John Lednicky, Glynis Dunn, et al., "Some Oral Poliovirus Vaccines Were Contaminated with Infectious SV40 After 1961," *Cancer Research*, vol. 65, no. 22, November 15, 2005, pp. 10273–10279.

[464] Paola Rizzo, Ilaria Di Resta, Amy Powers, Herbert Ratner, and Michele Carbone, "Unique Strains of SV40 in Commercial Poliovaccines from 1955 Not Readily Identifiable with Current Testing for SV40 Infection," *Cancer Research*, vol. 59, no. 24, December 15, 1999, pp. 6103–6108.

[465] F. Qi et al., "Simian Virus 40 Transformation, Malignant Mesothelioma and Brain Tumors," *Expert Review of Respiratory Medicine*,vol. 5, October 2011, pp. 683–697.

[466] Ibid.

[467] M. Carbone, R. A. Kratzke, and J. R. Testa, "The Pathogenesis of Mesothelioma," *Seminars in Oncology*, vol. 29, February 2002, pp. 2–17.

cultures) and to induce tumors when injected into volunteers[468] and rodents. However, it is not considered scientifically valid to implicate the contaminating SV40 viruses with these human tumors.

> *An association has been found between SV40 and certain types of cancer in humans. However, though the virus or its DNA have been found in certain types of cancer, it has not been determined that SV40 causes these cancers. Finding that two events are "associated" is not the same as establishing that one event caused the other.*[469]

Certain scientists who have had careers in polio and SV40 research know firsthand that inconvenient scientific truths can be abrogated by industry and politics. Two of the world's most respected scientists in the SV40 realm, Dr. Harvey Pass and Dr. Michele Carbone, commented on how science was censored.

> *I [Michele Carbone] wanted to have a press statement . . . and to be able to talk to the media if contacted by them. I also believe that the public and the media have the right to ask us any question they wish once our work has been accepted by a peer-review journal and that scientists should not decide what the media should or should not know . . . [Dr. Levine] told me that if I, or Harvey, talked to the press, against his wishes, we would be "punished." . . . Pass was shocked at the uproar, particularly the threat. "I didn't think you got punished for science."*[470]

There are still the rare truth seekers, like attorney Stanley Kops, who continue to voice opposition to the claims that SV40 is no longer an issue with vaccines.

---

[468] F. Jensen, H. Koprowski, J. S. Pagano, J. Ponten, and R. C. Ravdin, "Autologous and Homologous Implantation of Human Cells Transformed in Vitro by SV40," *Journal of the National Cancer Institute*, vol. 32, 1964, pp. 917–932.
[469] *Vaccine Safety: Frequently Asked Questions About Cancer, Simian Virus 40 (SV40), and Polio Vaccine,* Centers for Disease Control and Prevention, 2012.
[470] D. Bookchin and J. Schumacher, *The Virus and the Vaccine,* St. Martin's, Griffin, New York, 2004, p. 163.

The news article by Nancy J. Nelson repeats the current scientific dogma that simian virus 40 (SV40) was removed from all oral polio vaccine sold and administered in the United States. In a recent article, however, I have challenged this accepted "fact" based on legal documents and the absence of test results from at least one of the principal vaccine manufacturers, Lederle. As noted in that article, internal Lederle documents indicate that the company has not been able to document that it tested all vaccine seeds to confirm the absence of SV40 contamination.

Every scientist who is attempting to determine the role of SV40 as a cause of cancer in humans and every news reporter who is interested in this issue should demand all of the records of both the government and the vaccine manufacturer so that there can be a full scientific and independent investigation as to whether there was full compliance with the removal of SV40 from all oral polio vaccine used in the United States from 1962 until 2000.[471]

How a virus dubbed "the perfect war machine"[472] by Dr. Carbone because it affects at least four major cellular mechanisms that either promote cancer or interfere with cancer-fighting defenses, could be impacting countries that continue using oral polio vaccines by the ton today, is anyone's guess. How much of the abrupt rise in human cancer rates since the introduction of monkey products into the human population is due to SV40 will also remain uncertain due to a lack of precise research.

Monkeys are still used in polio vaccine production today. According to Stanley Kops' allegations, SV40 was and still is a potential risk in both the OPV and the inactivated polio vaccine (IPV). The IPV used in the developed world is still treated with formaldehyde, but SV40 has been known since 1961 to survive formaldehyde beyond the usual

---

[471] S. Kops, "Re: Debate on the Link Between SV40 and Human Cancer Continues," *Journal of the National Cancer Institute*, vol. 94, no. 3, February 6, 2002, pp. 229–230.

[472] D. Bookchin and J. Schumacher, *The Virus and the Vaccine,* St. Martin's, Griffin, New York, 2004.

12-day minimum.[473] Vaccine manufacturers today cite a minimum of 12 days of formaldehyde treatment.[474]

History repeats itself

In India today, as the WHO tracks polio during the vaccination campaigns, reports of paralytic cases associated with wild-type poliovirus have declined, and AFP has increased annually, reaching 60,000 new cases in 2011.

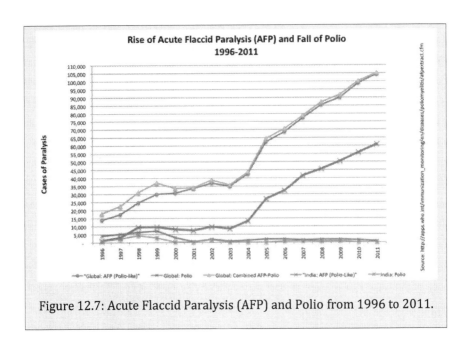

Figure 12.7: Acute Flaccid Paralysis (AFP) and Polio from 1996 to 2011.

The causes of AFP that have been identified are as follows:

---

[473] P. Gerber, G. A. Hottle, and R. Grubbs, "Inactivation of Vacuolating Virus (SV40) by Formaldehyde," *Proceedings of the Society for Experimental Biology and Medicine,* vol. 108, October 1961, pp. 205–209.
[474] Sanofi Pasteur, *Poliovirus Vaccine Inactivated, IPOL,* October 15, 2012, www.fda.gov/downloads/biologicsbloodvaccines/vaccines/approved products/ucm133479, accessed June 17, 2013.

Poliomyelitis, non-polio enterovirus, vaccine-associated polio-myelitis (which can include polio vaccines), rabies virus, vari-cella zoster virus, Japanese encephalitis virus, Guillain-Barré syndrome, cytomegalovirus, sciatic neuritis from injection, transverse myelitis, epidural abscess, spinal cord compression, exotoxin of corynebacterium diptheriae, toxin of clostridium botulinum, Karwinskia, tick bite paralysis, Lyme borreliosis, myasthenia gravis, polymyositis autoimmune, viral myositis, trichinosis, toxic myopathies among others.[475]

In spite of (or perhaps because of) the aggressive OPV campaigns in India, there has been a steep ascent in AFP diagnoses. Nonetheless, the WHO and its sister organizations celebrate because the number of documented cases of *wild* poliovirus-associated paralysis has declined.

It just so happens that DDT is still heavily used in India. Despite the well-documented connection between poliomyelitis and DDT[476,477] symptoms, including anterior horn spinal cord damage, respiratory paralysis, muscle spasm, and weakness, multi-billion dollar polio eradication campaigns march on. Often, an Indian child is vaccinated 15 times (or more) with live vaccine by age five.

In fact, at the end of 2005, **children under 5 years old were reported to have received on average 15 doses of tOPV [triva-lent OPV]** *in UP and Bihar, compared with 10 in the rest of India,*

---

[475] Marx et al., "Differential Diagnosis of Acute Flaccid Paralysis," *Epidemiologic Reviews*, vol. 22, 2000, pp. 298–316.

[476] F. Burgess and G. R. Cameron, "The Toxicity of D.D.T.," *British Medical Journal*, vol. 1, June 23, 1945, pp. 865–871.

[477] M. Biskind, "DDT Poisoning and the Elusive 'Virus X': A New Cause for Gastroenteritis," *American Journal of Digestive Diseases*, vol. 16, no. 3, 1949, pp. 79–84. Paper contains 13 references to the effect of DDT and poliomyelitis symptoms.

and only 4% of children were reported to have received fewer than 3 doses, of whom 90% were under 6 months old.[478]

Pulse Polio is an immunization campaign established by the government of India beginning in 1995 to eradicate poliomyelitis by vaccinating all children under the age of five against poliovirus. The initial goal for India to be free of polio by 2005 was not met. The Pulse program involves setting up vaccine booths in all parts of the country; arranging employees, volunteers, and vaccines; vaccinating children with OPV on National Immunization Days; and identifying children missing from the immunization process.

A major oversight on the part of the press and the medical establishment as they observe the WHO's version of history is that massive "pulse" vaccination campaigns have done nothing to eliminate childhood paralysis and, in fact, there is strong evidence pointing to the likelihood that experimental polio vaccination is related to the sharp rise in AFP. It has been reported in the *Lancet*[479] that the incidence of AFP, especially non-polio **AFP, increased drastically in India after an experimental, high-potency polio vaccine was introduced**. Worse still is that children identified with non-polio AFP are at more than twice the risk of dying than those with wild polio infection.[480] Isn't vaccination really about eliminating paralysis . . . or is it simply to replace wild virus with a vaccine virus regardless of the outcome?

Non-polio AFP rate increases in proportion to the number of polio vaccine doses received in each area. . . . Nationally, the non-polio AFP rate is now 12 times higher than expected. In the states of Uttar Pradesh (UP) and Bihar, which have pulse polio rounds nearly every month, the non-polio AFP

---

[478] Grassly et al., "New Strategies for Elimination of Polio from India," *Science*, vol. 314, November 17, 2006, pp. 1150–1153.

[479] J. Puliyel, C. Sathyamala, and D. Banerji, "Protective Efficacy of a Monovalent Oral Type 1 Poliovirus Vaccine," *The Lancet*, vol. 370, 2007, pp. 129–130.

[480] C. Sathyamala., "Polio Eradication Programme in India," *The Indian Journal of Medical Research*, vol. 125, 2007, pp. 695–696.

rate is 25- and 35-fold higher than the international norms. . . . The non-polio AFP rate during the year best correlates to the cumulative doses received in the previous three years . . . Association of the non-polio AFP rate with OPV doses received in 2009 was 41.9%. Adding up doses received from 2007 increased the association (R2 = 55.6% p < 0.001).[481]

The WHO says that wild polio is declining in India, but will it really be eradicated? It could still circulate in the future, just as it could still be circulating in the United States today. In order to say it is eradicated, they would have to examine the stools of everyone more than just once. However, they only examine the stool of those who develop paralysis—most of whom have been vaccinated with live vaccine virus, which often displaces wild virus in the intestine. Could the increase in AFP in India be the result of the release of so much vaccine virus into the population? Are these people getting more polio paralysis as a result of natural recombination and mutation?

Wild polioviruses, vaccine polioviruses, and neurovirulent Coxsackie viruses can all interact, recombine, and evolve into seriously neurovirulent entities.[482,483,484,485] Why would a vaccine virus be stable and not follow the laws of nature, which involve the clear likelihood of recombination?

---

[481] N. Vashisht and J. Puliyel, "Polio Programme: Let Us Declare Victory and Move On," *Indian Journal of Medical Ethics,* vol. 9, April–June 2012, pp. 114–117.

[482] S. Jegouic et al., "Recombination Between Polioviruses and Co-Circulating Coxsackie A Viruses: A Role in the Emergence of Pathogenic Vaccine-Derived Polioviruses," *PLoS Pathology,* vol. 5, no. 5, May 2009.

[483] R. Crainic et al., "Measles and Poliomyelitis: Vaccine, Immunization, and Control," in *Natural Evolution of Oral Vaccine Poliovirus Strains,* pp. 371–390.

[484] S. Guillot et al., "Natural Genetic Exchanges Between Vaccine and Wild Poliovirus Strains in Humans," *Journal of Virology,* vol. 74, no. 18, September 2000, pp. 8434–1843.

[485] M. M. Georgescu, F. Delpeyroux, and R. Crainic, "Tripartite Genome Organization of a Natural Type 2 Vaccine/Nonvaccine Recombinant Poliovirus," *Journal of General Virology,* vol. 76, September 1995, pp. 2343–2348.

The response to the rise in AFP in India by the WHO and the Global Alliance for Vaccines and Immunisation[486] (GAVI) has been to ramp up the oral polio vaccination campaigns in recent years. Now some children are reported to have received 32 vaccines by five years of age. In the past, there was never such an aggressive effort to inoculate children up to 30 times *for one disease* by their fifth birthday.

> *At a vaccinators' meeting in Sultangunj Referral Hospital held Tuesday, supervisors reported a "new"* **resistance coming from the "educated middle class people"** *who were getting tired of several rounds of immunisation: one family claimed that their* **five year old child had received pulse polio vaccination 32 times**.[487]

Just what are GAVI members trying to accomplish? Does it look like the sustainable health and betterment of India's people are the main goals? Dr. V. I. Agol commented in *Nature* that vaccination against poliomyelitis might have to continue indefinitely.[488]

---

[486] GAVI members include WHO, the World Bank, Unicef, and the Bill and Melinda Gates Foundation, www.gavialliance.org.

[487] "Multiple Doses of Pulse Polio Vaccine Irritate People," *Times of India*, August 25, 2002.

[488] V. I. Agol, "Don't Drop Current Vaccine Until We Have New Ones," *Nature*, June 16, 2005.

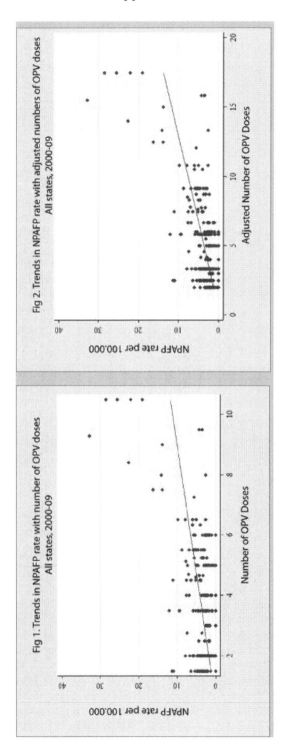

Figure 12.8: Non-Polio Acute Flaccid Paralysis (NPAFP) correlation to Oral Polio Vaccine (OPV).

The charts (Figure 12.7) on the previous page unequivocally reveal how the rate of AFP has risen with the number of OPV doses. Given all the information available to scientists and politicians today and a century of polio literature to reflect upon, one must surely wonder... what in the world are they thinking? The rising numbers of paralyzed children in India deserve a better explanation than "It is for the greater good," because clearly it is not.[489]

Conclusion

By now it should be obvious that there was more to the "polio" story than a crippling virus and a world that was saved by a vaccine. Isn't it strange that the reasoning behind polio epidemics in the United States in the 1940s was increased societal hygiene?[490,491,492] Filth, back then, was thought to be protective against polio! The explanation given was that babies in areas with better hygiene (unlike the native people who were known to be immune without developing poliomyelitis) were not exposed to wild virus early enough due to societal cleanliness and therefore did not develop early natural immunity.

Today India is told that paralytic poliovirus infections are a result of poor societal hygiene. Such doublespeak demonstrates how the tenet changes to accommodate the vaccine agenda and deny the true causes of paralysis.

As of today, no programs have been funded to investigate or validate the scientific findings that implicate associations between chemicals like DDT and arsenic and the syndrome of poliomyelitis. Instead, the

---

[489] "National Polio Surveillance India Data 2000–2010, NPSP Polio Surveillance Data on Acute Flaccid Paralysis (AFP) and Non-Polio AFP and Demographic Data," http://jacob.puliyel.com/download.php?id=248.

[490] Nidia H. De Jesus, "Epidemics to Eradication: The Modern History of Poliomyelitis," *Virology Journal*, 2007, 470.

[491] "Polio," Massachusetts Society for Medical Research, Inc., 2004.

[492] Albert B. Sabin, "Paralytic Consequences of Poliomyelitis Infection in Different Parts of the World and in Different Population Groups," *American Journal of Public Health*, vol. 41, October 1951.

world is reliant upon blemished vintage research that was funded by the major medico-political powers of the first half of the 20th century.

The National Foundation for Infantile Paralysis was overseen by the major medical monopoly, the Rockefeller Institute. Vaccination continues as the sole intervention for the perceived problem of poliomyelitis in India and other undeveloped countries, even in the face of vaccine-induced paralysis, vaccine virus mutations, and obvious failures. When vaccine programs don't live up to their promises, the blame is always placed on the unvaccinated, or a new angle is drawn to the tune of "five vaccines per child may not be enough." By sleight of hand—changing the diagnosis of old-time polio to AFP—any ongoing paralysis will be covered while the dimes continue to roll in.

In addition to the rise in AFP that correlates with rising OPV dosing in India, there are numerous reports of vaccine viruses mutating to virulence, causing polio outbreaks in China, Nigeria, and India. As always, the finger is pointed at under-vaccinated populations rather than at the vaccine itself or the myriad other causes of viral mutation.

> Apart from the resilience of circulating wild-type viruses, major problems have emerged as a result of intrinsic properties of the OPV. It has the propensity to escape its designated role as a protecting immunogen by circulating in poorly immunized populations, thereby evolving into highly neurovirulent poliovirus strains **after recombination with other enteroviruses** (Kew et al, 2005; P. Jiang, J.A.J. Faase, A.E. Gorbalenya and E. Wimmer, unpublished data). This independent occurrence in different parts of the world causes yearly outbreaks of poliomyelitis.[493]

---

[493] E. Wimmer, "The Test-Tube Synthesis of a Chemical Called Poliovirus: The Simple Synthesis of a Virus Has Far-Reaching Societal Implications," special issue, *European Molecular Biology Organization Report*, vol. 7, July 2006, pp. S3–S9.

We often hear that OPV circulating in poorly immunized populations is wonderful because the unvaccinated get the benefit. But OPV vaccines will always be able to recombine with enteroviruses no matter how highly vaccinated the population, and dangerous recombination viruses that cause paralysis will not be called "polio." This is one way that a mountain of new AFP cases builds, while GAVI and WHO celebrate eradication of polio.

Today the GAVI deserves criticism and examination of its goals. This is a time when the developing world needs improved nutrition, clean and chemical-free water, sustainable farms with clean soil, and the luxury of being free from war, famine, and spiritual persecution. If philanthropists want to go down in history as truly making the world a better place, is $10 billion best spent on vaccines?

The Bill and Melinda Gates Foundation will donate $10 billion over the next decade to research new vaccines and bring them to the world's poorest countries . . . they said the money will produce higher immunization rates and aims to make sure that 90 percent of children are immunized against dangerous diseases such as diarrhea and pneumonia in poorer nations. "We must make this the decade of vaccines," Bill Gates said in a statement. "Innovation will make it possible to save more children than ever before."[494]

Perhaps a $10 billion decade of sustainable farming, nutrition, and sanitation would have a long-lasting impact on saving the children under discussion.

The WHO's current strategy calls for cessation of oral polio vaccination three years after the last report of wild poliovirus-induced poliomyelitis.[495]

---

[494] A. Higgins, "Bill Gates Makes $10 Billion Vaccines Pledge," *Huffington Post*, January 29, 2010.
[495] WHO, "Framework for National Policy Makers in OPV-Using Countries," 2005, www.polioeradication.org/Posteradication.aspx, accessed June 17, 2013.

It is ironic that the vaccine on which the world has depended for polio eradication will itself become a risk to eradication once the transmission of wild poliovirus has been interrupted.[496]

If WHO's plan succeeds, the artificially immune herd stands to become the completely non-immune herd, as new children are born who have not been infected with wild-type viruses or even exposed to vaccine poliovirus. This **condition has never existed in human history.** Under these conditions, any reintroduction of poliovirus could be disastrous to this newly virgin population. The people of India, Pakistan, and Nigeria stand to become more vulnerable to viral reintroduction than any population ever before.

During the United States epidemics, roughly 50–80 percent of the population was naturally immune to at least one type of poliovirus. Wild poliovirus alone in healthy people was never a major threat. Natural herd immunity has always been protective (recall Xavante natives). In due time, India's people will have the lowest level of herd protection ever, and in the face of continued DDT use, intramuscular injections of antibiotics, diets high in sugar and low in essential vitamins, and stress, their susceptibility to paralytic disease is enormous.

If poliovirus is reintroduced into the toxic, unhealthy, immunologically naive population—from residual samples stored in laboratories, some of which are highly neurovirulent (recall 1916 New York City); circulating vaccine-derived polioviruses; or poliovirus that is chemically synthesized—the potential outcome is unfathomable.

Today children are forced to submit to vaccines because the WHO and others are just targeting wild poliovirus and not the problem of paralysis. Once this very shortsighted goal is met, there will undoubtedly be future trouble. The WHO knows this and already has

---

[496] D. L. Heymann et al., "A Vision of a World Without Polio: The OPV Cessation Strategy," *Biologicals*, vol. 34, June 2006, pp. 75–79.

considered the steps necessary to deal with the immunologically naive population if viral reintroduction occurs.[497]

History books of the future may reflect upon a disaster with this conclusion: Wild poliovirus should have been left alone and the real sources of paralysis pursued and addressed.

---

[497] WHO, "Framework for National Policy Makers in OPV-Using Countries," 2005, pp. 6–12.

~ 13 ~

WHOOPING COUGH

*The disease is not infrequently complicated by inflammation
of the lungs, and the violent coughing which occurs is apt to produce a harmful dilation of the lung tissue itself. It is by no means
uncommon in underfed children for the disease to be followed by
tuberculosis of the lungs. Cases of paralysis complicating whooping
cough have been reported, and changes in the eye due to hemorrhages
into that organ produced by coughing have also been noted.
It is thus seen that whooping cough, which is estimated killed over
10,000 American children in the year 1911, is a disease seriously
affecting the public health and demanding earnest attention.*

– Dr. W. C. Rucker, Assistant Surgeon General,
United States Public Health Service, 1911

*It may be questioned whether universal vaccination against
pertussis is always justified, especially in view of the increasingly
mild nature of the disease and of the very small mortality.*

– Dr. Justus Ström, 1960

*Most cases of whooping cough are relatively mild. Such cases are
difficult to diagnose without a high index of suspicion because
doctors are unlikely to hear the characteristic cough, which may
be the only symptom. Parents can be reassured that a serious
outcome is unlikely. Adults also get whooping cough, especially
from their children, and get the same symptoms as children.*

– Douglas Jenkinson, 1995

Because whooping cough was once a devastating disease in a large
proportion of children, a campaign to develop a vaccine was under-

taken, but not until after deaths had already fallen to historic lows in the 1940s. From its peak in the 1800s, whooping cough deaths had declined by more than 99 percent before a vaccine was in widespread use.

The national vaccination program began in the United States in the late 1940s and in England by 1957.

Adverse events

Very early on, there were indications of problems. A 1946 article discussed twin boys aged 10 months (D. M. and G. M.) who both died on June 19, 1945, after receiving their second injection of diphtheria and pertussis vaccine.

> *After the second immunizing injections, both infants cried considerably on reaching home; they vomited and consumed excessive amounts of water, each taking about two full bottles. They then "feel asleep" and when next noticed by their parents appeared "lifeless." . . . At 11:30 p. m. when his diaper was changed, he was found to be ice cold and wringing wet with perspiration. The parents explained that they regarded these symptoms as expected effects of the injections and therefore did not summon medical aid until 5:30 a.m., when D. M. appeared to be dead and G. M. gravely ill.[498]*

A 1948 article in *Pediatrics* discussed cases of brain damage following use of the vaccine. The article is hauntingly similar to the large number of cases of autism that would escalate decades later. The children, mostly boys, had been developing normally and showed no problems prior to receiving the vaccine. They manifested "acute cerebral" symptoms within hours of injection. A regression or "failure of further development" occurred afterwards.

---

[498] Jacob Werne, MD, and Irene Garrow, MD, "Fatal Anaphylactic Shock: Occurrence in Identical Twins Following Second Injection of Diphtheria Toxoid and Pertussis Antigen," *Journal of the American Medical Association*, vol. 131, no. 9, June 1946, pp. 731–732.

*Inspection of the records of the Children's Hospital for the past ten years has disclosed 15 instances in which **children developed acute cerebral symptoms within a period of hours after the administration of pertussis vaccine.** The children varied between 5 and 18 months in age and, in so far as it is possible to judge children of this age range, were developing normally according to histories supplied by their parents. None had convulsions previously . . . Twelve of the children were boys and three were girls, a sex difference also encountered in relation to other substances, such as lead, causing gross injury to the developing nervous system. At inoculation time, the children varied in age between 5 and 18 months. Developmental data were obtained in detail on all but two of the children, whose mothers simply stated that they had developed normally. Reference to the case histories showed that such objective activities such as sitting, walking, and talking had appeared in many of the children prior to the inoculations; and the regressions or failure of further development occurred after the encephalopathies [any disease or symptoms of disease referable to disorders of the brain] in several instances. In so far as it was possible to judge none of the children were defective prior to their acute illness.*[499]

The authors discussed these children's cases at length. At the end of their paper, they conclude that the risk of the vaccine seems too great if the only thing to be avoided was "the average attack of pertussis." At the time of their paper, death from whooping cough had become relatively rare.

In common with many other biologic materials used parenterally [not by mouth], an important risk of encephalopathy attends the use of prophylactic pertussis vaccine . . . The universal use of such vaccine is warranted only if it can be

---

[499] Randolph K. Byers, MD, and Frederic C. Moll, MD, "Encephalopathies Following Prophylactic Pertussis Vaccine," *Pediatrics*, vol. 1, no. 4, April 1948, pp. 438–439, 443.

shown to be effective in preventing encephalopathy or death from pertussis itself in large groups of children. **If avoidance of the inconvenience of the average attack of pertussis is all that is expected, the risk seems considerable.** *Efforts to diminish the hazard by modification of the vaccine or new methods of administration seem indicated.*[500]

As use of the DTP vaccine widened, reports in medical journals that focused on the serious consequences from the vaccine also became more common. Even though some authors determined that there were no problems or that they were rare, others reported significant neurologic damage. In 1958 Dr. Berg reported on a case of mental retardation following the use of the vaccine.

A case is reported of an 8-months-old normal child who, within 24 hours of a combined diphtheria-pertussis inoculation, became pyrexial [with fever], drowsy, and hypotonic. Convulsions and evidence of mental deterioration followed rapidly. At 3 years of age convulsions still persisted and mental retardation was gross. (I.Q. = 23).[501]

Dr. Berg noted that, although some recovered after a serious reaction, others were left with permanent damage or died.

Since Madsen (1933) first drew attention to the possibility of serious consequences following active immunization against whooping-cough, **reports of neurological sequelae [secondary consequences] of such immunization have come from various parts of the world. These sequelae have ranged from transient convulsions with complete recovery to gross crippling, mental retardation, and death.**[502]

---

[500] Randolph K. Byers, MD, and Frederic C. Moll, MD, "Encephalopathies Following Prophylactic Pertussis Vaccine," *Pediatrics*, vol. 1, no. 4, April 1948, p. 444.
[501] J. M. Berg, "Neurological Complications of Pertussis Immunization," *British Medical Journal*, July 5, 1958, p. 27.
[502] Ibid., p. 24.

Since whooping cough had become much milder and there was an increased risk of neurologic complications from vaccination, the necessity of vaccination at all was intermittently called to question. For example, this 1960 paper by Dr. Justus Ström, once again questioned the idea of universal vaccination.

> In the light of these circumstances the attitude to vaccination cannot be the same in all countries. When there is a risk, and when the neurological complications may either be fatal or lead to serious consequences for the individual and the family, the situation needs to be reconsidered. Thus **it may be questioned whether universal vaccination against pertussis is always justified, especially in view of the increasingly mild nature of the disease and of the very small mortality.** I am doubtful of its merits at least in Sweden, and I imagine that the same question may arise in some other countries. We should also remember that the modern infant must receive a large number of injections and that a reduction in their number would be a manifest advantage.[503]

Dr. Ström detailed the neurologic problems after vaccination and noted that complications were higher from vaccination than from naturally acquired disease.

> In Sweden, as in several other countries, neurological complications after pertussis (triple) vaccination have been observed. A nation-wide investigation showed that 36 cases of such complications had occurred in about 215,000 vaccinated children (1 in 6,000) during 1955-8. Most of these consisted of convulsions, coma, or collapse, and the children were restored to health; but there were four deaths, of which two were sudden, and nine cases indicative of encephalopathies with severe lesions (1 in 17,000). **An investigation of the incidence of neurological complications after pertussis [natu-**

---

[503] Justus Ström, "Is Universal Vaccination Against Pertussis Always Justified?" *British Medical Journal*, October 22, 1960, p. 1186.

ral disease] showed that this was not so high as after vaccination.[504]

Dr. Ström was not the only professional calling for discontinuation of pertussis vaccination. In 1981 Dr. Gordon Stewart stated that vaccination was not justified because most cases of whooping cough were mild and recovery provided lasting immunity.

> *In the United Kingdom and in many other countries, whooping cough (and measles) are no longer important causes of death or severe illness except in a small minority of infants who are usually otherwise disadvantaged. In these circumstances, I* **cannot see how it is justifiable to promote mass vaccination of children everywhere against diseases which are generally mild, which confer lasting immunity, and which most children escape or overcome easily without being vaccinated.**[505]

In 1979 four infants died within 24 hours of receiving a specific lot of the DTP vaccine. A report noted that the vaccine had been tested before its release and that the tests were found to be "satisfactory."

> *On March 9, 1979, the Tennessee State Department of Public Health reported to CDC 4 deaths in infants 2 to 3 months of age who had received within 24 hours of their deaths a dose of DTP vaccine from a single lot, No. 64201, manufactured by Wyeth Laboratories, Inc. . . . Autopsies were performed on 2 children, and all 4 deaths were listed as unexplained sudden infant deaths on the death certificates . . . An investigation of unexplained sudden infant deaths in Tennessee during the periods August 1977 through March 1978 through March 1979 revealed 74 and 77 deaths, respectively . . . Eight deaths*

---

[504] Justus Ström, "Is Universal Vaccination Against Pertussis Always Justified?" *British Medical Journal*, October 22, 1960, p. 1186.
[505] Gordon T. Stewart, "Whooping Cough in Relation to Other Childhood Infections in 1977–9 in the United Kingdom," *Journal of Epidemiology and Community Health*, vol. 35, 1981, p. 145.

had occurred within 1 week of vaccination in the 1978-79 period; 2 were recorded in the 1977-78. Of the 151 infants who died suddenly, the proportion who had received DTP immunization in public clinics was significantly higher for the 1978-79 period.[506]

On March 11, just a couple of days after the report, Tennessee withdrew lot No. 64201 from public clinics within that state. The *Morbidity and Mortality Weekly Report* (MMWR) on March 21 stated that Wyeth Laboratories withdrew this bulk lot from further distribution and use in the United States. It was not specified if that lot was destroyed.

A follow-up report confirmed that 4 deaths occurred within 24 hours after receipt of vaccine from lot 64201. The report also noted that among the data on 114 children who died at 6 weeks of age or older, there was a significantly higher proportion "who had ever received DTP immunization." An editorial note concluded that there was no suggestion of greater risk of sudden deaths with other DTP lots and that the "cluster of deaths in Tennessee in possible association with 1 particular lot of DTP vaccine should not interfere with current recommended childhood immunization practices."[507]

Most medical experts continued to ignore these reports and insisted that the vaccine only rarely led to neurologic problems. To them, any encephalopathy was thought to be a mere coincidence that would have occurred even without the vaccine. Most authorities concluded that permanent brain damage as a result of DTP was a myth. As had occurred with the smallpox vaccine years earlier, there was a medical bias against admitting that a heavily promoted medical procedure was actually harmful.

---

[506] "DTP Vaccination and Sudden Infant Deaths—Tennessee," *MMWR*, vol. 28, no. 11, March 23, 1979, pp. 131–132.

[507] "Follow-Up on DTP Vaccination and Suddent Infant Deaths—Tennessee, *MMWR*, vol. 28, no. 12, March 30, 1979, pp. 134–135.

Fortunately, there were a few scientists who carefully examined the issue and honestly sought to determine if the adverse outcomes were related to the DTP vaccine. A 1974 study stated that the association between the vaccine and neurologic illness was not mere chance.

> **We do not think, however, that the majority of cases we report here represent a chance association because of the clustering of illness in the 7 days after inoculation, and particularly in the first 24 hours.** *This clustering is outstanding in the records of the Department of Neurology where there has been a sustained attempt to document both the date of onset of all neurological illness and also the timing of inoculations. It is assumed that the pertussis component is responsible because the reactions described after DTP inoculation are similar to those seen after pertussis vaccine alone.*[508]

In order to placate the concerns over the vaccine and determine if they were significantly toxic, a test using mice was developed. This crude test attempted to determine vaccine safety simply by measuring weight loss and "vaccine-related" deaths.

> *Vaccine is tested for toxicity by the mouse weight gain test. For this test, 14- to 16-g mice are injected . . . at the end of 72 hours, the average weight per mouse may be no less than the average weight of the mice before injection . . .* **at the end of seven days there may be no more than 5% vaccine-related deaths of mice in all the toxicity tests performed.**[509]

Although that was the accepted standard test for safety, a 1962 Eli Lily report showed that there was no relationship between that mouse toxicity test and neurologic damage in children.

---

[508] M. Kulenkampff, J. S. Scwartzman, and T. J. Wilson, "Neurological Complications of Pertussis Inoculation," *Archives of Disease in Childhood*, 1974, vol. 49, pp. 48–49.

[509] James D. Cherry, MD MSc; Philip A. Brunell, MD; Gerald S. Golden, MD; and David T. Karzon, MD, "Report on the Task Force on Pertussis and Pertussis Immunization—1988," *Pediatrics*, vol. 81, no. 6, June 1998, Part 2, p. 954.

*It is obvious that severe neurologic reactions have occurred in children after immunization with pertussis vaccines which have passed the toxicity and potency tests currently in use . . . **It was clear that there was no correlation between the mouse toxicity test and the reaction rates in children.***[510]

The debate regarding neurologic damage from the vaccine continued. Many still contended that the risk was low; however, in 1977 Dr. Gordon Stewart wrote that the risk from getting the vaccine was greater than contracting whooping cough.

*Because of the national deficit in epidemiological data and in intelligence, it is impossible to estimate the prevalence of the pertussis reaction syndrome or of subsequent brain damage and mental defect. It is unlikely to be lower than 1 in 60,000, but it might be as high as 1 in 10,000, or in its transient form, still higher. If it is 1 in 20,000 then at least 30 children will suffer permanent brain damage in the U.K. each year and many more might be started, early in life, on the early stages of an organic dementia which, in its ultimate form, has the features of a demyelinating disease and cerebral atrophy. **This risk far exceeds the present risk of death or permanent damage from whooping-cough** or even, in some parts of the country, the chance of contracting it.*[511]

A 1983 study stated that reactions of some type were common and that convulsions occurred in approximately 1 in 1,750 vaccinations.

. . . pertussis vaccine has been noted to be reactogenic, with minor reactions occurring in 50 to 60% of vaccine recipients and convulsions and hypotonic-hyporesponsive episodes occurring in approximately 1:1,750 immunizations. Encephalopathy

---

[510] C. N. Christensen, "Pertussis Vaccine Encephalopathy," *Eli Lilly Report*, 1962, p. 10.

[511] Gordon T. Stewart, "Vaccination Against Whooping-Cough: Efficacy Versus Risks," *The Lancet*, January 29, 1977, p. 237.

has been variously estimated to occur in from 1:6,500 to 1:510,000 vaccines.[512]

This 1980 report tied the use of the DTP vaccine to seizures. The author noted that these severe damages were especially abominable because they originated from a medical treatment performed on perfectly healthy children.

> *. . . since there is **a significant difference between the incidence of spontaneous fits in children of the same age group and the incidence after DTP, a causal relationship between the DTP and the seizures appears to be confirmed**. . . the severe damages are particularly tragic as they are iatrogenic [medically caused] and in most cases affect primarily completely healthy children.[513]*

The Institute of Medicine (IOM) was established in 1970 as an independent nonprofit organization that worked outside of government to provide unbiased and authoritative advice to decision makers and the public. The 1985 IOM report of the U.S. National Academy of Sciences reported on the problem of adverse reactions to the whole-cell pertussis vaccine. The panel estimated that there were 17,994,600 doses of whole-cell vaccine given each year. The result was 7,197,840 cases of minor reactions, 10,283 convulsions, 164 cases of encephalitis, and 58 cases of chronic disability, with costs running into the millions. The panel also estimated that the whole-cell DTP caused two to four deaths per year.[514]

[512] Larry J. Baraff, MD; Wendy J. Ablon; and Robert C. Weiss, MD, "Possible Temporal Association Between Diphtheria-Tetanus Toxoid-Pertussis Vaccination and Sudden Infant Death Syndrome," *Pediatric Infectious Disease*, vol. 2, no. 1, January 1983, p. 10.
[513] O. T. S. Bajc, "Convulsions After Pretussis Vaccination," *Schwiez Med Wochenschr,* vol. 110, December 20, 1980, p. 13.
[514] *New Vaccine Development Establishing Priorities, Volume I, Diseases of Importance in the United States,* Part One of a Two-Part Study by the Committee on Issues and Priorities for New Vaccine Development Division of Health Promotion and Disease Prevention, Institute of Medicine, National Academy Press, Washington, D.C., 1985, pp. 172–173, 175.

As a result of their findings, the IOM recommended a switch to the acellular version, or DTaP, which contained inactivated pertussis toxin (PT) and, depending on the manufacturer, one or more other bacterial components. The hope was that it would greatly reduce the number of reactions by virtue of being a less antigenic substance.

Even after the IOM's objective report, most officials continued to believe that serious reactions were very rare. But in 1991, Professor Wolfgang Ehrengut, a former director of the Institute of Vaccinology and Virology in Hamburg, Germany, wrote that there was a strong bias against believing that central nervous system (CNS) complications followed whooping cough vaccination. His 35 years of studying whooping cough's post-immunization complications qualified him as an expert.

> In conclusion *I am convinced that pertussis CNS complications are a reality and they are, in my view, underestimated.* *The controversy on the legal acceptance of the existence of pertussis vaccine encephalopathy has found its end.*[515]

The primary concern continued to focus on encephalopathy after vaccination. In 1992 analysis of the DTP vaccine showed a connection with encephalopathy whereas the DT shot did not.

> *Significant associations were revealed between encephalopathy and receipt of the DTP vaccine less than 7 days before onset of illness* or between encephalopathy and receipt of measles vaccine within 7-14 days prior to onset of illness, but no association was detected prior to DT vaccination.[516]

---

[515] Wolfgang Ehrengut, "Bias in Evaluating CNS Complications Following Pertussis Immunization," *Acta Paediatrica Japonica*, vol. 33, no. 4, August 1991, p. 426.

[516] Paul E. Fine and Robert T. Chen, "Confounding in Studies of Adverse Reactions to Vaccines," *American Journal of Epidemiology*, vol. 136, no. 2, 1992, p. 127.

The 1993 "Parent's Guide to Childhood Immunizations" published by the CDC promoted the idea that although there could be a reaction to DTP, possible brain damage had "not been proven." The possibility of death from the vaccine was not mentioned. Previous studies, including the 1985 Institute of Medicine report showing 10,300 seizures, 164 cases of encephalitis, 60 cases of chronic disability, and 2 to 4 deaths each year from DTP, must have been missed by CDC's authors.

> *About 1 child in 100 may cry for a long time (3 hours or more) after getting the shot. About one in 1,750 shots a child will have complications. Also, about one child in 1,750 shots may become limp or pale afterwards. These side effects are not long-lasting and have not been known to cause any permanent harm . . . Permanent brain damage has been reported on rare occasions after a child has been vaccinated with DTP. However, most experts believe that a connection between DTP and brain damage has not been proven.*[517]

Evidence of the danger from whole-cell DTP vaccines mounted. Another major report by the Institute of Medicine published in 1994 confirmed that there was a relationship between the DTP vaccine and encephalopathy.

> *Evidence is consistent with a causal relation for acute encephalopathy, shock and "unusual shock-like state."*[518]

Most developed countries use the acellular vaccines, but the whole cell vaccine is still used throughout the world. [519]

---

[517] "Parent's Guide to Childhood Immunization," CDC, 1993, pp. 13–14.

[518] *Adverse Events Associated with Childhood Vaccines: Evidence Bearing on Causality,* Vaccine Safety Committee, Institute of Medicine, 1994, p. 316.

[519] "Recommendations for Whole-Cell Pertussis Vaccine," WHO Technical Report Series, Annex 6, no. 941, 2007, p. 304.

Risk of death from pertussis: History and complete data

The views of Dr. Stewart and other doctors with similar thinking were still in the minority. Those who conceded that the historic severity of whooping cough was unchanged concluded that the benefits of the vaccine somehow must outweigh the risks. This erroneous assumption was based in part on an illusion that the introduction of the vaccine caused the reduction in whooping cough deaths. A lengthy study on whooping cough and the whooping cough vaccine was published in 1988 in *Pediatrics.* The very first paragraph of the paper states the following.

In the United States, pertussis has been successfully controlled by routine mass immunization of infants and children. In the prevaccine era, there were 115,000 to 270,000 cases of pertussis and 5,000 to 10,000 deaths due to the disease each year. During the last 10 years, there have been 1,200 to 4,000 cases and five to ten deaths per year.[520]

That paragraph set the tone for the rest of the article by indicating that thousands of people died each year from whooping cough, but after the DTP vaccine was introduced, very few died. Anyone who believed this statement would, of course, believe in the benefit of the vaccine.

The authors reference a document titled "Historical Statistics of the United States Colonial Times to 1957." From this paper, it was clear that between 1900 and 1934, anywhere from 5,000 to roughly 10,000 people died each year from whooping cough. Another document from the CDC also showed that from about 1970 to the time of the study in 1988, there were approximately 5 to 10 annual deaths from whooping cough. So, in fact, the authors' statement is true. However, it was based on selective data and did not represent the full picture.

---

[520] James D. Cherry, MD, MSc; Philip A. Brunell, MD; Gerald S. Golden, MD; and David T. Karzon, MD, "Report on the Task Force on Pertussis and Pertussis Immunization—1988," *Pediatrics*, vol. 81, no. 6, June 1998, Part 2, p. 939.

In order to examine an issue, it is important to ask the right questions. The title of the paper, "Report of the Task Force on Pertussis and Pertussis Immunization," implies that the focus is on vaccination. The opening paragraph indicates that the vaccine was the only factor in the decline of mortality from whooping cough.

Using the authors' reference documents, it is clear that the most marked decline in deaths from whooping cough occurred before the introduction of the vaccine in the late 1940s (Graph 13.1). Looking at percent decline from peak, the authors' data shows that the death rate from whooping cough in the United States had already fallen by approximately 92 percent before the vaccine was in widespread use and that the vaccine had no appreciable effect on the downward trend.

Data from England and Wales is even more impressive, showing that the death rate from whooping cough had dropped by more than 99 percent before the use of the vaccine. **The belief that vaccination was instrumental in the decline of death is not supported by the data.** Yet when reading the *Pediatrics* paper, the reader—a doctor—would have accepted the belief that the vaccine was the only factor.

This explains the behavior of doctors and their fear of pertussis as it drives them to push the vaccine even on those who don't want it. Doctors do not receive unbiased information in medical school or during their careers. In order for doctors to learn the full truth, they have to seek it and then deal with the resultant cognitive dissonance. It is very difficult to continue practicing medicine under conventional dictates once that truth is accepted.

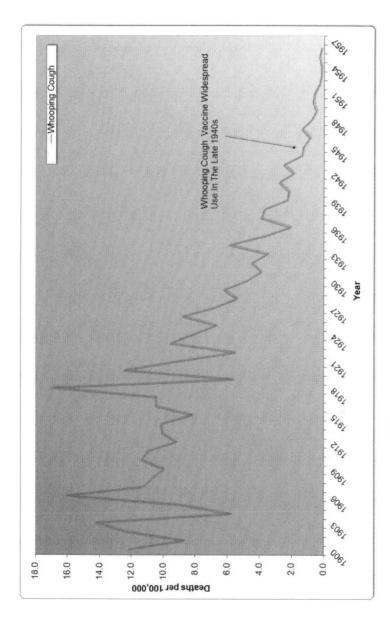

Graph 13.1: United States whooping cough mortality rate from 1900 to 1957.

A thorough examination of the complete official data shows an obvious and dramatic drop in whooping cough deaths between 1902 and 2008. The DTP vaccine coverage rate was officially recorded in England starting in 1970. But by 1957, when vaccination began on a national scale, deaths from whooping cough had already all but vanished (Graph 13.2 and Graph 13.3).

Because of the lower number of deaths in a country the size of England, it is difficult to determine the effect the vaccine may have had, or not had, on mortality prevention (Graph 13.4). However, authors of a 1984 article note that although there was a dramatic decline in vaccination rates in England in the mid-1970s to mid-1980s, there was not an increase in the number of deaths.

> *The 1974-5 outbreak of whooping cough in England affected a population in which 80% of the children had been immunised against pertussis. At that time fears about whooping cough vaccine caused **a dramatic fall in immunisation rates and in consequence a large increase of notifications. Despite this increase the number of deaths has not risen and it has been suggested that the disease may now be less severe.***[521]

A study published in 1984 determined that there had actually been a decrease in whooping cough hospital admissions and deaths after vaccination rates declined. This result was the exact opposite of what should have happened as a result of declining vaccination rates—if the vaccine was truly preventing serious disease.

> *Since the **decline in pertussis immunisation there has been an unexpected fall in whooping cough admissions and***

---

[521] T. M. Pollock, E. Miller, and J. Lobb, "Severity of Whooping Cough in England Before and After the Decline in Pertussis Immunisation," *Archives of Disease in Childhood*, vol. 59, 1984, p. 162.

death rates—a fall that has affected children of all ages and vaccination status.[522]

In Sweden, examinations in 1978 showed that 84 percent of children who were verified to have pertussis had previously received three doses of vaccine. As a result, the whole-cell DTP vaccine was deemed ineffective. Combined with the concerns over its safety, the Swedish health ministry recommended discontinuation of the whooping cough vaccination in 1979.

> *In 1978, 5,140 bacteriologically verified cases of pertussis were reported to the National Bacteriological Laboratory, Stockholm. Investigation of a subsample showed that out of 620 children aged 1-6 years with the disease, 521 (84%) had received three injections of pertussis vaccine. Another investigation disclosed that 84% of 38,015 preschool children born during 1974-8 in various regions of Sweden had been given three injections of pertussis vaccine ... Since the Swedish-made pertussis vaccine evidently lacked protective effect, vaccination was stopped in 1979.*[523]

> *... **confidence in the vaccine was so damaged that it was progressively reduced in potency and finally, in 1979, withdrawn on the grounds it was both ineffective and possibly unsafe.** The incidence of pertussis in Sweden is now returning to that before the immunization era, although the clinical disease is reported to be mild.*[524]

A 1995 letter from Victoria Romanus at the Swedish Institute of Infectious Disease Control indicated that deaths from whooping

---

[522] T. M. Pollock, E. Miller, and J. Lobb, "Severity of Whooping Cough in England Before and After the Decline in Pertussis Immunisation," *Archives of Disease in Childhood*, vol. 59, 1984, p. 164.

[523] B. Trollfors and E. Rabo, "Whooping Cough in Adults," *British Medical Journal*, vol. 283, September 12, 1981, p. 697.

[524] D. L. Miller, R. Alderslade, and E. M. Ross, "Whooping Cough and Whooping Cough Vaccine: The Risks and Benefits Debate," *Epidemiologic Reviews*, vol. 4, 1982, p. 15.

cough remained near zero. Sweden's population was 8,294,000 in 1979 and 8,831,000 by 1995. From 1981 to 1993, 8 children were recorded as dying, with the cause of death listed as pertussis. This averaged to be about 0.6 children per year possibly dying because of whooping cough. These numbers show that the odds of dying from pertussis in Sweden were about 1 in 13,000,000 even when there was no national vaccination program.[525]

---

[525] Letter from Victoria Romanus, MD, PhD, Department of Epidemiology Swedish Institute of Infectious Disease Control, Stockholm Sweden, August 25, 1995.

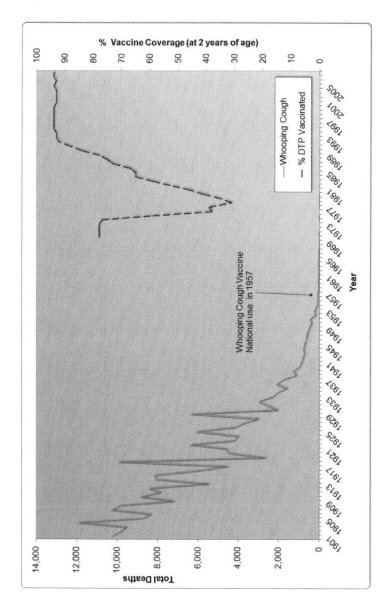

Graph 13.2: England and Wales whooping cough mortality vs. DTP vaccine coverage from 1901 to 2008.

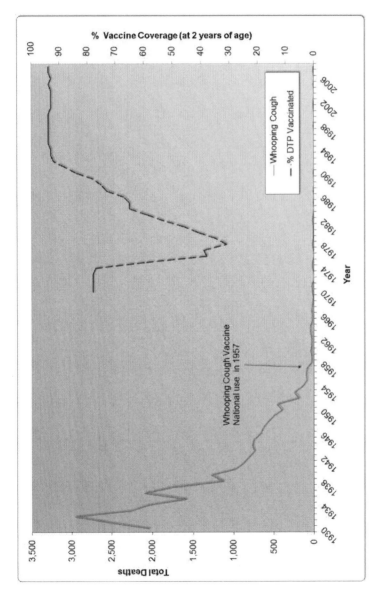

Graph 13.3: England and Wales whooping cough mortality vs. DTP vaccine coverage from 1930 to 2008.

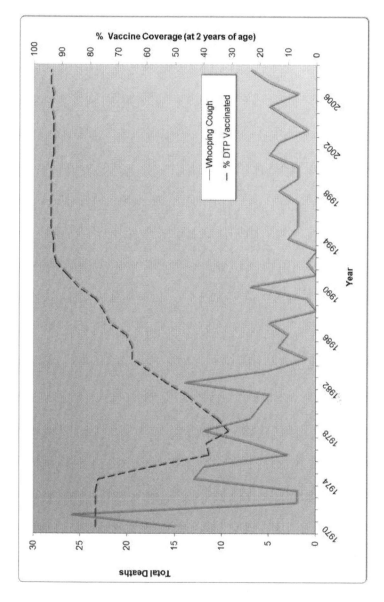

Graph 13.4: England and Wales whooping cough mortality vs. DTP vaccine coverage from 1970 to 2008.

Disease rate decline: Fact and fiction

The vaccine did not have much of an impact on the overall death rate, but the disease rate did *appear* to decline. How much credit should the vaccine receive?

> *When I entered practice in 1921, the death rate from whooping cough was 321.6 per 100,000 infants during their first year of life. This figure steadily declined through the years to reach 1.6 per 100,000 by 1960 and has steadily decreased since then.* **The decline in death rate, which accompanied the decline in incidence, could have been due to several factors including slow loss of virulence of the organism.** *It has been difficult to prove that the use of vaccine has been completely responsible for this diminished incidence.*[526]

Even though the vaccine may impart some small degree of antibody protection to a select few of the numerous antigens and toxins, the biased way in which children were tested could have played a role in the decreased recorded incidence and inflated reputation of the vaccine.[527] In 2012 Dr. Jenkinson commented that pertussis really never went away.

> *The increase in reported cases coincides with similar increases in the US and Australia. A large proportion of this increase is probably the result of better recognition and diagnosis.* **My data provide good evidence that it never went away. What went away was the ability of doctors to recognise it, and in the absence of a practicable diagnostic test, official figures fell** *. . . feedback from people who have had whooping cough indicates that, in the past five years, doctors in the UK, US, and Australia have become more willing to consider the diagnosis in adults. This coincides with the wider availability of a practicable blood test . . .*

---

[526] Edward B. Shaw, MD, "Pertussis Vaccine," *Pediatric Infectious Disease Journal*, vol. 2, no. 3, May/June 1983, p. 265.

[527] J. D. Cherry, "Why Do Pertussis Vaccines Fail?" *Pediatrics*, vol. 129, no. 5, May 2012, pp. 968–970.

I think the Health Protection Agency should be cautious when using its own possibly flawed data . . .[528]

Official statistics have shown a decrease in the incidence of whooping cough; however, the disease is still widespread. In a 1996 seminar on pertussis and pertussis vaccination, Dr. Paul Fine noted just how difficult it can be to diagnose whooping cough. He also pointed out that, because there is a strong belief in vaccination, the bias among doctors and nurses cannot help but skew the results to overestimate vaccine efficacy.

> *I think diagnosing pertussis is difficult. I know that there is **one of the world's pertussis experts in this room right now, medically qualified, whose own child coughed for six weeks before a diagnosis of pertussis was even thought about** . . . I wonder how much we're missing out there?*[529]

A prolonged cough in adolescents and adults may be the only symptom of whooping cough. Many people do not seek medical care for this annoying cough. When they do visit a doctor, their illness is often not diagnosed as whooping cough, in part because the medical community perceives it to be a childhood disease that is controlled by vaccination.

Doctors often do not consider whooping cough in children who are fully vaccinated or in the older population. Official statistics on incidence do not reflect the true amount of circulating whooping cough in persons of all ages.

> *Data generated during the last 15 years suggest that the circulation of B pertussis is occurring in adolescents and adults and*

---

[528] D. Jenkinson, "Increase in Pertussis May Be Due to Increased Recognition and Diagnosis," *British Medical Journal*, vol. 21, August 2012, p. 345.
[529] Paul Fine, MD, "Perspectives on Pertussis Efficacy Studies," Interagency Group to Monitor Vaccine Development, September 22–24, 1996, p. 13.

is manifested by prolonged cough illnesses, which most often go unrecognized as pertussis.[530]

Recent epidemiologic studies have shown that the incidence and prevalence of Bordetella pertussis infection in adults are much greater than previously reported. **In studies of adults with chronic cough, 20 to 25 percent were found to have serologic evidence of recent B. pertussis infection.** *However, pertussis is rarely considered in adults because the signs and symptoms are nonspecific.*[531]

Reports are highest during peak epidemics, partly due to increased cases but mostly due to enhanced awareness and community anxiety that is stoked by the media. Many parents are full of dread and doom, only to find out that the medical system's offer of antibiotics does nothing to alter the severity of the cough and to later discover the much greater power of vitamin C treatment, which they often use on their subsequent children.

There was another contribution to the period of perceived decline in whooping cough, and that involved a policy change in the 1990s. Similar to what happened with polio in 1954, the **case definition of whooping cough was refined in the 1990s, eliminating many cases that would have previously been tagged as pertussis**.

At the time of the pediatric diphtheria and tetanus toxoid and acellular pertussis (DTaP) vaccine efficacy trials in the early 1990s, it was hoped that a universal case definition could be developed so that the results of the various trials could be compared. To this end, the World Health Organization (WHO) case definition was developed. The primary case definition required laboratory confirmation and 21 days of paroxysmal cough. I was

---

[530] James D. Cherry, MD, "The Epidemiology of Pertussis: A Comparison of the Epidemiology of the Disease Pertussis with the Epidemiology of Bordetella Pertussis Infection," *Pediatrics*, vol. 115, no. 5, May 2005, p. 1422.

[531] Jeffrey T. Kirchner, "Manifestations of Pertussis in Immunized Children and Adults," *American Family Physician*, vol. 60, November 1, 1999, p. 2148.

*a member of the WHO committee and disagreed with the primary case definition because it was clear at that time that **this definition would eliminate a substantial number of cases and therefore inflate reported efficacy values**.*[532]

Broken promises

As had been the promise with all vaccines at their inception, there was an expectation that vaccinated people would be protected for life against whooping cough.

The primary course of pertussis vaccination is considered sufficient to confer lifelong protection . . .[533]

Just as the promise of lifelong protection for the other vaccines was never met, it was unmet for whooping cough. It is not readily admitted that vaccination provides inferior immunity, but today it is generally recognized that vaccination does not produce lifelong immunity.

Immunity after [natural] clinical disease is believed to be relatively complete and permanent. Second attacks were documented in the prevaccination era but apparently were uncommon.[534]

*The limited data available on the duration of pertussis vaccine-induced immunity suggest that **vaccinated persons become susceptible to pertussis disease approximately 5-10 years following vaccination**.*[535]

---

[532] J. D. Cherry, "Why Do Pertussis Vaccines Fail?" *Pediatrics*, vol. 129, no. 5, May 2012, pp. 968–970.

[533] *Hugo & Russell's Pharmaceutical Microbiology 8th Edition*, Wiley-Blackwell, 2011, p. 161.

[534] James D. Cherry, MD, MSc; Philip A. Brunell, MD; Gerals S. Golden, MD; and David T. Karzon, MD, "Report on the Task Force on Pertussis and Pertussis Immunization—1988," *Pediatrics*, vol. 81, no. 6, June 1998, Part 2, p. 951.

[535] Dalya Güriş, Peter M. Strebel, Barbara Bardenheier, Muireann Brennan, RaffiTachdjian, et al., "Changing Epidemiology of Pertussis in the United

Experience has shown that the vaccine's efficacy degrades over time. Early studies on the more antigenic whole-cell DTP vaccine indicated that immunity had all but faded in as little as 12 years.

> *The efficacy of pertussis vaccine remains controversial. Social, cultural, nutritional, and therapeutic changes occurred concomitantly with vaccine introduction and partially account for the declining incidence. However, most authors agree that the vaccine is protective, although the relative contribution to control remains undocumented . . . The acceptance of significant risks associated with pertussis vaccine is further complicated by evidence that immunity is not sustained. **Susceptibility to pertussis 12 years after immunization may be as high as 95%, as noted in an epidemic among hospitalized personnel in Cincinnati.**[536]*

A 1993 whooping cough epidemic demonstrated that the illness had shifted from younger to older children. Those who had received the appropriate number of vaccines still became infected.

> *In the 1993 pertussis epidemic in Cincinnati there was a dramatic shift in the age distribution of patients from infants toward older immunized children, adolescents, and adults. **Most disturbing was the occurrence of epidemic pertussis among children who were appropriately immunized for their age.**[537]*

States: Increasing Reported Incidence Among Adolescents and Adults, 1990–1996," *Clinical Infectious Diseases*, vol. 28, 1999, p. 1235.

[536] Roger M. Barkin, MD, and Michael E. Pichichero, MD, "Diphtheria-Pertussis-Tetanus Vaccine: Reactogenicity of Commercial Products," *Pediatrics*, vol. 63, no. 2, February 1979, p. 260.

[537] Celia Christie, Mary L. Marx, Colin D. Marchant, and Shirley F. Reising, "The 1993 Epidemic of Pertussis in Cincinnati—Resurgence of Disease in a Highly Immunized Population of Children," *New England Journal of Medicine*, vol. 331, 1994.

A 2007 study in adults showed that the acellular DTaP vaccine-induced antibodies wane significantly after just one year.[538] In 2004 Dr. Cherry published results from a prospective trial involving 1,793 adolescents and adult subjects who received acellular pertussis vaccines. **Only 20 percent had measurable concentrations of IgG antibodies to pertussis toxin after one month.** Other less specific antigens were also low, at 68, 59, and 39 percent for filamentous hemagglutinin, pertactin, and fimbriae types 2 and 3, respectively.[539] According to the author, antibody to pertussis toxin is specific for past infection with *Bordetella pertussis (B. pertussis)*, whereas antibody to FHA, PRN, and FIM can also be due to infection with other *Bordetella* species. In addition, antibody to FHA may also be the result of cross-reacting antibodies to *Mycoplasma pneumoniae* proteins and other unidentified agents. Thus, anti-pertussis antibody is the most specific antibody measured, and those levels were the lowest of all after only one month.[540]

But the story is even more complicated because, even if antibodies are generated, this does not mean bacteria will be killed. According to Weingart, booster immunization of adults with acellular pertussis vaccines does not necessarily increase bactericidal activity over preimmunization levels.[541] Instead of recognizing the futility in trying to control this endemic disease with vaccines, the conclusion, even in papers that demonstrate the lack of effectiveness and efficacy, is always to vaccinate older people and to vaccinate them often.

---

[538] C. U. Meyer et al., "Cellular Immunity in Adolescents and Adults Following Acellular Pertussis Vaccine Administration," *Clinical and Vaccine Immunology*, vol. 14, no. 3, March 2007, pp. 288–292.

[539] J. D. Cherry et al., "Prevalence of Antibody to Bordetella Pertussis Antigens in Serum Specimens Obtained from 1793 Adolescents and Adults," *Clinical Infectious Diseases*, vol. 39, no. 11, December 2004, pp. 1715–1718.

[540] Ibid.

[541] C. L. Weingart et al., "Characterization of Bactericidal Immune Response Following Vaccination with Acellular Pertussis Vaccines in Adults," *Infection and Immunity*, vol. 68, no. 12, December 2000, pp. 7175–7179.

A very recent study by Dr. David Witt, chief of infectious diseases at the Kaiser Permanente Medical Center in San Rafael, California, found that the DTaP vaccine lost its effectiveness in children in as little as three years.

The whooping cough vaccine given to babies and toddlers loses much of its effectiveness after just three years—a lot faster than doctors believed . . . *"I was disturbed to find maybe we had a little more confidence in the vaccine than it might deserve," said the lead researcher, Dr. David Witt.*[542]

The 2012 study by Dr. Witt and colleagues showed that the majority of children who had whooping cough—as confirmed by laboratory testing—had been vaccinated.

Of the 132 patients 18 years of age or under at time of illness, 81% were fully vaccinated, 11% under-vaccinated, and 8% never vaccinated. Of the 103 individuals 12 years of age or younger 85% were fully vaccinated, 7% under-vaccinated, and 8% never vaccinated.[543]

Contrary to broad medical belief, the disease did not strike the unvaccinated more than the vaccinated as is generally expected by vaccine proponents. The highest incidence of disease was actually in the 8- to 12-year-olds who had previously been fully vaccinated.

Our unvaccinated and under-vaccinated population did not appear to contribute significantly to the increased rate of clinical pertussis. **Surprisingly, the highest incidence of disease was among previously vaccinated children in the eight to twelve year age group. . . Surprisingly, in the 2-7 and 8-12 age groups, there was no significant difference**

---

[542] "Study: Whooping Cough Vaccination Fades in 3 Years," *Associated Press*, September 19, 2011.
[543] Maxwell A. Witt; Paul H. Katz, MD, MPH; and David J. Witt, MD, "Unexpectedly Limited Durability of Immunity Following Acellular Pertussis Vaccination in Pre-Adolescents in a North American Outbreak," *Clinical Infectious Diseases*, March 15, 2012.

in attack rates between fully vaccinated and under- and un-vaccinated children . . .[544]

Some estimate that as many as one-third of adolescents and adults with a prolonged cough are infected with *B. pertussis* bacteria. This applies even to those who have been vaccinated or had natural disease.

> *It is important to note that all 13 studies of adolescents and adults with prolonged cough illnesses have found evidence of B. pertussis infection. These studies have been conducted in 6 countries and 7 geographic areas of the United States over a 16-year period.* ***These data suggest that B. pertussis infection in adolescents and adults is endemic . . .***[545]

> *Although pertussis traditionally has been considered a disease of childhood, it was well-documented in adults nearly a century ago and is currently recognized as an important cause of respiratory disease in adolescents and adults, including the elderly. Because of waning immunity, adult and adolescent pertussis can occur even when there is a history of full immunization or natural disease . . . Studies from Canada, Denmark, Germany, France, and the United States indicate that* ***between 12 and 32% of adults and adolescents with a coughing illness for at least 1 week are infected with Bordetella pertussis.***[546]

Why is whooping cough so widespread when there has been a vaccine available since the 1940s? A 2003 study showed that the

---

[544] Maxwell A. Witt; Paul H. Katz, MD, MPH; and David J. Witt, MD, "Unexpectedly Limited Durability of Immunity Following Acellular Pertussis Vaccination in Pre-Adolescents in a North American Outbreak," *Clinical Infectious Diseases,* March 15, 2012.

[545] James D. Cherry, MD, "The Epidemiology of Pertussis: A Comparison of the Epidemiology of the Disease Pertussis with the Epidemiology of Bordetella Pertussis Infection," *Pediatrics*, vol. 115, no. 5, May 2005, p. 1425.

[546] Edward Rothstein, MD, and Kathryn Edwards, MD, "Health Burden of Pertussis in Adolescents and Adults," *Pediatric Infectious Disease Journal,* vol. 24, no. 5, May 2005, p. S44.

vaccine was nowhere near as effective as generally believed. Although the vaccination rate in New Zealand was at least 80 percent, the effective protection against the disease may have been as low as 33 percent, which indicates that the vaccine has a high failure rate.

> The obtained figures indicate that in New Zealand the effective vaccination rate against pertussis is lower than 50%, and perhaps even as low as 33% of the population. These figures contradict the medical statistics which claim that more than 80% of the newborns in New Zealand are vaccinated against pertussis. This contradiction is due to the mentioned unreliability of the available vaccine. **The fact that the fraction of immune population obtained here is considerably lower than the fraction of vaccinated population implies a high level of vaccination failure.**[547]

Much like smallpox about a century ago and measles more recently, the realization that vaccination is not lifelong has resulted in calls for whooping cough revaccination of eight-year-olds, adolescents, adults, and seniors.

> Although the current rate of immunization uptake is high (estimated at about 93%), Bordetella pertussis continues to cause significant morbidity and mortality. Pertussis is frequently underreported as although culture is very specific it is at best 80% sensitive. The total morbidity and mortality from infection with this organism may be greatly underestimated.[548]

> The epidemiology of pertussis that nearly all physicians learned in medical school has been stood on its head, Dr. John Ogle said at a conference on pediatric infectious diseases

---

[547] A. Korobeinikova, P. K. Mainia, and W. J. Walker, "Estimation of Effective Vaccination Rate: Pertussis in New Zealand as a Case Study," *Journal of Theoretical Biology*, vol. 224, 2003, p. 274.

[548] Sarath Ranganathan, Robert Tasker, Robert Booy, ParvizHabibi, Simon Nadel, et al., "Pertussis Is Increasing in Unimmunised Infants: Is a Change in Policy Needed?" *Archives of Disease in Childhood*, vol. 80, 1999, p. 297.

*in Aspen, Colo. It was formerly believed that infection or immunization conferred lifetime immunity, but it now appears that any resultant immunity is in fact short lived. Thus, there is a growing interest in the selective reimmunization of adults, he said. And, while pertussis was once considered uncommon in adults and older adolescents, it's now believed that the disease is endemic in these populations, who actually serve as the primary reservoir for pertussis, explained **Dr. Ogle, professor of pediatrics at the University of Colorado, Denver. Studies from throughout the developed world suggest 25%-30% of persistent coughing illness in these age groups is pertussis**, he added.*[549]

The frequent occurrence of mildly symptomatic B. pertussis infection in adults refutes the previously held belief that infection-acquired immunity is lifelong.[550]

Protection after natural infection was never lifelong, but it can endure for 30 years, which would yield far better herd immunity than unpredictable, short-lived, and incomplete vaccine-type immunity.

A very noteworthy study was published in 2013, looking at baboons, which are susceptible and manifest whooping cough like humans do.[551] Baboons who were either vaccinated or not vaccinated were later exposed to pertussis bacteria, something that cannot be done experimentally in humans (due to ethical considerations), but which yields very important data. Expectedly, the baboons that had never

---

[549] Mike Bykowski, "Pertussis in Adults," *International Medical News Group*, 1999.

[550] Aaron M. Wendelboe, MSPH; Annelies Van Rie, MD, PhD; Stefania Salmaso, PhD; and Janet A. Englund, MD, "Duration of Immunity Against Pertussis After Natural Infection or Vaccination," *Pediatric Infectious Disease Journal*, vol. 24, no. 5, May 2005, p. S58.

[551] Jason M. Warfel, Lindsey I. Zimmerman, and Tod J. Merkel, "Acellular pertussis vaccines protect against disease but fail to prevent infection and transmission in a nonhuman primate model," Proceedings of the National Acadamy of Sciences, 2013.

been infected got the cough and remained colonized with bacteria for a maximum of 38 days. **Baboons that were previously vaccinated and immune vaccine-style, became colonized upon later exposure for a longer time than the naïve baboons; 42 days. However unvaccinated baboons that recovered naturally and were later exposed to the bacteria did not become colonized at all – zero days.**

So, who is providing better herd immunity in the face of bacterial exposure? Vaccinated individuals who presume they are immune, yet remain asymptomatically colonized for 42 days spreading bacteria? Unvaccinated kids who get infected and remain colonized for 38 days? Or the naturally convalesced who are not able to be colonized and therefore do not spread bacteria at all upon re-exposure? Better still: natural convalescence makes for decades longer, solid immunity than vaccination.

Original antigenic sin committed by vaccination

Before the vaccine era, naturally acquired disease usually provided comprehensive long-term immunity because natural immunity involves a more broad-spectrum response to the entirety of the bacteria and their toxins. Remember that being immune to any degree does not stop the bacteria from flying around and entering the airway. When a naturally immune person reencounters whooping cough bacteria, the body will efficiently respond and clear them from the system. This is not necessarily true of vaccinated people.

The concept of original antigenic sin (OAS) was coined by Dr. Thomas Francis, who became well known during the Salk vaccine era when he oversaw and interpreted the results of the largest (and most controversial) vaccine trial in history. He explained the phenomenon of OAS using natural influenza virus as an example.[552]

---

[552] T. Francis, "On the Doctrine of Original Antigenic Sin," *Proceedings of the American Philosophical Society*, vol. 104, no. 6, December 15, 1960, pp. 572–578.

First, let's define how the body responds to natural infection. When a person gets an infectious disease for the first time, the body's immune system uses its innate powers, which mostly involve cellular immunity. In the process, it prepares for the future. The next time that same infectious agent comes around, the body will use its memory of the first experience so that it can react faster.

But after a vaccine, when the natural microorganism comes along later, the body will act according to how it was programmed by the vaccination—and that is what is meant by original antigenic sin (OAS).

When it comes to B. pertussis, OAS is very important and well described. The bacteria secrete several toxins, one of which only emerges after the infection takes place. That is called adenylate cyclase toxin (ACT). Once whooping cough bacteria attach to cells in the bronchi, a gene in the bacteria switches on, and ACT, which acts like a force field against the immune system, is produced. ACT stops the immune system from recognizing the bacteria by acting as an anti-inflammatory and antiphagocytic factor. This gives the bacteria about a two-week advantage until the immune system wakes up to the fact that it has been duped. **In the case of natural whooping cough immunity, ACT forms the basis of the initial immune response. That front-line immune response is not only critical for eliminating the first round of pertussis bacteria, but it is also crucial for removing bacteria upon later reinfection.**

In natural immunity, the body reacts very strongly to ACT, but because of original antigenic sin and the absence of ACT in the vaccine, the vaccinated are not programmed to respond to it at all. Vaccines do not boost antibody to this toxin, because as of yet, nobody has figured how to put that antigen into the vaccine. The naturally convalesced have more than 17 times the amount of antibody to ACT than DTaP recipients and more than 9 times than DTP vaccinated, as measured after pertussis infection.[553] There is only a miniscule level of ACT antibody in the vaccinated, which is the result of the immune system's paralyzed effort to mount a response after programming by the vaccine.

When a vaccinated person contracts pertussis again, the bacteria can get a good hold because there is little to stop them. The immune system will not respond to ACT in the future, because the programming has been set by the first contact (which was the needle, not the bacteria). Dr. Cherry admitted as much in his 2010 paper.

> *Of particular interest is the lack of a significant ACT antibody response in children for whom the DTP or DTaP vaccines failed. This induced tolerance is intriguing and may be due to the phenomenon called "original antigenic sin."*[554]

Cherry later sanitized the wording when referring to the phenomenon. His new terminology, which pointed to the exact same problem, was changed to "linked epitope suppression."

> *In a previous study, it was observed that children who were DTaP vaccine failures had a blunted antibody response to the nonvaccine antigen ACT, whereas unvaccinated children with pertussis had a vigorous antibody response to this antigen . . . **Linked epitope suppression** applies as the immune response to the new epitopes is suppressed by the strong response to the original vaccine components.*[555]

---

[553] J. D. Cherry et al., "Determination of Serum Antibody to Bordetella Pertussis Anenylate Cyclase Toxin in Vaccinated and Unvaccinated Children and in Children and Adults with Pertussis," *Clinical Infectious Diseases*, vol. 15, no. 4, February 2004, pp. 502–507.

[554] Ibid.

[555] J. D. Cherry et al., "Antibody Response Patterns to Bordetella Pertussis Antigens in Vaccinated (Primed) and Unvaccinated (Unprimed) Young Chidren with Pertussis," *Clinical and Vaccine Immunology*, vol. 17, no. 5, May 2010, pp. 741–747.

This was later affirmed by another doctor in the *Journal of the American Medical Association*.

> *The lesser protection provided by DTaP, both as the initial vaccine or full primary course, may be due to linked epitope suppression, when the initial exposure locks in the immune response to certain epitopes and inhibits response to other linked epitopes on subsequent exposures.*[556]

The reason immunologists and vaccine scientists don't talk about original antigenic sin is because if they had to explain to the public just what it means in principle and in practical fact, they'd have to explain that vaccination breaches a fundamental immunological tenet.

Dr. Humphries: I've personally seen, in unvaccinated families, one child have clinical whooping cough, and the other children did not. When those children had their blood antibodies measured to see if they were going to be a risk to their schoolmates, they were measured as having had experience with pertussis by IgG or both IgM and IgG. In retrospect, some mothers could recall a cold-like illness, and others could not. I mention the fact that they were unvaccinated, not because I believe that is the reason they were infected, but because I believe that is the reason the children had subclinical infections that went unrecognized, and they developed immunity.

They would have to admit that whooping cough vaccine immunity is vastly inferior and that vaccine immunity has immunologic unintended consequences in the future. As an aside, OAS was also a factor in morbidity of the influenza vaccinated when H1N1 infection arrived.[557,558]

---

[556] S. L. Sheridan et al., "Number and Order of Whole Cell Pertussis Vaccines in Infancy and Disease," *Journal of the American Medical Association*, vol. 308, no. 5, August 1, 2012, pp. 454–456.

[557] L. C. Rosella, "Assessing the Impact of Confounding (Measured and Unmeasured) in a Case-Control Study to Examine the Increased Risk of Pandemic A/H1N1 Associated with Receipt of the 2008–9 Seasonal Influenza Vaccine," *Vaccine*, vol. 29, no. 49, November 15, 2011, pp. 9194–9200.

The other reason ACT is important is that it is also a component to parapertussis. If you have recovered naturally from *B. pertussis,* you have high levels of ACT immunity that not only protect you from *B. pertussis* but also are active against *B. parapertussis* and, of course, you won't get that from a vaccine.

Far from being eliminated as a disease, whooping cough is endemic in highly vaccinated populations. It is important to understand that the pertussis vaccine can only prevent serious infection in *some* vaccinated people, but it will never prevent **carriage and spread** in anyone, vaccinated or not. Because of original antigenic sin, the vaccinated will be unable to clear the bacteria as efficiently and, thus, are more likely to be vectors for the disease.

Most people believe that all whooping cough is a serious and easily identifiable disease of children. But the truth is that whooping cough circulates freely, often without ever making a peep.

> *. . . the shortfall in reported disease was due largely to atypical, asymptomatic or forgotten infections. First,* ***recent authors have estimated that an appreciable proportion (e.g. 25%) of infections are asymptomatic (Linneman, 1979), and B. pertussis has repeatedly been isolated from symptomless individuals*** *(Broome, Fraser & English, 1979; Broome et al. 1981; Lambert, 1965; PHLS, 1969). Secondly, given the varied spectrum of clinical response to B. pertussis infection, it is reasonable to suppose that some attacks will not be recognized as whooping-cough.*[559]

The mainstream media only reports, by and large, the supposedly deadly nature of whooping cough. However, in actuality, most cases of pertussis are mild and probably escape reporting.

---

[558] R. Bodewes et al., "Annual Vaccination Against Influenza Virus Hampers Development of Virus-Specific CD8 T Cell Immunity in Children," *Journal of Virology*, vol. 85, no. 22, November 2011, pp. 11995–12000.

[559] P. E. M. Fine and J. A. Clarkson, "Distribution of Immunity to Pertussis in the Population of England and Wales," *Journal of Hygiene*, vol. 92, no. 1, February 1984, pp. 21–26.

Rates of reported pertussis are 40- to 160-fold less than actual illness rates, and asymptomatic infections are 4–22 times more common than symptomatic infections.[560]

Portraying disease as severe, whether it is or not, is admittedly done because it helps to increase vaccine uptake. Recent CDC PowerPoint presentations[561] reveal this tactic with influenza, and doctors have written about it regarding pertussis as well.

Publicity given to the more severe consequences of whooping cough has created a widely held perception that the disease is always severe, debilitating, and dangerous. Such a perception helps to encourage immunization, but if untrue it degrades diagnostic accuracy...[562]

There was the fear that this would interfere with many other forms of immunization which are far more beneficial and important to the infant. Those who expressed their disagreement with the broadcast conclusions stated that it might have the effect of increasing the incidence of death from pertussis and urged and secured publicity of opinions favoring continued use of the vaccine.[563]

Conclusion

By the mid-1900s, whooping cough deaths had declined by more than 99 percent. The fact that all infectious disease mortality had also declined was noted in a report by Gordon T. Stewart in 1981.

---

[560] J. D. Cherry, "Epidemiology of Pertussis," *Pediatric Infectious Disease Journal*, vol. 25, no. 4, April 2006, pp. 361–362.

[561] Glen Nowak, PhD, "Communicating in Changing and Difficult Communication Environments," 2005 Safer Healthier People, CDC; "Planning for the 2004–05 Influenza Vaccination Season: A Communication Situation Analysis," CDC, DHHS.

[562] D. Jenkinson, "Natural Course of 500 Consecutive Cases of Whooping Cough: A General Practice Population Study," *British Medical Journal*, vol. 310, Februrary 1995, pp. 299–302.

[563] Edward B. Shaw, MD, "Pertussis Vaccine," *Pediatric Infectious Disease Journal*, vol. 2, no. 3, May/June 1983, p. 265.

*Historically, the dominant and obvious fact is that most, if not all, major communicable diseases have become less serious in all developed countries for 50 years or more. Whooping cough is no exception. It has behaved in this respect like measles and similarly to scarlet fever and diphtheria, in each of which at least **80% of the total decline in mortality, since records began to be kept in the United Kingdom in 1860, occurred before any vaccine or antimicrobial drugs were available and 90% or more before there was any national vaccine progamme.**[564]*

Instead of acknowledging the true cause for this extraordinary mortality decline before vaccination took hold, the medical profession embraced vaccination as a profitable and core medical tool. The problems with vaccines were consigned to oblivion or ensconced—and ultimately replaced with myth. Few ever bother to investigate or consider that anything else happened besides what they've been told.

Vaccination is not a simple, straightforward cut-and-dry issue. It is complicated. The diseases are complicated and, moreover, the immune system is very superficially understood by even the most accomplished immunologists today.

. . . "the immune system remains a black box," says Garry Fathman, MD, a professor of immunology and rheumatology and associate director of the Institute for Immunology, Transplantation and Infection . . . "Right now we're still doing the same tests I did when I was a medical student in the late 1960s . . ." It's staggeringly complex, comprising at least 15 different interacting cell types that spew dozens of different molecules into the blood to communicate with one another and to do battle. Within each of those cells sit tens of thousands of genes whose activity can be altered by age, exercise, infection, vaccination status, diet, stress, you

---

[564] Gordon T. Stewart, "Whooping Cough in Relation to Other Childhood Infections in 1977–9 in the United Kingdom," *Journal of Epidemiology and Community Health*, vol. 35, 1981, p. 144.

name it. . . . That's an awful lot of moving parts. And we don't really know what the vast majority of them do, or should be doing . . . **We can't even be sure how to tell when the immune system's not working right, let alone why not, because we don't have good metrics of what a healthy human immune system looks like. Despite billions spent on immune stimulants in supermarkets and drugstores last year, we don't know what—if anything—those really do, or what "immune stimulant" even means.**[565]

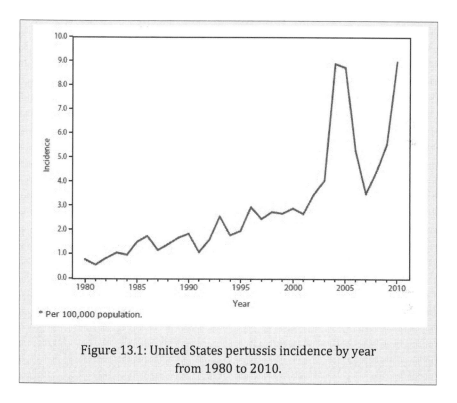

Figure 13.1: United States pertussis incidence by year from 1980 to 2010.

Every infectious disease cannot be viewed through the same lens or measured by the same standard of comparison. Some, like smallpox, were eliminated by an improved hygienic environment. Others, like poliovirus, were fallaciously blamed for sicknesses they were

---

[565] B. Goldman, "The Bodyguard: Tapping the Immune System's Secrets," *Stanford Medicine*, Summer 2011.

not totally responsible for. Some will never be eliminated by any mechanism.

Whooping cough reports are now increasing despite very high vaccination rates (Figure 13.1). In fact, the disease rates, especially in young infants today, are even higher than they were when vaccine uptake was much lower. It wasn't until 1978 that pertussis vaccination was required for school entry in the United States, but at the same time infants of age six to eight weeks began to be vaccinated routinely.

How many whooping cough shots did children get when you were growing up? Now we are in a situation where whooping cough vaccines are pretty much a regular event, cradle to grave, and the incidence of clinical whooping cough today—in the most heavily vaccinated populations—is increasing, inciting panic where the drug-sponsored media ramps up unnecessary fear.

In the midst of all the panic and revaccinations, vaccine resistance by pertussis bacteria is now emerging. The prolonged whooping cough epidemic in Australia that began in 2008 has predominantly been caused by a new genotype of *B. pertussis*. The strain was responsible for 31 percent of cases in the 10 years before the current epidemic, but has accounted for 84 percent since. This represents a nearly three-fold increase, indicating that the bacteria have genetically evolved under the selection pressure from the present vaccine. Dr. Lan of the

> **Dr. Humphries**: Generally speaking, antibiotic-treated children fare no better than their untreated counterparts. In my experience they often fare worse. Breastfeeding makes a major difference in how well the child handles the infection. Infants as young as two weeks of age have fared quite well at home with the vitamin C treatment and breast milk alone. This makes sense given that antibiotics alter the bowel immunity and, during the dying off of bacteria in the gut, release even more toxin into the already toxic child.

2012 study has been quoted[566] as saying that the vaccine is less effective against the evolving strain, and any immunity that is gained wanes rapidly.[567] Pertussis bacterial vaccine resistance has also begun to be reported in the United States.

How futile does it seem to keep battling and essentially strengthening such a huge and potentially innocuous force with clumsy weapons? Properly managed, natural whooping cough is but an irksome nuisance that will impart true and lasting immunity upon the convalesced. However, through the onslaught of vaccination, the herd was robbed of its ability to efficiently deal with this disease.

The future could bring a continuous evolution of vaccine-resistant strains that will no doubt require newer pertussis vaccines. In fact, the development of live inhaled pertussis vaccines for newborns has already occurred.[568] You would think that one live intranasal vaccine would be enough to impart long-term immunity in a newborn. But apparently, it isn't. This new vaccine is going to be added to the already dysfunctional pertussis vaccination program.

The reason that the live intranasal vaccines can't be enough to provide herd immunity, even if they could provide full-spectrum long-term immunity, has to do with how the rest of the population has been programmed with vaccines—committing original antigenic sin.

Adults, whose immune systems were only primed for "back end" immunity rather than for ACT and numerous surface antigens, can no longer respond in any other way. So, an intranasal vaccine won't give front-end immunity to adults any more than re-exposure to

---

[566] J. Norrie, "Vaccine Resistant Whooping Cough Takes Epidemic to New Level," *The Conversation*, March 21, 2012.

[567] Octavia et al., "Newly Emerging Clones of Bordetella Pertussis Carrying Prn2 and Ptxp3 Alleles Implicated in Australian Pertussis Epidemic in 2008–2010," *Journal of Infectious Diseases*, vol. 205, no. 8, April 15, 2012, pp. 1220–1244.

[568] R. Cornford-Nairns, "Construction and Preliminary Immunobiological Characterization of a Novel, Non-Reverting, Intranasal Live Attenuated Whooping Cough Vaccine Candidate," *Journal of Microbiology and Biotechnology*, vol. 22, no. 6, 2012, pp. 856–865.

whooping cough or booster injections would. Given that booster shots don't increase the bactericidal qualities in the blood and do contribute to bacterial resistance, why even recommend them? Until those DTaP-vaccinated adolescents and adults die, they will be the main source of carriage and spread in the community—whether a safe, live, effective vaccine is put to broad use or not.

There's still another problem with pertussis vaccines, and that is that the vaccines themselves are now a source of false-positive pertussis PCR tests.[569] How do you think this complicates the doctor's task, and how is it affecting humanity overall, given the rampant and unnecessary use of antibiotics for all cases that test positive?

The paradox is that the incidence of *B. pertussis* has increased again as the vaccine era has progressed, but mortality was down significantly long before the vaccine was deployed. The decline in mortality was not due to antibiotics. Conventional medical literature acknowledges that antibiotics do not necessarily decrease the severity of the disease, and when the drugs are given they are prescribed not to treat the disease but to decrease the length of contagion. Antibiotic treatment is believed to be effective in improving the course of the disease if started early. However, some studies have found that antibiotic treatment has the opposite effect and actually prolongs the illness.[570] Antibiotic-treated children can have a duration of cough 6 to 11 days longer and spasmodic cough 4 to 13 days longer than untreated patients.[571]

If vitamin C in adequate doses was given to children, and even the youngest infants with pertussis, the reputation of *B. pertussis* as the devastating 100-day cough would fade away. Parents would also be less likely to fall victim to pressure by the medical system's ac-

---

[569] Hossein et al., "Aerosolized Vaccine as an Unexpected Source of False-Positive Bordetella Pertussis PCR Results," *Journal of Clinical Microbiology*, vol. 50, no. 2, February 2012, pp. 472–474.

[570] A. E. Tozzi et al., "Clinical Presentation of Pertussis in Unvaccinated and Vaccinated Children in the First Six Years of Life," *Pediatrics*, vol. 112, no. 5, November 2003, pp. 1069–1075.

[571] Ibid.

ceptance of a vaccine that imparts only short-lived and partial protection. And who would benefit from that?

If whooping cough is commonly a mild disease and apt to be missed, what are the implications for clinical practice? If whooping cough was perceived as a less severe disease, it might have a negative effect on vaccination uptake. If more people understood that the incidence of whooping cough has increased with increasing vaccines, bacterial resistance is emerging, and there is a nontoxic treatment available, surely vaccine uptake would decline further. Since early diagnosis is difficult and treatment with antibiotics is not sufficiently effective.[572] a reevaluation of the necessity of the entire medical approach is warranted. But that won't happen until the "delicate fabric" of interlaced pharmaceutical companies, government, and academia becomes torn. The following conclusion from a special article by the National Vaccine Advisory Committee should indicate to you exactly whose best interests are at the core of vaccine policy.

Collaboration and cooperation of government agencies, such as NIH, CDC, FDA, USAID, DOD, large vaccine companies, small research companies, and academia are essential to continue success and fulfill the promise of recent advances in science and technology.

Threats to any part of the delicate vaccine research and development network *jeopardize the rapid development and supply of new life-saving and life-enhancing vaccines for the American people. What is the optimal size, scope, and configuration of the US vaccine enterprise? These questions should be debated only in the context of a full understanding of how the current system works and its record of effectiveness. These National Vaccine Advisory Committee recommendations **will help to ensure that public policies take into consideration this research and development network and foster and sustain it** to facili-*

---

[572] D. Jenkinson, "Natural Course of 500 Consecutive Cases of Whooping Cough: A General Practice Population Study," *British Medical Journal,* vol. 310, Februrary 1995, pp. 299–302.

tate the timely introduction and supply of new vaccines.[573]

When the function of academic research is to foster and sustain a delicate fabric of collaboration, no one will bite any hand that feeds them—particularly in the climate that exists today.

> *To serve the public interest, government advisory committees must be independent of industry, but such committees cannot be relevant and effective if isolated from the expertise and experience of the industry, which is the principal funder of vaccine research and development.*[574]

Until this political triangle is broken, parents must know that the health of their children rests upon their own research and good judgment.

---

[573] E. K. Marcuse, "United States Vaccine Research: A Delicate Fabric of Public and Private Collaboration," *Pediatrics*, vol. 102, no. 4, Part 1, October 1998, pp. 1002–1003.

[574] E. K. Marcuse, "United States Vaccine Research: A Delicate Fabric of Public and Private Collaboration," *Pediatrics*, vol. 102, no. 4, Part 1, October 1998, pp. 1002–1003.

~ 14 ~

MEASLES

First in 1935, I was in private practice in the coal-mining town of Bedlington, England when the triennial measles epidemic struck. Walking or cycling, I would visit the homes of sick children, and in one day would see 20-30 new measles cases. Those were the Depression years, and the children's diets were decidedly subnormal. It was also the days before antibiotics, so that the treatment was mostly symptomatic and ineffectual. Yet out of more than 500 sick children under my care, not a single one died.

– Aidan Cockburn (1912–1981), 1971

For over 100 years, there has been a strong association with vitamin A deficiency and adverse measles outcomes, especially in young children. Has the time come for the medical community to recognize that any child presenting with measles complications should be given vitamin A and evaluated for overall nutritional status? If not, what has history taught us?

– Adrianne Bendich, 1992

Introduction

Throughout the 1800s, measles epidemics occurred about every two years in the United States and England. During these epidemics, some hospital wards overflowed with children, up to 20 percent of whom died. However, by the 1960s, the deaths had dropped to extremely low numbers in both England and the United States (Graph 14.1). In England, the percent decline from its peak level reached an astonishing 99.96 percent by the time the vaccine was introduced in 1968 (Graph 14.2).

> *Before the general nutrition status of European children reached the high level it is today, measles infection was*

337

something to be feared . . . measles accounted for 11% of all deaths in Glasgow in the years 1807-1812. Case fatality rates were high. For example, during the years 1867-1872 in a Paris orphanage, the Hospice des Enfants Assistés, 612 of the 1256 (49%) children who developed measles died . . . During the last century, the burden of measles had dropped remarkably in Europe. In Glasgow, 14.2% of children younger than 5 years of age contracted measles in 1908 and had a mortality rate of 5.8%. Even in the absence of a vaccine, by 1960, notification of childhood measles in England and Wales was only 2.4% and mortality fell to 0.030%, which is 1/200th of the 1908 Glasgow mortality rate.[575]

In England and in the United States, the chance of dying from measles had dropped to 1–2 percent by the 1930s.[576]

Many think that antibiotics were responsible for the vast decline in mortality. For measles, scarlet fever, typhoid, whooping cough, and diphtheria, the overall downward trend in mortality was unaffected by the introduction of penicillin, which was not mass produced until 1944 (Graph 14.3 and Graph 14.4).

Word of the measles vaccine development effort was out by the late 1950s. In anticipation, by the early 1960s news reports emphasized the potential seriousness of the disease. This *New York Times* report highlighted the number of deaths each year from measles.

Measles is more feared for its complications than for itself. It renders its victims highly susceptible to other infections. It seems to nullify the patient's resistance to tuberculosis. The most dread complication is encephalitis, which attacks the brain and spinal cord . . . In the United States alone, it is estimated that 1,000,000 persons a year get measles. The

---

[575] Clive E. West, PhD, DSc, "Vitamin A and Measles," *Nutrition Reviews*, vol. 58, no. 2, February 2000, p. S46.
[576] Richard D. Semba, "Vitamin A as 'Anti-Infective' Therapy, 1920–1940," *American Society for Nutritional Sciences*, 1999, p. 786.

National Office of Vital Statistics reported that in 1960 there were 410 deaths from measles.[577]

The news report indicated the total number of deaths but failed to mention that, when normalized to deaths per 100,000, that number had nearly bottomed out and would likely continue to drop even more. The official 1960 number of deaths from measles in the United States was recorded as 380, with the population during that year at 180,671,000. This equaled a mortality rate for measles of 0.24 per 100,000. Statistics from 1963 show that, relative to many other causes of death, measles was extremely low.[578] By the year of the *New York Times* report, the US measles death rate had plummeted by more than 98 percent from that peak.

When the measles vaccine was licensed in 1963, the measles death rate in Massachusetts had reached zero (Graph 14.5). Similarly, in Washington State, as in other locations throughout the Western world, the measles death rate had been steadily trending toward zero for years (Graph 14.6). By 1963 Washington State had a measles death rate of 0.3 per 100,000.

In 1963 some New England states had no deaths at all from measles. During this year, the whole of New England had only 5 deaths attributed to measles. Deaths from asthma were 56 times greater, accidents 935 times greater, motor vehicle accidents 323 times greater, other accidents 612 times greater, and heart disease 9,560 times greater.[579]

---

[577] William L. Laurence, "Measles Vaccine: Tests with Live and Killed Virus Are Reported 96% Effective," *New York Times*, November 19, 1961.
[578] *Vital Statistics of the United States 1963, Vol. II—Mortality, Part A,* pp. 1–18, 1–19, 1–21.
[579] Ibid.

State	Measles	Asthma	Accidents	Motor Vehicle Accidents	Other Accidents	Heart Disease
Maine	1	41	514	194	320	4,734
New Hampshire	0	21	305	132	173	2,937
Vermont	3	11	222	110	112	1,871
Massachusetts	0	138	2,299	714	1,585	23,611
Rhode Island	1	28	341	103	238	4,356
Connecticut	0	44	998	366	632	10,301
New England	5	283	4,679	1,619	3,060	47,804

Table 14.1: Causes of death in six New England states in 1963.

High measles death rates are still reported in countries where children are undernourished and lack the vitamins and nutrients necessary to support the immune system. Yet statistics on measles mortality never distinguish the countries with good nutrition from those without, which leads the public to believe that measles is still something to fear. Child mortality due to measles is 200 to 400 times greater in malnourished children in less developed countries than those in developed ones. In addition, measles brings about consumption of nutrients in marginally nourished children, so they will also do worse if not supplemented during infection.[580] As nutrition improves, complications from measles diminish.

---

[580] M. Gabr, "Undernutrition and Quality of Life," *World Review of Nutrition & Dietetics,* vol. 49, 1987, pp. 1–21.

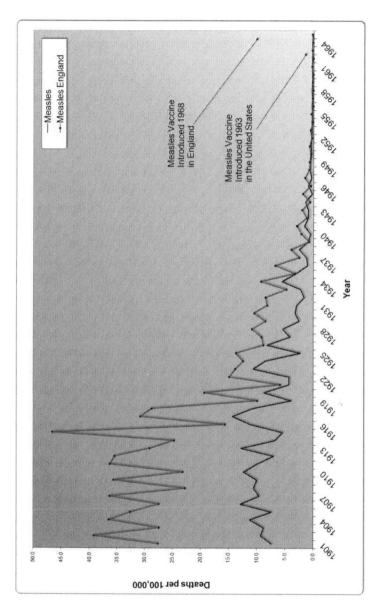

Graph 14.1: Comparison United States and England in mortality rates for measles from 1901 to 1965.

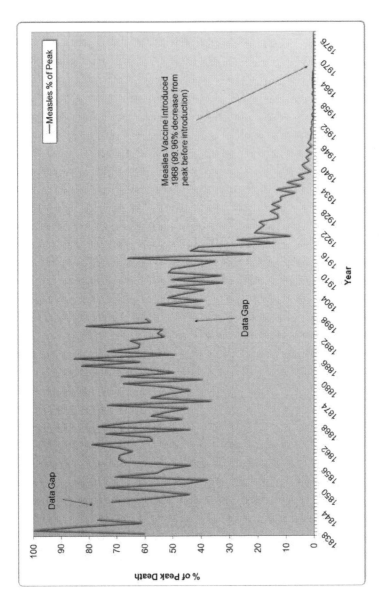

Graph 14.2: England percent decline in mortality rate for measles from 1838 to 1978.

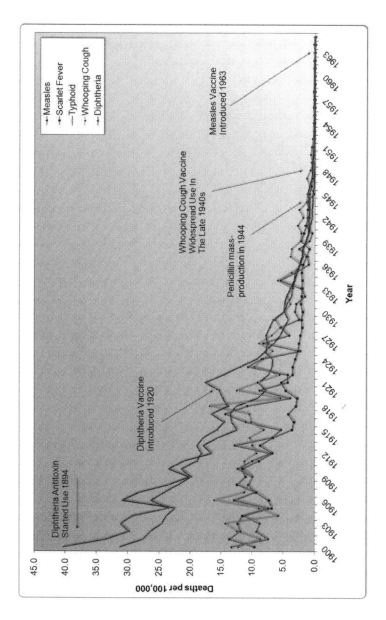

Graph 14.3: United States mortality rates from various infectious diseases from 1900 to 1965.

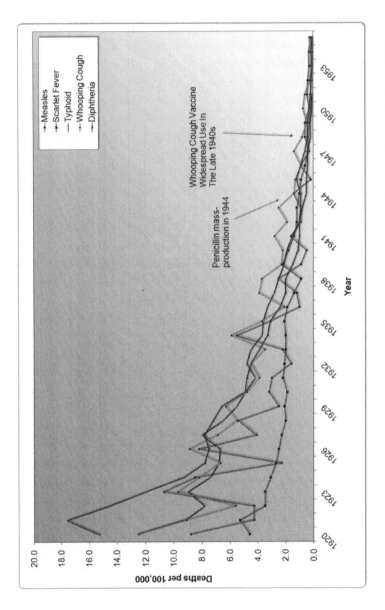

Graph 14.4: United States mortality rates from various infectious diseases from 1920 to 1955.

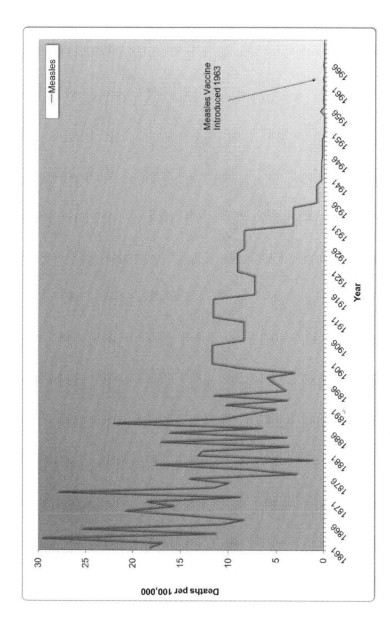

Graph 14.5: Massachusetts mortality rate from measles from 1861 to 1970.

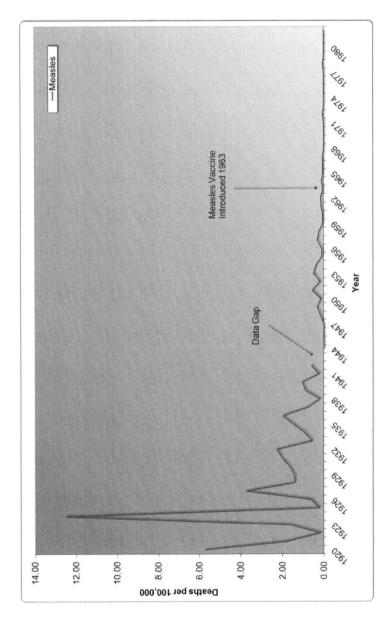

Graph 14.6: Washington State measles mortality rate from 1920 to 1982.

The safety record you may not know about

The early measles vaccine that contained "killed" virus was an aluminum-precipitated vaccine produced from formaldehyde-inactivated monkey kidney cell cultures. A study from 1967 revealed that the vaccine could cause pneumonia as well as encephalopathy (inflammation of the brain).

> *Pneumonia is a consistent and prominent finding. Fever is severe and persistent and the degree of headache, when present, suggests a central nervous system involvement. Indeed one patient in our series who was examined by EEG, **evidence of disturbed electrical activity of the brain was found, suggestive of encephalopathy . . . These untoward results of inactivated measles virus immunization was unanticipated.** The fact that they have occurred should impose a restriction on the use of inactivated measles virus vaccine. We now recommend that inactivated measles virus vaccine should no longer be administered.*[581]

In addition to being dangerous, killed vaccines were very ineffective. Whatever vaccine induced immunity was present declined rapidly, and recipients again became susceptible. They were later advised to be revaccinated with live vaccine in the hope of rectifying the problem. But this approach only led to more problems. Those who encountered wild measles or live vaccine measles, after having the killed vaccine, had a tendency to develop a more severe disease, atypical measles.

Atypical measles occurred because people who were previously vaccinated had their immune systems wrongly programmed and

---

[581] Vincent A. Fulginiti, MD; Jerry J. Eller, MD; Allan W. Downie, MD; and C. Henry Kempe, MD, "Altered Reactivity to Measles Virus: Atypical Measles in Children Previously Immunized with Inactivated Measles Virus Vaccines," *Journal of the American Medical Association*, vol. 202, no. 12, December 18, 1967, p. 1080.

committed original antigenic sin.[582] The problematic effect often lasted up to 16 years.

> *Atypical measles was characterized by a higher and more pro-longed fever, unusual skin lesions and severe pneumonitis com-pared to measles in previously unvaccinated persons. The rash was often accompanied by evidence of hemorrhage or vesiculation. The pneumonitis included distinct nodular paren-chymal lesions and hilar adenopathy. Abdominal pain, hepatic dysfunction, headache, eosinophilia, pleural effusions and edema were also described.* **Cases of atypical measles were reported up to 16 years after receipt of the inactivated vaccine. Admin-istration of the live virus vaccine after 2 to 3 doses of killed vaccine did not eliminate subsequent susceptibility to atypi-cal measles and was often associated with severe reactions at the site of live virus inoculation.**[583]

The killed vaccines were quickly abandoned. But there were also significant issues with the live vaccines, which were not highly attenuated and produced a "modified measles" rash in about half of those injected—essentially equivalent to a case of measles. Forty-eight percent of people had rash, and 83 percent had fevers up to 106°F post-injection.[584] To temper this problem, measles-specific antibody was given in the form of immune serum globulin alongside the live vaccines. This practice blunted an otherwise obvious reac-tion (fever and rash) to the live virus in the vaccine, but had serious potential consequences.[585] This will be discussed shortly.

---

[582] Harrison C. Stetler, MD; Robert D. Gens, MD; and George R. Seatstrom, MPA, "Severe Local Reactions to Live Measles Virus Vaccine Following an Immunization Program," *American Journal of Public Health*, 1983, p. 899.

[583] D. Griffin et al., "Measles Vaccines," *Frontiers in Bioscience*, vol. 13, January 2008, pp. 1352–1370.

[584] "Measles Vaccine Effective in Test—Injections with Live Virus Protect 100 Per Cent of Children in Epidemics," *New York Times*, September 14, 1961.

[585] T. Rønne, "Measles Virus Infection Without Rash in Childhood Is Related to Disease in Adult Life," *The Lancet*, vol. 325, no. 8419, January 1985, pp. 1–5.

One of the major drawbacks in determining the problem with vaccines is that, because it is a scientific fact that mercury is unhealthy for nervous system tissue, the focus has been mostly on mercury. Unfortunately, the investigation into mercury alone is shortsighted. Measles vaccines, although they have never contained mercury, have nonetheless been associated with neurological damage.

Aseptic meningitis, or nonbacterial meningitis, is a condition in which the layers lining the brain become inflamed. In the early 1990s, a mass immunization campaign in Brazil deployed a modern product—the highly attenuated MMR vaccine. The use of that vaccine on a large scale over a short period of time made it possible to detect a significant increase in aseptic meningitis that is more difficult to see when vaccination is spread out over longer periods.[586] The Brazilian situation should be carefully considered

A similar connection was seen in 1976 when the United States mass vaccinated 45 million people in four weeks with the swine flu vaccine. The resultant damage from that vaccine is etched in the American psyche—most older adults know someone who was damaged. The official toll of people who qualified by government standards as having Guillain-Barré syndrome (GBS) was more than 200, 11 of whom died.* There was a clustering of cases in the second and third weeks after vaccination. The epidemic never arrived, and the ill-conceived campaign was labeled a fiasco. Only one person died with swine flu that year. CDC and IOM today agree that the vaccine led to "an increased risk" of GBS.

One has to wonder how many of today's vaccine campaigns would be deemed fiascos by the public if synchronous vaccination was carried out within weeks.

* Phillip M. Boffey, "Guillain-Barré: Rare Disease Paralyzes Swine Flu Campaign," Science, vol. 195, no. 4274, January 14, 1977, pp. 155–159.

---

[586] Sérgio Souza Da Cunha, Laura C. Rodrigues, Mauríco L. Barreto, and InêsDourado, "Outbreak of Aseptic Meningitis and Mumps After Mass Vaccination with MMR Vaccine Using Leningrad-Zagreb Mumps Strain," Vaccine, vol. 20, 2002, p. 1111.

because it afforded a unique opportunity to detect brain disease after the vaccine.

The reason that vaccines are not done in "pulse" fashion to interrupt transmission is that if they were administered on specified days, any damage from vaccination would become blindingly obvious to both parents and authorities. It is much more difficult to make any connection between vaccines and reactions when they are given to individuals, spread out over the whole year, as per the childhood age-based schedule, or the gradual administering of flu shots over several months. Pulse days eliminate the ability of the authorities to claim coincidence due to "background incidence."

The British National Childhood Encephalopathy Study conducted in the 1970s was a case-control study comparing vaccination histories of more than 1,000 encephalopathy cases.[587] The authors reported a relative risk of serious neurologic illness of 3.9 in previously neuro-logically normal children admitted to the hospital 7 to 14 days after the measles vaccine. Dr. Ward published results from a separate study in 2007 that validated these findings.[588]

Incomplete clearance of measles virus and deranged immune responses have a known association with chronic clinical and sub-clinical infection. Peer-reviewed reports of vaccinated children have shown that residual measles virus is of pathological significance.

MV [measles virus] was predominantly detected in dendritic cells in reactive follicular hyperplastic centres in ileal biopsies from affected children, but was also identified in mature

---

[587] R. Alderslade et al., "The National Childhood Encephalopathy Study: A Report on 1000 Cases of Serious Neurological Disorders in Infants and Young Children from the NCES Research Team," *Whooping Cough: Reports from the Committee on Safety of Medicines and the Joint Committee on Vaccination and Immunisation,* Her Majesty's Stationery Office, London, United Kingdom, 1981, pp. 79–169.

[588] K. N. Ward et al., "Risk of Serious Neurologic Disease After Immunization of Young Children in Britain and Ireland," *Pediatrics,* vol. 120, no. 2, August 2007, pp. 314–321.

lymphocytes in these hyperplastic areas. This result indicates a possible interaction between MV and the immune response in the pathogenesis of ileocolitis in these children. **MV may be a potential "immunological trigger" in the pathogenesis of lymphoid hyperplasia and ileocolitis.** *Potential initiators for this type of immunological response are dendritic cells . . . The presence of MV antigen in follicular dendritic cells may reflect a transient stage in the progression from latent to persistent MV infection.*[589]

In 1998 Dr. Andrew Wakefield published a case series[590] in the *Lancet* which revealed regressive autism associated with ileal nodular enterocolitis in children vaccinated with MMR vaccines. In a bizarre move by the General Medical Council 12 years later, Dr. Wakefield's *Lancet* study was retracted under duress. This retraction occurred in February 2010 just as he had published another study[591] that revealed abnormal early neurodevelopmental responses in male infant rhesus macaques receiving a single dose of thimerosal-containing hepatitis B vaccine at birth. Among a number of neurologic dysfunctions in that study was a significant delay in the acquisition of three survival reflexes—root, snout, and suck—compared with unvaccinated primates. The manuscript was accepted, published electronically, and then abruptly removed without explanation. In 2010 it was printed in another journal[592] without Dr Wakefield's name. In both studies, there was no claim as to causation—just the suggestion that "further investigation is merited."

---

[589] V. Uhlmann et al., "Potential Viral Pathogenic Mechanism for New Variant Inflammatory Bowel Disease," *Molecular Pathology*, vol. 55, no. 2, April 2002, pp. 84–90.

[590] A. Wakefield et al., "Ileal-Lymphoid-Nodular Hyperplasia, Non-Specific Colitis, and Pervasive Developmental Disorder in Children," *The Lancet*, vol. 351, no. 9103, February 28, 1998, pp. 637–641.

[591] L. Hewitson et al., "Delayed Acquisition of Neonatal Reflexes in Newborn Primates Receiving a Thimerosal-Conatining Hepatitis B Vaccine: Influence of Gestational Age and Birth Weight," *Neurotoxicology*, vol. 73, no. 19, 2010, pp. 1298–1313.

[592] Ibid., *Journal of Toxicology and Environmental Health, Part A,* vol. 73, no. 19, 2010, pp. 1298–1313.

Since the attacks on Dr. Wakefield, another group of scientists has been working to address three valid critiques of the earlier studies:

1. Lack of demonstration of the vaccine-strain measles versus wild measles in intestinal lesions

2. Lack of validation of finding the measles virus in bowel tissue from patients other than those associated with the Wakefield/*Lancet* and Uhlmann studies

3. Lack of demonstration of the measles virus in developmentally delayed versus typically developing children

All three critiques were addressed by Dr. Stephen Walker's group in a preliminary report in 2006. Vaccine-strain measles was found in the bowel lesions of his series of autistic children.[593] That work is stalled due to lack of funding.

A Japanese group published results showing that vaccine-strain measles is found in peripheral blood mononuclear cells. The group carried out detection of measles genomic RNA in peripheral mononuclear cells in eight patients with Crohn's disease, three patients with ulcerative colitis, and nine children with autistic enterocolitis. The sequences obtained from the patients with ulcerative colitis and children with autism were consistent with vaccine strains.[594]

---

[593] S. J. Walker et al., "Persistent Ileal Measles Virus in a Large Cohort of Regressive Austistic Children with Ileocolitis and Lymphonodular Hyperplasia: A Revisitation of an Earlier Study," International Meeting for Autism Research, Montreal, Canada, June 3, 2006.

[594] H. Kawashima et al., "Detection and Sequencing of Measles Virus from Peripheral Mononuclear Cells from Patients with Inflammatory Bowel Disease and Autism," *Digestive Diseases and Sciences*, vol. 45, no. 4, April 2000, pp. 723–729.

During a class-action case in Australia over Merck's heart-attack and stroke-inducing drug, Vioxx, it was revealed that a "doctor hit list" circulated within the ranks of the hierarchy. This list contained names of the doctors who spoke out against the drug using labels such as "neutralize," "neutralized," and "discredit." During the testimony, Julian Burnside, QC, acting for the plaintiff, read one email from a Merck employee that said, "We may need to seek them out and destroy them where they live."*

Also reported in the Australian were documents that surfaced in the Federal Court in the Melbourne hearing regarding the criminal intent of Merck staffers who admitted they intended to "stop funding to institutions" and "interfere with academic appointments." Identical to the backlash on scientists who reported the contamination of polio vaccines with SV40 monkey virus, academic freedom was jeopardized when research exposed giant and potentially costly† errors on the part of pharmaceutical companies.

It is not surprising that research on the topic of persistent vaccine-strain measles in children with autoimmune diseases or brain damage has not been aggressively funded and encouraged. If parents thought that the MMR vaccine could result in brain damage, painful colon disease, or autoimmune disease of the liver, surely vaccine revenues would plummet, and the financial loss would dwarf that of Vioxx.

* Milanda Rout, "Vioxx Maker Merck and Co Drew Up Doctor Hit List," April 1, 2009, www.theaustralian.com.au/news/drug-company-drew-up-doctor-hit-list/story-e6frg6n6-1225693586492.

† Merck set aside 4.85 billion USD for legal claims and withdrew the drug from the market in 2004.

Dr. Kawashima has also isolated vaccine-strain measles RNA in peripheral blood monocytes of children with autoimmune hepatitis. He concluded that those children can have persistence of the vaccine strain in vivo for many years after vaccination, and the persistence of the measles virus might play some role in the pathology of autoimmune hepatitis.[595]

Vaccine-induced measles: Off the record

Many of today's measles cases are not counted or recognized, because the sickness that comes with vaccine measles is incorrectly thought to be more innocuous than natural measles. Numerous literature reports speak to the fact that not only do vaccinated people have live measles virus that is not cleared from the body, it is shed in urine and presumably other secretions.

Measles vaccine virus can be detected in urine after vaccination.

> *We describe a 17-month-old child* **with fever and rash [fifteen days post]** *after measles-mumps-rubella vaccination. Detection of* **vaccine-strain measles virus in his urine** *by polymerase chain reaction confirmed the diagnosis of a vaccine reaction rather than wild-type measles. We propose that measles virus should be sought and identified as vaccine or wild-type virus when the relationship between vaccination and measles-like illness is uncertain.*[596]

The vaccine has essentially induced cases of measles that were either benign,[597] crippling,[598] or deadly.[599]

---

[595] H. Kawashima et al., "Polymerase Chain Reaction Detection of the Hemagglutinin Gene from Attenuated Measles Vaccine Strain in the Peripheral Mononuclear Cells of Children with Autoimmune Hepatitis," *Archives of Virology*, vol. 141, no. 5, 1996, pp. 877–884.

[596] G. Jenkin et al., "What Is the Cause of a Rash After Measles-Mumps-Rubella Vaccination?" *Medical Journal of Australia*, vol. 171, August 1999, pp. 194–195.

[597] Ibid.

[598] R. E. Weibel et al., "Acute Encephalopathy Followed by Permanent Brain Injury or Death Associated with Further Attenuated Measles Vaccines: A Review of Claims Submitted to the National Vaccine Injury Compensation Program," *Pediatrics*, vol. 101, March 1998, pp. 383–387.

Today, reports of "modified measles" are synonymous with attenuated vaccine virus cases and are available to anyone who does a literature search. Reports conclude that doctors should be considering vaccine-strain measles infections in aseptic meningitis and encephalitis cases.

> *A 72-year-old man with subacute right upper limb palsy was diagnosed with cerebral infarction at another hospital. However, the head magnetic resonance imaging (MRI) scans showed no abnormalities. The scans showed an abnormality in the left frontal-parietal lobe, and the serum measles IgM level was elevated. Measles encephalitis was consequently diagnosed and steroid pulse therapy was immediately initiated.* **With widespread administration of the measles vaccine, we expect that the incidence of modified measles will increase in the future.** *Hence the serum titer of the measles virus should be measured when patients with subacute meningoencephalitis of unclear origin are identified.*[600]

As this 2011 Japanese paper suggests, the problems with measles vaccines are going to get worse, not better, in the future.

The data suggests that immunity to measles may not be absolute but rather a continuum of clinical illnesses.[601] Some levels of preexisting antibody may protect against classic measles but not against mild clinical infections.[602] Seroconversion after vaccination is no guarantee against developing typical or atypical measles during exposure. Vaccine immunity is known to wane to varying degrees, and the relative importance of waning immunity remains poorly

---

[599] A. Bitnun et al., "Measles Inclusion-Body Encephalitis Caused by the Vaccine Strain of Measles Virus," *Clinical Infectious Diseases,* vol. 29, no. 4, October 1999, pp. 855–861.

[600] T. Nishiwaki et al., "Suspected Measles Encephalitis Caused by Modified Measles That Was Difficult to Diagnose: A Case Report," *Brain Nerve*, vol. 63, no. 1, January 2011, pp. 75–78.

[601] R. T. Chen et al., "Measles Antibody: Reevaluation of Protective Titers," *Journal of Infectious Diseases*, vol. 162, no. 5, November 1990, pp. 1036–1042.

[602] Ibid.

understood.[603] Illness without rash is known to occur after exposure to measles, even in persons with PRN titers[604] above the level thought to be protective.[605]

Measles breaks through the most densely immune, vaccinated populations that have had two doses of vaccine. But it doesn't always look like measles. It can be "atypical" or rashless. If you have measles virus and only two of three required symptoms for diagnosis, you could be called a "symptomatic noncase."[606]

The risks and benefits of vaccinating should be undestood by practitioners advising for consent and parents agreeing to the vaccine. But the finer details are rarely, if ever, understood by any doctor, nurse, or pharmacist.

The failed plan

Despite the greatly diminished danger of measles, news reports in 1965 urgent-

Some of the major reasons cited in the literature on the high degree of vaccine failure prior to 1980 are as follows:

1. Vaccination under the age of one year when maternal antibodies interfere with the growth of vaccine virus.

2. The simultaneous use of gamma globulin where the response is often less satisfactory if the dose of gamma globulin is too great.

3. The use of killed vaccine before live vaccine has been found to be less efficient in giving protection in the MRC (Medical Research Council) trial and serologically in Canadian trials.

4. The vaccine is labile, and observation in several clinics and pediatricians' offices in the United States has revealed suboptimal handling of vaccine.

5. The decline in antibody titers has been found to be greater with attenuated vaccines than with natural disease, and the decline is greater with the more attenuated modern vaccines.

---

[603] R. T. Chen et al., "Measles Antibody: Reevaluation of Protective Titers," *Journal of Infectious Diseases*, vol. 162, no. 5, November 1990, pp. 1036–1042.
[604] PRN is Plaque Reduction Neutralization Titer. Plaques are areas on cell culture dishes where virus attacks cells, demonstrating viral activity and lack of immunity. Reduction of plaque indicates viral neutralization.
[605] Chen et al.
[606] Ibid.

ly called for children to quickly be vaccinated against the disease. Theoretical claims were made that a single shot would provide life-long immunity.[607]

> The United State Public Health Service licensed a new, refined, live-measles vaccine. Although **several live vaccines have been licensed since 1963—all of them one-shot treatments that give life immunity without serious side-effects**—the new one is considered by epidemiologists as "the best so far in minimizing the side-effects."[608]

The plan began in 1963 **with an expectation of eradication by 1967 ...**

> Effective use of these vaccines during the coming winter and spring should insure the eradication of measles from the United States in 1967.[609]

... if enough of the "right" children were vaccinated.

> Measles, the "harmless" childhood disease that can kill, will be nearly eradicated from most areas of the country a year from now, officials of the United States Public Health Service predict ... Although there are still more than 12 million susceptible children, **vaccination of the "right" two million to four million youngsters could wipe out the disease**, according to Dr. Robert J. Warren of the Communicable Disease Center in Atlata.[610]

---

[607] The Medical Officer, vol. 118, 1967, p. 79.

[608] "Thaler to Hold State Senate Hearing to Find Fastest Way to Expedite Plan," New York Times, February 24, 1965.

[609] David J. Sencer, MD; H. Bruce Dull, MD; and Alexander D. Langmuir, MD, "Epidemiologic Basis for Eradication of Measles in 1967," Public Health Reports, vol. 82, no. 3, March 1967, p. 256.

[610] Jane E. Brody, "Measles Will Be Nearly Ended by '67, U.S. Health Aides Say," New York Times, May 24, 1966.

More than one shot has always been needed for vaccine-style measles protection, and as time marches on it appears that, like pertussis, more vaccines for older people will be called for.[611]

More than a decade later, the objective of measles elimination was still not achieved. There were repeat epidemics that happened throughout the United States.

Not only was one shot insufficient, it turned out that even two could be insufficient. In addition, there is no telling if boosters had much effect past one year.

> ... in the booster vaccines, there was only a modest initial rise in titer, and after a year the level was almost back to where it had been before the booster. In addition, we noted a lack of "take" in 14 other children, most of whom probably had been immunologically stimulated previously. In short, the data suggested that a booster dose might not have any lasting effect on waning immunity.[612]

Essentially, what happened as a result of vaccination was a shift in the susceptible group to an older age where symptoms can also be atypical. During the pre-vaccine era, infants were more solidly protected, and it was mostly children under the age of 10 who developed measles. After the vaccine, infants and older children became susceptible whereas they had not been during the natural measles epidemics.

Dr. James Cherry, a well-known vaccinationist and pediatrician, commented that, in the post-vaccine era, measles had become a "time bomb." (Cherry, *Hospital Practice*, 1980, pp. 49–57.) There is reason to believe that the bomb is still ticking.

By 1989 the new theory on failure to eradicate was that the earlier vaccines were not as effective as originally believed.

---

[611] "Recommended Adult Immunization Schedule, by Vaccine and Age Group," United States, Centers for Disease Control, 2013, www.cdc.gov/vaccines/schedules/hcp/imz/adult.html.

[612] J. D. Cherry, "The 'New' Epidemiology of Measles and Rubella," *Hospital Practice*, vol. 15, no. 7, July 1980, pp. 49–57.

Some of the first vaccines mass produced in 1963 contained a killed virus. In 1989 Dr. Feigin of Texas Children's Hospital stated that he believed the 1963 vaccine was "not widely effective" and that the 1967 vaccine was unstable and lost its "effectiveness" if not properly refrigerated. **It was not until 1980 that a stable live measles vaccine became available.**[613]

In the same year, after three types of measles vaccines had failed to produce eradication or even predictable herd immunity, vaccine scientists changed course from one shot and stated that, in using the new live vaccine, two doses would be required for reliable protection. They also recommended that everyone under the age of 32 be revaccinated because the old vaccines they received were inadequate. The single shot once promised to provide lifelong immunity against measles in the 1960s was never produced.

Outbreaks of measles continued into the 1990s—this time because of an immunity gap among children in the 10- to 12-year-old age group.[614]

Once again, there was no perceived problem with the vaccine or the theory of vaccination, but with the people who didn't get enough injections. As still happens today, the unvaccinated or partially vaccinated were unjustly blamed for the outbreaks occurring in highly vaccinated populations. Twenty-one cases of measles occurred in Sangamon County, Illinois, in 1984. The CDC reports:

> This outbreak demonstrates that **transmission of measles can occur within a school population with a documented immunization level of 100%.** This level was validated during the outbreak investigation. Previous investigations of measles outbreaks among highly immunized populations have revealed risk factors such as improper storage or handling of vaccine,

---

[613] Lisa Belkin, "Measles, Not Yet a Thing of the Past, Reveals the Limits of an Old Vaccine," *New York Times*, February 25, 1989.

[614] "Measles Risk Linked to Gap in Vaccinations," *New York Times*, August 16, 1996.

vaccine administered to children under 1 year of age, use of globulin with vaccine, and use of killed virus vaccine. However, these risk factors did not adequately explain the occurrence of this outbreak.[615]

A 1994 study indicated that as vaccination rates increased, measles became a disease of vaccinated people. This "startling" surprise challenged the theory that vaccine-induced "herd immunity" would protect against outbreaks of measles.

> *... multiple measles outbreaks have occurred in school populations in which 71% to 99.8% of the student body had been vaccinated appropriately . . .* **Startling at the time was the finding that measles outbreaks developed in these school populations even though more than 98% of the students had previously been vaccinated** *. . . In the particular case of measles,* **"herd immunity" is not completely effective** *in preventing an outbreak of measles despite extraordinarily high immunization rates.*[616]

In the year 2000, measles was declared eliminated from the United States. However, in 2012 the CDC pulled back from that declaration, stating that measles reappeared and was spreading. Like the threat from polio, though, the danger was from abroad, not the heavily vaccinated children of the United States. Of the total number of cases, 200 were attributed to foreign travel, but the source for 22 cases was never determined.[617] No deaths or adverse outcomes were reported.

It is clear that the reported measles incidence rate did decline, although it took much longer than originally promised and required

---

[615] "Measles Outbreak Among Vaccinated High School Students—Illinois," *MMWR*, Centers for Disease Control and Prevention, June 22, 1984, p. 349.

[616] Gregory A. Poland, MD, and Robert M. Jacobson, MD, "Failure to Reach the Goal of Measles Elimination: Apparent Paradox of Measles Infections in Immunized Persons," *Archives of Internal Medicine*, August 22, 1994, pp. 1816–1818.

[617] "Measles Outbreaks in 2011 Were Worst in 15 Years: CDC," *Health Day News*, April 19, 2012.

more than one shot of a vaccine that had significant side effects. In the United States and England, this trend was probably boosted through the use of an extensive vaccination program, with all the "unintended consequences" and inherent unknowns.

Plan for future failure

One key factor to consider is that measles vaccine does not create lifelong immunity. The only way to remain immune with artificial immunity via vaccines is to be vaccinated several times during a lifetime. We have not yet seen how the vaccine will play out over several generations of exclusively vaccinated people. Epidemics are likely to become more common in the future.

One study predicted that, even with good response to vaccination, immunity wanes in as little as 25 years. If this is true, then there could be a resurgence of measles after a period of relatively low measles incidence, which we are in now.

> *Because measles-specific antibody titer after vaccination is lower than after natural infection, there is concern that vaccinated persons may gradually lose protection from measles. Secondary vaccine failure (loss of immunity over time), in contrast to primary vaccine failure (no protection immediately after vaccination), is a concern because of the potential insidious challenge to measles elimination. For instance, if vaccine-induced immunity wane to nonprotective levels in a high proportion of vaccinated adults, the level of population protection might decline to allow recurrence of endemic disease. By means of statistical modeling, Mossong et al. **predicted waning of vaccine-induced immunity 25 years after immunization.**[618]*

---

[618] Mark S. Dine, Sonja S. Hutchins, Ann Thomas, Irene Williams, and William J. Bellini, et al., "Persistence of Vaccine-Induced Antibody to Measles 26–33 Years After Vaccination," *Journal of Infectious Diseases*, 2004, p. S123.

The estimate of 25 years for waning vaccine immunity is generous. Reports of waning immunity or vaccine failure, even with the live vaccines, show that immunity can wane in as few as 10 years.[619]

A 2009 study published in *Proceedings of the Royal Society* investigated what could happen with waning measles vaccine immunity even with high vaccine coverage among children. They predicted that, after a long disease-free period in the population, the introduction of infection will lead to far larger epidemics than predicted by standard models.

> *We can foresee that vaccination will have two conflicting effects . . . it will reduce the number of newborn susceptibles and hence should have some of the usual associated public-health benefits reducing the number of cases in young children. However, this reduction in cases will lead to a reduction in boosting and therefore a greater susceptibility to infection in older age classes . . . When immunity wanes, vaccination has a far more limited impact on the average number of cases. While this observation has clear public-health implications, the dynamic consequences of the interaction between vaccination, waning immunity and boosting are far more striking. For* **high levels of vaccination (greater than 80%) and moderate levels of waning immunity (greater than 30 years), large-scale epidemic cycles can be induced.**[620]

Levy estimated in a 1984 report[621] that by 2050 the proportion of susceptibles may be greater than in the pre-vaccine era. His computer model, while unproven in 1984, has come to pass as very accurate, since it predicted the epidemics of the year 2000.

---

[619] J. D. Cherry, "The 'New' Epidemiology of Measles and Rubella," *Hospital Practice,* vol. 15, no. 7, July 1980, pp. 49–57.

[620] J. M. Heffernan and M. J. Keeling, "Implications of Vaccination and Waning Immunity," *Proceedings of the Royal Society B*, vol. 276, 2009.

[621] D. L. Levy, "The Future of Measles in Highly Immunized Populations: A Modeling Approach," *American Journal of Epidemiology*, vol. 120, no. 1, July 1984, pp. 39–48.

Recovery without antibodies: A disconcerting discovery

Antibodies are a marker of what happened after infection or vaccination but are not the essential tool for the primary mission of "search and destroy."

> *A paradoxical observation involving AMI [antibody-mediated immunity] is **that specific IgG is often made after the host has recovered.** In fact, a rise in serum IgG titer is a time-honored method for diagnosing many infectious diseases. This observation **begs the question of why IgG is made after recovery from most infectious diseases. Invoking a need to prevent recurrences is a somewhat unsatisfactory answer if the initial innate and cellular response was adequate to clear the first bout of disease.**[622]*

Vaccine scientists know that the immune system responds with more than just antibody, yet because markers of cell-mediated immunity are elusive, antibody has become the measure of whether or not a person is immune. By priming the immune system with disease particles in a vaccine, the intention is to produce memory immunity that will later respond rapidly to similar infections. Theoretically, the body should quickly respond and destroy invaders before they can multiply and cause noticeable disease.

Is the antibody just a marker of a more complex process? Scientists were surprised when they learned that individuals with a deficit in antibody production, called agamma-globulinemia, recovered from measles just as well as normal antibody producers.[623] This "disconcerting" discovery was made in the 1960s when measles vaccinations were just getting under way.

---

[622] A. Casadevall et al., "A Reappraisal of Humoral Immunity Based on Mechanisms of Antibody Mediated Protection Against Intracellular Pathogens," *Advances in Immunology,* vol. 91, 2006, pp. 1–44.

[623] Sallie R. Permar et al., "Limited Contribution of Humoral Immunity to the Clearance of Measles Viremia in Rhesus Monkeys," *Journal of Infectious Diseases*, vol. 190, no. 5, 2004, p. 998.

One of the most disconcerting discoveries in clinical medicine was the finding that children with congenital agamma-globulinaemia, who could make no antibody and had only insignificant traces of immunoglobulin in circulation, contracted measles in normal fashion, showed the usual sequence of symptoms and signs, and were subsequently immune. No measles antibody was detectable in their serum [the water part of blood minus clotting factors and cells].[624]

Therefore the antibody part of immunity is not at all necessary for the natural recovery from measles.

*. . . children with antibody deficiency syndromes have quite unremarkable attacks of measles with the characteristic rash and normal recovery. Furthermore, they are not unduly prone to reinfection. It therefore seems that serum **antibody, at any rate in any quantity, is not required for the production of the measles rash; nor for the normal recovery from the disease; nor to prevent reinfection.***[625]

Humoral immunity does not seem to play a major role in natural resistance against the disease.[626]

If humoral immunity does not "play a major role in natural resistance" against measles, then what does? The reason most people completely recover after acute infections is because of something called innate immunity. This involves a part of the immune system that requires no memory or previous exposure and does not involve preformed specific antibodies. Instead, it involves the activation of white blood cells, including macrophages, natural killer cells, and antigen-specific T lymphocytes, as well as the release of

---

[624] "Measles as an Index of Immunological Function," *The Lancet*, September 14, 1968, p. 611.

[625] P. J. Lachmann, "Immunopathology of Measles," *Proceedings Royal Society of Medicine*, vol. 67, November 1974, p. 1120.

[626] H. Valdimarsson, Gudrun Agnarsdottir, and P. J. Lachmann, "Cellular Immunity in Subacute Scelrosing Panenecephalitis," *Proceedings Royal Society of Medicine*, vol. 67, November 1974, p. 1125.

various cytokines (immune system proteins) in response to a foreign invader.

This aspect of immunity is present regardless of vaccination and is highly dependent on essential nutrients. When cellular immunity is impaired—for instance, in leukemia—measles is disastrous.[627,628]

The pro-vaccine argue that the reason to vaccinate all healthy people is to protect those at highest risk. Huge amounts of money are spent figuring out why so many vaccinated remain susceptible to infection[629] and why the same people who are susceptible to disease complications don't respond to the vaccine.[630]

The appearance of one case of measles in the highest vaccinated populations always promotes widespread fearmongering by public health officials **because they know the fragility of vaccine immunity**.

> *Measles outbreaks are occurring where they are least expected . . . Since 2005 these outbreaks have occurred in the U.S.—with surprising numbers of cases occurring in persons who previously received one or even two documented doses of measles-containing vaccine. In fact, as of September 2011, the U.S. has*

---

[627] Diane E. Griffin and Michael B. A. Oldstone, *Measles: Pathogenesis and Control*, 2009, p. 155.

[628] Sallie R. Permar et al., "Limited Contribution of Humoral Immunity to the Clearance of Measles Viremia in Rhesus Monkeys," *Journal of Infectious Diseases*, vol. 190, no. 5, 2004, p. 998.

[629] G. A. Poland and R. M. Jacobson, "The Re-emergence of Measles in Developed Countries: Time to Develop the Next-Generation Measles Vaccines?" *Vaccine*, vol. 30, no. 2, January 5, 2012, pp. 103–104.

[630] I. H. Haralambieva, I. G. Ovsyannikova, V. S. Pankratz, R. B. Kennedy, R. M. Jacobson, and G. A. Poland, "The Genetic Basis for Interindividual Immune Response Variation to Measles Vaccine: New Understanding and New Vaccine Approaches," *Expert Review of Vaccines*, vol. 12, no. 1, January 2013, pp. 57–70.

had 15 measles outbreaks with 211 confirmed cases—the highest number of cases since 1996.[631]

If they understood the innate immune system, the real history of measles, and the use of vitamins C and A, their official response would not always be to promote fear.

Why does it make sense to subject all healthy people who are not usually susceptible to disease complications, to the known and unknown risks of MMR vaccines, when the result could be leading the world to a situation worse than the pre-vaccine days?[632] What will be the response to that? Revaccinating all of us every five years?

Antibody Dependent Enhancement (ADE)

Vaccine scientists have long relied on antibody as a measure of a vaccine's efficacy. It is a little-known fact that any antibody, even a vaccine-induced one, can render a person more vulnerable to disease. There is an undeniably delicate balance between protective immunity and the induction of enhanced susceptibility not only to the disease vaccinated for, but other diseases as well, and often this enhanced susceptibility comes from a vaccine that was administered to protect.

A virus recognizes and binds one or several specific cell surface receptor(s), enabling the entrance into cells. Some antibodies increase the ability of viruses to infect their target cells. This phenomenon is called antibody dependent enhancement (ADE) of infection.[633]

---

[631] G. A. Poland and R. M. Jacobson, "The Re-emergence of Measles in Developed Countries: Time to Develop the Next-Generation Measles Vaccines?" *Vaccine,* vol. 30, no. 2, January 5, 2012, pp. 103–104.

[632] D. L. Levy, "The Future of Measles in Highly Immunized Populations: A Modeling Approach," *American Journal of Epidemiology,* vol. 120, no. 1, July 1984, pp. 39–48.

[633] A. Takada and Y. Kawaoka, "Antibody-Dependent Enhancement of Viral Infection: Molecular Mechanisms and in vivo Implications," *Reviews in Medical Virology,* vol. 13, no. 6, November–December 2003, pp. 387–398.

There is no controversy over the fact that the inactivated measles vaccines led to an abnormal immune response and, later, a form of original antigenic sin.[634] Several mechanisms have been proposed over the years.

Measles virus has two important proteins on the surface—H (hemagglutinin) and F (fusion). The killed vaccine only programmed the recipient to manufacture antibodies to H. Then, when the natural virus or a live attenuated vaccine virus was encountered, the recipient could only respond to H protein because of faulty initial immune programming. Meanwhile, the F protein permitted viral access to human cells, causing victims to be more vulnerable than they would have been if not vaccinated at all.[635]

The measles literature contains many admissions of how much is still not understood regarding measles virus pathogenesis and what actually constitutes immunity.

> *Development of new vaccines has been hampered by an incomplete understanding of protective immunity and of the priming for enhanced disease by the inactivated vaccine.*[636] [This "priming" refers to the Antibody Dependent Enhancement.]

The phenomenon of ADE has also been a problem with dengue fever, RSV, rickettsial, trachoma, and Mycoplasma pneumoniae vaccines and is one of the reasons there is no HIV vaccine to date.[637,638] It also has been seen with Coxsackie virus.[639]

---

[634] Sukathida Ubol and Scott B. Halstead, "How Innate Immune Mechanisms Contribute to Antibody-Enhanced Viral Infections," *Clinical and Vaccine Immunology*, vol. 17, no. 12, December 2010, pp.1829–1835.

[635] I. Iankov et al., "Immunoglobulin G Antibody-Mediated Enhancement of Measles Virus Infection Can Bypass the Protective Antiviral Immune Response," *Journal of Virology*, September 2006, pp. 8530–8540.

[636] D. Griffin et al., "Measles Vaccines," *Frontiers in Bioscience*, vol. 13, January 2008, pp. 1352–1370.

[637] W. Huisman et al., "Vaccine-Induced Enhancement of Viral Infections," *Vaccine*, vol. 27, 2009, pp. 505–512.

Original antigenic sin (OAS) and ADE are different aspects of a similar phenomenon. They both apply to vaccines as well as infections and can lead the immune system astray, crippling the innate ability to fight disease upon exposure and rendering the victim more susceptible.

The more scientists learn about the immune system, the more they realize their profound lack of understanding. Regardless of the fact that not even the tip of the iceberg has been breached in immunology, immune systems have been manipulated by vaccines for more than 200 years. Excerpts from the following immunology journal of 2006 are revealing and have startling implications for vaccine science.

*It is increasingly apparent that, rather than being inherently good or bad, the effects of Abs (antibodies) are either beneficial or deleterious in a host, depending on the type of microbe–host interaction, including the setting in which damage occurs as a function of the host immune milieu and response. A logical extension of this concept is that an Ab that is protective in one host may not be protective in another if the nature of their immune responses to the relevant agent places them on different parts of the damage response curve. These concepts have important ramifications for vaccine design since vaccine efficacy could depend on enhancement of the immune response for those with weak immune responses, but **enhanced responses could be detrimental in those who naturally generate strong immune responses**. . . . Hence, rather than being a static or stable characteristic, the ability of an Ab to mediate protection is likely to be dynamic, changing as a function of time, the host response, available host receptors and inflammatory mediators, and the state of the microbe in the host . . . Considering that the immune response to pathogenic microbes includes Abs to many Ags (anti-*

---

[638] A. Z. Kapikian et al., "An Epidemiologic Study of Altered Clinical Reactivity to Respiratory Syncytial Virus Infection," *American Journal of Epidemiology*, vol. 89, no. 4, April 1969, pp. 405–421.
[639] W. Huisman et al.

*gens) differing in the predominant isotype and amount, one can easily **envision unfathomable complexity** that becomes even more daunting if one considers host genetic variation. Clearly, **defining protective efficacy of an Ab molecule in a predictive fashion is currently beyond the state of immunological science and may not be possible with current reductionistic approaches to scientific problems . . . Immunological knowledge is insufficient to predict the Ab characteristics that will be protective. Therefore, in most instances, determining the efficacy of Ab remains an empiric rather than predictive discipline.**[640]*

Measles reports declined, but why?

Because the number of deaths in the pre-vaccine era had already reached record low levels, the mortality rate for measles could not have been significantly affected by the vaccine program. Yet there was an apparently steep drop in incidence of the disease from 1963 onward (Graph 14.7 and Graph 14.8).

But was that dramatic downtrend in the curve all because of vaccines? As of 1968, the US immunization survey showed that only 50–60 percent of children between one and nine years old had been vaccinated. And vaccinated children still got a lot of measles. During the epidemic days, even when three vaccines were given to children, more than 50 percent of measles cases were fully vaccinated.[641]

If vaccine herd immunity requires 95 percent vaccinated using two doses of an effective vaccine (which was not begun until at least 1980 when a stable vaccine was marketed), why is it that, by 1968, the reported incidence had plummeted when only 50–60 percent of children were vaccinated with an ineffective vaccine?

---

[640] A. Casadevall et al., "A Reappraisal of Humoral Immunity Based on Mechanisms of Antibody Mediated Protection Against Intracellular Pathogens," *Advances in Immunology,* vol. 91, 2006, pp. 1–44.

[641] E. A. Mitchell et al., "Measles Immunization in South Auckland," *New Zealand Medical Journal,* vol. 98, no. 791, November 27, 1985, pp. 1016–1017.

Since the introduction of vaccination, vaccine uptake has risen from around 50% in 1968 to 76% in 1988.[642]

In the 1960s, only a few states required children to be vaccinated against measles to attend school.[643]

Isn't it astonishing that there was such a large drop in measles incidence by 1969, and relatively low (compared to today) uptake of admittedly ineffective vaccines?[644]

The area on the curve of Graph 14.7 between 1963 and 1968 needs to be understood within a fuller context.

---

[642] V. A. A. Jansen, N. Stollenwerk, H. J. Jensen, M. E. Ramsay, W. J. Edmunds, et al., "Measles Outbreaks in a Population with Declining Vaccine Update," *Science*, vol. 301, August 8, 2003, p. 804.

[643] Saad B. Omer, MB, BS, PhD, MPH; Daniel A. Salmon, PhD, MPH; Walter A. Orenstein, MD; M. Patricia deHart, ScD; and Neal Halsey, MD, "Vaccine Refusal, Mandatory Immunization, and the Risks of Vaccine-Preventable Diseases," *The New England Journal of Medicine*, May 7, 2009.

[644] *Measles—Q&A About Disease & Vaccine,* Centers for Disease Control and Prevention, November 2012, www.cdc.gov/vaccines/vpd-vac/measles/faqs-dis-vac-risks.htm.

Here are some probable contributions to the decline in the reported cases of measles:

First:

As always happens after a vaccine campaign, the criteria for diagnosing the disease was narrowed. The vaccinated who developed measles were not counted in the tally of wild measles, even though they were infected with measles virus.

The accelerated decline seen on the curve could have been due to the fact that if someone received a vaccine and developed a rash and high fever, but did not have wild-type measles, it wasn't measles. So because of the new classification, measles was bound to drop in the vaccinated. The CDC admits today that:

> . . . *many measles cases in previously vaccinated or immunosuppressed individuals do not meet the clinical case definition.*[645]

Modern clinical case confirmation criteria are very stringent:

- Laboratory confirmation by any of the following
    - Positive serologic test for measles immunoglobulin M antibody;
    - Significant rise in measles antibody level by any standard serologic assay;
    - Isolation of measles virus from a clinical specimen; or
    - Detection of measles-virus specific nucleic acid by polymerase chain reaction
    - Note: A laboratory-confirmed case does not have to have generalized rash lasting ≥3 days; temperature ≥101°F or 38.3°C; cough, coryza, or conjunctivitis.

    OR

---

[645] "Measles Serologic Techniques," Centers for Disease Control and Prevention, www.cdc.gov/measles/lab-tools/serology.html, accessed July 19, 2013.

- An illness characterized by
  - Generalized rash lasting ≥3 days; and
  - Temperature ≥101°F or 38.3°C; and
  - Cough, coryza, or conjunctivitis; and
  - Epidemiologic linkage to a confirmed case of measles.[646]

Serologic verification and contact with another verified case was not necessary before the vaccination era, even though there are at least 10 other infections that clinically resemble measles. Today there are numerous reports of missed diagnoses in the vaccinated because it is assumed they don't have measles; therefore only the differential diagnoses are considered. Rota et al. reported on just such an instance, where Kawasaki's disease—not measles—was suspected in the patient. The two attending physicians (with a history of three vaccines each) contracted measles, but it was not suspected, and they continued working.[647]

When does a vaccinated person have measles?

- **Vaccine-induced "measles"** is a modified form of measles occurring 5-12 days after measles vaccination. It is not transmissible and **should NOT be classified as measles**.
- Serologically-diagnosed cases who received a measles-containing vaccine 8 days to 8 weeks before testing may be

---

[646] "Measles," in *Manual for the Surveillance of Vaccine-Preventable Diseases,* 5th ed., 2012, Centers for Disease Control and Prevention, www.cdc.gov/vaccines/pubs/surv-manual/chpt07-measles.html#case, accessed July 5, 2013.

[647] J. S. Rota, C. J. Hickman, S. B. Sowers, P. A. Rota, S. Mercader, et al., "Two Case Studies of Modified Measles in Vaccinated Physicians Exposed to Primary Measles Cases: High Risk of Infection but Low Risk of Transmission," *Journal of Infectious Disease*, vol. 204, suppl. 1, July 2011, pp. S559–63.

classified as confirmed measles **ONLY if they are also epidemiologically linked to a confirmed case**.[648]

Do measles-vaccinated individuals contract, and have potential to spread measles? Apparently so. In a December 2013 report[649] of a vaccinated child who became ill with verified vaccine-strain clinical measles, concern was raised about 45 of 87 contacts. Those contacts were treated with either vaccines or immune globulin, which skews any analysis of spread.

The index case received her first dose of MMR vaccine 37 days prior to the onset of illness. Acute phase measles antibodies were noted and virus genotype was determined by the National Microbiology Laboratory in Winnipeg, Canada as vaccine strain, genotype A, MVs/British Columbia/39.13 [A] (VAC). Investigations clarified that there were no shipping, handling or cold-chain deviations for the specific vaccine used, and that it was administered by a public health nurse trained in immunisations. Post exposure prophylaxis was given to 45 of the 87 contacts, and included measles vaccines and immune globulin. Had the health authorities not vaccinated or given immune globulin to the contacts, we would have been able to see whether the vaccine, that is supposed to provide herd immunity, did infect other people.

Clinically significant vaccine-associated illness is thought to be rare, but when it occurs it is indistinguishable from wild-type measles, except by genotyping. Vaccine-strain measles should be considered in any outbreak, and tested for accordingly. Yet in the real world, testing for vaccine strains rarely happens, because doctors presume it's impossible, and public health officials consider it unnecessary

---

[648] Measles factsheet, New South Wales Ministry of Health, Australia, www0.health.nsw.gov.au/factsheets/guideline/measles.html, accessed December 10, 2012.

[649] Murti M, Krajden M, Petric M, Hiebert J, Hemming F, Hefford B, Bigham M, Van Buynder P, "Case of vaccine-associated measles five weeks post-immunisation, British Columbia, Canada, October 2013." Eurosurveillance, vol. 18, Issue 49, December 5, 2013.

except in special circumstances.

Because correct measles diagnoses are around 2.5-7% of all suspected cases, it would seem that doctors may not be very good at detecting the disease, whether vaccine-associated or not.[650] Which begs a couple of questions: 1) How often were doctors correct in their measles diagnosing prevaccine, and before PCR testing and salivary testing was done? 2) How many cases of vaccine strain measles today continue to go undiagnosed or incorrectly diagnosed as something else?

Up to 54 percent of vaccinated cases in some reports[651] developed rash with vaccination, which was in part why the immune globulin was administered with it. Still today, by the CDC's admission, 5–10 percent of vaccinees develop a rash and fever. Since measles rash is often missed by clinicians and parents and attributed to something else, that 5–10 percent would be a gross underestimate.

Given that at least 5–10 percent of measles vaccines result in fever and rash, then there are approximately 650,000–1,300,000 cases of measles in the United States per year from the 13–14 million yearly doses of vaccine injected.

Second:

Gamma globulin use during measles infection began in the 1940s and was given prolifically from 1963 to 1968 and even after. The reason it was given at the same time as the live and killed vaccines was to limit the negative (measles infection) effects of the injection,

---

[650] Irga Davidkin, Mia Kontio, Mikko Paunio, and Heikki Peltola, "MMR vaccination and disease elimination: the Finish experience," *Expert Review of Vaccines*, 2010, pp. 1045-1053; David Brown, Mary Ramsay, Alison Richards, and Elizabeth Miller, "Salivary diagnosis of measles: a study of notified cases in the United Kingdom, 1991-3," *British Medical Journal*, April 1994, vol. 308, pp. 1015-1017.

[651] J. Brody et al., "Measles Vaccine Field Trials in Alaska," *Journal of the American Medical Association*, vol. 189, August 1964, pp. 339–342.

but it was and still is[652] also prescribed as prophylaxis to those exposed to measles cases.

Measles can be prevented or modified after exposure by passive immunization with the use of immune serum globulin.[653] (But it comes with a price: potential development of tumors and connective tissue disease later in life.[654] Not to mention all the problems that can occur in giving a pooled human blood product.) It would therefore have contributed to decreasing severity of acute measles disease manifestation when used alone or with the vaccine. Yet the attribution would have been given to the vaccine.

Rashless infection would have led to fewer measles *reports*, but not because measles was not circulating and causing occult infections. So, on one hand, the early vaccines were leading to cases of atypical measles and causing a different disease (which were not counted as wild measles), and on the other hand, the gamma globulin given to prevent the side effects of the vaccines was also interfering with normal cell-mediated processing of the virus.

Third:

Before the introduction of the 1963 vaccine, the incidence of measles was already on a slow decline (Graph 14.9). Was measles slowly becoming less prevalent anyway? We know that measles can be subclinical 30 percent of the time.[655] The death rate had already plummeted. Like smallpox, was the disease slowly burning out? Was

---

[652] "Measles, Mumps, and Rubella—Vaccine Use and Strategies for Elimination of Measles, Rubella, and Congenital Rubella Syndrome and Control of Mumps: Recommendations of the Advisory Committee on Immunization Practices (ACIP)," *MMWR*, vol. 47, no. RR-8, Centers for Disease Control and Prevention, May 22, 1998, pp. 1–57.

[653] T. Rønne, "Measles Virus Infection Without Rash in Childhood Is Related to Disease in Adult Life," *The Lancet*, vol. 325, no. 8419, January 1985, pp. 1–5.

[654] T. Rønne, "Measles Virus Infection Without Rash in Childhood Is Related to Disease in Adult Life," *The Lancet*, vol. 325, no. 8419, January 1985, pp. 1–5.

[655] R. S. Sharma, "An Epidemiological Study of Measles Epidemic in District Bhilwara, Rajasthan," *Journal of Communicable Diseases*, vol. 20, December 1988, pp. 301–311.

the rise in breastfeeding and improved nutrition contributing to fewer diagnosed cases?

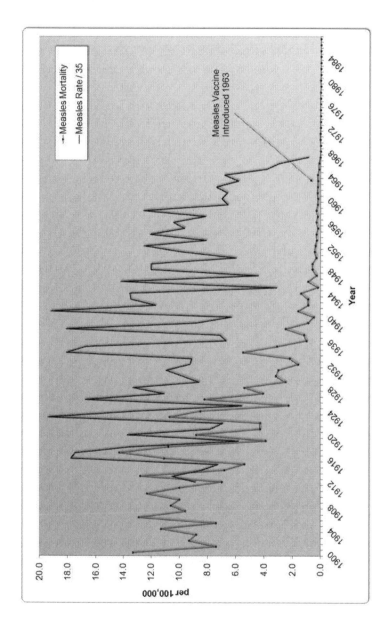

Graph 14.7: United States measles mortality rate with 1/35 measles disease rate from 1900 to 1987.

Measles

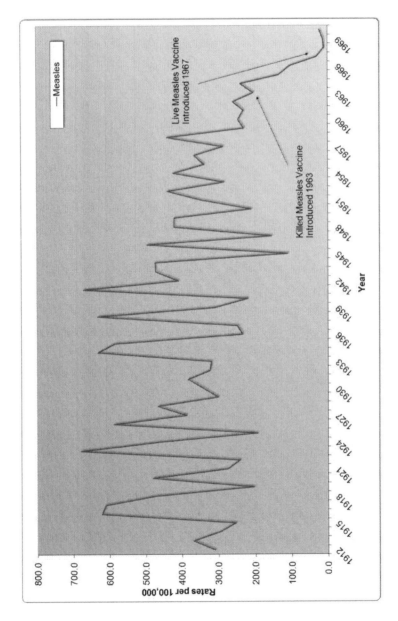

Graph 14.8: United States measles incidence from 1912 to 1970.

Measles

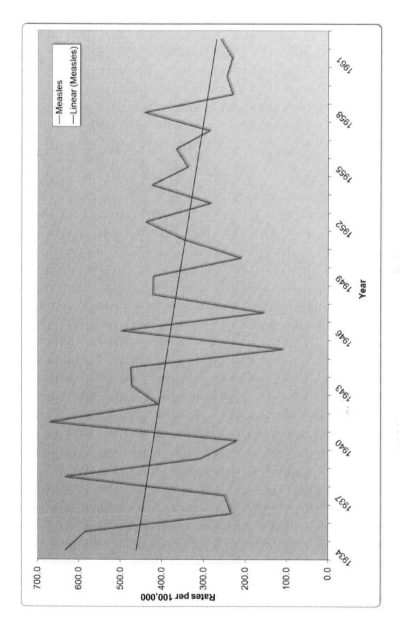

Graph 14.9: United States measles incidence from 1934 to 1962.

Is going rashless a good thing?

Measles virus itself does not cause any rash. The red spots are the physical manifestation of a cell-mediated reaction in the epithelial cells, which damages cells that have been infected with measles. Those cells then die, limiting ongoing viral reproduction. Yet measles virus can infect and not manifest any rash at all.

Consider the fact that agammaglobulinemics get a rash and throw off measles just fine because their innate immunity/cellular immunity is intact. Consider that **those with cellular immunity impairment, either from disease or malnutrition, develop NO rash and often die** with giant cell (coalesced cells of lymphoid origin) accumulation, usually in the lungs.

As you can probably imagine, any type of infection (vaccine or wild type) with measles that doesn't manifest with a rash could mean there was an incomplete response by the T cells and that measles virus escaped complete neutralization. So how is rashless measles created?

Immune globulin was used to prevent infection before the vaccine was invented, and its use continued for years alongside the live vaccines. This combination of immune globulin before virus can prime the immune system in such a way that it won't manifest a rash. The absence of rash may seem like a good thing, but considering that the rash is physical evidence of cellular immunity destroying virus-containing cells, its absence may not be so wonderful.

In 1985 Dr. Rønne published the results of a study where numerous adults were noted to have no history of measles rash but were infected in the past, as measured by blood antibody titers.

*Adults who have not had measles have either escaped exposure, or have **responded without manifesting the pathognomonic rash**. In general, the presence of measles virus antibodies is taken as evidence of past infection; in the present investigation, it was regarded as evidence of viral infection, but not necessarily of* *clinical measles . . . **Specific IgG antibody was detected in 53 out of 56 individuals with a negative history of measles,** and in all 59 controls [controls had a known history of measles].*[656]

This scenario of evidence of prior infection without clinical knowledge of measles occurred because of the administration of measles immune globulin and from vaccinating individuals who had measles-specific antibody that was either maternally derived or injected by clinicians. These rashless individuals would have numbered in the millions. Dr Cherry reported[657] that the practice of concomitant immune globulin went on long after its discontinuation was recommended in 1968.

Immune serum globulin (ISG) that was injected upon measles exposure and given to millions at the time of vaccination in the 1960s could have had serious health consequences that are manifesting today, yet nobody is making the connection. The antibody had the potential to interfere with normal cell-mediated processing of the virus.

Those who were infected by a live vaccine or a natural virus later but did not form a rash appear to be most at risk. Chen et al.[658] reported that illness without rash due to measles may occur in persons with antibody titers above the accepted target of 120.

---

[656] T. Rønne, "Measles Virus Infection Without Rash in Childhood Is Related to Disease in Adult Life," *The Lancet*, vol. 325, no. 8419, January1985, pp. 1–5.

[657] J. D. Cherry, "The 'New' Epidemiology of Measles and Rubella," *Hospital Practice,* vol. 15, no. 7, July 1980, pp. 49–57.

[658] R. T. Chen et al., "Measles Antibody: Reevaluation of Protective Titers," *Journal of Infectious Diseases,* vol. 162, no. 5, November 1990, pp. 1036–1042.

There are several scenarios regarding preexisting antibody and measles:

1. Preexisting antibody prior to any measles exposure (which is a setup for primary vaccine failure). This can happen in infants who have maternal antibody and are vaccinated anyway. The other situation in which this can happen is when there is gamma globulin administered, followed by an encounter with wild measles or vaccine measles. This is what Dr. Rønne wrote about. It is also a setup for limited response to the virus and later chronic diseases.

2. No injected antibody and subsequent natural measles after weaned from extended breastfeeding, which is the ideal situation for full recovery and immunity for life.

3. No antibody and then a subsequent vaccine. This can go either way, and any of the above can happen. Primary vaccine failure is possible. Additionally, the route of infection being a syringe needle gives access to the nervous system in a way that natural measles does not and provokes an immune response that differs from inhaled exposure in several ways.

4. Vaccinated with inactivated virus, and then subsequent vaccination with a different virus or subsequent infection with natural measles. This has the potential of committing original antigenic sin, which could leave the vaccine recipient unable to respond fully and allow for persistent infection.

Acute natural infection and presumably even vaccination during a time when measles-specific antibody is present may induce a long-term suppressive effect on measles immune response. The presence of such antibodies at the time of infection interferes with the cellular immunological response to measles virus, especially with the development of specific cell-mediated immunity (and/or other cytotoxic reactions).[659]

---

[659] T. Rønne, "Measles Virus Infection Without Rash in Childhood Is Related to Disease in Adult Life," *The Lancet*, vol. 325, no. 8419, January 1985, pp. 1–5.

Intracellular measles virus may then survive the acute infection and later cause diseases which develop in adulthood. This is quite a startling revelation; however, there is a highly significant association between a negative history of known measles with evidence of prior rashless infection (detected by antibody before and after later re-exposure) and four disease categories: immunoreactive diseases, sebaceous skin diseases, degenerative diseases of bone and cartilage, and tumors.[660]

Those children who received ISG (immune serum globulin), after 1941 and through the 1960s and 1970s and, in some cases, even today as part of measles prevention, were/are most at risk. This is yet another unintended consequence of interfering with a virus that really needed to be met with a cellular immune system replete with vitamins A, C, and D and not with a vaccine-primed immune system or immune globulin.

The interaction of preexisting measles antibodies with measles virus disrupts the normal cellular immune response and has implications for infants who are vaccinated at a time when they still have circulating

> Although vaccinating a malnourished person or a child with any illness in progress is clearly dangerous due to the immunosuppressive effects of vaccination, in 1997 the World Health Organization stated that measles vaccines should be given to any sick child regardless of illness or nutrition. Shockingly, they stated: "Since there are virtually no contraindications to measles vaccination, measles vaccine should be administered regardless of the patient's health status. Measles vaccination is particularly important for malnourished children and for those with chronic illnesses, as they are at increased risk of complications due to measles. An exception to this recommendation is children who, on admission, are so ill that they are at serious risk of dying. Although administration of measles vaccine is not dangerous in such cases, parents may incorrectly attribute a death to the vaccination." (R. J. Biellik et al., *Bulletin World Health Organization*, 1997)

---

[660] T. Rønne, "Measles Virus Infection Without Rash in Childhood Is Related to Disease in Adult Life," *The Lancet*, vol. 325, no. 8419, January 1985, pp. 1–5.

maternally derived antibody, which persists for about 12 to 15 months. (Vaccination of mothers, however, has reduced the longevity of maternal antibody. See next section.) It is well known that infants do not respond in the desired fashion to a vaccine given in the early months of life, and if they are vaccinated too early (before 15 months of age) they can become nonresponders even after revaccination.[661] For this reason, the vaccine is delayed in the United States until 12 months of age. However, the WHO recommends vaccination as early as 6 months of age in undeveloped countries where they deem the risk of infection to be greater than adverse consequences of a vaccine that has "virtually no contraindication."[662]

It is known that vaccinating an infant too early will result in primary vaccine failure due to interference by maternal immunity as well as limited response of the immature infant immune system, which is by design not highly reactive initially. But what are the potential consequences of vaccinating while maternal-specific anti-measles antibody is present? Dr. Rønne's research[663] (discussed previously) revealed significantly higher rates of cancer and autoimmune diseases in humans vaccinated while immune globulin was present.

*The decreasing maternal antibody levels in children under one year of age are inversely related to increasing responsiveness of infants to measles vaccine. In those who receive a primary vaccination against measles before 10 months of age, revaccination several years later is often unsuccessful, indicating **that***

---

[661] De Serres et al., "Higher Risk of Measles When the First Dose of a 2-Dose Schedule of Measles Vaccine Is Given at 12–14 Months Versus 15 Months of Age," *Clinical Infectious Diseases,* vol. 55, no. 3, August 2012, pp. 394–402.

[662] R. J. Biellik et al., "Strategies for Minimizing Nosocomial Measles Transmission," *Bulletin World Health Organization*, vol. 75, no. 4, 1997, pp. 367–375.

[663] T. Rønne, "Measles Virus Infection Without Rash in Childhood Is Related to Disease in Adult Life," *The Lancet*, vol. 325, no. 8419, January 1985, pp. 1–5.

immunization performed while antibody is present may induce a long-term suppressive effect.[664]

How many vaccines result in a suppressive effect and scenarios that are immunologically identical to rashless measles? Is the suppression and occult carriage of a disease like measles worth the risk, given the potential long-term consequences? How would people with the diseases mentioned by Dr. Rønne ever know that they were a consequence of suppressing cellular response to measles by a vaccine or immune globulin? Who would make the connection between a medical intervention and its long-term consequences? **How does this all fit into the present-day epidemic of connective tissue diseases, immunoreactive diseases, and degenerative and tumorous ailments?** Have any studies of completely vaccinated versus never vaccinated children been done? No. Vaccine science will not and has not ventured anywhere near Dr. Rønne's provocative report.

Pulling off the blanket: Loss of maternal protection

All mothers provide some degree of disease protection to their infants by passing immunity through both placenta and breast milk. The degree of protection depends on the vaccination history or infection history of the mother, the continuous infection rate in the population, and the nutrition of the mother.

Breastfeeding infants borrow the mother's innate immune system and memory immunity that was acquired through her previous natural infection. Also relevant to measles is that infants are fed vitamin A through breast milk.

Some literature incorrectly assumes that the protection afforded to the infant is derived solely from passively acquired antibodies. But breast milk carries a host of viral-neutralizing agents other than immune globulins, which is why fewer breastfed infants get measles

---

[664] T. Rønne, "Measles Virus Infection Without Rash in Childhood Is Related to Disease in Adult Life," *The Lancet*, vol. 325, no. 8419, January1985, pp. 1–5.

than non-breastfed infants. Silfverdal reported a negative association between a diagnosis of clinical measles infection and duration
of breastfeeding, even after adjusting for vaccination status. There
was a 30 percent decreased risk in children who were breastfed for
more than three months in comparison with those who were never
breastfed.[665]

Breast milk is not just food, and its immunoprotective properties
involve more than just antibodies. Colostrum contains viable T
lymphocytes that impart immunity to the newborn.[666]

A flood of immune cells ready and primed to do battle comes from
maternal milk. Immunocompetent measles-convalesced mothers are
known to transfer memory-activated T lymphocytes that have accumulated in the breast. The T cells in mammary glands are predominantly activated ones and far exceed the concentration in
maternal blood.[667] Those cells enter the infant's intestine, pass
through to infant lymph nodes, and are used by that infant to resist
disease. This type of immunity is not from placental transference and
is only present in breastfed infants, not formula-fed ones.[668]

Breastfeeding was at a historic low in the United States in the 1940s,
with only 25 percent of infants initiated with breast milk, most of
whom were rapidly weaned by two months.[669] There was an upward
trend in the 1970s to about a 35 percent initiation rate,[670] which

---

[665] S. A. Silfverdal et al., "Breast-Feeding and a Subsequent Diagnosis of
Measles," *Acta Paediatr,* vol. 98, no. 4, April 2009, pp. 715–719.
[666] M. Parmely et al., "Colostral Cell-Mediated Immunity and the Concept of a
Common Secretory Immune System," *Journal of Dairy Science,* vol. 60, no. 4,
April 1977, pp. 655–665.
[667] C. Le Jan, "Cellular Components of Mammary Secretions and Neonatal
Immunity: A Review," *Veterinary Research,* vol. 27, nos. 4–5, 1996,
pp. 403–417.
[668] J. Schlesinger et al., "Evidence for Transmission of Lymphocyte Responses
to Tuberculin by Breast-Feeding," *The Lancet,* September 1977, pp. 529–532.
[669] C. Hirschman and M. Butler, "Trends and Differentials in Breast Feeding: An
Update," *Demography,* vol. 18, no. 1, February 1981, pp. 39–54.
[670] Ibid.

slowly continued to rise to today's initiation rate of approximately 75 percent.[671]

Breast milk contains stem cells, myoepithelial progenitors, immune cells, interferon, and cytokines. A vast array of "new" immune cells are being added to the list every year. There is ample evidence that breast milk has an immunomodulating effect via interferon and Th1 cell response to measles that formula does not have.[672]

There are lower levels of virus-specific immunity in the serum and milk in vaccinated mothers compared to naturally immune mothers. Although the overall clinical case rate may have declined with measles vaccination, the most sensitive members of the herd are at an increased risk today—because of vaccination.

Breastfed infants of vaccinated mothers have nearly three times the risk of measles infection than those of naturally immune mothers—even in the era of vaccination when there is supposedly less measles virus in the environment.

> *Infants whose mothers were born after 1963 had a measles attack rate of 33%, compared to 12% for infants of older mothers.* **Infants whose mothers were born after 1963 are more susceptible to measles than are infants of older mothers. An increasing proportion of infants born in the United States may be susceptible to measles** . . . *the adjusted odds ratio for maternal year of birth (born after 1963) was 7.5 (95% confidence interval 1.8, 30.6).*[673]

---

[671] *CDC Breastfeeding Report Card—United States, 2012,* www.cdc.gov/breastfeeding/data/reportcard.htm.

[672] C. Le Jan, "Cellular Components of Mammary Secretions and Neonatal Immunity: A Review," *Veterinary Research,* vol. 27, nos. 4–5, 1996, pp. 403–417.

[673] M. Papania et al., "Increased Susceptibility to Measles in Infants in the United States," *Pediatrics,* vol. 1045, no. 5, e59, November 1999, pp. 1–6.

In 2005 nearly 60 percent of 503 hospitalized children with measles were younger than nine months old. And there was a specific reason for that.

> **Our results suggest that infants born to mothers who acquired immunity to measles by vaccination may get a relatively small amount of measles antibody, resulting in loss of the immunity to measles before the vaccination age.** *Measures to improve the immunity in young infants not eligible for measles vaccination would be critical to interrupt the measles transmission in China.*[674]

The fact that vaccinated people have inferior immunity in comparison to the naturally convalesced has led to the recommendation of revaccinating women before pregnancy. But this type of artificial immunity will not be transferred as well as natural immunity.

> *Waning immunity may become an increasing problem as vaccine coverage increases: because more mothers will have been vaccinated and since they have not been exposed or had natural measles, they will transmit lower levels of maternal antibody.* **Thus their babies become susceptible to measles by 3 to 5 months of age.**[675]

> *The starting concentrations of maternal antibodies in infants in this study depended highly on the concentration of antibodies in the mother and on her vaccination status. Infants of vaccinated women started with significantly fewer antibodies than did infants of naturally immune women. Infants of women vaccinated against measles receive fewer maternal antibodies*

---

[674] Hong Zhao, Pei-Shan Lu, Yali Hu, QiaozhenWu, Wenhu Ya1, et al., "Low Titers of Measles Antibody in Mothers Whose Infants Suffered from Measles Before Eligible Age for Measles Vaccination," *Virology Journal,* 2010.
[675] *Oxford Textbook of Medicine,* vol. 1, 2005, p. 357.

and thus have shorter protection than infants of women with naturally acquired immunity.[676]

The authors refer to antibody level differences because nobody has figured out how to tell for certain who is truly immune. People without antibodies can be completely protected from clinical illness by cellular immunity. Therefore antibody is a mere surrogate that has questionable significance.

In contrast to a vaccinated mother, if a naturally immune mother's infant is exposed to the virus during breastfeeding, the baby has access to the mother's innate and acquired cellular and humoral immunity. Medical literature suggests that the **lower risk of contracting clinical measles after being breastfed can last up to 10 years**.[677]

When Silfverdale evaluated thousands of vaccinated and unvaccinated breastfed and non-breastfed children looking at the risk of measles, breastfeeding had a significant impact on lowering measles risk when compared to non-breastfeeding, independent of vaccination.

*The inverse association of measles diagnosis with breast-feeding was found also in children vaccinated against measles with an **odds ratio** (and 95% confidence interval) **of 0.74** (0.60–0.90) for those breast-fed for more than three months compared with those who were never breast-fed. Among children **not vaccinated** against measles **the odds ratio** for breast-feeding for more than three months was **0.63** (0.50–0.79) compared with those who were never breast-fed.*[678]

---

[676] E. Leuridan, N. Hens, V. Hutse, M. Ieven, M. Aerts, et al., "Early Waning of Maternal Measles Antibodies in Era of Measles Elimination: Longitudinal Study," *British Medical Journal*, 2010.

[677] S. A. Silfverdal et al., "Breast-Feeding and a Subsequent Diagnosis of Measles," *Acta Paediatr*, vol. 98, no. 4, April 2009, pp. 715–719.

[678] Ibid.

Interestingly in Silfverdal's paper, 27.9% of all measles cases were vaccinated (1558 vaccinated cases out of 5569 vaccinated children).

Now that children who were vaccinated in the 1970s and later are of childbearing age, accumulating evidence shows that infants are not as well protected as they were when measles circulated widely, infecting nearly every child by the age of 15. Today the only solution to the issue of waning vaccine immunity is to keep vaccinating and to vaccinate childbearing-age mothers again. But this will always carry more risk than letting the disease circulate and be dealt with normally by T cells in well-nourished populations. Because the morbidity and mortality associated with measles is most severe among infants, the early loss of passive immunity demonstrated in recent studies of vaccinated mothers[679] should be of major concern.

Today, because of vaccination, young infants are more susceptible than ever. Scientists are searching for ways to vaccinate them and bypass the vaccine neutralization that comes from placental and breast milk immunity.[680] Why? That immunity protects the infant from measles. This is just another example of how vaccines have created a situation that requires even more vaccines and more manipulation of the immune system. This is financially efficient for vaccine manufacturers but scientifically and immunologically unsound.

Vitamins A and C

The cellular arm of immunity is not simple to measure and track. For this reason, it is somewhat of a guess as to how often any population requires revaccination. The general rule of thumb has always been that if there are measles outbreaks, there must be a population that needs more vaccines. The absence of deaths during outbreaks in the

---

[679] Ohsaki et al., "Reduced Passive Measles Immunity in Infants of Mothers Who Have Not Been Exposed to Measles Outbreaks," *Scandinavian Journal of Infectious Diseases,* vol. 31, pp. 17–19.
[680] Kim et al., "Insights into the Regulatory Mechanism Controlling the Inhibition of Vaccine-Induced Seroconversion by Maternal Antibodies," *Blood,* vol. 117, no. 23, June 9, 2011, pp. 6143–6151.

developed world and the importance of nutrition are always omitted from news reports.

Vitamin A stops the measles virus from rapidly multiplying inside cells by up-regulating the innate immune system in uninfected cells which helps to prevent the virus from infecting new cells. It is well known today that a low vitamin A level correlates with low measles-specific antibodies and increased morbidity and mortality.[681] Vitamin A is a well-proven intervention for reduction of mortality, concomitant infections, and hospital stay.

It made no more sense to vaccinate against measles in 1963 than it does to put an infected child in a dark room instead of just giving vitamin A, which protects the retinas and the uninfected cells. In Africa, it's the massive bodily demand for vitamin A that causes xeropthalmia (dry eyes) which, even long term, is reversible with vitamin A supplements.[682]

The efficiency of the cellular immune system is tied to the intake of dietary nutrients, including vitamin A, vitamin C, zinc, selenium, and protein rich in vitamin B. Poor nutrition leads to impaired cellular immune responses, which results in worse outcomes after measles infection or exposure.[683]

When the body fights any infection, especially measles, vitamin A stores become depleted by various mechanisms. Measles infections and high-titer measles vaccines both impair cell-mediated immunity, in part because of vitamin A depletion. Some of that depletion is a result of consumption by the epithelial cells of the body, and some is

---

[681] D. Stephens et al., "Subclinical Vitamin A Deficiency: A Potentially Unrecognized Problem in the United States," *Pediatric Nursing Journal*, vol. 22, no. 5, September–October 1996, pp. 377–389.

[682] E. Mayo-Wilson, A. Imdad, K. Herzer, M. Y. Yakoob, and Z. A. Bhutta, "Vitamin A Supplements for Preventing Mortality, Illness, and Blindness in Children Aged Under 5: Systematic Review and Meta-Analysis," *British Medical Journal*, August 25, 2011.

[683] D. N. McMurray, "Cell-Mediated Immunity in Nutritional Deficiency," *Progress in Food & Nutrition Science*, 1984, p. 193.

due to rapid immune cell turnover. But other mechanisms, which involve sequestering of vitamin A, are also probably responsible. A low vitamin A level due to malnutrition or dietary insufficiency sets the stage for an even worse outcome. Death from secondary infections is a known risk during measles, but it is mostly because of depressed cellular immune responses, due to vitamin deficiencies.

> *... cell-mediated immune responses are profoundly depressed during measles. This is important in Nigeria for measles affects the young who are often malnourished, and in such children the disease is severe and prolonged. As a result intercurrent [occurring at the same time] infections such as tuberculosis, candidiasis, and herpes simplex, which are normally controlled by cell-mediated immunity, become rampant after measles and contribute to the alarmingly high mortality rate.[684]*

> **Measles remains one of the leading causes of childhood mortality in countries where malnutrition, poor sanitation, and inadequate medical care are prevalent ... Measles is often a fatal disease among socioeconomically deprived children in tropical countries.[685]**

This also explains why during the 1800s and into the 1900s, when the general nutritional status of the Western world was improving, there was a dramatic decrease in deaths from measles.

In the 1920s, it was theorized that vitamin A could be used to fight disease. Dubbed the "anti-infective" vitamin, Dr. S. W. Clausen and Dr. A. B. McCoord of the University of Rochester Medical School found that it was effective against a variety of infections.[686]

---

[684] H. C. Whittle, J. Dossetor, A. D. M. Brysceson, and B. M. Greeenwood, "Cell-Mediated Immunity During Natural Measles Infection," *Journal of Clinical Investigation*, September 1978, p. 684.

[685] Paul D. Hoeprich, *Infectious Diseases: A Modern Treatise of Infectious Processes*, Harper and Row Publishers, 1977, pp. 691, 696.

[686] "Vitamin A Is Found to Attack Disease," *New York Times*, September 9, 1936.

Dr. Ellison reported in 1932 that well-nourished children rarely died or had serious complications from measles, even without sulfonamides and other primitive antibiotics.[687]

As early as 1932, scientists found that mortality dropped by 58 percent when children hospitalized with measles were given cod liver oil, which contains vitamins A and D and omega-3 fatty acids.[688]

In the 1970s, there were calls to ensure increases in dietary vitamin A for the management of measles in developing countries.[689]

In 1987 scientists in Tanzania used vitamin A during measles outbreaks and watched the impressive protective effects.[690]

During the 1990s, when mortality reductions of 60–90 percent were measured in poor countries using vitamin A in hospitalized measles cases, there was even more publicity of the vitamin A depletion theory in measles mortality and morbidity.

> *Combined analyses showed that massive doses of **vitamin A given to patients hospitalized with measles were associated with an approximately 60% reduction in the risk of death overall, and with an approximate 90% reduction among infants** . . . Administration of vitamin A to children who developed pneumonia before or during hospital stay reduced mortality by about 70% compared with control children.*[691]

---

[687] Adrianne Bendich, "Vitamins and Immunity," *Journal of Nutrition,* vol. 122, no. 3, March 1, 1992, p. 603.

[688] D. Stephens et al., "Subclinical Vitamin A Deficiency: A Potentially Unrecognized Problem in the United States," *Pediatric Nursing Journal,* vol. 22, no. 5, September–October 1996, pp. 377–389.

[689] David C. Morley, "Measles in the Developing World," *Proceedings Royal Society of Medicine*, vol. 67, November 1974, p. 1114.

[690] A. Foster and A. Sommer, "Corneal Ulceration, Measles and Childhood Blindness in Tanzania," *British Journal of Ophthalmology*, vol. 71, 1987, pp. 331–343.

[691] Wafaie W. Fawzi, MD; Thomas C. Chalmers, MD; M. Guillermo Herrera, MD; and Frederick Mosteller, PhD, "Vitamin A Supplementation and Child

By 2010 it was well accepted that supplementing with vitamin A during acute measles illness led to significant drops in both adverse outcomes and death.

> *Vitamin A administration also reduces opportunistic infections such as pneumonia and diarrhea associated with measles virus-induced immune suppression. Vitamin A supplementation has been shown to reduce risk of complications due to pneumonia after an acute measles episode. A study in South Africa showed that the **mortality could be reduced by 80% in acute measles with complications, following high-dose vitamin A supplementation.**[692]*

Finally, vitamin A (which is found in high concentrations in breast milk) was given credit in the battle against measles, but only after a vaccine was well accepted throughout the world.

In the United States, studies have found that vitamin A deficiency is not just a thing of the past. Even children with normal diets were vitamin deficient upon measles infection. A 1992 California study showed that 50 percent of children hospitalized with measles had a vitamin A deficiency. But there was also vitamin A deficiency in 30 percent of the sick controls who did not have measles. None of the uninfected controls showed significant deficiency.

> *We studied 20 children with measles in Long Beach, Calif., and found that 50% were vitamin A deficient. This frequency among presumably well nourished American children supports evaluation of vitamin A status as a part of acute management of measles in the United States.[693]*

Mortality: A Meta-Analysis," *Journal of the American Medical Association*, February 17, 1993, p. 901.

[692] Prakash Shetty, *Nutrition Immunity & Infection*, 2010, p. 82.

[693] Antonio C. Arrieta, MD; Margaret Zaleska, RN; Harris R. Stutman, MD; and Melvin I. Marks, MD, "Vitamin A Levels in Children with Measles in Long Beach, California," *The Journal of Pediatrics*, July 1992, p.75.

This study also implied that non-measles infections can deplete vitamin A stores, though to a lesser degree than measles.

Could even well-nourished children have suboptimal vitamin A levels due to being vaccinated? Naturally acquired measles[694] *and* measles vaccination both deplete the body of vitamin A.

> *Previous studies have shown* **excess mortality and immune abnormalities among girls immunized with high titer measles vaccine 2 to 4 years after immunization** . . . *our results showed that serum vitamin A concentrations were depressed after measles vaccination, irrespective of whether it was the monvalent or combined measles vaccine.*[695]

This "unexpected" consequence of measles vaccination was due to reduced vitamin A levels from the vaccine, which increased susceptibility to other infections.

> *High titre vaccines, like natural measles, cause long term disruption of immune function, including an imbalance in the type of helper T cell response* . . . *The message is clear.* **Strategies involving vaccination in infants with maternal antibody, or new measles vaccines, must be tested in randomized trials in which the end point is mortality and not a surrogate effect such as measles antibody titre.**[696]

> *Measles vaccine has been associated with other unexpected adverse findings in long-term studies.* **In developing countries, the use of high-titre vaccine at 4-6 months of age was associated with an unexpectedly high mortality in**

---

[694] Clive E. West, PhD, DSc, "Vitamin A and Measles," *Nutrition Reviews*, vol. 58, no. 2, p. S47.

[695] S. Songül Yalçin, MD, and Kadriye Yurdakök, MD, "Sex-Specific Differences in Serum Vitamin A Values After Measles Immunization," *The Pediatric Infectious Disease Journal*, 1999, p. 747.

[696] A.J. Hall and F.T. Cutts, "Lessons from Measles Vaccination in Developing Countries," *British Medical Journal*, vol. 307, November 1993, pp. 1205.

girls by the age of 2 years from infectious childhood illness.[697]

The other essential nutrient in measles cases is vitamin C. Lymphocyte mitogenic factor and distinct populations of T cells are known to be suppressed during measles infection. Vitamin C treatment has a beneficial effect in reversing this viral immune suppression.[698]

Availability of vitamin C-rich fruits and vegetables was another factor in disease morbidity and mortality reduction. There were improving trends in overall nutrition as seen by a parallel in the decline in deaths from measles and the vitamin C deficiency diseases. Experiments done in the 1940s showed that vitamin C was effective against measles, especially when used in higher doses.

During an epidemic [of measles] vitamin C was used prophylactically and all those who received as much as 1000 mg. every six hours, by vein or muscle, were protected from the virus. Given by mouth, 1000 mg. in fruit juice every two hours was not protective unless it was given around the clock. It was further found that 1000 mg. by mouth, four to six times each day, would modify the attack; with the appearance of Koplik's spots and fever, if the administration was increased to 12 doses each 24 hours, all signs and symptoms would disappear in 48 hours.[699]

Otitis media and pneumonia can be compounding factors in measles infections. Bacterial superinfection during a virus infection is usually

---

[697] N. P. Thompson, S. M. Montgomery, R. E. Pounder, and A. J. Wakefield, "Is Measles Vaccination a Risk Factor for Inflammatory Bowel Disease?" *The Lancet*, April 29, 1995, p. 1073.

[698] M. Joffe et al., "Lymphocyte Subsets in Measles: Depressed Helper/Inducer Subpopulation Reversed by in vitro Treatment with Levamisole Nad L-Ascorbic Acid," *The Journal of Clinical Investigation*, vol. 72, no. 3, May 1983, pp. 971–980.

[699] Fred R. Klenner, MD, "The Treatment of Poliomyelitis and Other Virus Diseases with Vitamin C," *Southern Medicine & Surgery*, July 1949.

due to vitamin C and D deficiency. Butler[700] reported that bacterial pneumonia was not significantly associated with lower vitamin A levels. That makes sense since vitamins C and D have important roles in combatting bacterial infections.

Nutrient levels may seem lacking today, but during the 1800s when disease mortality was more than 9 times higher, nutrient levels were far worse. Back then, people were dying of scurvy, and today we are simply having illness that doctors don't connect to focal or subclinical scurvy. Overall, society is much better nourished today than 200 years ago.

Nutrient deficiency is known to have a direct effect on the virulence of microorganisms. This means that a nutrient-deficient neighbor can actually influence your health.

> ... current work suggests that not only can the nutritional status of the host affect the immune response, but it can also affect the viral pathogen . . . a benign strain of coxsackievirus B3 became virulent and caused myocarditis in selenium—and vitamin E— deficient mice. . . . changed an avirulent virus into a virulent one. Once these mutations occurred, even mice with normal nutriture developed disease from the mutated virus.[701]

This raises an interesting argument in terms of herd immunity. But for some reason, we never see nutrition being mentioned in media ads that warn of disease epidemics.

SSPE

Although some may say that all the problems with measles vaccines were worth the risk because the morbidity of measles was cut down,

---

[700] J. C. Butler et al., "Measles Severity and Serum Retinol (Vitamin A) Concentration Among Children in the United States," *Pediatrics*, vol. 81, no. 6, June 1993, pp. 1176–81.
[701] M. A. Beck and O. A. Levander, "Host Nutritional Status and Its Effect on a Viral Pathogen," *The Journal of Infectious Diseases*, vol. 182, suppl. 1, September 2000, S93–S96.

they miss the bigger picture. That picture involves numerous neurologic diseases, including SSPE (subacute sclerosing panencephalitis, which is a rare, chronic progressive encephalitis that nearly universally ends in death), even in those who are appropriately vaccinated.[702]

Contrary to popular belief, SSPE is now a disease of the vaccinated. In a study of nine SSPE cases, three had been fully vaccinated against measles. There was no history of rash in any who were vaccinated and developed SSPE.

> *Also, three patients had been vaccinated against measles and there was **no clinical feature of measles before the vaccination**. Subclinical measles might be responsible for the early development of SSPE in these cases . . . There are cases occurring in vaccinated children. In these cases it is not clear whether SSPE occurred as a result of subclinical measles infection.[703]*

And:

> *Three SSPE patients did not have clinical measles infection, and they all received two doses of measles vaccine at 1 and 6 years . . . **As measles vaccination had been reported to cause SSPE, this issue definitely requires a wider epidemiologic survey** . . . we expect to encounter more measles infection despite vaccination, and more SSPE cases in the near future.[704]*

In 1989 Dyken[705] reported an increase in the proportion of cases of SSPE following measles vaccination. There is also a shorter incubation period for SSPE following vaccination compared with that

---

[702] Yilmaz et al., "Subacute Sclerosing Panencephalitis: Is There Something Different in the Younger Children?" *Brain & Development*, vol. 28, no. 10, November 2006, pp. 649–52.

[703] Ibid.

[704] P. Ip et al., "Subacute Sclerosing Panencephalitis in Children: Prevalence in South China," *Pediatric Neurology*, vol. 31, no. 1, July 2004, pp. 46–51.

[705] P. R. Dyken, S. C. Cunningham, and L. C. Ward, "Changing Character of Subacute Sclerosing Panencephalitis in the United States," *Pediatric Neurology*, vol. 5 no. 6, November–December 1989, pp. 339–341.

which develops after measles infection. SSPE is far from a closed-book issue in the era of vaccination.

Measles inclusion body encephalitis is another term for SSPE in immunocompromised persons. When it occurs in healthy children, they are deemed immunocompromised, even if there is no evidence of immunocompromise.

> We report a case of measles inclusion-body encephalitis (MIBE) occurring in an apparently healthy 21-month-old boy 8.5 months after measles-mumps-rubella vaccination. He had no prior evidence of immune deficiency and no history of measles exposure or clinical disease. . . . The nucleotide sequence in the nucleoprotein and fusion gene regions was **identical to that of the Moraten and Schwarz vaccine strains**. . . . On hospital day 51, the patient died after ventilatory support was withdrawn. . . . An immunologic evaluation of this patient was prompted by the diagnosis of MIBE. While we cannot ascribe his condition to any classic immunodeficiency syndrome, our findings support the presence of a primary immunodeficiency.[706]

Could most cases of SSPE now during the vaccine era, and in the past before vaccines, have had some sort of immunodeficiency that was never diagnosed? How many supposedly normal children actually have subtle ways their bodies work differently, that the medical profession misses because they assume so much? Why does the medical profession ignore what they don't know? Even more important, they don't even consider the fact that they don't know what they don't know.

Antipyretics and immune globulin have been administered to blunt the immune response to live vaccine measles and to wild measles, perhaps trapping measles virus in the body indefinitely. The fact that

---

[706] A. Bitnun et al., "Measles Inclusion-Body Encephalitis Caused by the Vaccine Strain of Measles Virus," *Clinical Infectious Diseases,* vol. 29, no. 4, October 1999, pp. 855–861.

SSPE is related to incomplete viral clearance and that measles-specific immune globulin caused much of the incomplete viral processing, potentially places SSPE into the category of both an immunodeficiency and an iatrogenic disease. Those who have probed the topic of vaccine-strain measles as a cause of disease have wound up in dangerous territory. As with the scientific exploration of SV40, the cancer virus from polio vaccines, the discussion of vaccine-strain measles virus as a cause of serious disease is shunned.

Kidney disease improvement after measles

Infection with measles virus during severe unrelenting episodes of childhood nephrotic syndrome[707] has been a topic of much discussion in the medical literature since the early part of the 20th century, beginning with Pirquet in 1908.[708] Numerous reports reflecting varying degrees of resolution after measles infections exist in conventional medical journals.[709,710]

At first glance, some of the results seem lackluster, as many of the children had recurrence after a period of becoming disease-free. However, upon closer examination of how these children were treated, nearly all the relapses occurred in those who were also treated with gamma globulin, which reduces the full expression and immune response to measles. Or they were given sulfa drugs or mercurials. The reports that reflect cases of nephrotic syndrome and untampered measles infection, with limited or no radical treatment of the nephrosis, had the most long-lasting and dramatic recoveries. One case of interest appeared in the journal *Archives of Disease in Childhood* in 1978. It was a reflection on a boy who developed

---

[707] Large amounts of protein lost into the urine from the blood characterized by proteinuria, hypoalbuminemia, hyperlipidemia, and edema.
[708] C. von Pirquet, "Das verhalten der kutanen Tuberculin Reaktion wahrend Masern," *Deutsche Medizinische Wochenschrilt*, vol. 34, 1908, p. 1297.
[709] R. W. Blumberg and H. A. Cassady, "Effect of Measles on the Nephrotic Syndrome," *Archives of Disease in Childhood,* vol. 73, no. 2, February 1947, pp. 151–166.
[710] G. Oberg, "Effect of Measles on the Nephrotic Syndrome," *Upsala Lakareforen Forh,* vol. 15, no. 54(1–2), March 1949, pp. 85–89.

nephrosis 60 years prior. He was not given any drugs and had a full and lifelong recovery.

What makes his case even more interesting is that it followed Dr. Constantine Hering's laws of disease. It is obvious that a superficial entity was driven deeper by suppressive treatments, resulting in his nephrosis.

> *R. was a healthy 10-year-old boy who in 1916 developed a rash on the legs, diagnosed as eczema. After prolonged treatment with an ointment the rash disappeared. A specimen of urine routinely examined during this time had been noted to contain albumin and casts.*[711]

Doctors continued draining his abdomen of liters upon liters of fluid, making his case worse, to the point where his death was predicted to be imminent.

> *His poor swollen face with its horrible waxen pallor was scarcely recognisable. So certain did death now seem that the whole family was taken to be outfitted with mourning clothes.*[712]

Before the doctors' treatments of repeated abdominal fluid drainage with development of an abscess were able to kill him, wild measles developed and restored his health.

> *Once more hopes rose, only to be extinguished yet again by what appeared at the time to be the inevitably final catastrophe—the onset of a high fever and what proved to be an attack of measles. Miraculously, as it seemed to those about him, he survived this and thereafter his gradual return to full health was uninterrupted. Some 6 months had elapsed since he had first become oedematous, a trace of albumin in the urine*

---

[711] D. Gairdner, "A Notable Case of Nephrosis," *Archives of Disease in Childhood*, vol. 53, no. 5, May 1978, pp. 63–365.
[712] Ibid.

only remained.[713]

The boy enjoyed lifelong recovery. His blood pressure, blood chemistry, and creatinine clearance were normal more than 60 years later. He became a pediatrician. And he was most likely cured *because* corticosteroids, gamma globulin, and antibiotics were not used.

Conclusion

Alexander Langmuir, MD, is known today as "the father of infectious disease epidemiology." In 1949 he created the epidemiology section of what became the CDC. He also headed the Polio Surveillance Unit that was started in 1955 after the polio vaccine misadventures. Dr. Langmuir knew that measles was not a disease that needed eradication when he said:

> *To those who ask me, "Why do you wish to eradicate measles?,"*
> *I reply with the same answer that Hillary used when asked why*
> *he wished to climb Mt. Everest. He said, "Because it is there." To*
> *this may be added, "... and it can be done."*[714]

Langmuir also knew that by the time vaccine was developed, measles mortality in the United States had already declined to minimal levels when he described measles as a:

> *... self-limiting infection of short duration, moderate severity, and*
> *low fatality ...*[715]

The vaccine was created because it could be done, not necessarily because it was needed.

---

[713] D. Gairdner, "A Notable Case of Nephrosis," *Archives of Disease in Childhood,* vol. 53, no. 5, May 1978, pp. 63–365.
[714] A. Langmuir, "The Importance of Measles as a Health Problem," *American Journal of Public Health*, vol. 52, no. 2, 1962, pp. 1–4.
[715] Ibid.

Today Merck has been accused, by two of its inside virologists, of falsifying documents in order to keep its mumps vaccine patent, all the while knowing that the vaccine is not effective. A lawsuit was filed in 2010[716] and an amended complaint in 2012,[717] detailing Merck's efforts to allegedly "defraud the United States through an ongoing scheme to sell the government a mumps vaccine that is mislabeled, misbranded, adulterated, and falsely certified as having an efficacy rate that is significantly higher than it actually is." Merck allegedly did this from the year 2000 onward to maintain its exclusive license to sell the MMR vaccine and keep its monopoly of the US market. Interestingly, this ongoing event has been widely shielded from mainstream media.

During the alleged fraudulent activity occurring in Merck's labs, two courageous scientists voiced their objection. They claim to have been told by upper management that if they called the FDA they would be jailed. They were also reminded of the very large bonuses that were to be rewarded after the vaccines were certified.

If what these scientists claim is true, the net result of Merck's questionable activity were mumps epidemics and outbreaks that have led to the perceived need for more boosters and, thus, increased revenue for Merck.

It is known that the mumps component of all MMR vaccines from the mid-1990s has had a very low efficacy, estimated at 69 percent.[718] The mumps portion has lost efficacy (the ability to stimulate immune response), but not necessarily its ability to multiply and remain in the body. What do you think happens to a live attenuated virus that

---

[716] Krahling and Wlochowski v. Merck & Co., Inc., civil action # 10-4374(CDJ), complaint for the violations of the federal false claims act, United States District Court for the Eastern District of Pennsylvania, filed August 27, 2010.
[717] Ibid.
[718] R. Harling et al., "The Effectiveness of the Mumps Component of the MMR Vaccine: A Case Control Study," *Vaccine,* vol. 23, no. 31, July 2005, pp. 4070–4074.

is injected into a person and elicits only a sluggish immune response? It essentially amounts to persistent infection.

What disasters can befall those who accept injections of any vaccine virus that can live indefinitely within?

Person-to-person measles transmission seems to have been interrupted after years of experimental vaccinations and some surprising and unintended consequences. Much of the interruption was done by intentionally subjecting children to measles viruses through needle injection which the immune system can react to in abnormal ways, creating other diseases in the process.

What we have now is a population of increasingly unhealthy children—with rates of many chronic disorders increasing dramatically. Vaccination, for many, is a matter of swapping one set of possible risks for another set of probable risks, which are said to be "coincident."

~ 15 ~

STARVATION, SCURVY, AND VITAMIN C

A large number of men in our army were attacked by a certain pestilence, against which the doctors could not find any remedy in their art. A sudden pain seized their feet and legs; immediately afterwards the gums and teeth were attacked by a sort of gangrene, and the patient could not eat any more. Then the bones of the legs became horribly black, and so, after having continued pain, during which they showed the greatest patience, a large number of Christians went to rest on the bosom of our Lord.

– Jacques de Vitry (1160–1240), the First Crusade

I wish my colleagues who discourse so prolixly about the treatment of this disease would recognize that the grass in the fields, inconspicuous as it is, has a greater power to heal this disease than all their fancied wisdom and unsurpassed panaceas.

– Abraham Bogaert, Dutch physician (1663–1727), 1711

Vitamin C can truthfully be designated as the antitoxic and antiviral vitamin.

– Dr. C. W. Jungeblut (1897–1976), 1930s

Most vitamins are required by essentially all species of animals. Vitamin C is required by only a few species, including man.

– Linus Pauling (1901–1994), Nobel Prize in Chemistry (1954); Nobel Peace Prize (1963)

Infectious diseases such as smallpox, measles, and whooping cough were not the only health perils faced by the people of the past.

Starvation

Scarcity of food and periodic famines have historically resulted in deadly malnutrition. Vitamin deficiency is a common consequence of starvation that can lead to scurvy, pellagra, beriberi, anemia, and other nutrient-deficiency illnesses. Because vitamins have a strong impact on the immune system, people who are deficient can become susceptible to all types of infections. Poor housing, deplorable and extremely stressful working conditions, and other negative consequences of poverty, combined with malnutrition, opened the door for a wide variety of infectious diseases.

> *Famines always provide a fertile breeding ground for many diseases. The lack of food not only produced oedemas [excessive watery swelling] and specific deficiency diseases among the people, but also, by lessening their resistance, made them an easy prey to all kinds of infections. Since famines disorganized normal life, people's living conditions became worse. The louse thrived and typhus spread.*[719]

An article written in 1836 described the miserable state of people throughout the world who were near starvation.

> *In France, beggars are numerous, and people die of hunger. In fruitful and vine-clad Portugal, a pilot will prostate himself on the deck of a vessel, in his gratitude for the boon of a hard biscuit. The Arabs, half-starved themselves, devour half-starved sheep. In luxuriant Chili, the inhabitants feed on sea-weed in the intervals of their crops, and those, who are of delicate constitutions, do not survive. In Canada, during the winter, many are starved to death. In Buenos Ayres, numbers live on offals [waste], at the public shambles. In upper Peru, the natives eat animals that die of disease. The Chinese do the same and likewise convert other disgusting matters into food. Thousands of infants are destroyed in China; nor is it considered a crime;*

---

[719] Henry E. Sigerist, *Civilization and Disease*, Cornell University Press, New York, 1943, pp. 8–9, 55.

since the babe suffers a less cruel death by its mother's hand, that it would by starvation. In Norway and Sweden, the people mix their bread with saw-dust.[720]

A letter recorded in an 1851 House of Commons report detailed the plight of the people on the island of Skye in Scotland. Many were without land, food, or work, which left numerous families on the verge of starvation.

The people are in the depth of misery, they have nothing to eat, and they have no employment, and no prospect whatever before them but death! . . . There are about 400 persons this night without 400 ounces of meal among them all . . . At Roag I found a family of Rory Campbell in actual starvation. The wife in bed unable to rise from pure want. Four children, ragged, lank, and lean. The oldest fourteen years, the youngest three and a half years . . . For four days, this family lived on three pounds of oatmeal.[721]

The Irish people suffered horribly from shortages of food in the early 1800s. Millions were in a state of near starvation, and many starved to death. An 1835 report describes the horrendous situation.

. . . there were half a million fewer human beings in Ireland between 1831 and 1841 than there had been between 1821 and 1831. The Commissioners of Poor-law Inquiry, in 1835, report that 2,300,000 of the agricultural population are in a constant state approaching starvation.[722]

During the Great Irish Potato Famine that took place from 1846 to 1847, people died not only from starvation, but also from diseases that took hold as a result of malnutrition.

---

[720] "Scanty Sustenance," *The American Magazine of Useful and Entertaining Knowledge*, vol. II, Boston, 1836, p. 348.
[721] Sir John McNeil, GCB, *Report of the Board of Supervision on the Western Highlands and Islands,* 1850, p. 50.
[722] "The State of Ireland," *The Spectator*, vol. 19, 1846, pp. 174–175.

*In Ireland, which had a soaring population, potato blight caused famine and thousands of deaths in 1810, 1820, and 1830, leading in the years after to **the notorious Great Famine in which perhaps two million people died, some from starvation, but far more from typhus and other epidemics consequent upon malnutrition and social collapse.**[723]*

Mrs. Asenath Nicholson described the situation suffered by the people in her book *Annals of the Famine in Ireland in 1847, 1848, and 1849* published in 1851. Mrs. Nicholson, a native of Vermont, wrote of her eyewitness account of the condition of the Irish people.

So that they, the people, were under the necessity of cutting down their potatoes and giving them to their cattle to keep them alive. All these circumstances connected together, have brought hunger to reign among them to that degree, that the generality of the peasantry are on the small allowance of one meal a day, and many families cannot afford more than one meal in two days, and sometimes one meal in three days. Their children are crying and fainting with hunger, and their parents weeping, being full of grief, hunger, debility, and dejection, with glooming aspect, looking at their children likely to expire in the jaws of starvation.[724]

A *New York Times* article described the meager conditions of the people living in St. Petersburg, Russia, in 1899. Lack of food and poor living conditions left the population susceptible to numerous diseases.

The newspapers of the city publish accounts of the condition of the so-called famine districts of Russia, especially Samara, in the eastern part of European Russia. The efforts of the Red Cross Society have staved off the horrors of actual starvation;

---

[723] Roy Porter, *The Greatest Benefit to Mankind*, Harper Collins, New York, 1997, p. 398.

[724] A. Nicholson, *Annals of the Famine in Ireland in 1847, 1848, and 1849*, New York, 1851, p. 90.

but the society's funds are almost exhausted; and the dire distress, compelling the consumption of all kinds of garbage, had produced an epidemic of terrible mortality, with typhus, scurvy, and other pestilential diseases. The peasants are compelled to sell everything and are living in cold, damp, and filthy cabins. Weakened by hunger, they fall ready victims to typhus and acute scurvy.[725]

From 1919 to 1923, people in Soviet Russia suffered a dreadful famine. Twenty-two million faced starvation so severe that cannibalism became an option for survival.

> *. . . conditions in Russia are getting worse every day. Starvation is increasing . . . We are quite helpless in the growing distress . . .* **Cannibalism is spreading to a terrific degree . . . Twenty-two million people are now directly endangered by starvation . . . Seven or eight million people might perhaps be saved by us next autumn. But the rest (i.e., 14 or 15,000,000) inevitably face starvation** *. . . The truth is: Starvation is going to be worse next year, and even the year after the next will be a terrible one.*[726]

> *Winter is bringing immense misery, and hundreds of thousands of deaths from hunger and disease have occurred throughout the Middle East, Caucasus and South Russia. The flight of refugees of all nationalities throughout Asia Minor into South Russia has begun. Reports indicate that the unprecedented hardships are increased by various little wars and also by little bands who prey on one another, when there are no other victims. It is believed that cannibalism is frequent. The Smyrna district is a fair example of Asia Minor. It is estimated that*

---

[725] "The Famine in Russia, Red Cross Funds Have Run Low and Peasants Are Dying," *New York Times*, March 24, 1899.

[726] Harold Henry Fisher, *The Famine in Soviet Russia, 1919–1923: The Operations of the American Relief Administration*, 1927, p. 300.

there are more than 150,000 Turks homeless, living in the open in that district, and most of them starving.[727]

This 1873 report discussed the poor quality of food available in US cities. The unhealthy food left many children malnourished and susceptible to all types of disease. Adulterated meats would often be made into sausages or disguised to hide the fact that they were diseased or rancid.

*A great evil is creeping into our city through the avarice and inhumanity of certain butchers, who kill diseased cattle which they buy cheap, and cut up and sell in sausages and other forms of disguise . . . In our large cities there is no more frequent cause of disease than the sale of unwholesome food. The lower classes, victims of poverty and the avarice of dealers, habitually consume food that is most unwholesome, indeed poisonous, and as a consequence, often from that cause alone, drag out a miserable physical existence, **and their children are puny, wretched specimens of humanity, who fall easy prey to epidemics.**[728]*

Scurvy and Vitamin C

Scurvy is a disease that results from a deficiency of dietary vitamin C, which is essential for the formation of healthy collagen. Collagen is the protein that forms connective tissue in skin, bones, and blood vessels and also gives support to internal organs. In scurvy, the body is not able to generate adequate collagen or extracellular matrix proteins that serve as mortar holding cells together. As a result, the body literally comes unglued and falls apart. A 1907 article describes a person who suffered with severe scurvy. His body slowly disintegrated until he died.

---

[727] "Great Hosts Perish in Wake of War, Hundreds of Thousands of People Said to Have Died of Hunger and Disease, Talk of Cannibalism," *New York Times*, December 16, 1919.
[728] *Second Annual Report of the Board of Health of the District of Columbia*, 1873, p. 121.

No one who has not seen with his own eyes the victim of scurvy can image what torment that plague entails. It is a disease that comes on very gradually—the patient usually complaining at **first of only a general weakness and apathy.** *He moves with difficulty, preferring to sit or lie down and his face becomes drawn and pale. Soon his gums become painfully tender, blood oozing from them at the slightest pressure, and his teeth get loose in their sockets;—he can eat noth-*

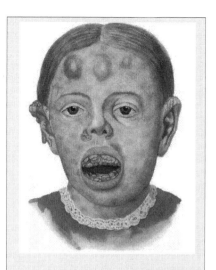

Photo 15.1: Infantile Scurvy. Ellen S. Five years old. The gums are swollen or beefy and hanging in tumor-like masses. There are also blood-tumors on the forehead. (1914)

ing solid, so in a few days he becomes too weak to move about, and takes to his bed. Little by little the sufferer's legs begin to swell, angry red spots appear on the skin, and rapidly become violet, blue and black, like bad bruises. These spots are caused by the rupture of superficial blood vessels, just as in true bruises, and as the swelling of the lower limbs increases, the spots become so numerous that all the leg appears like a polished black log. The patient cannot stretch his swollen legs and lies motionless with his legs drawn up. Often the distended skin bursts, and large open sores add to the torture of the stricken man. At the same time the gums become one mass of bleeding and decaying tissue which sometimes assumes the aspect of a fungoid growth that half fills the cavity of the mouth. The patient's breath smells unbearably, so that the air of the room soon becomes poisoned by the putrid odor. At this stage if medical assistance and constant careful nursing are not available, the sufferer rapidly loses his last strength and **soon dies from exhaustion.**[729]

Note the quote above says the first symptoms of scurvy are apathy and weakness, and they soon die from exhaustion. Vitamin C has numerous functions in the body. Probably the most important action involves the part of vitamin C called ascorbic acid, which is essential for normal mitochondrial metabolism.

Ascorbic acid is protective against reactive oxygen species (free radical damage) in the mitochondria and keeps the mitochondria healthy.

A brief mention of mitochondria is called for in any discussion of scurvy. If you are unfamiliar with these amazing intracellular organelles, they are sometimes called "cellular powerhouses" because they are responsible for the production of chemical energy. The oxygen you breathe is used within mitochondria to produce chemical energy called adenosine triphosphate, or ATP. In addition to supplying cellular energy, mitochondria are involved in other tasks such as signaling, cellular differentiation, control of the cell cycle, and cell growth.

Since levels of mitochondrial AA can be augmented with dietary vitamin C supplementation, our data suggest the pharmacological relevance of vitamin C in the protection of the mitochondrial genome against oxidative injury.[730]

Ascorbic acid is also necessary for transport of one of three types of substrates used for fuel. Proteins, sugars, and fats are used for energy production to generate ATP, which is the main energy source for the majority of cellular functions of the body. Without ATP, cell

---

[729] Nicolai Shiffkoff, "In the Valley of the Shadow," *The Friend—A Religious and Literary Journal*, vol. LXXX, Philadelphia, 1907, p. 244.

[730] K. D. Sagun, J. M. Cárcamo, and D. W. Golde, "Vitamin C Enters Mitochondria via Facilitative Glucose Transporter 1 (Glut1) and Confers Mitochondrial Protection Against Oxidative Injury," *The FASEB Journal*, vol. 19, no. 12, October 2005, pp. 1657–1667.

energy flatlines, and critical cell functions stop. The fats cannot get through the mitochondrial membrane without ascorbic acid because an essential molecule called carnitine, which shuttles the fat inside the mitochondria, is dependent upon ascorbic acid for its generation. The biosynthesis of carnitine requires ascorbic acid as a cofactor for two separate hydroxylation steps.[731] Therefore, if there is scurvy, core metabolism shuts down, resulting in **profound fatigue** and fatty acid buildup elsewhere. This type of functional fatty acid deficiency manifests in the form of neurological disorders, cardiac disease, and muscle weakness.[732] The fatigue marks the beginning of a breakdown of the body. Without normal mitochondrial function, the immune system breaks down as do all the systems that maintain bone and flesh structure. The result is obvious—death.

The Recommended Dietary Allowance levels for vitamin C do not prevent "scurvy." They merely keep you from dying from complete mitochondrial shutdown.

William A. Guy, dean of the Medical Department of King's College, described the poor diet of gold miners in California in the 1850s. Thousands of miners subsisted on meat, fat, coffee, and alcohol while working long, hard days under the unrelenting California sun. The vitamin C-deficient diet led many to develop scurvy.

> *Scurvy has been very prevalent among the gold miners of California ... the emigrants upon the overland journeys and at the mines, as living almost entirely upon fried bacon or fat pork and flour made into batter-cakes, and fried in the fat, which completely saturates it. This is washed down with copious libations of strong coffee, and large quantities of brandy or whiskey are taken in the intervals of the meals ... this has been*

---

[731] C. S. Johnston and C. Corte, "Tissue Carnitine Fluxes in Vitamin C Depleted-Repleted Guinea Pigs," *Journal of Nutritional Biochemistry*, vol. 10, no. 12, December 1999, pp. 696–699.

[732] S. Sharma and S. M. Black, "Carnitine Homeostasis, Mitochondrial Function, and Cardiovascular Disease," *Drug Discovery Today: Disease Mechanisms*, vol. 6, nos. 1–4, 2009, pp. e31–e39.

the diet of thousands for months, under a scorching sun, when the temperature was over a hundred in the shade, the men being at the same time subjected to the most intense labour.[733]

Although many died of cholera during the California Gold Rush of the mid-1800s, an estimated 10,000 men died from scurvy.

*Anthony Lorenz, who had made an intensive study of the subject and read much unpublished material, estimated that **at least 10,000 men died "of scurvy, or its sequelae, in the California Gold Rush** . . . Its victims outnumbered those of cholera." Dr. Praslow, the German physician who was in the Sacramento area in the winter of 1849-50, testified to the weakening effect of the disease: "I frequently saw patients who suffered from scurvy . . . die within a few days from an acute diarrhea."*[734]

Cause of Death	Number	%
Diarrhoea [sic]	254	37
Scorbutus (Scurvy)	202	30
Dysentery	52	8
Other diseases	63	9
Smallpox	1	
Gangrene	2	
Typhus	2	
Pneumonia	10	
Wounds	7	1
Killed	2	< 1
No causes listed	108	15
Total	688	100

The US Civil War (1861–1865) is often examined nostalgically with a focus on politics and military engagements. While many soldiers died during battle, many more died without "glory" from extreme nutritional deficiencies or otherwise preventable diseases. For instance, the causes of death listed for Indiana soldiers buried at the National Ceme-

---

[733] William A. Guy, "Lectures on Public Health, Addressed to the Students of the Theological Department of King's College," *Medical Times*, vol. 23, January–June 28, 1851, p. 283.
[734] Kenneth Carpenter, *The History of Scurvy and Vitamin C*, 1986, p. 112.

tery in Andersonville (see table on prior page), Georgia, shows that diarrhea and scurvy directly accounted for at least two-thirds.[735] Dysentery was the next common cause of death, with the infamous diseases such as smallpox, typhus, pneumonia, and gangrene responsible for only a small fraction. **Those who were killed in actual battle or who died as a result of their wounds accounted only for 1 percent of the total deaths.**

An 1882 *New York Times* article described scurvy in miners in Pottsville, Pennsylvania. These miners not only suffered from tissue degradation but from one of the other major factors in vitamin C deficiency—immune system impairment.

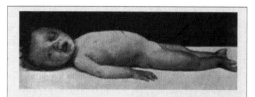

Photo 15.2: Characteristic position of the legs in scurvy. The legs are practically always tender, usually exquisitely so, so that the slightest movement or pressure causes the most severe pain. (1922)

Within the last few weeks 30 Hungarians and Poles suffering from scurvy in its worst form, as well as pneumonia, have been admitted to the county hospital. The alarming increase of such cases has provoked much comment, and the matter will be laid before the Medical Society. The disease is ascribed to the almost exclusive use of salt meat by the imported laborers about the mines and their unclean habits.[736]

Scurvy caused an enormous number of deaths, especially on long naval journeys or during wars. During the naval battles of the Seven Years' War (1754–1763), more men died of disease than from actual battle.

---

[735] *Report of the Unveiling and Dedication of Indiana Monument at Andersonville, Georgia (National Cemetery), Thursday, November 26, 1908,* pp. 73–102.
[736] "Scurvy in Pottsville," *New York Times,* June 25, 1882.

... in the Crimean war 23,000 cases of scurvy developed in the French army alone, and in all the naval battles of the Seven Years' War there were but 1512 sailors and marines killed by implements of war, yet 133,078 men died of disease or were missing, the principal being scurvy.[737]

Rickets is a softening of bones in children caused by a deficiency of vitamin D, magnesium, phosphorus, and calcium. This disease can lead to fractures and deformities. Few people are aware that vitamin C is also very important for healthy bone mineralization and for bone formation.

Industrial towns above all proved breeding ground of the archetypal diseases of poverty and overcrowding such as rickets, the crippling bone disease in infants, especially ominous for females who, as a result of pelvic deformities would often suffer fatal childbirth difficulties. Though widely known as "the English disease," Britain enjoyed no monopoly, for everywhere dinginess and deprivation provided an ideal seedbed. A 1907 survey of Paris revealed that every other child between the ages of six months and three years suffered more or less from rickets, and New York reported the same.[738]

Through the 1800s into the 1900s, a myriad of changes took place that allowed people to improve their diets. A better supply of food, including more fruits and vegetables, resulted in a slow decline of scurvy as a cause of death (Graph 15.1). The fact that scurvy is a disease of poor diet was eventually accepted by the medical profession and the public. The *New Albany Medical Herald* reported in 1907:

Infantile scurvy is a disease of modern times and is attributable to altered conditions arising from over-civilization and from the crowding into cities, which makes it difficult or

---

[737] C. Marsh Beadnell, RN, "On the Decline of Scurvy," *Guy's Hospital Gazette*, 1899, p. 349.

[738] Roy Porter, *The Greatest Benefit to Mankind*, Harper Collins, New York, 1997, p. 401.

impossible for children to be fed in an ideal manner . . . It is less than thirty years since the nature of the disease was recognized by Cheadle, his paper appearing in 1878 . . . his views were somewhat slow in gaining general acceptance, and the truth of his contention was not thoroughly established until a paper was read by Sir Thomas Barlow on this subject before the Royal Medical Society in 1883. "Scurvy is a constitutional disease due to some prolonged error in diet."[739]

By 1900 deaths from scurvy were rare and steadily decreased. Simultaneously, death from infectious diseases also drastically declined. This is because immune cells are highly dependent on a component of vitamin C called ascorbic acid.

Today we know that vitamin C is vital to several components of the human immune system, including white blood cells. About 50–70 percent of all white blood cells are neutrophils, the primary immune cell type that utilizes vitamin C. This 2004 study shows that vitamin C is also used by granulocytes, or polymorphonuclear leukocytes (PMNs). PMNs are white blood cells that contain a segmented lobular nucleus; they can be further classified into eosinophil, basophil, or neutrophil.

*. . . the ascorbate [vitamin C] pool in the PMNs is used by the PMNs to destroy the engulfed pathogens, as suggested by our results and also by earlier observations that dietary supplementation with **vitamin C augments innate immunity**.*[740]

Innate immunity is the part of cellular immunity that requires no memory of previous infection.

Data from England shows that deaths from scurvy decreased in parallel with deaths from other infectious diseases, including whooping cough (Graph 15.2) and measles (Graph 15.3).

---

[739] "Infantile Scurvy," *New Albany Medical Herald*, 1907, p. 240.

[740] P. Sharma et al., "Ascorbate-Mediated Enhancement of Reactive Oxygen Species Generation from Polymorphonuclear Leukocytes: Modulatory Effect of Nitric Oxide," *Journal of Leukocyte Biology*, vol. 75, June 2004, pp. 1075–1076.

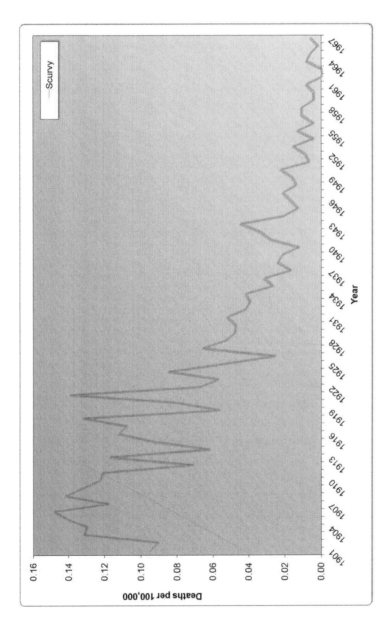

Graph 15.1: England mortality rate from scurvy from 1901 to 1967.

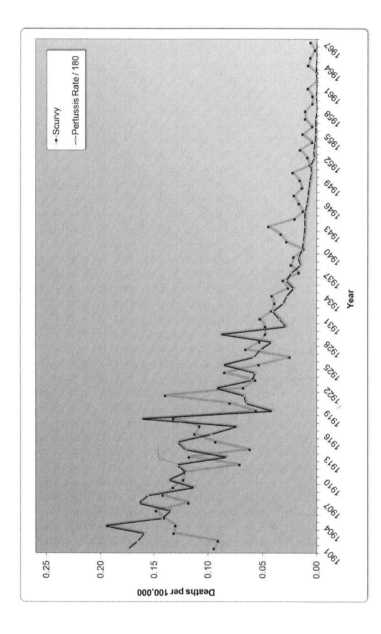

Graph 15.2: England mortality rates from scurvy vs. whooping cough from 1901 to 1967.

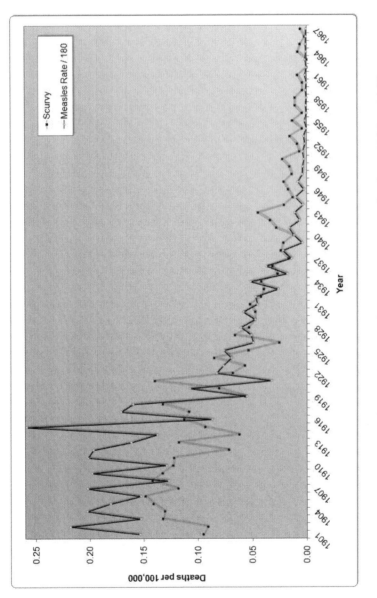

Graph 15.3: England mortality rates from scurvy vs. measles from 1901 to 1967.

A paper published in 1949 by Dr. Fred R. Klenner showed the impressive positive effects of ascorbic acid against a number of diseases. One of the diseases discussed was herpes zoster, also known as shingles. It is a disease that can cause severe pain. Dr. Klenner effectively used large doses of ascorbic acid to treat this condition and described how the pain rapidly disappeared in a number of cases.

> *In herpes zoster 2000 to 3000 mg. of vitamin C was given every 12 hours, this supplemented by 3000 mg. in fruit juice by mouth every two hours. Eight cases were treated in this series, all of adults. Seven experienced cessation of pain within two hours of the first injection and remained so without the use of any other analgesic medication. Seven of these cases showed drying of the vesicles within 24 hours and were clear of lesions within 72 hours . . . One of the patients, a man of 65, came to the office doubled up with abdominal pain . . . He was given 3000 mg. of vitamin C intravenously and directed to return to the office in four to five hours . . . He returned in four hours completely free of pain. He was given an additional 2000 mg. of vitamin C, and following the schedule given above he recovered completely in three days.*[741]

A later paper published in 1953 by Dr. Klenner also showed that vitamin C was effective against measles. He found that, when used in large doses, there was a definite positive response manifested by an increased white blood cell count (unlike bacterial infections, viral infections often drop the white blood count, which can be devastating), a drop in fever, and general all-around improvement of the patient. This rise in white blood cell count indicated a mobilizing of the immune system against the measles virus. Dr. Klenner discussed his first attempts at using vitamin C to treat a child with measles.

---

[741] Fred R. Klenner, MD, "The Treatment of Poliomyelitis and Other Virus Diseases with Vitamin C," *Southern Medicine & Surgery*, July 1949.

In the Spring of 1948 measles was running in epidemic propor-
tions in this section of the country. Our first act, then, was to
have our own little daughters play with children known to be
in the "contagious phase." When the syndrome of fever, redness
of the eyes and throat, catarrh [inflammation of a mucous
membrane], spasmodic bronchial cough, and Koplik spots
[measles skin spots] had developed and the children were obvi-
ously sick, vitamin C was started. In this experiment it was
found that 1000 mg every four hours, by mouth, would modify
the attack . . . When 1000 mg was given every two hours all
evidence of the infection cleared in 48 hours . . . the drug (vit-
amin C) was given 1000 mg every 2 hours around the clock for
four days . . . These little girls did not develop the measles rash
during the above experiment and although exposed many
times since still maintain this "immunity."[742]

Dr. Klenner described several other remarkable cases of recovery
using vitamin C. One was a 10-month-old baby with measles. The
baby had a fever of 105°F, red eyes and throat, catarrh (mucous
inflammation), spasmodic cough, and Koplik spots.

1000 mg of vitamin C was given intramuscularly every four
hours. After 12 hours the fever was 97.6°F, the conjunctivitis
and red throat had cleared, there was no cough . . . the baby
made an uneventful recovery . . . Four years have now elapsed
and there has been no measles.[743]

Another case was an eight-year-old boy who suffered from poliomyelitis. He had conjunctivitis, a sore throat, a high fever of 104°F,
nausea and vomiting, and a headache of such intensity that adult
doses of aspirin given by his mother had no effect. During the examination, he either rubbed his neck or held his head between his hands,
begging for someone to relieve the pain.

---

[742] Fred R. Klenner, MD, "The Use of Vitamin C as an Antibiotic," *Journal of Applied Nutrition*, 1953.
[743] Ibid.

Six hours after commencing therapy the neck pain was gone, the headache completely relieved, he could tolerate the ceiling light, his eyes were dry and the redness was definitely clearing. Nausea and vomiting had disappeared, the fever was down to 100.6°F., and he was sitting up in "a straight position in bed" and in a jovial mood while he drank his glass of lime ade. **He was discharged from the hospital after receiving 26 grams of vitamin C in a 48-hour period, clinically well.**[744]

A 1952 article published by Dr. McCormick described positive results using vitamin C for a number of infectious conditions.

The writer [Dr. McCormick] has previously reported spectacular results by this method in the treatment of tuberculosis, scarlet fever, pelvic infection, septicemia, etc. Concurrently, by this same method, Klenner has reported dramatic results in the treatment of virus diseases, including poliomyelitis, encephalitis, measles, herpes zoster, virus pneumonia, etc.[745]

Vitamin C's benefit during infection has much to do with the neutralization of bacterial and viral toxins and with the supply of ascorbic acid to white blood cells. But there is another more direct effect on bacteria. Today, scientists are validating the antimicrobial effect of vitamin C on certain bacterial infections. The effect involves oxidative killing via the Fenton reaction, with vitamin C essentially acting as an antibiotic.

In Escherichia coli, a common mechanism of cell death by bactericidal antibiotics involves the generation of highly reactive hydroxyl radicals via the Fenton reaction. Here we show that **vitamin C, a compound known to drive the Fenton reaction, sterilizes cultures of drug-susceptible and drug-resistant Mycobacterium tuberculosis,** *the causative agent*

---

[744] Fred R. Klenner, MD, "The Use of Vitamin C as an Antibiotic," *Journal of Applied Nutrition*, 1953.
[745] W. J. McCormick, MD, "Ascorbic Acid as a Chemotherapeutic Agent," *Archives of Pediatrics*, vol. 69, no. 4, April 1952.

of tuberculosis. The bactericidal activity of vitamin C against M. tuberculosis is dependent on high ferrous ion levels and reactive oxygen species production, and causes a pleiotropic effect affecting several biological processes.[746]

An earlier work in 1937 by Dr. Claus W. Jungleblut showed that injections of natural vitamin C were effective in preventing poliomyelitis paralysis in infected monkeys. In his experiment, he found that six times as many animals escaped paralysis following treatment with natural vitamin C than control animals.

The data presented in this paper, which are based on a number of experimental animals almost thrice as large as previously reported, leave no doubt that the administration of natural vitamin C during the incubation period of experimental poliomyelitis is followed by a definite alteration in the severity of the disease.[747]

Pertussis is another disease that consumes large amounts of vitamin C and is effectively ameliorated with high enough doses. A 1936 pilot study by Otani[748] documents more rapid improvement than expected in the majority of his cases, even though his dosing was far too low to have reached an effective threshold. He only used 50 to 200 mg per injection.

Vermillion published a similar study in 1938.

In this small series of twenty-six cases of whooping cough, cevitamic acid seemed to be strikingly effective in relieving

---

[746] C. Vilchèze, T. Hartman, B. Weinrick, and W. R. Jacobs Jr., "Mycobacterium Tuberculosis Is Extraordinarily Sensitive to Killing by a Vitamin C-Induced Fenton Reaction," *Nature Communications*, vol.4, no. 1881, May 2013, pp. 1–10.

[747] Claus W. Jungleblut, "Further Observations of Vitamin C Therapy in Experimental Poliomyelitis," *Journal of Experimental Medicine*, September 1937, pp. 470–471.

[748] T. Otani, "Concerning the Vitamin C Therapy of Whooping Cough," *Klinische Wochenschrift*, vol. 15, no. 51, December 1936, pp. 1884–1885.

and checking the symptoms in all but two of the cases which apparently received little if any relief. It is our opinion that it should be given further trial in all cases of whooping cough regardless of the age of the patient, or the length of time already elapsed since the original symptoms.[749]

But he also used very low doses of cevitamic (ascorbic acid) acid. In 1937 Ormerod reported in a small study group:

Ascorbic acid has a definite effect in shortening the period of paroxysms from a matter of weeks to a matter of days.[750]

His doses were also very low—150 to 500 mg. Given that pertussis is a toxin-mediated disease, these low doses would not have come close to tissue saturation. Sessa[751] and Meier[752] also reported positively on low-dose vitamin C in pertussis.

There are no randomized controlled trials (RCTs) to demonstrate the effect of high-dose vitamin C on the duration and severity of pertussis. However, there are practices that have been caring for very young infants and children for 30 years using high-dose vitamin C, and they have not lost or damaged one of those children. There are thousands of happy mothers who know that vitamin C saved their children from suffering the feared ravages of pertussis. Vitamin C has no known toxic dose and, when used properly, makes whooping cough far more manageable.

Doctors have used vitamin C effectively in cases of measles, scarlet fever, poliomyelitis, pertussis, opiate withdrawal, coronary artery

---

[749] E. L. Vermillion et al., "A Preliminary Report on the Use of Cevitamic Acid in the Treatment of Whooping Cough," *Journal of the Kansas Medical Society*, vol. XXXIX, no. 11, November 1938, pp. 469, 479.

[750] M. J. Ormerod et al., "Ascorbic Acid (Vitamin C) Treatment of Whooping Cough," *Canadian Medical Association Journal*, vol. 36, no. 2, August 1937, pp. 134–136.

[751] T. Sessa, "Vitamin Therapy of Whooping Cough," *Riforma Medica*, vol. 56, 1940, p. 38.

[752] K. Meier, "Vitamin C Treatment of Pertussis," *Ann Pediatr* (Paris), vol. 164, 1945, p. 50.

disease, cancer, life-threatening sepsis, encephalitis, pneumonia, and other conditions. Unfortunately, their work has been forgotten or actively denied.

~ 16 ~

LOST REMEDIES

*The greatest obstacle to discovery is not
ignorance—it is the illusion of knowledge.*

– Daniel J. Boorstin (1914–2004)

*Any person who has been exposed need have no fear
of smallpox if he will take two or three tablespoonfuls
of pure cider vinegar three or four times a day.*

– J. P. MacLean, PhD, 1901

There are hundreds of examples in the field of medicine where fundamentally flawed ideas have gained public support and were kept alive by belief momentum. Eugenics, numerous psychiatric diagnoses, harmful drugs like thalidomide, fever reducers, diethylstilbestrol, bloodletting, and unbalanced hormone replacement are several examples of faulty ideas that have historically attained a level of scientific and societal legitimacy. Not only have these strange types of beliefs been accepted, but in the midst of their unquestioned superiority, better ideas were overlooked.

In the hope of preventing disease, vaccination took hold as the only way to combat smallpox. The original belief was that vaccination was a safe way to acquire lifelong immunity. This turned out to be untrue, and thus had to be redressed as a "temporary way of making smallpox milder." Even though revaccinations were required yearly for some people, even though there was great success using isolation and disinfection after abandoning vaccination in Leicester, and even though there were large numbers of vaccination-related deaths and vaccine failures, devotion to vaccination by the medical profession became firmly established.

What you might not know is that there were always other simpler, cheaper, and more helpful means to combat diseases, many of which provided remarkable successes yet, unfortunately, never attained legitimacy in the mainstream. If a remedy couldn't be patented or given the AMA seal of acceptance, it generally would not have ranked in the public or medical eye. Here are a few examples.

Herbs

Cinnamon is a common and familiar spice that has anti-infective properties. A 2009 study in the *Journal of Cranio-Maxillofacial Surgery* showed it to be effective in hospital-acquired infections and antibiotic-resistant bacteria, which are major health concerns worldwide.[753] Cinnamon's use as an anti-infective has been known for a long time. A letter to the editor in 1878 to the medical journal the *Lancet* indicated that, during an outbreak of cholera, all cases survived through the use of cinnamon. This is an impressive claim since cholera had a very high fatality rate during the 1800s.

I see in your issue of last week that a surgeon in India has tried the injection of chloral in cholera, and lost 60 per cent of his patients. I have tried oil of cinnamon in an outbreak on board an Indian emigrant ship, and every case recovered. I have no doubt that the above medicine is a specific for cholera.[754]

In 1889 Dr. Knaggs used a combination of ingredients, including cinnamon, with good outcomes in all 75 patients who suffered with the bacterial infection diphtheria. The therapeutic mixture was precipitated sulphur, chocolate powder, glycerine, and cinnamon water.

Mix the powders in a mortar; then gradually add the glycerine with constant trituration, and lastly the cinnamon-water.

---

[753] Patrick H. Warnke et al., "The Battle Against Multi-Resistant Strains: Renaissance of Antimicrobial Essential Oils as a Promising Force to Fight Hospital-Acquired Infections," *Journal of Cranio-Maxillofacial Surgery*, vol. 37, no. 1, October 2007.

[754] T. D. Atkins, MRCS (Royal College of Surgeons), "Treatment of Cholera—To the Editor of The Lancet," *The Lancet*, March 23, 1878, p. 445.

Dose, half a teaspoonful every hour or oftener. Dr. Knaggs reports the treatment of seventy-five cases of diphtheria by this drug alone, with no fatal results.[755]

In 1899 Dr. C. G. Grant observed that cinnamon protected from malaria. He recommended it for intestinal problems, typhoid, and influenza.

*Cinnamon is recommended as an internal antiseptic by Dr. C. G. Grant (British Med. Journal). When in Ceylon he discovered that **persons working in cinnamon gardens seemed to be immune to malaria.** On trial he found it valuable in gastro-enteritis, recurrent boils, and, he thinks, in typhoid fever. He was astonished by its wonderful influence in influenza, and earnestly recommends its free use by others.*[756]

In 1907 Dr. Ross reported on his use of cinnamon oil for 16 years to help patients quickly recover from influenza. Weeks of illness from the flu were reduced to three or four days.

Ross states that for nearly sixteen years he has employed cinnamon in various forms in treating this [influenza] disease, but for many years now he has always employed the oil of Ceylon cinnamon bark . . . We all of us have heard only too often of bad cases of influenza where the unhappy patients have been confined to their beds or their rooms for a fortnight, three weeks, a month, or even longer . . . he has invariably treated influenza with cinnamon, his patients have generally been perfectly fit to return to their avocations, whatever they may have been, within three or four days, and that in no single case has a

---

[755] Cornelius E. Billington, MD, *Diphtheria: Its Nature and Treatment*, William Wood and Company, New York, 1889, p. 183.

[756] "Cinnamon as an Internal Antiseptic," *Cincinnati Lancet-Clinic*, July 1, 1899, p. 352.

patient suffering from influenza been on his hands for more than a week.[757]

In 1917 Dr. Drummond used cinnamon in the treatment of head colds and recommended its use for measles. At that time, measles was still considered a serious condition, with approximately 10,000 people, mainly children under five, dying each year in England and Wales.[758]

Dr. W. B. Drummond, Medical Superintendent of Baldovan Institution for the Feebleminded, describes in The British Medical Journal his experience with cinnamon in the preventative treatment of German measles. He urges that it be tried extensively in the endeavor to prevent epidemics of the ordinary variety of measles . . . Cinnamon is a drug whose therapeutic virtues are not sufficiently recognized. The essence of cinnamon in twenty-five-drop doses is one of the most effective remedies in cases of acute coryza, [inflammation of nasal mucous membraes] *. . . some years ago an article was published in The Journal strongly advo-cating cinnamon as a preventative of measles.*[759]

In 1919 Dr. Drummond commented that cinnamon oil was an effective prophylactic against measles or that it made measles milder.

It has been my practice, when I meet with a case of measles in a family, to prescribe a course of cinnamon for all unprotected members of the family. **In the majority of cases the person so treated [with cinnamon] escaped the disease [measles] altogether, or else had it in very mild form.**[760]

---

[757] "Cinnamon Oil in the Treatment of Influenza," *The Kansas City Medical Index-Lancet*, vol. XXVIII, no. 1, January 1907, p. 92.

[758] T. Shadick Higgins, MD, "The Prevention of Measles Mortality," *Maternity and Child Welfare*, vol. 1, no. 2, February 1917, p 7.

[759] "Cinnamon Stops Measles," *New York Times*, August 12, 1917.

[760] "Cinnamon as a Preventive of Measles," *American Druggist Pharmaceutical Record*, New York, November 1919, p. 47.

It is difficult to know exactly why cinnamon was so helpful, but today we do know that it possesses many beneficial properties, is an anti-oxidant, and contains vitamins A and C and minerals like zinc, potassium, magnesium, and manganese.

For centuries, garlic has been believed to ward off sickness. It has been used for the common cold, high blood pressure, and the prevention of gangrene. Onion is a close relative of garlic and has also been used in the treatment of many diseases. A 1903 article reported that people who ate onions were immune to smallpox. The article also stated that these same people were rarely vaccinated.

> *Dr. A. P. Seligman,* **vaccine physician to the city Board of Health, who has given considerable attention to the study and pathology of smallpox, declares that onion-eating people are virtually immune from the disease.** *Not a single case has broken out among the inhabitants of the Italian, Polish and Hungarian settlements. These people consume large quantities of onions. Vaccination is extremely rare among them.*[761]

In 1901 garlic was used to treat 200 patients with tuberculosis in the City Hospital of Venice. Improvement was noted in all stages of the disease.

> *Over 200 patients were thus treated in addition to the ordinary hygienic and symptomatic treatment. An improvement is said to have taken places in all stages of tuberculosis, especially in the early cases . . . the cough is lessened, the local physical signs disappear, as do the night-sweats and hemoptyses [coughing up of blood], and there is a remarkable improvement in appetite and the general condition.*[762]

---

[761] "Vegetables' Medicines," *The Small Farmer*, September 1903, p. 179.
[762] "Garlic in Pulmonary Tuberculosis," *Merck's Archives of Materia Medica and Drug Therapy*, vol. III, 1901, p. 357.

In 1902 Dr. Minchin published an article entitled "The Successful Treatment of Tuberculosis and Lupus by Garlic." He was quoted as saying:

> *I look upon it as a perfectly safe treatment, and also an effi-*
> *cient one in all cases of pulmonary tuberculosis in nearly all*
> *moderately-advanced cases, and in those in a very advanced*
> *stage. Its action is fairly rapid . . . I have had so much success*
> *with it that I have come to look upon few cases of consumption*
> *as hopeless.*[763]

In 1904 an interesting study was published about guinea pigs who were exposed to tuberculosis. The group that was fed a daily diet of garlic stayed free of infection. However, the control group that was not fed garlic became infected.

> *[Dr. Carrazzani] believes that a sufficiently generous use of*
> *garlic in tuberculosis will produce immunity against infection.*
> *Of a group of guinea pigs kept in an atmosphere charged with*
> *tubercle bacilli, those whose daily diet had contained one gm.*
> *of garlic were found at the end of three months to be free from*
> *tuberculosis, while the others were badly infected . . . The views*
> *of Dr. Carrazzani include a hint at an explanation for the com-*
> *paratively low death rate from pulmonary tuberculosis among*
> *the Italians, both in their own country, and in America.*[764]

A 1917 article showed that, of 56 different treatments tried in the Metropolitan Hospital in New York, garlic proved to be the best against tuberculosis. Garlic was also found to be effective against whooping cough.

> *William Charles Minchin writing in the Medical Press and Cir-*
> *cular for June 13, 1917, gives the results of years of special*
> *study of the therapeutic action of oil of garlic. This oil is*

---

[763] "Garlic for Consumption," *Otago Witness*, no. 2530, September 10, 1902, p. 64.
[764] "Garlic," *The Medical Council*, vol. IX, 1904, p. 420.

composed of allylsulphide with volatile terpenes, and would appear to be Nature's antiseptic for internal use, destroying many pathogenic germs within the body, and being at the same time harmless to the tissues . . . In the treatment of whooping cough Minchin has found garlic to be most efficacious. In the case of adults an inhalation of fresh succusallii sativa, rapidly relieves the distressing symptoms. It must be used, however, continuously from three to five hours for two or three days in order to produce the best results. In the case of infants and young children 20 minims to half a dram of the juice of garlic taken internally every four hours in a little syrup gives speedy relief in the early stages. The author lays special emphasis upon the beneficial effects of garlic in the treatment of tuberculosis, and he quotes the results obtained by the staff of the Metropolitan Hospital, New York, in **the treatment of 1082 cases of tuberculosis according to fifty-six different methods, out of which garlic gave the best results.**[765]

Modern science is confirming what has been known for hundreds of years—garlic is effective in helping the body fight infections. A 2003 study examined the use of orally ingested garlic against Methicillin-resistant Staphylococcus Aureus (MRSA), which is now a common and deadly pathogen that is resistant to many conventional antibiotics. They concluded that garlic "inhibited the growth of and killed MRSA. . . . in a dose-dependent manner."[766]

Echinacea, also called purple coneflower, has a long history of use in treating infections. It works by strengthening the immune system to better fight off infections, particularly in the early onset of a cold or the flu. This 1901 article describes the remarkable effect of echinacea on smallpox. Even in the worst type known as confluent

---

[765] "The Therapeutic Uses of Garlic," *Medical Record—A Weekly Journal of Medicine and Surgery*, September 1, 1917, p. 376.
[766] Shyh-ming Tsao, Cheng-chin Hsu, and Mei-chin Yin, "Garlic Extract and Two Diallyl Sulphides Inhibit Methicillin-Resistant Staphylococcus Aureus Infection in BALB/Ca Mice," *Journal of Antimicrobial Chemotherapy*, October 2003, p. 979.

smallpox, there was a steady improvement when echinacea was taken internally and used as a body lotion.

> Dr. Joseph Adolphus writes: "I have seen the beneficial action of Echinacea in two epidemics. The remedy in smallpox modified the severity of the disease, restrained suppuration [discharge of pus], checked the severity of symptoms and promoted convalescence. I frequently saw cases of severe confluent type, wherein the symptoms were of a serious kind, high fever, delirium, some with coma, abominably offensive odor of body and breath, urine nearly suppressed, steadily improve when taken internally, and used as a lotion over the whole body."[767]

In 1904 Dr. Mathews discussed the remarkable effects of echinacea, not only in blood infections but also in treating smallpox and anthrax. He noted that in cases of anthrax, the formation of boils could be "stopped" with the use of echinacea. It was also known to relieve burn pain almost "instantly."

> . . . with the gratifying experiences in relieving many almost helpless conditions of the various forms of blood poison, leads me to believe that in echinacea we have the best and at the same time the safest of all the remedies of its class. In the treatment of typhoid fever it seems especially valuable and can be given without interruption from the start to the close of the disease with any kind of temperature without any fear of dosing the patient any irreparable damage, but with an assurance that if properly administered the severity of the disease will be modified and less liable to have complications, and shorten its duration . . . Given **in smallpox it lessens aching and shortens the febrial [fever] period, and beyond question robs the stage of postulation of its frightful consequences. As a remedy for anthrax it exerts such an influence that the formation of new colonies of boils can almost certainly be**

---

[767] "Echinacea in Smallpox," *The Medical Summary*, 1901, p. 303.

stopped . . . As a remedy for burns I have never seen its equal. It relieves pain and burning sensation almost instantly . . .[768]

In 1905 Dr. C. S. Chamberlin extolled the virtues of echinacea in sepsis, which is an infection that has spread into the bloodstream. He believed it was a very powerful treatment that prevented the loss of life and limb.

> *In my own experience the results attending in the use of Echinacea have convinced me that there is no remedy of so great a treatment of cases of septic infection, and I have repeatedly used it in cases of septicemia following wounds of the extremities, which I am confident, by any other means of treatment, would have resulted in the loss of the limb and possibly the life of the patient.*[769]

It is likely that most people were so nutrient deficient that supplementing with substances containing vitamins and enzymes made a big difference.

Jicama

In the 1890s, General Rivera of the Mexican Army was faced with the illness of typhus fever in many of his men. A local woman administered a remedy to the soldiers with surprisingly good results. The remedy was a preparation of jicama, a sweet root vegetable native to Mexico and Central and South America. This lost hero of history used a root vegetable to treat more than 4,000 cases of pneumonia or typhus for free. Amazingly, every person was cured, and there were no reported deaths. This is especially remarkable considering that those particular diseases had very high mortality rates during that time.

---

[768] A. B. Mathews, MD, "Echinacea—Some of Its Uses in Modern Surgery," *Transaction of the Medical Association of Georgia*, 1904 , pp. 394, 395.
[769] "Value of Echinacea," *The Medical Bulletin: A Monthly Journal of Medicine and Surgery*, vol. 27, 1905, pp. 177–178.

*Gen. Aureliano Rivera, one of the bravest and most celebrated officers of the Mexican Army, has done more during the past five months toward suppressing the typhus fever epidemic in Mexico than all the physicians of the country combined. In one of his campaigns in the State of Oajaca, about a year ago, Gen. Rivera had among his troops a number of men ill with typhus fever. A woman in the town near which he was camped was permitted to administer a remedy to the patients. The results were surprisingly good, all the men recovering speedily from the disease. The General asked the woman if the medicine was a secret. She answered that it was merely a preparation of jicama, a farinaceous root . . . Within the past few months, it having been noised abroad that Gen. Rivera was gratuitously distributing a medicine that was a cure for typhus, so many Indians besieged his residence that he was obliged to open there a room as a dispensary, and daily he gives doses of the jicama free to hundreds of poor people who ask for it. In the past year it is estimated that Gen. Rivera has treated **over 4,000 cases, and there has not been one death. Every person attacked with pneumonia or typhus who has taken the marvelous remedy had been cured.** The root has never been analyzed by chemists and its properties are unknown.*[770]

Fresh juice

A 1905 article in the *New York Times* discussed a cure for tuberculosis that was developed by Dr. Russell. His treatment was vegetable juices, which cured patients who suffered from active tuberculosis.

Dr. Russell says he has found a combination of foods which seems effective in the destruction of the bacilli of tuberculosis. The most beneficial item in the food combination—consisting of butter, bread, eggs, milk, and emulsion—is, he says, vegetable juices. Since the introduction of this juice the report records

---

[770] "A Cure for Typhus Fever—Gen. Rivera Has Saved Thousands of Lives by the Use of Jicama Root," *New York Times*, May 15, 1893.

remarkable results among the tuberculosis patients. The fluid, which Dr. Russell and his colleagues at the Post-Graduate believe to have beneficial properties, is the combined juice of every kind of vegetable to be had in the market. It has been in regular use at the hospital along with the regular diet since Jan. 7. It is now recorded that in the first five months of this year eleven patients were discharged "apparently cured," against a record number of thirteen cures effected during the whole of 1904. This sudden increase, and the fact that the patients are still thriving upon the vegetable-juice treatment, lead the examiners to believe that Dr. Russell has discovered a fluid, the properties of which are fatal to the progress of tuber-culosis . . . The vegetables first used were potato, onion, beet, turnip, cabbage, and celery. Later were added sweet potato, apple, pineapple, carrot, parsnip, and later still rhubarb, (pieplant), summer squash, tomato, spinach, radishes, string beans, and green peas with the pods.[771]

In 1906 Dr. Russell published a 126-page book on his treatment for tuberculosis. The first part of the book discussed the treatment protocol. The rest was devoted to the detailed case histories of the 55 patients who were carefully studied. People were allowed in the study only if they were confirmed to have tuberculosis, and they were only declared cured after they were determined to be free of tubercle bacilli. Dr. Russell's treatment protocol involved a healthy lifestyle, including vegetable juices. Remarkably, all 55 people treated in the study were cured.

---

[771] "Vegetable Juice a New Consumption Remedy, Tried with Success at Post-Graduate Hospital, 11 Believed to be Cured," *New York Times*, August 25, 1905.

Pulmonary Tuberculosis is a disease of malnutrition. The plan of treatment is based upon what is universally accepted as the most rational method for the relief of the disease, viz.: fresh air and sunlight in abundance, good food, plenty of sleep, regulated exercise, care of sputum and attention to the small things of daily life which are known to influence nutrition favorably . . . The coming of the patients to the dispensary twice each day gives the opportunity to educate them how best to live according to their means. They come ostensibly only to drink emulsion and vegetable juice . . .[772]

Later research in the 1950s showed that at least part of the beneficial anti-bacterial effect of vegetable juices was lycopene.

. . . in the 1950s, investigators at the Karolinska Institute, in an attempt to extract an anti-bacterial substance from non-pathogenic bacteria, discovered that the tomato juice used in the culture media contained an effective anti-bacterial agent. Further characterization of the lipophilic fraction resulted in the discovery that the lycopene in the tomato juice was the active agent.[773]

Dr. Max Gerson was another pioneer doctor who, in the 1930s to 1950s, used fruit and vegetable juices, a carefully selected vegetarian diet, and vitamin and mineral therapy to heal tuberculosis, type 2 diabetes, heart disease, kidney failure, cancer, and other chronic conditions. His legacy lives on today through his daughter Charlotte in San Diego California's Gerson Institute. The Gerson Therapy activates the body's extraordinary ability to heal itself through an organic, vegetarian diet, raw juices, coffee enemas, and natural supplements.

---

[772] John F. Russell, MD, *Report of Fifty-Five Apparent Cures of Pulmonary Tuberculosis Occurring in Working People Who Were Treated at a Dispensary Without Interruption to Their Work*, New York, February 1906, p. 9.
[773] Adrianne Bendich, "β-Carotene and the Immune Response," *Proceedings of the Nutrition Society*, 1991, p. 263.

Apple cider vinegar

Vinegar is a common food product made through fermentation of a variety of sources. Apple cider vinegar is an old folk remedy for high cholesterol, sore throats, sinus infections, and many other conditions. An 1877 article described Dr. Roth's success using vinegar for smallpox prophylaxis.

> D. G. Oliphant, M.D., of Toronto, Canada, having read the article on the use of Acetic acid in scarlet fever, writes of a "vinegar cure" as applied to small pox. Dr. Roth first claimed wonderful success in treatment regarding vinegar more reliable as a prophylactic in small-pox than Belladonna in scarlet fever. **Dr. Roth gave both to the sick and to the exposed two table-spoonfuls of vinegar, after breakfast and at evening, for fourteen days. Few persons thus treated took the disease at all. None who adopted the prophylactic treatment died, while among those under ordinary treatment the mortality was as usual.**[774]

In 1899 Dr. Howe also demonstrated vinegar's ability to protect a person from acquiring smallpox. Those who used the vinegar protocol were able to take care of other people with smallpox without fear of contracting the disease. The author notes that, despite several hundred exposures, vinegar was protective against smallpox and was considered an "established fact."

> The vinegar treatment as a preventative against the contagion of smallpox, discovered by Dr. C. F. Howe, county health officer of Atchison, Kansas, has passed the point of mere theory and is now an established fact, having been efficient in several hundred cases of exposure in the city of Atchison and Atchison county. Many of these exposures have been the nurse, as well as many others that it was impossible to isolate from the original

---

[774] "Acetic Acid in Scarlet Fever," *American Homoeopathist—A Monthly Journal of Medical Surgical and Sanitary Science*, vol. 1, no. 1, July 1877, p. 73.

*case of smallpox for the want of room. In other words, **anyone, vaccinated or not, can nurse a case of smallpox without fear of contracting the disease if, at the same time, they use the vinegar in tablespoonful doses four times daily in half a cup of water.** It can be taken in less amount for small children or more by adults.*[775]

Again, in 1901 Professor MacLean promoted the idea of using apple cider vinegar three or four times a day to protect a person from contracting smallpox.

*J.P. MacLean Ph.D., the renowned "anti" Secretary of the Western Reserve Historical Society, having readily overthrown the conclusions of all the great men who for a century past have been convinced of the efficacy of vaccination for the prevention of smallpox, now comes to the front in the newspapers with the real preventative. **"Any person who has been exposed need have no fear of smallpox if he will take two or three tablespoonfuls of pure cider vinegar three or four times a day." The discussion may now be regarded as closed, and smallpox at last is conquered!** What a pity Secretary MacLean Ph.D. has been so long in expounding his great discovery . . . Acetic acid from the juice of the grape must by no means be substituted for acetic acid from the juice of the apple.*[776]

Today we know that apple cider vinegar is a highly effective disinfectant and also alkalizes the body, which would naturally lead it to be more disease resistant. In addition, it contains potassium and numerous enzymes that aid in digestion, has antiscorbutic properties, and has been used effectively for numerous health issues since ancient times. Prebiotics that feed probiotics are also present in quantity.

---

[775] "Vinegar to Prevent Smallpox," *The Critique*, January 15, 1899, p. 289.
[776] *Cleveland Journal of Medicine*, vol. VI, no. 1, 1901, p. 58.

In 1902 Dr. G. W. Harvey discussed the merits of vinegar in the use against smallpox. He also stated that, from his experience, it was effective in diphtheria.

> *Vinegar and cider are both known to possess prophylactic and curative properties against smallpox, and should be tried thoroughly. I know from personal experience that vinegar is an antidote to the poison of diphtheria, and I have so much confidence in it that I use it in every case of that malady, and I have my first case to lose.*[777]

The apple cider vinegar used in these instances would have been raw unfiltered and unpasteurized, which is what most health experts recommend today.

Apple cider vinegar might seem silly, but only because most people have been conditioned to accept the age-old prophylaxis for smallpox: raw, disease-laden, contaminated pus scrapings from an infected animal's (usually a cow) belly, diluted in glycerin, and scratched into the human arm with a metal prong until the arm was raw and bleeding. What seems sillier now?

Cod liver oil

Cod liver oil is a nutrient-rich supplement that helps maintain a healthy immune system. Physicians of past generations bestowed great confidence in the therapeutic virtues of cod liver oil, especially in the treatment of infections such as tuberculosis.

> *The unquestioned value possessed by cod-liver oil in all conditions of reduced vitality . . . has won for it the most extensive use and firmly established it in the medical profession's favor. Not alone in chronic mal-nutrition, has its worth been demonstrated, but also as a builder of tissue and a restorative in*

---

[777] G. W. Harvey, MD, "Vaccination," *Transactions of the National Eclectic Medical Association of the United States of America*, vol. 30, 1902, p. x.

convalescence, especially in that state following acute lung and bronchial inflammations.[778]

. . . there is no doubt that cod-liver oil is an important remedy in tuberculosis, even if only for the fact that it contains a considerable proportion of easily assimilable fat, and may be used as a food rather than a drug.[779]

Puerperal fever, also known as childbed fever, is a bacterial infection contracted by women during childbirth or miscarriage. Before doctors were knowledgeable about bacteria, they caused the majority of cases of puerperal fever themselves because they did not believe in hand washing and would not heed the sound words of Drs. Ignaz Semmelweis and Oliver Wendell Holmes. In 1929 Mellanby and Green published work that showed an amazing 66 percent decline in the death rate of needlessly infected women after they were given cod liver oil.

*Physicians at the County of Lanark Maternity Hospital near Edinburgh conducted a large trial that confirmed the findings of Green and Mellanby. **Treatment with cod-liver oil reduced the incidence of puerperal fever by an impressive two-thirds.***[780]

Silver

Colloidal silver is a liquid suspension of microscopic silver particles. It is still recommended by many in the alternative medicine field as a broad-spectrum anti-infective agent. In 1901 Dr. Dworetzky reported on 10 cases in which he used silver to treat various types of serious infections. The patients all greatly improved with the

---

[778] "Cod-Liver Oil in Convalescence from Acute Lung Diseases," *Annals of Gynecology and Pediatry*, vol. 21, 1909, p. 24.
[779] Maurice Fishberg, MD, *Pulmonary Tuberculosis*, Lea & Febiger, Philadelphia and New York, 1919 , p. 632.
[780] Richard D. Semba, "Vitamin A as 'Anti-Infective' Therapy, 1920–1940," *American Society for Nutritional Sciences*, 1999, p. 786.

treatment, and many were described as being "entirely cured" within a short period of time.

> *Colloidal silver has the property of killing and destroying all the pathogenic bacteria that may be circulating in the blood after they have broken through the natural barriers that oppose their entrance into the circulation, and probably also of neutralizing their toxins and rendering them harmless. The action of this "metallic antitoxin" was manifested by the rapid disappearance of all the symptoms of general intoxication, the fall in the temperature, and the improvement in the pulse that was apparent in all cases . . . There is a great future before this new remedy, which is one of the most reliable weapons for the combating of septic wound infection and septic general infection.[781]*

In 1918, during the flu pandemic when millions died, an outbreak of influenza aboard a ship appeared to have been successfully controlled through the use of colloidal silver applied to the eyes and nose.

> *During a part of the month of September, 1918, the ship was moored to the dock at Norfolk, Va. An influenza epidemic was in evidence, so the crew was immediately restricted to ship. Plans were devised by the medical officer by which the disease might be retarded in its rapid spread. A prophylactic treatment consisting of colloidal silver, 10 per cent in the eyes and nose twice each daily, proved very successful in every way, as the cases developing in the crew diminished rapidly.[782]*

These successful interventions were all essentially forgotten. If they had been more widely used, and used in combination, they may have changed the world view of disease management into one that

---

[781] A. Dworetzky, MD, "Some Further Experiences with Soluble Silver," *New England Medical Monthly*, vol. XXI, no. 1, January 1902, p. 202.
[782] W. L. Martin, "Susquehanna," *The Supplement to the United States Naval Medical Bulletin*, no. 10, July 1919, p. 77.

supports what nature has already provided. Instead, the dominant medical paradigm stepped up and employed diseased animal matter injections into the skin of healthy people to supposedly impart immunity.

~ 17 ~

BELIEF AND FEAR

*The one permanent emotion of the inferior man is fear—
fear of the unknown, the complex, the inexplicable.
What he wants above everything else is safety.*

– Henry Louis Mencken (1880–1956)

*Figures often beguile me, particularly when I have the
arranging of them myself; in which case the remark
attributed to Disraeli would often apply with justice and force:
"There are three kinds of lies: lies, damned lies and statistics."*

– Mark Twain (1835–1910)

*Not a scintilla of truth as to the benefit of vaccination or
of anti-diphtheritic serum, is in existence, except statistics. And
statistics are lies. Two kinds of lies. Deliberate lies and stupid
lies. I have spent too much time behind the scenes where
medical statistics are made to have a particle of faith in them.*

– F. N. Seitz, Mechano-Therapy Specialist, 1908

*The great enemy of the truth is very often not the lie—
deliberate, contrived and dishonest, but the myth, persistent,
persuasive, and unrealistic. Belief in myths allows the
comfort of opinion without the discomfort of thought.*

– John Fitzgerald Kennedy (1917–1963)

Belief and fear are powerful influences to the psyche. Because hierarchical powers have exploited these human vulnerabilities, they have unfortunately shaped the world.

People are led to believe that because the world is a dangerous place, only governments and large institutions can provide protection because they are bigger and more knowledgeable than small communities. Rules and restrictions are put in place. Those who believe this lose trust in their own capability and thus surrender thinking and decision making to others.

Doctors are no exception to this phenomenon. Medical practitioners cede their independent thinking to texts, advisory panels, and traditions, which vary depending on political influences of the times.

In medical school, doctors are taught to view the human body as a random mistake-ridden vessel that has to be forced into submission with surgery, antibiotics, antihypertensives, antihistamines, anti-inflammatories, and other medical interventions. The natural extension of this paradigm over the past 100 years has been for the medical profession to condition human beings not to trust anyone but certified medical doctors to fix these defective aberrations of creation.

In the late 1800s, Dr. Charles Creighton wrote a comprehensive report that was published in the *Encyclopedia Britannica*.[783] His contribution, which presented a great deal of detail, found many serious problems with the medically promoted procedure of the time called vaccination. He critiqued numerous facets, including the history of Edward Jenner's discovery, risks of vaccination, effectiveness of vaccination and revaccination, and vaccination legislation.

His piece also contained numerous data tables that did not reinforce the benefit of vaccination, including figures of deaths from the skin disease erysipelas after smallpox vaccination. By 1903 the

---

[783] "Vaccination," *Encyclopædia Britannica*, The Henry G. Allen Company, New York, vol. XXIV, 1890, pp. 23–30.

*Encyclopedia Brit*annica contained the same piece, but with all the tables removed.[784]

By 1922 Dr. Creighton's vaccination contribution was completely eliminated and replaced with a new entry, "Vaccine therapy."[785] This item contained only a brief paragraph that referred to the original smallpox vaccine invented by Edward Jenner. It stated that smallpox vaccination provided immunity, and if by chance smallpox was contracted in a vaccinated person, the disease would only run a "mild" course.[786]

The rest of the article discussed different applications of vaccine therapy and concluded that vaccination would eventually find even more applications and become recognized as an important tool to combat disease. Ideology and myth had displaced verified historical documentation. The history of the phenomenally successful non-vaccinating experience in Leicester, the documented vaccine-related diseases and deaths, the 1872 smallpox pandemic, the fact that smallpox had shifted to a mild disease in spite of declining vaccination rates, the spreading of foot-and-mouth disease via vaccines, and the amazingly successful use of apple cider vinegar against smallpox were all trampled under the heels of conventional medicine's growing dominance.

The new literature that was distributed to the public and doctors was predominantly mythology about "Jenner's great discovery." From here, the idea of dangerous germs and lifesaving vaccines came to dominate medical and societal thinking.

Vaccination was successfully implanted into the minds of the masses as the most effective means to prevent disease. Next came diphtheria antitoxin in 1895, and then diphtheria vaccination starting in 1920.

---

[784] *Encyclopedia Britannica*, The Saalfield Publishing Company, Akron, Ohio, 1903, pp. 6119–6121.

[785] "Vaccine Therapy," *Encyclopædia Britannica*, The Encyclopædia Britannica Company, New York, vol. XV, 1922, pp. 319–321.

[786] Ibid.

A cascade of research on vaccines for other diseases was subsequently funded and pursued with great enthusiasm. Not surprisingly, after 1900, while provocation polio was on the rise, so was the practice of many intramuscular injections for many vaccines and medical treatments. Here are the vaccines that were used in New Zealand at the end of 1911:

- Acne Vaccine (Mixed)
- Acne Bacillus vaccine
- Coley's Fluid
- Coli Bacillus Vaccine
- Combined Vaccines for colds.
- Catarrhalis Micrococcus Vaccine
- Dipth. Anti Sera,
- Friedlander Bacillus Vaccine
- Gonococcus Vaccine
- Influenza Bacillus Vaccine
- Meningococcus Anti Serum.
- Plague (Haffkine's Prophylactic)
- Pituitary Extract (Valporole)
- Pneumococcus Vaccine
- Staphylococcus vaccine (mixed)
- Staphylococcus Vaccine (Aureus)
- Staphylococcus Anti Serum, (Polyvalent)
- Staphylococcus Anti Sera, Puerperal Fever
- Staphylococcus Anti Sera, Pyogenes
- Staphylococcus Anti Sera, Rheumatic Fever
- Staphylococcus Anti Sera, Erysipelas,
- New Tuberculin T.R. (Koch)
- New Tuberculin T.R. (Azoules)
- New Tuberculin T.R. (Koch), (Lucius and Bruning.)
- Tuberculin for Von Piquet's reaction.
- Tuberculin (Old) Human (Koch)
- Tuberculin (Old) Bovine (Koch)
- Tubercle Emulsion (Lucius and Bruning)
- Tubercle Vaccine 0.0005 mgm
- Tubercle Vaccine 0.0001 mgm.
- Normal Horse Serum.
- Tubercle, Moist, for opsonic estimation.

- Staphylococcus Albus Vaccine,
- Tubercle for conjunctival test.
- Typhoid Bacillus Vaccine
- Tetanus Anti Serum[787]

That list might seem bizarre, but the same type of bamboozlement was occurring in the United States. Senate hearing minutes from 1972 reveal the details of the 32 "worthless vaccines" that were licensed and on the market.[788] The estimated cost of the vaccines, which were "of little value and perhaps even harmful," was estimated to be "astronomical." Some of the vaccines had been on the market for 20 years.

Here is the list:

1. Product A   Bacterial vaccine mixed respiratory
2. Product B   Respiratory UBA
3. Product C   Staphylococcus-streplococcus UBA
4. Product D   Combined vaccine No. 4 with catarrhalis
5. Product E   Mixed vaccine No. 4 with H. influenzae
6. Product F   Staphylococcus vaccine
7. Product G   Entoral
8. Product H   Typhoid H. antigen
9. Product I   Vacagen tablets
10. Product J   Brucellin anhgen
11. Product K   Staphylo-strepto serobacterin vaccine
12. Product L   Catarrhalis serobacterln vaccine mixed
13. Product M   Sensitized bacterial vaccine H. influenzae serobacterin in vaccine mixed
14. Product N   Staphage lysate type I
15. Product O   Staphage lysate type III
16. Product P   Staphage lysate lypes I and III

---

[787] House of Representatives, 1912, Appendices to Parliamentary Journals, Session 2 V. iv. Page 108 of the Director General of Health's report.
[788] Consumer Safety Act of 1972, Hearings before the subcommittee on executive reorganization and government research, 92nd congress, second session, S. 3419, April 20, 23, and May 3, 4, pp. 346–348, 435.

17. Product Q   Catarrhalis combined vaccine
18. Product R   Strepto-staphylo vatox
19. Product S   Staphylococcus toxoid-vaccine vatox
20. Product T   Respiratory vatox
21. Product U   Respiratory B.A.C
22. Product V   Gram·negative B.A.C.
23. Product W   Pooled stock B.A.C. No,
24. Product X   Pooled stock B.A.C. No. 2
25. Product Y   Staphylococcal B. A.C Do.
26. Product Z   Pooled skin B.A.C
27. Product AA   Mixed infection phylacogen
28. Product BB   Immunovac oral vaccine
29. Product CC   lmmunovac respiratory vaccine (parenteral)_
30. Product DD   Streptococcus immunogen arthritis
31. Product EE   N. catarrhalis vaccine (combined)
32. Product FF   N.catarrhalis vaccine immunogen (combined)

The manufacturers included Eli-Lilly, Merck Sharp & Dohme, and Parke Davis.

From the beginning, vaccination was promoted by vastly exaggerating the benefits, and unrealized promises were repeatedly made. Whenever possible, any problems or disasters were concealed from the public. In the early 1900s, Dr. Charles Cyril Okell, a high-ranking expert in the field of infectious diseases,[789] wrote numerous articles published in a wide variety of medical journals. He pioneered the first attempts (on himself) using a scarlet fever bacteria toxin in the United States. Shortly before his premature death in 1939, he wrote his final work, which was effectively a deathbed confession. In it, he noted the gross distortion of the benefits of vaccination and the concealment of mistakes.

> *. . . the immunisation of the masses has been undertaken with almost a religious fervour. The enthusiast rarely stopped to*

---

[789] H. J. Parish, "Charles Cyril Okell," *Journal Hygiene*, May 1939, vol. XXXIX, no. 3, pp. 217–224.

*wonder where it would all finish or whether **the fulsome
promises made to the public in the form of "propaganda"
would ever be honoured. Without propaganda there can,
of course, be no large-scale immunisation, but how peri-
lous it is to mix up propaganda with scientific fact. If we
baldly [in plain or basic language] told the whole truth it
is doubtful whether the public would submit to immunization** . . .* Accidents and mistakes must inevitably happen
and when they take place what might have been a highly in-
structive lesson is usually suppressed or distorted out of
recognition. Those who have had to take detailed notice of the
immunisation accidents of the past few years know that to get
the truth of what really went wrong generally calls for the resources of something like the secret service.*[790]

During this time of vaccine obsession, infectious agents were mistakenly envisaged as causative for many medical conditions. Pellagra
caused diarrhea, dermatitis, dementia, and death. Today it is known
to be caused by niacin or tryptophan deficiency. However, there was
a time when doctors believed that pellagra was induced by a virus.
Dr. Ralph Scobey remarked on pellagra in 1952.

*Harris (1913) was able to inject . . . filtered tissue mate-
rial from pellagra victims into monkeys to cause a corresponding disease in these experimental animals.* He
*concluded from these experiments that a virus was present in
the injected material and that was the cause of pellagra. If the
work of Harris had been followed exclusively, various strains
of "virus" might have been discovered and a vaccine, effective
in experimental animals might have been developed . . .*[791]

Perceived risk of a disease seems to increase after the development
of a vaccine. For instance, measles and chicken pox were widely

---

[790] Charles Cyril Okell, "From a Bacteriological Back-Number," *The Lancet*,
January 1, 1938, pp. 48–49.
[791] Ralph R. Scobey, MD, "The Poison Cause of Poliomyelitis and Obstructions
to Its Investigation," *Arch Pediatr*, April 1952, pp. 172–93.

thought to be routine childhood illnesses until the vaccines were available. Then, concern over complications of infection moved to the forefront of discussion. After the risks were broadcast, fear set in, and most people quickly give up their responsibility and decision making. They thought they were accepting a smaller risk to avoid a bigger one. Belief and fear merge and keep the majority obedient to vaccine mandates. There may have been some protest from parents who knew measles and chicken pox were normal and harmless childhood illnesses, but eventually those voices became silent.

Opposition to vaccination was and still is deemed to be only from those who don't understand science and, because of their foolhardy resistance, can bring on more disease and death. From his 2011 book *Deadly Choices: How the Anti-Vaccine Movement Threatens Us All*, Dr. Paul Offit discusses his belief in Edward Jenner and the first vaccine.

> In 1796, Edward Jenner invented a vaccine that eliminated smallpox from the face of the earth . . . In 1898, the British government finally gave in, appeasing angry citizens by passing a conscientious-objection law. People who didn't want to get a vaccine didn't have to. Within a year, the government issued more than two hundred thousand certificates of conscientious objection. By the late 1890s, vaccine rates plummeted. In Leicester 80 percent of babies were unvaccinated . . . Antivaccine forces had won the day . . . As a result, England became Europe's epicenter of smallpox disease and death. For antivaccine activists in England, the freedom to choose had become the freedom to die from that choice.[792]

What is conspicuously missing is evidence to support the statements made. Data and graphs are not presented to prove what he says, which in turn influences what other doctors believe. Paul Offit simply makes the statement that England had become an "epicenter of smallpox disease and death" in the late 1800s. The belief that Offit

---

[792] Paul A. Offit, MD, *Deadly Choices—How the Anti-Vaccine Movement Threatens Us All*, 2011, pp. 106, 125.

is an expert in infectious diseases and thus an expert on history and vaccination overrides any need for his readers to request proof of his statements.

In a 2011 article, Saad Omer made a similar statement on how the decrease in the use of the smallpox vaccine resulted in a resurgence of smallpox. The decline in vaccination was, according to Omer, a result of "irregular physicians" who did not follow the orthodox medical model.

> *Despite the challenges inherent in establishing a reliable and safe vaccine delivery system, vaccination became widely accepted as an effective tool for preventing smallpox through the middle of the 19th century, and the incidence of smallpox declined between 1802 and 1840. In the 1850s, "irregular physicians, the advocates of unorthodox medical theories," led challenges to vaccination. Vaccine use decreased, and smallpox made a major reappearance in the 1870s.*[793]

Statements like this that influence mass belief are not borne through evidence or historical documentation. In many places in the world, including Leicester, England, vaccination rates had been high through the 1800s. Strict laws in England, Massachusetts, Chicago, and other places ensured extremely high vaccination rates of 90 percent or more. Despite this, there were repeat epidemics of smallpox which culminated in the 1872 smallpox pandemic that killed large numbers throughout the world, even in populations that were highly vaccinated.

---

[793] Saad B. Omer et al., "Vaccination Refusal Endangers Public Health," *Epidemics*, 2011, p. 171.

By the 1880s, vaccination rates had declined in Leicester and in England. Conventional thinking of the time falsely predicted that there would be a resurgence of disease and death from smallpox as it would "spread like wildfire" through the unvaccinated population. Despite the dire predictions, the Leicester Method was effectively implemented in place of vaccination for the next 60 years (Graph 17.1).

> Note that the graph (17.1) shows that there was almost always a spike up in smallpox deaths coincident with increased vaccination coverage. This fact is opposite to conventional medical belief.

There were those in the medical community who were relieved that the failure of compulsory vaccination never gained much public scrutiny. Instead, the focus was shifted to new types of vaccinations.

> *Compulsory vaccination which once had the suffrage of the nation has now hardly a serious supporter. We are ashamed to jettison the idea completely and perhaps afraid that if we did the accident of some future epidemic might put us in the wrong. **We prefer to let compulsory vaccination die a natural death and are relieved that the general public is not curious enough to demand an inquest.** In the meantime our attention is diverted to other and newer forms of immunisation.*[794]

All the problems from smallpox vaccination have long been forgotten. Officially recorded deaths from cowpox and other effects of vaccination, including the dreaded skin condition of erysipelas, are never mentioned. Jaundice and syphilis were also spread through the practice of arm-to-arm vaccination.

Smallpox vaccination's virtually unchallenged belief momentum has existed for so many decades that it is rarely contemplated, let alone challenged. Most history books that make mention of Edward Jenner's discovery quickly conclude, without any or with only scant evidence, that it was only of enormous benefit. Some mention in more

---

[794] Charles Cyril Okell, "From a Bacteriological Back-Number," *The Lancet*, January 1, 1938, pp. 48–49.

detail the anti-vaccine movement, but it is always cast in the light that foolish, uneducated protestors were in dangerous opposition to settled science.

In actuality, the facts show the opposite of the belief (Graph 17.2). As vaccination rates declined in England, so did the deaths from smallpox.

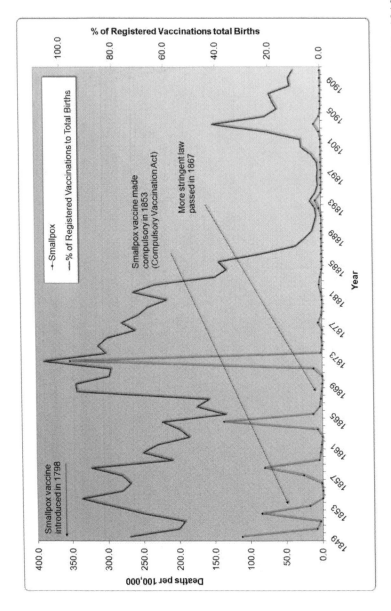

Graph 17.1: Leicester, England, smallpox mortality rate vs. smallpox vaccination coverage from 1849 to 1910.

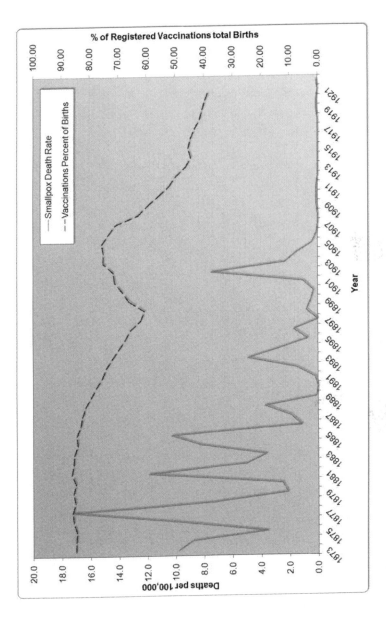

Graph 17.2: England and Wales smallpox mortality rate vs. smallpox vaccine coverage rates from 1873 to 1922.

In his book, Paul Offit also states that, before the use of the pertussis vaccine, 7,000 deaths occurred each year from whooping cough, and afterward there were only about 30 deaths.

> *Whooping cough (pertussis) is a devastating infection. Before a vaccine was first used in the United States in the 1940s, about three hundred thousand cases of whooping cough caused seven thousand deaths every year, almost all in young children. Now, because of the pertussis vaccine, fewer than thirty children die every year from the disease. But times are changing.*[795]

Year	Total	Population	Deaths
1926	10,331	117,399,000	8.8
1927	8,095	119,038,000	6.8
1928	6,507	120,501,000	5.4
1929	7,550	121,770,000	6.2
1930	5,908	123,077,000	4.8
Average	7,678	120,357,000	6.4
1946	1,273	141,389,000	0.9
1947	2,018	144,126,000	1.4
1948	1,173	146,631,000	0.8
1949	746	149,188,000	0.5
1950	1,062	150,688,000	0.7
Average	**1,254**	146,404,000	0.8
% Change	83.6%	25.2%	87.5%

A 1988 paper in the medical journal *Pediatrics* made a similarly inaccurate claim. The table to the left shows the official numbers from two 5-year periods 20 years apart. By the time the pertussis vaccine was introduced in the late 1940s, the total deaths were on average about 1,200, not 7,000.[796]

What is more notable is that, during those 20 years, the population increased by about 25 percent. Such a large increase in population makes it important to determine a normalized death rate. From

---

[795] Paul A. Offit, MD, *Deadly Choices—How the Anti-Vaccine Movement Threatens Us All*, 2011, p. xii.

[796] Vital Statistics of the United States 1937 Part I, US Bureau of the Census, 1939, pp. 11–12; 1938 Part I, US Bureau of the Census, 1940, p. 12; 1943 Part I, US Bureau of the Census, 1945; 1944 Part I, US Bureau of the Census, 1946, p. XXII–XXIII; 1949 Part I, US Public Health Service, 1951, p. XLIV; US Census Bureau, Statistical Abstract of the United States: 2003; www.census.gov/statab/hist/HS-01.pdf.

normalized numbers, we can see that the deaths per 100,000 had decreased by 85 percent during those 20 years. **The odds of dying from whooping cough had dramatically decreased from 1 in 15,625 to 1 in 125,000. This change occurred before the use of any vaccine.** The clear downward trend in the death rate before the introduction of the vaccine is never acknowledged.

Many vaccine enthusiasts claim that antibiotics were also responsible for the decline in morbidity and mortality. But the death rate from whooping cough had been declining since the 1920s, long before antibiotics were used in the United States. An examination of the data from 1920 onward shows a continuous downward trend in the death rate from whooping cough (Graph 17.3). It is difficult to see any significant impact on overall death rate after the introduction of the whooping cough vaccine program. A magnified view of the same data from 1940 to 1970 also shows a continuous downward decline in death rate (Graph 17.4).

If pertussis vaccination was important to the overall decline in deaths, there should be a large noticeable drop in the death rate shortly after the introduction of the vaccine. Yet there is no observable effect. The statement "because of the pertussis vaccine, fewer than thirty children die every year from the disease" is not supported by the official data. Clearly, like smallpox, other factors were involved in the change of whooping cough from a significant killer to a milder disease.

In the 1970s, England experienced a large drop in pertussis vaccination rates. The data shows that there was no massive increase in deaths as would have been expected if vaccination impacted mortality. Authors from a 1984 study confirm that "fears about whooping cough vaccine caused a dramatic fall in immunisation rates and in consequence a large increase of notifications. Despite this increase the number of deaths has not risen . . ."[797]

The prediction that there would be 7,000 annual deaths from whooping cough without vaccination had absolutely no basis in reality.

Paul Offit discussed the same decrease in DTP vaccination in England in the early 1970s. As vaccination rates dropped, it was believed that there would be a severe epidemic which would result in increased deaths from whooping cough.

Year	Total	% DTP
1970	15	78
1971	26	78
1972	2	78
1973	2	78
1974	13	77
1975	12	59
1976	3	38
1977	7	39
1978	12	31
1979	7	35
1980	6	41
1981	5	46
1982	14	53
1983	5	59
1984	1	65

The year before [1975] Wilson's paper, 79 percent of British children were immunized. By 1977, the rate had fallen to 31 percent. As a consequence, more than a hundred thousand children contracted whooping cough, five thousand were hospitalized; two hundred had severe pneumonia; eighty suffered seizures; and thirty-six died. It was one of the worst epidemics of whooping cough in modern history.[798]

Was this, in fact, an out-of-the-ordinary epidemic? Since Dr. Offit does not specify the years he used to obtain his 36 deaths or provide any reference, we have to go to the official data ourselves and locate

---

[797] T. M. Pollock, E. Miller, and J. Lobb, "Severity of Whooping Cough in England Before and After the Decline in Pertussis Immunization," *Archives of Disease in Childhood*, vol. 59, 1984, p. 162.

[798] Paul A. Offit, MD, *Deadly Choices—How the Anti-Vaccine Movement Threatens Us All*, 2011, p. 16.

the area in question.[799] The years from 1976 to 1980 (shaded box in the table) were the ones when vaccination rates were at their lowest. Using official statistics, the number of deaths in those years totaled 35, which is almost exactly the same number that Dr. Offit used in his claim. **The deaths from the previous 5 years, 1971 to 1975 (dash outlined box in the table), while vaccination rates were higher, totaled 55, or about 1.5 times greater than what Dr. Offit describes as the "worst epidemic in modern history."**

Deaths from 1974, when vaccination rates were near their peak of 77 percent, were about the same as the year with the lowest vaccination rate of 31 percent in 1978. Even more startling is that, **during the year 1971, when vaccination rates were at their peak of 78 percent, deaths were the highest, at more than two times the rate of 1978 when vaccinations were at their lowest, 31 percent.**

Examining data starting from 1940, 17 years before pertussis vaccination began in England in 1957, it is clear that there was a general downward trend in deaths (Graph 17.5). Whooping cough deaths were on the decline as they had been for about 100 years and were essentially unaffected by the amount of vaccination coverage. The official data does not match Paul Offit's declaration that the pertussis vaccine is responsible for the enormous decline in deaths.

A similar interpretation of historical data on measles can be found in a 1980 paper from the *American Journal of Public Health*. The authors state:

> *Death rates due to measles have paralleled measles case rates and have shown a striking decline since the licensure of measles vaccine in 1963.*[800]

---

[799] Record of Mortality in England and Wales for 95 years as provided by the office of National Statistics, 1997; Health Protection Agency Table: Notification of Deaths, England and Wales, 1970–2008.

[800] Sister Jeffrey Engelhardt; Neal A. Halsey, MD; Donald L. Eddins; and Alan R. Hinman, MD, "Measles Mortality in the United States 1971–1975,"

The authors include a graph (17.6) showing a large decline in measles deaths after 1963. This information is presented as a logarithmic graph that magnifies the small change in the death rate after 1963. On the other hand, a graph (17.7) displaying the percent decline from the peak death using the exact same data shows that before 1963, the death rate had already decreased by more than 98 percent. A "striking" decline of 98 percent before 1963 is not mentioned at all by the study authors.

In a 2007 article from the *Journal of the American Medical Association (JAMA)*, the authors indicated that from 1953 to 1962, an average of 440 people died from measles. By 2004, however, the death rate had fallen to zero, indicating a 100 percent reduction in deaths attributed completely to the vaccine.[801] Again, although this information is technically accurate, it misleads by omission of the understanding of the massive reduction in deaths before the introduction of the vaccine. From the data, it is evident that through the 1930s, 1940s, and 1950s, the death rate had significantly declined, and any impact from the measles vaccine was minimal (Graph 17.8).

Data from England and Wales shows that there was a massive decline in death from measles well before the introduction of the measles vaccine. The graph (17.9) displaying the percent decline from the peak death rate exhibits that the mortality rate for measles had fallen by almost 100 percent before the use of the vaccine in England in 1968.

In that same 2007 *JAMA* article, the authors show that from 1934 to 1943, 4,034 people died from whooping cough, and by 2004 there were a mere 27 deaths. They state that there was a decline in "pertussis deaths by 99.3 percent" because of the vaccine. This statement

---

American Journal of Public Health, vol. 70, no. 11, November 1980, pp. 1166–1169.

[801] Sandra W. Roush, MT, MPH; Trudy V. Murphy, MD; and the Vaccine-Preventable Disease Table Working Group, "Historical Comparisons of Morbidity and Mortality for Vaccine-Preventable Diseases in the United States," *Journal of the American Medical Association*, vol. 298, no. 18, November 14, 2007, pp. 2155–2163.

is disingenuous and, as usual, leaves out the details of the bigger picture. As you can see in Graph 17.3, whooping cough deaths had been on the decline well in advance of the vaccine, which was obviously not the major factor in that decline. A bigger infectious killer during the 1800s, scarlet fever, which was eradicated without the use of a mass vaccination program and before the use of antibiotics, is not mentioned at all in the *JAMA* paper, presumably because it is not considered a vaccine-preventable disease.

Actually, there was a scarlet fever vaccine made of strep toxin, but most people today are unaware of it. The vaccine was first used in 1912 in Russia and later widely in the United States, Hungary, and Poland.[802] By the 1930s, the toxin vaccine was known to have serious consequences.

Immunization against scarlet fever through the use of the Dick toxin has found but limited application because of the number of the injections required and the severity of the attendant reactions.[803]

Active immunization against scarlet fever has been practiced rather haphazardly since it was first introduced by the Dicks in 1924. Their method required the inoculation of the raw unmodified erythrogenic toxin at five weekly intervals using 500, 2,000, 8,000, 25,000, and 80,000 skin test doses. In some series, reversal of the Dick reaction was reported in 90% to 95% of the persons so treated. A subsequent attack rate of 0.5% in the inoculated as compared to 14% in some uninoculated control groups was observed. However, such severe reactions were encountered in from

---

[802] U. Friedemann, "Epidemiology of Children's Infectious Diseases," *The Lancet*, vol. 2, August 1928, pp. 211–217.

[803] Gaylord W. Anderson, "Scarlet Fever Immunization with Formalinized Toxin: A Preliminary Report," *American Journal of Public Health*, vol. 28, no. 2, February 1938, pp. 123–136.

10% to 30%, occasionally more, of the immunized subjects that this offered serious objection to its widespread use.[804]

Perhaps one of the saddest chronicles of such medical betrayal to its own is reflected in a case report series of student nurses who succumbed to lupus after they underwent vaccination with typhoid-paratyphoid vaccines followed by numerous mandatory scarlet fever toxin injections. All were healthy upon admission to nursing school, and all died about one year after vaccination, following drawn-out, painful illnesses.

. . . first injection of 500 skin test doses (STD) of scarlet fever streptococcus toxin with no ill results. One week later, the second injection of 2000 STD's was given and was followed by joint pains and fever. She remained in bed for 3 days at that time, but did not report to the health office. Nine days later, she returned and received the third injection of 8000 STD's, after which she developed severe arthralgia in the fingers and knees and a sore throat. She was hospitalised for 5 days, during which a low grade fever was found. Physical findings showed a red throat and a large area of hyperemia extending from the site of the injection on the left arm down the forearm midway to the wrist. She received aspirin with some improvement and discharged on December 7, with the diagnosis Dick-toxin reaction. She returned to the clinic on December 12 and her inoculations were continued. Epinephrine usually accompanied these injections.[805]

The case description continued. Two months after the last lot of injections, the trainee nurse was readmitted to the hospital with swelling and pain of the ankles and toes and tenderness of the joints of both hands, which had been constant since the first Dick test five

---

[804] M. Schaeffer and J. Toomey, "Immunization Against Scarlet Fever with Tannic Acid-Precipitated Erythrogenic Toxin," *Pediatrics*, vol. 1, 1948, pp. 188–194.
[805] L. F. Ayvazian and T. L. Badger, "Disseminated Lupus Arythematosus Occurring Among Student Nurses," *The New England Journal of Medicine*, vol. 239, no. 16, October 1948, pp. 565–570.

months earlier. The diagnosis was "rheumatic arthritis." She was given aspirin, but two weeks later the pain came back and she developed chills and fever, sore throat, and cough. One month later, the trainee nurse was readmitted to the hospital for two weeks, and during this admission a streptococcus vaccine was started in small doses, but because of her severe reaction further vaccines were refused. The diagnosis after this admission was "rheumatoid arthritis and infectious mononucleosis." Four months later, the trainee nurse noticed skin eruptions over her nose and both cheeks, and her saliva became foul. The skin and cheeks, upper lips, and the bridge of the nose were covered with purplish-red, mottled, and indurated rash eruptions. Two months later, the eruptions spread over much of the body. A year later, the trainee nurse died. All three cases in this report are equally stunning regarding the complete persistence and lack of regard for the damage to the nurses as it was being done.

So, there is a reason most people haven't heard of the scarlet fever vaccine. Vaccination belief today will hold up better if nobody knows about it. Certainly mandatory vaccines to health-care workers would come under closer scrutiny if nurses today had any idea how apparently disposable they have been in the past.

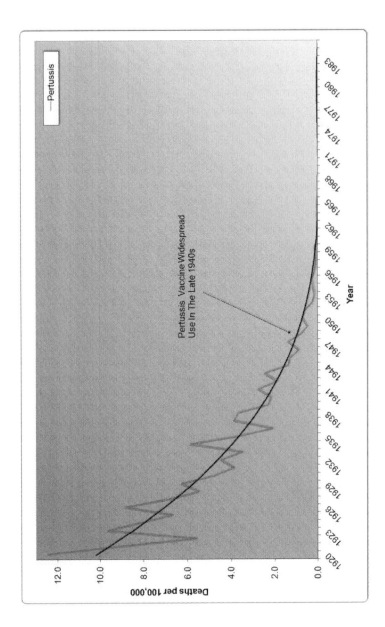

Graph 17.3: United States whooping cough mortality rate from 1920 to 1985.

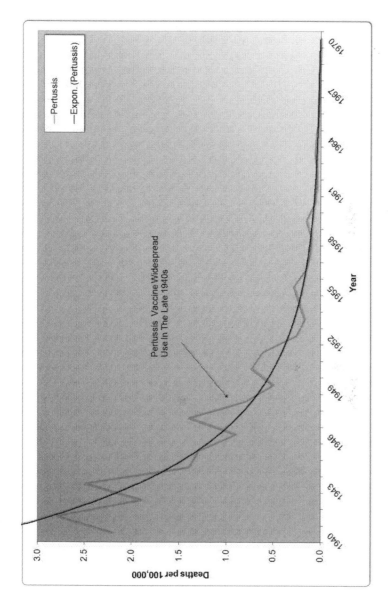

Graph 17.4: United States whooping cough mortality rate from 1940 to 1970.

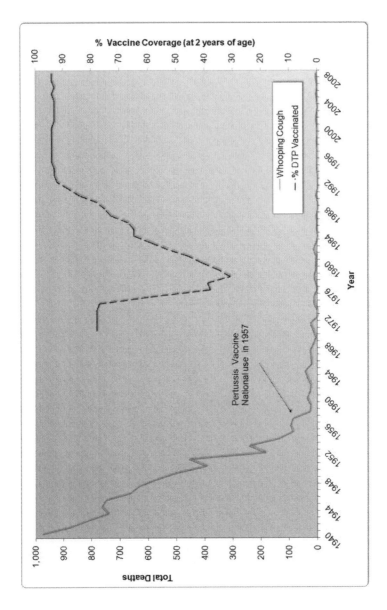

Graph 17.5: England and Wales whooping cough mortality from 1940 to 2008.

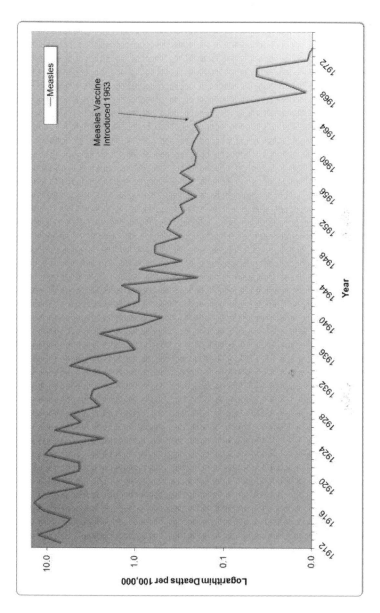

Graph 17.6: United States measles mortality rate from 1912 to 1975 on a logarithm plot.

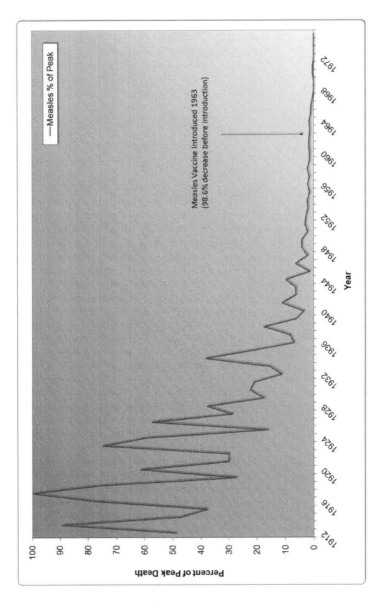

Graph 17.7: United States measles mortality rate from 1912 to 1975 in percent from the peak.

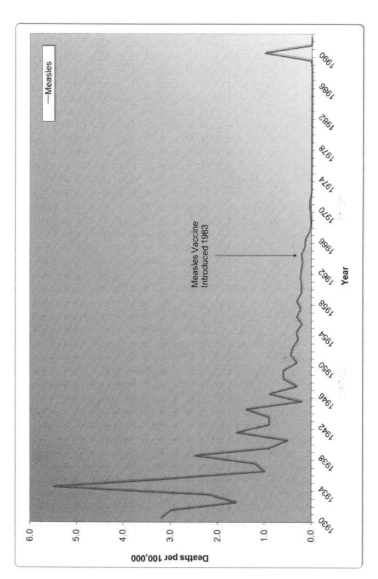

Graph 17.8: United States measles mortality rate from 1930.

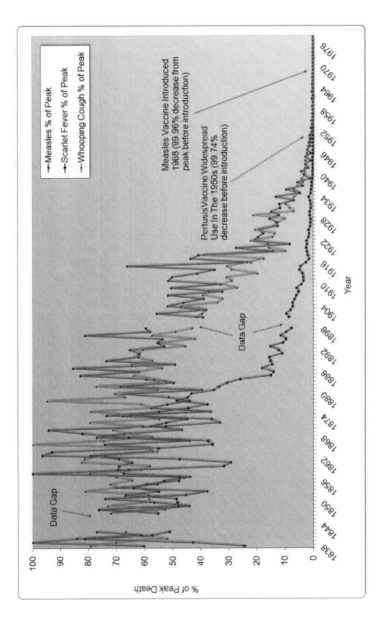

Graph 17.9: England and Wales scarlet fever, measles, and whooping cough percent from peak mortalityrates from 1838 to 1978.

We are not saying that vaccines had absolutely no impact on deaths from these infectious diseases, but by using historical statistics, it is clear that most authors' claims regarding the lifesaving effect of vaccination are markedly exaggerated, and **risk is continuously denied or underplayed**. Despite the fact that "vaccines were responsible for the massive decline in deaths" is based on a false foundation, it permeates medical thinking all over the world. Statements found in medical literature uniformly exaggerate the benefit of vaccination.

> *Today we might not think of these diseases as being very serious because, thanks to vaccines, we don't see them as often as we used to. But they can still be deadly. Measles used to kill hundreds—sometimes thousands—of people a year . . . Years ago, diphtheria was a widespread and greatly feared disease. Through the 1920s, it struck about 150,000 people a year and killed about 15,000 of them. Since then, these figures have dropped considerably, thanks to parents who have gotten their children vaccinated against this terrible disease.*[806]

> *It is difficult to underestimate the contribution of immunization to our well-being. It has been estimated that, were it not for childhood vaccinations against diphtheria, pertussis, measles, mumps, smallpox, and rubella, as well as protection afforded by vaccines against tetanus, cholera, yellow fever, polio, influenza, hepatitis B, bacterial pneumonia, and rabies, childhood death rates would probably hover in the range of 20 to 50%. Indeed, in countries where vaccination is not practiced, the death rates among infants and young children remain at that level.*[807]

Nobody can deny the truth that, during the 1800s, infant mortality was extremely high. Even though there were decades of vaccination for smallpox, the overall child mortality remained unchanged (Graph

---

[806] "Parent's Guide to Childhood Immunizations," US Department of Health and Human Services, 1994.

[807] Irwin W. Sherman, *Twelve Diseases That Changed Our World*, 2007, p. 66.

17.10). By the late 1800s and into the early 1900s, extraordinary changes were made that radically altered the landscape. If the small-pox vaccine was as important as claimed by officials, then during the era of strict vaccination laws child mortality should have decreased. Instead, the death rate remained flat, or in the case of children under one year of age the death rate actually increased during the era of strict vaccination laws and high vaccination rates.

Earlier work by Dr. Robert Watt showed that, although there had appeared to be a decrease in deaths after the introduction of vaccination, deaths from other causes increased. The overall death rate for children remained unchanged.

> . . . the work of Dr. Robert Watt, who tabulated the deaths of children less than 10 years of age in Glasgow during the **30 years centering around the introduction of vaccination, and showed that as smallpox decreased other children's diseases increased and that child mortality had been little affected by the change.**[808]

Not only were all infectious diseases declining during the late 1800s, other poverty-related deaths such as those from diarrhea also waned (Graph 17.11). By the early 1900s, life had dramatically improved. Children were less likely to die from many diseases they had suc-cumbed to only decades earlier. Most vaccines and other medical interventions appeared much later and were only minor players in comparison to all other interventions that took place.

---

[808] Walter F. Willcox, "Decrease in the Death Rate," *Introduction to the Vital Statistics of the United States, 1900 to 1930*, p. 20.

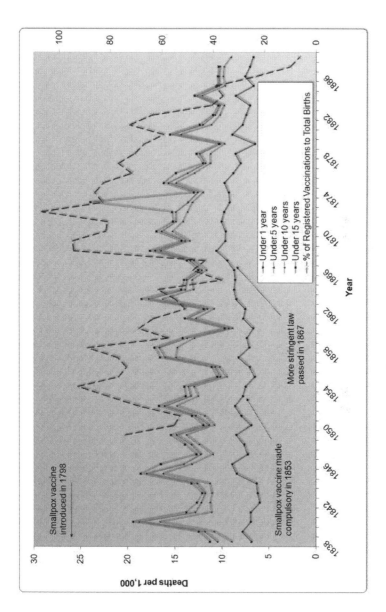

Graph 17.10: Leicester, England, mortality rates by age categories and smallpox vaccine coverage from 1838 to 1888.

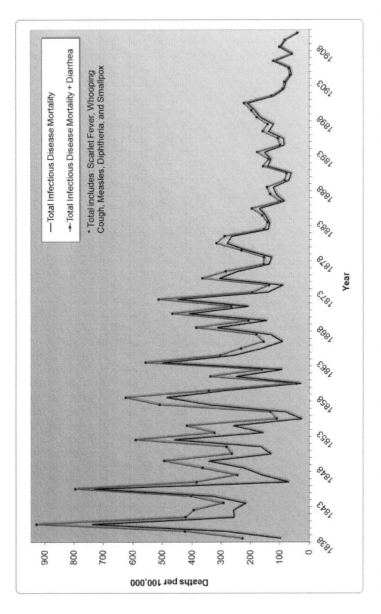

Graph17.11: Leicester combined mortality rates from various infectious diseases and diarrhea from 1838 to 1910.

In the big picture, the belief that vaccines were instrumental in changing our world from a disease-plagued horror to our modern environment is not reflected by the evidence. Nonetheless, this deeply ingrained ideology penetrates societal consciousness. Popular present-day books such as *The Panic Virus* reinforce a flawed concept of successful vaccination beginning with smallpox.

In the book, the story of Edward Jenner and the "relative safety" of the vaccine are introduced, along with the misunderstood concept of "herd immunity." Using this lore, the stage is set for the author to discuss the reasons some of us resist such a spectacular discovery. As is customary by vaccine proponents, the case for vaccination is never supported with real data but only assumptions. Instead of attempting to think for himself or analyze any of the numerous available data on his own, the author defers to "experts."

> *This leaves us with two choices: We can either take it upon ourselves to do a systematic analysis of all the available information—which becomes ever less feasible as the world grows more complex—or we can **trust experts and the media to be responsible about the information and advice they provide**. When they're not, whether it's because they're naïve or under resourced or lazy or because they become true believers themselves, the consequences can be severe indeed.*[809]

Fear of disease, plagues, and death underlie the narrative of the book. The struggle, according to the author, is between those who believe in vaccination and those who question the paradigm. It is a battle between those who understand the so-called "well-established history and evidence-based medicine" and those who do not. We are told that we must accept the belief of the media and experts unless they too are misinformed and do not recognize the already established pro-vaccine position. Thus, all bases are covered in order to delineate anyone with an education and a well-informed

---

[809] Seth Mnookin, *The Panic Virus*, Simon & Schuster, 2011, p. 18.

opinion that is against the theory of vaccination as unscientific and dangerous.

The belief momentum is so great that the authors of these types of books never take into consideration the possibility that there could be a fundamental problem with their base assumption, and neither does the media that supports them or their readers. The authors become another layer in the false belief, which further builds upon itself. Those who accept the belief are accepted by the group. Anyone who questions the belief in vaccination is attacked and vilified both within and outside the medical profession. Vaccine faith is supposed to be unquestioned because history has allegedly demonstrated the value of vaccination.

Do you think it has?

Fundamentally, we must evaluate the soundness of all ideas no matter how deeply ingrained. British philosopher John Stuart Mill said:

> *The fatal tendency of mankind to leave off thinking about a thing when it is no longer doubtful, is the cause of half their errors.*

Often, when one objectively searches for information, facts are uncovered that can be in shocking contrast to the original understanding. The truth may be uncomfortable, inconvenient, and unpopular, but in the end, if it is the truth, it must be embraced regardless of the cost.

Year after year, layer after layer, the vaccine belief built upon itself until today children are subjected to dozens of vaccines by second grade. Most parents are uncomfortable with this barrage of chemicals, disease, and animal residual. They pray and worry after their children are injected. If they seem unscathed after a few days, they think all is well, and they did a good thing. They may not consider the potential for long-term effects from vaccines or the complete absence of safety data on the vaccine program their children are participating in.

What if the hierarchy is wrong? What if the idea of vaccination is fundamentally flawed? What if we have yet to see the real effects on the immunity of the herd?

To date, despite the existence of thousands of never-vaccinated children, there has not been a "completely vaccinated" versus "never vaccinated" study to compare the difference between the short- and long-term health of both groups.

Nobody—not even the most educated immunologists—understands or can describe the complete cascade of events that occurs after injecting a vaccine. If physicians realized how little is known today about the immune system and vaccines, they would be duty bound to tell patients that there are no accurate scientific answers.

Because the whole truth isn't told, adults are the only line of defense for themselves. Until the minds of pediatricians are emancipated, parents will remain the best line of defense for their children.

The reality . . . is that vaccinology, as portrayed to the public today, amounts to writing religion on the back of ignorance.

LIST OF PHOTOGRAPHS

Chapter 1—The Not So Good Ol' Days

1.1: Syracuse, NY—Shanties Back to an Open Sewer. (*Charities—A Weekly Review of Local and General Philanthropy,* vol. VII, no. 23, December 7, 1901, p. 498)

1.2: Jefferson Street. The shed barn at right contains three horses. The barn next in view contains six horses and two goats. The house in the center of the picture is full of Italian families and presents no redeeming feature. On the left are other tenements full of families. (*Fifteenth Biennial Report of the Bureau of Labor and Industrial Statistics, Part V, Basement Tenements in Milwaukee, State of Wisconsin, 1911–1912,* p. 152)

1.3: A so-called room of a three-room tenement, but it is merely a large size closet with a slanting ceiling, located under the main entrance stairs of the building. Here, in a three-quarter bed, sleep the father and mother and a little child. The rest of the family sleep in the front room and kitchen. This "room" has absolutely no light or ventilation. (*The Women's Municipal League of Boston Bulletin,* vol. VII, no. 3, February 1916, p. 43)

1.4: The general insanitary conditions which surround the houses on both sides of the alley. The first house on the right is a small dilapidated frame house. Beyond it are three larger tenements. The outbuildings at the left are all dilapidated, and contain privies which are in a foul condition. There are not enough garbage boxes to supply the needs, and the ones provided are so seldom cleaned that the families dump their slops and garbage in the alley. (*Tenement Conditions in Chicago—Report by the Investigating Committee of the City Homes Association, 1901,* p. 39)

1.5: The conditions of the filth-strewn alleys, of courts and yards littered with rubbish, of ill-smelling stables and manure boxes find their climax and in part their cause in the accumulation of garbage. (*Tenement Conditions in Chicago—Report by the Investigating Committee of the City Homes Association, 1901,* p. 133)

1.6: Water-closet used by fourteen families. (*The Women's Municipal League of Boston Bulletin,* vol. VII, no. 3, February 1916, p. 32)

1.7: Public hall and sink. Sink supported only by string and flimsy wooden props. Hall floor covered with fecal matter and sewage. (*Tenement-House Reform Charities,* vol. XI, no. 16, for the week ending October 17, 1903, p. 359)

1.8: Kill Rats Poster. (*The Women's Municipal League of Boston Bulletin,* vol. VIII, no. 2, January 1917, p. 25)

1.9: A case of Acute Milk Poisoning Having Vomiting, Diarrhoea, Mucous and Bloody Stools, General Emaciation, Acute Cholera Infantum, and Dysentery. (Louis Fischer, MD, *Diseases of Infancy and Childhood: Their Dietetic, Hygienic, and Medical Treatment,* F. A. Davis Company, 1914, p. 257)

Chapter 2—Suffer the Little Children

2.1: Boy coal miners. (*The Child Labor Bulletin,* August 1914, p. 67)

2.2: Girl and older girl using a creel to move coal. (*Reports from Commissioners—Children Employment (Mines),* February 3–August 12, 1842, p. 93)

2.3: Typical passage a coal bearer traversed. (*Reports from Commissioners—Children Employment (Mines),* February 3–August 12, 1842, p. 92)

2.4: Child pulling corve. (*Reports from Commissioners—Children Employment (Mines),* February 3–August 12, 1842, p. 78)

2.5: The Lonely Trapper Boy. (*The Child Labor Bulletin,* August 1914, p. 68)

2.6: Boys in the manufacturing of medicine bottles. (*The Child Labor Bulletin,* August 1914, p. 52)

2.7: Children snipping beans in Maryland. (*The Child Labor Bulletin,* vol. 1, no. 4, February 1913, p. 39)

2.8: At a Dangerous Capping Machine. (*The Child Labor Bulletin,* vol. 1, no. 4, February 1913, p. 41)

2.9: A child employed as a doffer. (*Annual Report of the Massachusetts Child Labor Committee,* January 1, 1914)

2.10: Children 6, 8, and two of 12 years making hose supporters by lamplight. (*Annual Report of the Massachusetts Child Labor Committee,* January 1, 1913, p. 41)

2.11: Massachusetts Mill Workers. (*Annual Report of the Massachusetts Child Labor Committee,* January 1, 1914)

2.12: Child factory workers. (*Good Housekeeping,* October 1913, p. 507)

2.13: Only a box for a house, and railroad yard for a playground. (*The National Humane Review,* vol. VII, no. 4, April 1919, p. 73)

Chapter 4—Smallpox and the First Vaccine

4.1: Multiple site vaccination of 1898, showing a 'typically good arm.' (Derrick Baxby, "Smallpox Vaccination Techniques; from Knives and Forks to Needles and Pins," *Vaccine,* vol. 20, no. 16, May 15, 2002, p. 2142)

4.2: Mrs. L. H. age 27 lesions appeared 2 weeks after vaccination. (*Journal of Cutaneous Disease,* vol. XXII, 1904, p. 504)

4.3: Post-mortem photograph of child described in Case 1. Areas of gangrene are secondarily infected with Pseudomonas aeroginosa,

Micrococcus pyogenes and beta enterococcus. (*Pediatrics,* August 1958, p. 261)

Chapter 5—Contaminated Vaccines

5.1: Head of cow affected with foot-and-mouth disease. (*Bulletin No. 17,* Department of Agriculture, 1914, p. 27)

5.2: From the stable the calf is led to the operating room and strapped on the operating table. The shaved abdomen and thighs are again washed and then scarified with superficial linear incisions made with a surgeon's knife. Into the bleeding incisions made by the knife, vaccine (cowpox) virus is carefully smeared with an ivory or metal instrument. ("Vaccine Virus—Its Preparation and Its Use," *Scientific American,* January 19, 1901, p. 41)

5.3: Bullous dermatitis closely allied to acute pemphigus (*Diseases of the Skin and the Eruptive Fevers,* 1908, p. 89)

Chapter 8—The Power of the State

8.1: Portion of a Eugenics Chart. (*Eugenics, The Science of Human Improvement by Better Breeding,* 1910, p. 19)

8.2: Feeble-Minded at Vineland Colony in New Jersey. "They have the bodies of adults but the minds of children. It is not to the interest of the state that they should be allowed to mingle with the normal popu-lation; and it is quite as little to their own interest, for they are not capable of competing with people who are normal mentally." (Paul Popenoe, *Applied Eugenics,* the Macmillan Company, New York, 1918, p. 193)

Chapter 9—The Case of Arthur Smith Jr.

9.1: Arthur Smith, Jr. August 1915. (approximately 1 year after vaccination)

Chapter 11—The Amazing Decline

11.1: Extremely mild case of smallpox, bearing some resemblance to chickenpox. (*American Medicine,* vol. II, no. 23, December 7, 1901, p. 901)

11.2: Impetigo contagion in an adult. (*American Medicine,* vol. II, no. 23, December 7, 1901, p. 901)

11.3: Well marked eruption of chickenpox, showing lesions in varying stages of development. (*American Medicine,* vol. II, no. 23, December 7, 1901, p. 901)

Chapter 12—The "Disappearance" of Polio

12.1: George Clark walks on crutches and heavy braces. He had polio attack last April. (*Life,* March 5, 1956, p. 63)

12.2: Sister Kenny encourages a polio patient to stand for the first time. (*Life,* September 16, 1946, p. 82)

12.3: Iron lung encases 27-year-old Boyce Rash whose respiratory muscles have been paralyzed. Breathing function is so impaired that a mechanical apparatus is required to force air in and out of the patient's lungs. Seven iron lungs were shipped to Hickory, two of them from Boston. John Bryan, 8, uses oxygen inhalator. It feeds oxygen to nose of patient who has difficulty in breathing normally. Most severe cases involve paralysis of respiratory muscles. Tube extending from mouth collect saliva which boy cannot swallow because of paralyzed throat muscles. (*Life,* July 31, 1944, p. 27)

12.4: Knox Out DDT product advertisement. (*Life,* May 31, 1948, p. 102)

12.5: Flying and Biting Bugs on Jones Beach Die in a Cloud of DDT, New Insecticide—A truck-mounted for generator squirts the poison, mixed with oil droplets, over a four-mile area of the New York City playground. Spread by Army and Navy planes and by hand sprays, DDT routed dangerous disease-bearing flies and mosquitoes on

Pacific islands. DDT has a drawback—it kills many beneficial and harmless insects, but does not kill all insect pests. Birds and fish which eat large numbers of DDT-poisoned insects may be casualties too. (*National Geographic Magazine,* October 1945, p. 410)

12.6: "The great expectations held for DDT have been realized." Penn Salt chemicals advertisement. (*Time Magazine,* June 30, 1947)

12.7: Speaking of Pictures . . . These Demonstrate How DDT Paralyzes a Mosquito—In glass case mosquito feels effects of DDT, gives frantic kick, leaps into air. As DDT enters nervous system and starts to paralyze muscles, mosquito seems to be trying to kick of paralyzing sensation. Paralysis of the nervous system affects the mosquito legs. The mosquito staggers, falls over, tries to push back onto its legs. It makes one last violent effort to rise but topples back onto its head. On its back and almost completely paralyzed, the mosquito continues to battle against DDT but only succeeds in wiggling convulsively. It took DDT 45 minutes to knock the mosquito out completely. (*Life,* January 21, 1946, p. 11)

Chapter 15—Starvation, Scurvy, and Vitamin C

16.1: Infantile Scurvy. Ellen S. Five years old. The gums are swollen or beefy and hanging in tumor-like masses. There are also blood-tumors on the forehead. (Louis Fischer, MD, *Diseases of Infancy and Childhood: Their Dietetic, Hygienic, and Medical Treatment,* F. A. Davis Company, 1914, p. 257)

16.2: Characteristic position of the legs in scurvy. The legs are practically always tender, usually exquisitely so, so that the slightest movement or pressure causes the most severe pain. (Lewis Webb Hill, MD, *Practical Infant Feeding,* W. B. Saunders Company, 1922, p. 426)

Book back cover

Dr. Humphries' photo: Bonnie Farmer Photographer, www.bonniefarmerphotography.com

LIST OF GRAPHS

Chapter 3—Disease—A Way of Life

3.1: Six cholera pandemics. The first pandemic started in 1816, and the last ended in 1926.

Chapter 4—Smallpox and the First Vaccine

4.1: Boston smallpox mortality rate from 1811 to 1926. (Dozens of reports from the Board of Health of the City of Boston)

4.2: Boston smallpox mortality rate from 1841 to 1880. (Dozens of reports from the Board of Health of the City of Boston)

4.3: England and Wales total deaths from cowpox and other effects of vaccination from 1859 to 1922. (Written answer by Lord E. Percy to Parliamentary question addressed by Mr. March, MP, to the Minister to Health on July 16, 1923; Leicester: Sanitation Versus Vaccination, J. T. Biggs, JP, 1912, pp. 184–185)

4.4: England and Wales smallpox deaths vs. smallpox vaccination deaths from 1906 to 1922. (Written answer by Lord E. Percy to Parliamentary question addressed by Mr. March, MP, to the Minister to Health on July 16, 1923)

4.5: England and Wales smallpox and scarlet fever mortality rates from 1838 to 1922. (Record of mortality in England and Wales for 95 years as provided by the Office of National Statistics, published 1997; Report to The Honourable Sir George Cornewall Lewis, Bart, MP, Her Majesty's Principal Secretary of State for the Home Department, June 30, 1860, pp. a4, 205; Written answer by Lord E. Percy to Parliamentary question addressed by Mr. March, MP, to the Minister to Health on July 16, 1923; Essay on Vaccination by Charles T. Pearce, MD, Member of the Royal College of Surgeons of England)

4.6: England and Wales smallpox mortality rate vs. smallpox vaccine coverage rates from 1872 to 1922. (Written answer by Lord E. Percy to Parliamentary question addressed by Mr. March, MP, to the Minister to Health on July 16, 1923)

Chapter 7—The Rebel Experiment

7.1: Leicester, England, smallpox mortality rate vs. smallpox vaccination coverage from 1838 to 1910. (Leicester: Sanitation Versus Vaccination, J. T. Biggs, JP, 1912, pp. 720–722)

7.2: Leicester, England, mortality rates for various age groups vs. smallpox vaccination coverage from 1838 to 1910. (Leicester: Sanitation Versus Vaccination, J. T. Biggs, JP, 1912, pp. 720–722)

Chapter 11—The Amazing Decline

11.1: England and Wales scarlet fever mortality rate from 1838 to 1978. (Record of mortality in England and Wales for 95 years as provided by the Office of National Statistics, published 1997; Report to The Honourable Sir George Cornewall Lewis, Bart, MP, Her Majesty's Principal Secretary of State for the Home Department, June 30, 1860, pp a4, 205; Essay on Vaccination by Charles T. Pearce, MD, Member of the Royal College of Surgeons of England; Parliamentary Papers, the 62nd Annual Return of the Registrar General 1899 (1891–1898))

11.2: England and Wales mortality rates from various infectious diseases from 1838 to 1978. (Record of mortality in England and Wales for 95 years as provided by the Office of National Statistics, published 1997; Report to The Honourable Sir George Cornewall Lewis, Bart, MP, Her Majesty's Principal Secretary of State for the Home Department, June 30, 1860, pp. a4, 205; Essay on Vaccination by Charles T. Pearce, MD, Member of the Royal College of Surgeons of

England; Parliamentary Papers, the 62nd Annual Return of the Registrar General 1899 (1891–1898))

11.3: England and Wales whooping cough mortality rate from 1838 to 1978. (Record of mortality in England and Wales for 95 years as provided by the Office of National Statistics, published 1997; Report to The Honourable Sir George Cornewall Lewis, Bart, MP, Her Majesty's Principal Secretary of State for the Home Department, June 30, 1860, pp. a4, 205; Essay on Vaccination by Charles T. Pearce, MD, Member of the Royal College of Surgeons of England; Parliamentary Papers, the 62nd Annual Return of the Registrar General 1899 (1891–1898))

11.4: England and Wales measles mortality rate from 1838 to 1978. (Record of mortality in England and Wales for 95 years as provided by the Office of National Statistics, published 1997; Report to The Honourable Sir George Cornewall Lewis, Bart, MP, Her Majesty's Principal Secretary of State for the Home Department, June 30, 1860, pp. a4, 205; Essay on Vaccination by Charles T. Pearce, MD, Member of the Royal College of Surgeons of England; Parliamentary Papers, the 62nd Annual Return of the Registrar General 1899 (1891–1898))

11.5: United States whooping cough mortality rate from 1900 to 1967. (Vital Statistics of the United States 1937, 1938, 1943, 1944, 1949, 1960, 1967, 1976, 1987, 1992; Historical Statistics of the United States—Colonial Times to 1970 Part 1; Health, United States, 2004, US Department of Health and Human Services; Vital Records & Health Data Development Section, Michigan Department of Community Health; US Census Bureau, Statistical Abstract of the United States: 2003; Reported Cases and Deaths from Vaccine Preventable Diseases, United States, 1950–2008)

11.6: United States measles mortality rate from 1900 to 1987. (Vital Statistics of the United States 1937, 1938, 1943, 1944, 1949, 1960, 1967, 1976, 1987, 1992; Historical Statistics of the United States—Colonial Times to 1970 Part 1; Health, United States, 2004, US Department of Health and Human Services; Vital Records & Health Data

Development Section, Michigan Department of Community Health; US Census Bureau, Statistical Abstract of the United States: 2003; Reported Cases and Deaths from Vaccine Preventable Diseases, United States, 1950–2008)

11.7: Leicester, England, diphtheria mortality rate from 1880 to 1910. (Vital Statistics of the United States 1937, 1938, 1943, 1944, 1949, 1960, 1967, 1976, 1987, 1992; Historical Statistics of the United States—Colonial Times to 1970 Part 1; Health, United States, 2004, US Department of Health and Human Services; Vital Records & Health Data Development Section, Michigan Department of Community Health; US Census Bureau, Statistical Abstract of the United States: 2003; Reported Cases and Deaths from Vaccine Preventable Diseases, United States, 1950–2008)

11.8: New York City diphtheria mortality rates from 1880 to 1911. (Twenty-Ninth Annual Report 1900 City of Boston, Boston— Municipal Printing Office, 1901, p. 7; Thirty-Sixth Annual Report of the Board of Health of the City of Boston for the Year 1907, Muncipal Printing Office 1908, p. 17; Annual Report of the Board of Health of the City of Boston for the Year 1911, Muncipal Printing Office, 1912, p. 243; Scientific Features of Modern Medicine, Frederic S. Lee, PhD, New York, Columbia University Press, 1911, p. 92)

11.9: United States diphtheria mortality rate from 1900 to 1967. (Vital Statistics of the United States 1937, 1938, 1943, 1944, 1949, 1960, 1967, 1976, 1987, 1992; Historical Statistics of the United States— Colonial Times to 1970 Part 1; Health, United States, 2004, US Department of Health and Human Services; Vital Records & Health Data Development Section, Michigan Department of Community Health; US Census Bureau, Statistical Abstract of the United States: 2003; Reported Cases and Deaths from Vaccine Preventable Diseases, United States, 1950–2008)

11.10: Massachusetts tuberculosis, diphtheria, typhoid, measles, and smallpox mortality rates from 1861 to 1970. (Historical Statistics of the United States—Colonial Times to 1970 Part 1, Bureau of the Census, p. 63)

11.11: United States mortality rates from various infectious diseases from 1900 to 1965. (Vital Statistics of the United States 1937, 1938, 1943, 1944, 1949, 1960, 1967, 1976, 1987, 1992; Historical Statistics of the United States—Colonial Times to 1970 Part 1)

11.12: United States mortality rates from various infectious diseases from 1900 to 1965 magnified view. (Vital Statistics of the United States 1937, 1938, 1943, 1944, 1949, 1960, 1967, 1976, 1987, 1992; Historical Statistics of the United States—Colonial Times to 1970 Part 1)

11.13: United States mortality rates for age groups from 1900 to 1970. (Historical Statistics of the United States—Colonial Times to 1970 Part 1, Bureau of the Census, p. 60)

11.14: United States mortality rates for age groups from 1900 to 1970 magnified view. (Historical Statistics of the United States—Colonial Times to 1970 Part 1, Bureau of the Census, p. 60)

Chapter 12—The "Disappearance" of Polio

12.1: United States disease incidence from 1912 to 1970. (Historical Statistics of the United States Colonial Times to 1970 Part 1, Bureau of the Census, 1975, pp. 77)

Chapter 13—Whooping Cough

13.1: United States whooping cough mortality rate from 1900 to 1957. (Historical Statistics of the United States—Colonial Times to 1957, pp. 8, 26, 27)

13.2: England and Wales whooping cough mortality vs. DTP vaccine coverage from 1901 to 2008. (Record of Mortality in England and Wales for 95 years as provided by the office of National Statistics, published 1997; Health Protection Agency Table: Notification of Deaths, England and Wales, 1970–2008)

13.3: England and Wales whooping cough mortality vs. DTP vaccine coverage from 1930 to 2008. (Record of Mortality in England and Wales for 95 years as provided by the office of National Statistics, published 1997; Health Protection Agency Table: Notification of Deaths, England and Wales, 1970–2008)

13.4: England and Wales whooping cough mortality vs. DTP vaccine coverage from 1970 to 2008. (Record of Mortality in England and Wales for 95 years as provided by the office of National Statistics, published 1997; Health Protection Agency Table: Notification of Deaths, England and Wales, 1970–2008.)

Chapter 14—Measles

14.1: Comparison United States and England in mortality rates for measles from 1901 to 1965. (Vital Statistics of the United States 1937, 1938, 1943, 1944, 1949, 1960, 1967, 1976, 1987, 1992; Historical Statistics of the United States—Colonial Times to 1970 Part 1; Record of mortality in England and Wales for 95 years as provided by the Office of National Statistics, published 1997)

14.2: England percent decline in mortality rate from peak mortality rate for measles from 1838 to 1978. (Record of mortality in England and Wales for 95 years as provided by the Office of National Statistics, published 1997; Report to The Honourable Sir George Cornewall Lewis, Bart, MP, Her Majesty's Principal Secretary of State for the Home Department, June 30, 1860, pp. a4, 205; Essay on Vaccination by Charles T. Pearce, MD, Member of the Royal College of Surgeons of England; Parliamentary Papers, the 62nd Annual Return of the Registrar General 1899 (1891–1898))

14.3: United States mortality rates from various infectious diseases from 1900 to 1965. (Vital Statistics of the United States 1937, 1938, 1943, 1944, 1949, 1960, 1967, 1976, 1987, 1992; Historical Statistics of the United States— Colonial Times to 1970 Part 1; Health, United States, 2004, US Department of Health and Human Services; Vital Records & Health Data Development Section, Michigan Department of Community Health; US Census Bureau, Statistical Abstract of the

United States: 2003; Reported Cases and Deaths from Vaccine Preventable Diseases, United States, 1950-2008)

14.4: United States mortality rates from various infectious diseases from 1920 to 1955. (Vital Statistics of the United States 1937, 1938, 1943, 1944, 1949, 1960, 1967, 1976, 1987, 1992; Historical Statistics of the United States— Colonial Times to 1970 Part 1; Health, United States, 2004, US Department of Health and Human Services; Vital Records & Health Data Development Section, Michigan Department of Community Health; US Census Bureau, Statistical Abstract of the United States: 2003; Reported Cases and Deaths from Vaccine Preventable Diseases, United States, 1950-2008)

14.5: Massachusetts mortality rate from measles from 1861 to 1970. (Historical Statistics of the United States—Colonial Times to 1970 Part 1, Bureau of the Census, p. 63)

14.6: Washington State measles mortality rate from 1920 to 1982. (Communicable Disease Statistical Summary, Washington State 1920-1983, Office of Public Health Laboratory, Seattle, WA)

14.7: United States measles mortality rate with 1/35 measles disease rate from 1900 to 1987. (Vital Statistics of the United States 1937, 1938, 1943, 1944, 1949, 1960, 1967, 1976, 1987, 1992; Historical Statistics of the United States—Colonial Times to 1970 Part 1)

14.8: United States measles incidence from 1912 to 1970. (Historical Statistics of the United States—Colonial Times to 1970 Part 1; Bureau of the Census, 1975, pp. 77)

14.9: United States measles incidence from 1934 to 1962. (Historical Statistics of the United States—Colonial Times to 1970 Part 1; Bureau of the Census, 1975, pp. 77)

Chapter 15—Starvation, Scurvy, and Vitamin C

15.1: England mortality rate from scurvy from 1901 to 1967. (Record of mortality in England and Wales for 95 years as provided by the Office of National Statistics, 1997)

15.2: England mortality rates from scurvy vs. whooping cough from 1901 to 1967. (Record of mortality in England and Wales for 95 years as provided by the Office of National Statistics, 1997)

15.3: England mortality rates from scurvy vs. measles from 1901 to 1967. (Record of mortality in England and Wales for 95 years as provided by the Office of National Statistics, 1997)

Chapter 17—Belief and Fear

17.1: Leicester, England, smallpox mortality rate vs. smallpox vaccination coverage from 1849 to 1910. (Leicester: Sanitation Versus Vaccination, J. T. Biggs, JP, 1912, pp. 720–722)

17.2: England and Wales smallpox mortality rate vs. smallpox vaccine coverage rates from 1873 to 1922. (Written answer by Lord E. Percy to Parliamentary question addressed by Mr. March, MP, to the Minister to Health on July 16, 1923)

17.3: United States whooping cough mortality rate from 1920 to 1985. (Vital Statistics of the United States 1937, 1938, 1943, 1944, 1949, 1960, 1967, 1976, 1987, 1992; Historical Statistics of the United States—Colonial Times to 1970 Part 1; Health, United States, 2004, US Department of Health and Human Services; Vital Records & Health Data Development Section, Michigan Department of Community Health; US Census Bureau, Statistical Abstract of the United States: 2003; Reported Cases and Deaths from Vaccine Preventable Diseases, United States, 1950–2008)

17.4: United States whooping cough mortality rate from 1940 to 1970. (Vital Statistics of the United States 1937, 1938, 1943, 1944, 1949, 1960, 1967, 1976, 1987, 1992; Historical Statistics of the United States—Colonial Times to 1970 Part 1; Health, United States, 2004, US Department of Health and Human Services; Vital Records & Health Data Development Section, Michigan Department of Community Health; US Census Bureau, Statistical Abstract of the United States: 2003; Reported Cases and Deaths from Vaccine Preventable Diseases, United States, 1950–2008)

17.5: England and Wales whooping cough mortality from 1940 to 2008. (Record of Mortality in England and Wales for 95 years as provided by the office of National Statistics, 1997; Health Protection Agency Table: Notification of Deaths, England and Wales, 1970–2008)

17.6: United States measles mortality rate from 1912 to 1975 on a logarithm plot. (Vital Statistics of the United States 1937, 1938, 1943, 1944, 1949, 1960, 1967, 1976, 1987, 1992; Historical Statistics of the United States—Colonial Times to 1970 Part 1; Health, United States, 2004, US Department of Health and Human Services; Vital Records & Health Data Development Section, Michigan Department of Community Health; US Census Bureau, Statistical Abstract of the United States: 2003; Reported Cases and Deaths from Vaccine Preventable Diseases, United States, 1950–2008)

17.7: United States measles mortality rate from 1912 to 1975 in percent from the peak. (Vital Statistics of the United States 1937, 1938, 1943, 1944, 1949, 1960, 1967, 1976, 1987, 1992; Historical Statistics of the United States—Colonial Times to 1970 Part 1; Health, United States, 2004, US Department of Health and Human Services; Vital Records & Health Data Development Section, Michigan Department of Community Health; US Census Bureau, Statistical Abstract of the United States: 2003; Reported Cases and Deaths from Vaccine Preventable Diseases, United States, 1950–2008)

17.8: United States measles mortality rate from 1930. (Vital Statistics of the United States 1937, 1938, 1943, 1944, 1949, 1960, 1967, 1976, 1987, 1992; Historical Statistics of the United States—Colonial Times to 1970 Part 1; Health, United States, 2004, US Department of Health and Human Services; Vital Records & Health Data Development Section, Michigan Department of Community Health; US Census Bureau, Statistical Abstract of the United States: 2003; Reported Cases and Deaths from Vaccine Preventable Diseases, United States, 1950–2008)

17.9: England and Wales scarlet fever, measles, and whooping cough mortality rates from 1838 to 1978 in percent from the peak. (Record of mortality in England and Wales for 95 years as provided by the Office of National Statistics, published 1997; Report to The Honourable Sir George Cornewall Lewis, Bart, MP, Her Majesty's Principal Secretary of State for the Home Department, June 30, 1860, pp. a4, 205; Essay on Vaccination by Charles T. Pearce, MD, Member of the Royal College of Surgeons of England; Parliamentary Papers, the 62nd Annual Return of the Registrar General 1899 (1891–1898))

17.10: Leicester, England, mortality rates by age categories and smallpox vaccine coverage from 1838 to 1888. (Leicester: Sanitation Versus Vaccination, J. T. Biggs, JP, 1912, pp. 720–722)

17.11: Leicester combined mortality rates from various infectious diseases and diarrhea from 1838 to 1910. (Leicester: Sanitation Versus Vaccination, J. T. Biggs, JP, 1912, pp. 720–722)

LIST OF FIGURES

Chapter 5—Contaminated Vaccines

5.1: Connection between vaccines and foot-and-mouth disease. (Authors' original diagram)

Chapter 11—The Amazing Decline

11.1: Age-and Sex-adjusted Mortality Rates for the United States 1900-1973, Including and Excluding Eleven Major Infectious Diseases, Contrasted with the Proportion of the Gross National Product Expended on Medical Care. (John B. McKinlay and Sonja M. McKinlay, "The Questionable Contribution of Medical Measures to the Decline of Mortality in the United States in the Twentieth Century," The Milbank Memorial Fund Quarterly, *Health and Society,* vol. 55, no. 3, summer 1977, p. 415)

Chapter 12—The "Disappearance" of Polio

12.1: Spinal cross-section. ("The Spinal Cord," Nursing Care for Neurological Patients, SweetHaven Publishing Services, 2006, www.freeed.net/sweethaven/MedTech/NurseCare/NeuroNurse01.asp?iNum=4, accessed July 2013)

12.2: Michigan polio 1958 - epidemic virus identification via fecal analysis. (G. C. Brown, "Laboratory Data on the Detroit Poliomyelitis Epidemic 1958," *Journal of the American Medical Association,* vol. 172, February 20, 1960, pp. 807–812)

12.3: Michigan polio 1958 - epidemic viral antibody changes. (G. C. Brown, "Laboratory Data on the Detroit Poliomyelitis Epidemic 1958," *Journal of the American Medical Association,* vol. 172, February 20, 1960, pp. 807–812)

12.4: Polio incidence and persistent pesticide production. (c/o Jim West)

12.5: Polio morbidity. ("Polio Disease In-Short," Centers for Disease Control and Prevention, Department of Health and Human Services, www.cdc.gov/vaccines/vpd-vac/polio/in-short-both.htm, accessed June 17, 2013)

12.6: Paralytic poliomyelitis cases in Maryland from 1952 to 1959. (H. Ratner, "An Untold Vaccine Story," *Child and Family,* vol. 21, no. 3, 1993, pp. 253–263)

12.7: Acute Flaccid Paralysis (AFP) and Polio from 1996 to 2011. (http://apps.who.int/immunization_monitoring/en/diseases/polio myelitis/afpextract.cfm, accessed June 2102)

12.8: Non-Polio Acute Flaccid Paralysis (NPAFP) correlation to Oral Polio Vaccine (OPV).
(http://jacob.puliyel.com/download.php?id=248, accessed July 2013)

Chapter 13—Whooping Cough

13.1: United States pertussis incidence by year from 1980 to 2010. ("Summary of Notifiable Diseases—United States, 2009," MMWR, vol. 58, no. 53, May 13, 2011, www.cdc.gov/mmwr/preview/mmwrhtml/mm5853a1.htm, accessed July 2013)

INDEX

panencephalitis, 398
SV40, 279, 280, 281, 400
sweated industries, 179
syphilis, 90, 231, 243, 253, 255, 454

TCID, 272
tenement, 4
tenement industries, 30
Tissue Culture Infective Dose, 272
tonsillectomies, 230, 260
transverse myelitis, 240, 241, 242, 283
trapper, 24
tuberculosis, 51, 205, 206, 432, 438, 442
typhoid, 37, 38, 39, 43, 45, 47, 156, 167, 171, 175, 177, 178, 190, 191, 206, 217, 338, 429, 434, 464
typhus, 43, 44, 414

US Civil War, 6, 43, 414

Vaccination Act, 114, 126
vaccine virus, 65, 66, 68, 98, 101, 103, 267, 271, 273, 284, 285, 289, 354, 355, 367, 404
variolation, 60, 61, 97

vegetable juice, 438
Victoria Romanus, 309
Vitamin A, 391, 394, 442
vitamin C, 204, 205, 247, 261, 316, 334, 391, 396, 397, 410, 412, 413, 415, 416, 417, 421, 422, 423, 424, 425

waning immunity, 388
water supply, 9, 10, 168, 169, 170, 171, 173, 175, 181
WHO, 58, 138, 139, 282, 283, 284, 285, 286, 290, 291, 316, 384
whooping cough, 46, 47, 178, 184, 191, 192, 193, 194, 195, 206, 217, 219, 293, 295, 297, 298, 301, 303, 305, 306, 308, 309, 310, 314, 315, 316, 317, 318, 320, 321, 322, 324, 325, 327, 328, 329, 332, 333, 334, 335, 338, 405, 417, 424, 425, 432, 433, 458, 459, 460, 462
World Health Organization, 58, 139, 232, 316
Wyeth, 68, 271, 273, 298, 299

Xavante, 227, 291

yellow fever, 49

ABOUT THE AUTHORS

Roman Bystrianyk has been researching the history of diseases and vaccines for more than 15 years. He has an extensive background in health and nutrition as well as a BS in engineering and an MS in computer science.

Dr. Suzanne Humphries earned her medical degree in 1993 from Temple University in Philadelphia, Pennsylvania, and then became board certified in internal medicine and nephrology. Her career encompassed teaching medical students, residents, and graduate students, and included an assistant professorship at the clinical campus of Robert Wood Johnson Medical School in Camden, New Jersey, as well as 10 years in private practice affiliated with a large teaching hospital in Maine. In 2011 she chose to change directions and now practices as a holistic health consultant, and continues to research many aspects of medical practice, and write about the problems with vaccination. Her website is drsuzanne.net.

Made in the USA
Middletown, DE
26 October 2021